THE STRUCTURE OF SOCIAL ACTION

TALCOTT PARSONS

The Structure
of
Social Action

*A STUDY IN SOCIAL THEORY WITH SPECIAL
REFERENCE TO A GROUP OF RECENT EUROPEAN WRITERS*

VOLUME II

THE FREE PRESS, *New York*
COLLIER-MACMILLAN LIMITED, *London*

Library of Congress Catalog Card Number: 49–49353

FIRST FREE PRESS PAPERBACK EDITION 1968

printing number
2   3   4   5   6   7   8   9   10

INTRODUCTION TO THE
PAPERBACK EDITION

For an author who has had the good fortune to survive the
original publication of his book for so long, it is gratifying that
publication in paperback should occur just thirty years after the
original edition. That the decision of the Free Press is not wholly
without regard to financial matters is perhaps indicated by the fact
that just under 1200 hard cover copies were sold in the year 1966,
some eighty per cent of the number in the original McGraw-Hill
edition, which was exhausted only after approximately 10 years.

Of course, the rise in sales is partly because of the immense
growth of the American economy and, within it, the demand for
the output of books in the social sciences. The "survival value"
of the book, however, judging by the numerous critical comments,
is hardly accounted for by its seductive and charming literary
style or by its constituting a simple popularization of the work
of some famous European authors about whom many wished to
learn a little more without investing much intellectual effort.

It is perhaps a fair inference, then, that there is some more
substantive basis for its continued survival; one we may explain
partly in the familiar terms of the "sociology of knowledge." With
the general rise of the social sciences, sociology has become a
relatively "fashionable" discipline within the modern intellectual
community. In approaching its present prominence, however, it
has certainly followed economics, psychology, and political science.
As Nisbet[1] has recently shown, its rise has had much to do with
a new concern for the integrative problems of modern society—a
concern which was conspicuously lacking in much of the economic
and political thought of the nineteenth and the early part of the
present century. In dealing with some prominent authors of the
turn-of-the-century generation who were concerned with these
problems, notably Durkheim and Weber, the *Structure of Social*

---

[1] Robert A. Nisbet, *The Sociological Tradition*, Basic Books, 1967.

v

Action perhaps helped introduce a narrow group of rather technically minded American social scientists and a few other intellectuals to the analysis of some problems in this area. The book has, of course, been a beneficiary of the continuing growth of this type of concern. In other words, the growth of sociology is a function not only of the sheer scientific merits of the contributions of its practitioners, but also of larger intellectual currents of the time, which have been in part "existentially" determined. This being the case, the author evidently "got in" at a relatively early stage on a "good thing" and has been fortunate enough to ride on its "wave of success."

It is important to the story of the book that it dealt empirically with some of the broadest questions of the nature of modern industrial society—notably the nature of capitalism. Moreover, it did so at a time when the Russian Revolution, the Great Depression, the Fascist movements, and the approach of World War II were events and phenomena that raised many fundamental social questions. On the theoretical side, the book concentrated on the problem of the boundaries and limitations of economic theory. It did so in terms which did not follow the established lines of either the theory of "economic individualism" or its socialist opponents, even the British democratic socialists to say nothing of the Marxists. These orientations were probably of considerable importance in getting early attention for the book, since many intellectuals felt caught within the individualism-socialism dilemma, and economics seemed at the time to be the most important theoretical social science.

This does not seem to have been the case in more recent years, at least not to the same degree. Economic theory has become far more technical in this period and a certain dissociation seems to have emerged between the interests of economists in their technical theory and in their special concerns with matters of public policy and the interests of the other social sciences, especially sociology. Only recently is a new kind of rapprochement perhaps beginning to take shape, especially through collaboration among the disciplines with reference to the problems of development in the so-called underdeveloped nations, where only with difficulty can even the economic aspect of a society be treated as a purely economic problem in the analytical theoretical sense.[2]

---

[2] It is perhaps a significant symptom of this shift of attention that, among the books bearing my name, by far the least successful in sales

If substantive considerations of the sort just noted—on both broad empirical and theoretical levels that go somewhat beyond ideology in a crasser sense—have played a part in the survival value of this book, a further interesting question is raised. Throughout most of the present century, if not before, there has been in the social and behavioral sciences in this country a strong wish to be identified with the hard sciences. This has often gone so far as to generate rather extreme empiricist views of the philosophy of science that virtually relegate all theory to "soft-mindedness."[3] The tendency is endemic to the culture of the American behavioral sciences; indeed, one still hears very strident voices about the virtues of the sheerest empiricism—especially if quantitative, and about the dangers of theoretical speculation—especially if tending to produce "grand theory."

I have always maintained that the *Structure of Social Action* was an empirical work in a double sense. First, it is very much oriented to problems of the macroscopic developments in Western society, especially as seen through the eyes of the four principal authors discussed in the study. Secondly, it was an empirical study in the analysis of social thought. The writings treated are as truly documents as are manorial court rolls of the Middle Ages, and as such, present problems of understanding and interpretation. Whether an interpretation of Durkheim's *Division of Labor* is demonstrably valid is just as definitely an empirical question as whether Durkheim's view of the relation between Protestantism and high suicide rates is correct.

Nevertheless, the *Structure of Social Action* is, and was always meant to be, essentially a *theoretical* work. It was written under the aegis of a complex movement in the philosophy of science that ran counter to the sharp insistence on the exclusive virtue of hard science—especially, perhaps, as then expressed in the more

---

has been *Economy and Society* (with Neil J. Smelser, 1956), which I consider a more important theoretical contribution than several others. I think it literally "fell between stools" in that sociologists were put off by the level of economics it seemed to presume, while economists simply were not interested. Very likely most potential readers of *Economy and Society* thought that most of what I had to say on the topic was in the *Structure of Social Action* anyway, though this is far from being the case. On the contrary, it presented what I consider a major new theoretical advance.

[3] In sociology, the high point of this trend was perhaps William F. Ogburn's presidential address to the American Sociological Society in the 1930's.

popular interpretations of Bridgman's operationalism. To me the major prophet of this defense of theory was A. N. Whitehead, whose *Science and the Modern World* has remained an exceedingly important statement. In the background lay the work of Morris Cohen, *Reason and Nature*. A more direct influence was the work of L. J. Henderson (himself a physiologist with impeccable credentials as a hard scientist) on the importance of theory in general and the concept of system in particular—the latter he held to be Pareto's most important single contribution.

As noted in the book, I had also been impressed by two movements that opposed the empiricist atomism of the behaviorist movement in psychology, namely, *Gestalt* psychology and the "purposive" behaviorism of E. C. Tolman. Finally, the writings of James B. Conant in the general area of the popularization of science constituted a factor of encouragement. One statement by Conant which remains particularly salient is that the best measure of the process of advancement in a science is "reduction in the degree of empiricism."

The main thesis of the book was that the works of Marshall, Pareto, Durkheim, and Weber, related in complex ways to the works of many others, represented not simply four special sets of observations and theories concerned with human society, but a major *movement* in the structure of theoretical thinking. Against the background of the two underlying traditions of utilitarian positivism and idealism, it represented an altogether new phase in the development of European—which could then be practically equated with Western—thought about the problems of man and society. In retrospect, the most serious deficiency in this interpretation of intellectual history is its understatement of the independent significance of the special French tradition, with its complex, often conflicting, intertwining of the ideas of the "liberals" (Rousseau, St. Simon, and Comte), the "conservatives" (Bonald and De Maistre, and, not least, Tocqueville).

In any case, the main outline that emerged was clearly "grand theory," which put the analysis of social phenomena on a new track in the broadest possible terms.[4] Within limits, I think we

---

[4] Personal experience attested to its newness from the English-speaking, predominantly utilitarian perspective. In 1924-25 I spent a year as a research student in sociology at the London School of Economics without, so far as I can remember, ever hearing the name of Max Weber, though all

may say that this perspective of "grand theory" had a certain appeal, most importantly to younger people, especially graduate students, though gradually it spread rather widely.

Nevertheless, the controversy over the virtues and vices of "grand theory" shows no sign of subsiding. A particularly important episode occurred at the meeting of the American Sociological Society in 1948 when Robert Merton began to put forward his program for concentration on "theories of the middle range."[5] In retrospect this seems to have been a very constructive move that was necessary to integrate the empirically minded with the more theoretical. This evaluation does not, however, imply the advisability of abandoning a program of continuing work in the field of general theory. On the contrary, throughout what has now become a rather long career, I have held, with essentially complete constancy, a basic personal commitment to such a program.

This commitment began with my conviction of the unacceptability of the common view of the time, especially as expressed in Sorokin's *Contemporary Sociological Theories* (note the plural). He stated that the three sociologists in my study—Pareto, Durkheim, and Weber—belonged in radically different schools, and that Marshall, as an economist, belonged in a still different intellectual universe. I regarded their works not simply as four discrete and different alternative theories, but as belonging to a coherent *body* of theoretical thinking, understandable in terms of the major movements in the period's intellectual history.

The double concern, on the one hand with the status of economic theory as an analytical scheme, on the other hand with the interpretation of modern industrial society, carried the fruitful common implication that each theory, as an analytical scheme, must be part of a larger and more generalized theoretical organon. Thus, Marshall, the most prominent economic theorist of his generation, had to have an implicit if not explicit sociology. Pareto, who was explicitly both economist and sociologist, provided a most useful bridge. Weber, as a German-style "historical" economist who had a profound concern with the problem of "capitalism,"

---

of his most important work had been published by that time. Durkheim was of course known both in England and America, but discussions were *overwhelmingly* derogatory; he was regarded as the apostle of the "unsound group mind" theory.

[5] American Sociological Review, 1948, pp. 146-148; see also Chapters II and III in his *Social Theory and Social Structure*.

could then be fitted in. Finally, after all the discussion of his theory of the "group mind," I really came to understand Durkheim by grasping the significance of the fact that his point of departure, at least in one primary respect, lay in his critique (and hence relativizing) of the very central conception in the tradition of the classical economics, the *division of labor*.

My concern here is not to recapitulate the theoretical argument of the book. It is to call attention to the consequence of my decision not to present summaries of the works of leading spokesmen of four schools of sociological theory, but to demonstrate in them the emergence of a single, basically integrated, if fragmentary, theoretical movement. This made it necessary to work out independently the main structure of the theoretical scheme in terms of which the unity of the intellectual movement could be demonstrated. The general theory of the "structure of social action" which constitutes the framework of the book—and the justification for its title—was not simply a "summary" of the works of the four theorists. It was an independent theoretical contribution, incomplete and vulnerable, to be sure, but not in any simple sense "secondary." I do not think the survival value of the book could be explained without reference to it.

There is, however, an important further implication. It would be *most* unlikely and incongruous if any such generalized theoretical scheme should, as first formulated for a particular purpose, prove or claim to be definitive. If it were to be taken as more than a table of contents for the presentation of material, it had to undergo a continuing process of its own internal development and change. I think I can fairly claim that such a process has in fact gone on continually and that it shows no signs of coming to an end; in fact, it seems bound to continue long after the present author ceases to be involved in it.

It may be useful to distinguish three phases in this development in the thirty years since the publication of the *Structure*. The first may be thought of as the phase of "structural-functional" theory. It was most fully documented in the two publications, *Toward a General Theory of Action* (with Shils and other collaborators) and *The Social System* (both 1951). These works developed a shift of emphasis in the concept of system from primacy of a model derived from economics and physics (via Henderson, Pareto, and Schumpeter), to one derived primarily from biology and secondarily from anthropology (especially in W. B. Cannon's work and Radcliffe-Brown's interpretation of Durkheim). With respect to the conception of "action" in the narrower sense, the theory became more Durkheimian than Weberian, thus giving rise to Martindale's allegation that I had abandoned the whole Weber position, which surely was not the case.

This phase was also marked by a major coming to terms with two crucial neighboring disciplines, namely psychology, with special reference to the theory of personality, and social anthropology. The first led to a serious consideration of the implications of the work of Freud, mentioned in the preface to the second (first Free Press) edition of the *Structure* in 1949. I came to attribute great importance to the convergence of Durkheim and Freud in the understanding of the internalization of cultural norms and social objects as part of personality—a convergence which extended in an attenuated sense to Weber, but very importantly to the American sociological social psychologists, especially G. H. Mead. Secondly, I came to emphasize the relevance of the late Durkheim (especially that of the *Elementary Forms of the Religious Life*) to the theory of an integrated socio-cultural system, as this had come to be emphasized in the "functional" school of British social anthropology; perhaps in particular, Evans-Pritchard, Fortes, and Gluckman. A kind of "dialectic" relation of partial agreement and disagreement over these matters obtained with Clyde Kluckhohn and, somewhat more remotely, Raymond Firth, an old fellow student at London.

There was another central theme in this period which was only very partially related to that of the integration of sociology with social anthropology and the psychology of personality. This theme led to a path out of the old individualism-socialism dilemma that had come to dominate thought about modern society; it concerned the phenomenon of the professions, their position in modern society, and their relation to the cultural tradition and to higher education. More than any other interest, it provided the seed-bed of the pattern-variable scheme, only bare germs of which found expression in the *Structure of Social Action*. It was also the source of the perspective which made possible a new attack on the problem of the status of economic theory; one which produced, I think, quite far-reaching results.

The second major phase of development in general theory after the *Structure of Social Action* was initiated by the book mentioned above, *Economy and Society* (with Neil J. Smelser, 1956). In the background stood the *Working Papers in the Theory of Action* (with R. F. Bales and others), which among other things had greatly refined the pattern-variable scheme. *Economy and Society* (which in its original form constituted the 1953 Marshall Lectures at the University of Cambridge) departed from the Paretan conception that economic theory was abstract and partial relative to a theory of the social system as a whole. However, it proceeded to show that the economy is a clearly and precisely definable *subsystem* of a society that can be systematically related to other subsystems. The key to this analysis was the application of the "four-function paradigm" to the old economic conceptions of the factors of production and the corresponding shares of income (land-rent, labor-wages, capital-interest, organization-profit).

This conception of the economy as a societal subsystem proved capable of generalization. In the first instance, such generalization opened a new approach to the theoretical analysis of the "polity" by suggesting that it be treated as an analytically defined subsystem of a society strictly parallel to the economy. This eliminated a very serious asymmetry within the general theory of social systems between the status of economic and political theory. These developments have been closely associated with the analysis of generalized media involved in social interaction, starting with money as a basic theoretical model, but extending to political power and social influence. In turn, these extensions have entailed pressures to elaborate the analytical treatment of the other two primary functional subsystems of a society, the integrative—recently called the "societal community"—and the pattern-maintenance. It is in the context of establishing the framework for these developments that *Economy and Society* was not merely a recapitulation of the discussion of the relations of economic and sociological theory in the *Structure of Social Action*, but represented quite a new level of departure.

It was probably fair to criticise my theoretical work in its "structural-functional" phase for not adequately accounting for the problems of political structure and process, although it is hoped that the developments just outlined mitigate the criticism somewhat.[6] Legitimate objections could also be raised about the same phase with reference to the problems of accounting for

---

[6] Cf. William C. Mitchell, *Sociological Analysis and Politics; The Theories of Talcott Parsons*, Prentice-Hall, 1967.

change in societies and in their related cultural and psychological systems. The third main phase of my "post-Structure" theoretical development has come to center in these problem areas. Its keynote is a return to Weberian as distinct from Durkheimian interests, because Weber was overwhelmingly the most important of the post-linear social evolutionists. In respects that first began to take shape in *Economy and Society,* and were developed much farther by Smelser in his *Social Change in the Industrial Revolution,* not only has a rather general evolutionary scheme emerged, but also a paradigm for analyzing rather specific patterned processes of change. The paradigm has primarily to do with the relations among the processes of differentiation, inclusion, upgrading, and value-generalization. A few articles and two small books— one published and the other nearly completed—document this phase of development so far.[7]

The *Structure of Social Action* was not meant in the first instance to be a study in intellectual history. I chose a rather narrow sector within its time period and, except for background purposes, excluded previous contributions. In retrospect, in the broad spectrum of relevant intellectual developments, it seems that two figures who were de-emphasized in my book have come to influence the contemporary intellectual scene. Both belonged to the phase prior to the generation of my four principals; they were, namely, Tocqueville and Marx.

In the most generalized sense, especially as focused on the society as the crucial type of social system, Durkheim and Weber seem to me to be the *main* founders of *modern* sociological theory. Both were in explicit revolt against the traditions of both economic individualism and socialism—Weber in the latter context perhaps above all, because of the spectre of total bureaucratic "rationalization." In a sense, Tocqueville and Marx provided the wing positions relative to this central core. Marx was the apostle of transcending the limitations of the partial "capitalistic" version of rationalization through its completion in socialism. As Nisbet (op cit.) points out, this was to carry the doctrines of the Enlightenment to a drastic conclusion. Tocqueville, on the other hand, represented the anxious nostalgia of the *Ancien Regime* and the fear that the losses entailed in its passing could never be replaced.

---

[7] *Societies: Evolutionary and Comparative Perspectives,* Prentice-Hall, 1966; and *The System of Modern Societies,* Prentice-Hall, forthcoming.

Indeed, to a preeminent degree, Tocqueville was the apologist of a fully aristocratic society.[8]

Important as both of these authors have become in current discussion, they were antecedents of the generation treated in the *Structure of Social Action* who did not attain a comparable level of *technical* theoretical analysis. The appropriate characterization of Tocqueville's contribution seems to be insight rather than theoretical rigor. Marx's technical economic theory must now be regarded as largely superseded; particularly by men like Marshall and Keynes. His "laws" of history and class struggle require, to say the least, quite basic modification in the light of developments in both modern social theory and modern societies.[9]

Hence I still take the position that, given its European and macrosociological references, the selection which was inherent in the table of contents of the *Structure of Social Action* was in fact appropriate to the *core* line of development in sociological theory. Important as they have been, the influences of Tocqueville and Marx still seem to belong properly on the wings rather than at the core.[10] I hope it can be said that my own enterprise in general theory, sketched briefly above, has produced authentic developments from the potentialities present in this core, developments sufficiently catholic not to skew the possibilities for sociological theory too drastically because of positive preference or negative prejudice.

Talcott Parsons

Cambridge, Massachusetts
January, 1968

---

[8] This paragraph should be understood in a *theoretical,* not a political-ideological sense. In particular Tocqueville was very far from being a simple "conservative" defender of the Old Regime like Bonald and Maistre.

[9] Cf. "Some Comments on the Sociology of Karl Marx," Chapter IV in my forthcoming *Sociological Theory and Modern Society,* Free Press, 1967.

[10] Along with the American social psychologists, notably Cooley, Mead, and W. I. Thomas, the most important single figure neglected in the *Structure of Social Action,* and to an important degree in my subsequent writings, is probably Simmel. It may be of interest that I actually drafted a chapter on Simmel for the *Structure of Social Action,* but partly for reasons of space finally decided not to include it. Simmel was more a micro- than a macrosociologist; moreover, he was not, in my opinion, a *theorist* on the same level as the others. He was much more a highly talented essayist in the tradition of Tocqueville than a theorist like Durkheim. Again, however, his influence on subsequent sociological thought has been a major one.

PREFACE TO SECOND EDITION

Nearly twelve years have passed since the original publication of *The Structure of Social Action*. The post-war wave of interest in theoretical study and teaching in the relevant aspects of social science unfortunately found the book out of print, so that the decision of *The Free Press* to bring out a new edition is most welcome.

For a variety of reasons, it has been decided to reprint the original book without change. There is, in this decision, no implication that the book could not be substantially improved by revision. Nothing could be further both from the spirit of the work and from a number of explicit statements* in it. The author's own process of theoretical thinking has not stopped and if he were to undertake writing the book again at this time, it would come out a substantially different and, let us hope, a better book.

To present a revised version which would at all closely resemble what the book would be like if newly written in 1949 would, however, be a very heavy task. It would not only involve much actual rewriting, but, prior to that, a careful re-study and re-evaluation of the principal sources on which it was based. This would certainly be highly productive, but the problem is to balance judgment of the productiveness of such work compared to alternative uses of the time and energy it would require.

The most important consideration involved in the balance is the relative advantage to be derived from further refinement of the critical analysis of theoretical work done a generation and more ago as compared with the probable fruitfulness of proceeding with direct analysis of theoretical problems in relation to presently going empirical research interests without further refinement of critical orientation. The decision not to embark on a thorough revision of the book represents the judgment that in the present situation of social science, the latter constitutes the more fruitful channel for a major investment of time and energy.

The Structure of Social Action was intended to be primarily a

---

* See Chapter I, pages 40-41.

contribution to systematic social science and not to history, that is the history of social thought. The justification of its critical orientation to the work of other writers thus lay in the fact that this was a convenient vehicle for the clarification of problems and concepts, of implications and interrelations. It was a means of taking stock of the theoretical resources at our disposal. In the on-going process of scientific development, it constituted a pause for reconsideration of basic policy decisions, on principles which are serviceable in scientific work as in many other fields, namely, that "it is a good thing to know what you are doing," and that there may be resources and potentialities in the situation which in our absorption in daily work, we tend to overlook. The clarification gained from this stocktaking has opened up possibilties for further theoretical development of sufficient scope so that its impetus is as yet by no means exhausted. This is certainly true in a personal sense and it is reasonable to believe that it continues to be true for others.

The Structure of Social Action analyzed a process of convergent theoretical development which constituted a major revolution in the scientific analysis of social phenomena. The three principal authors treated in that study are by no means isolated but as contributors to the "sociological" side of the development, the added perspective of another decade does not diminish their relative stature as high points in the movement. There is an elevated range, not just three peaks, but these three peaks loom far higher than the lesser ones.

This is true on the sociological side. A major one-sidedness of the book is its relative neglect of the psychological aspects of the total conceptual scheme—a balance which a thorough revision would certainly have to attempt to redress. Here, at least, one figure in the same generation as the others, that of Freud, looms up as having played a cardinal role in a development which, in spite of the differences of his starting points and empirical concerns, must be regarded as a vital part of the same general movement of thought. Psychology is probably richer in significant secondary figures than is true on the sociological side, but no other one seems closely to approach the stature of Freud. So much is this the case that a full-dress analysis of Freud's theoretical development seen in the context of the "theory of social action"—and adaptation of the rest of the book to the results of such an analysis—would seem indispensable to the kind of revision which ought to be undertaken. This would, of course, necessarily result in a substantial lengthening of an already formidable work.

There may well be a difference of opinion whether there is any figure of comparable *theoretical* stature, who is classified as essentially a social or cultural anthropologist. It is the author's opinion that there is not. Though Boas, for example, may be of comparable *general* importance to social science and an equally great man, his contributions to systematic theoretical analysis in the same stream of development are not in the same category with a Durkheim or a Freud. In a diffuser sense, however, the contributions of anthropological thinking are, however, of first-rate importance and should receive distinctly more emphasis than has been given them in *The Structure of Social Action*. This is particularly true of the relations of the structure of social action to the "structure of culture." Further clarification of these issues is one of the most urgent needs of basic social science at present.

In its fundamentals, this basic theoretical development had taken place by, let us say, twenty-five years ago. But the frames of reference, the polemical orientations, the empirical interests and the intellectual traditions surrounding the authors were so various that the actual unity of their work was accessible only with a great deal of laborious critical interpretation. Indeed, it was worse than that, for the actual differentiations had already become overlaid with a welter of secondary interpretations and misinterpretations, which made the confusion even worse confounded. One of the principal services of *The Structure of Social Action* has been, I think, to clear away a great deal of this "underbrush" so that the bold outline of a theoretical scheme could stand out with some clarity.

A better understanding of the psychological and cultural aspects, which an analysis of Freud's work and of anthropological thought might have contributed would be desirable. Allowance should also be made for awkwardness of exposition. But even with qualifications of this sort, the book reached a point on which further developments can be built. Furthermore, given certain of the interpretive keys which it provides, the original works can be much more freely and fruitfully used. In a word, the outline of a theoretical scheme and the contributions of some of its principal creators have become much more the public property of a professional group rather than remaining the exclusive possession of a small coterie of

Pareto, Durkheim, or Weber scholars, which would more likely than not be rival coteries.

Assuming that, subject to the inevitable process of refinement, the basic theoretical outline developed in *The Structure of Social Action* is essentially sound, to place its significance in better perspective, something may be said about the nature and direction of the developments which can be built upon it.

It was emphasized that the scheme had developed in direct connection with empirical interests and problems of the authors. This is true and of the first importance. But only at a few points could this empirical orientation have been said at this stage to have approached the level of being "operationally specific." One of the most notable of these, with all its crudity, was Durkheim's analysis of suicide rates. Another, on a totally different level, was Weber's attempted test of the influence of religious ideas on economic development by the comparative analysis of the relationships between the relevant factors in a series of different societies. But on the whole, the major relation to empirical problems remained that of a broad "clarification of issues," elimination of confusion and untenable interpretations, and the opening up of new possibilities.

A central problem, therefore, has been and is, how to bring theory of this sort closer to the possibilities of guiding of and testing and refinement by technical research, especially with the use of technically refined instruments of observation, and of the ordering and empirical analysis of observational data.

At least at many points, an important series of steps in this direction seems to be made possible by a shift in theoretical level from the analysis of the structure of social action as such to the structural-functional analysis of social systems. These are, of course, "in the last analysis" systems of social action. But the structure of such systems is, in the newer version, treated not directly in action terms, but as "institutionalized patterns" close to a level of readily described and tested empirical generalization. This, in turn, makes it possible to isolate specific and manageable action processes for intensive dynamic study. Such processes, that is, are treated as action in relation to institutionalized roles, in terms of balances of conformity with and deviation from the expectations of the socially sanctioned role definitions, of conflicting role expectations impinging on the individual, and the constellations of motivational forces and mechanisms involved in such balances and conflicts.

The isolation of such problems to the point of empirical manageability can, however, within the framework of a structural-functional system of theory, be achieved with a relatively high level of attainment of the advantages of generalized dynamic analysis. Treating dynamic problems in the context of their relation both to the structure of a system and the relation of the processes to the functional prerequisites of its maintenance, provides a frame of reference for judging the general significance of a finding and for following out systematically its interconnections with other problems and facts.

The most promising lines of development of theory in the sociological and most immediately related fields, particularly the psychological and cultural, therefore, seem to be two-fold. One major direction is the theoretical elaboration and refinement of structural-functional analysis of social systems, including the relevant problems of motivation and their relation to cultural patterns. In this process, the structure of social action provides a basic frame of reference, and aspects of it become of direct substantive importance at many specific points. The main theoretical task, however, is more than a refinement of the conceptual scheme of the presently reprinted book—it involves transition and translation to a different level and focus of theoretical systematization.*

The second major direction is the development of technically operational formulations and adaptations of theoretically significant concepts. The development of techniques of empirical research has been exceedingly rapid in the recent past and promises much more for the future. Such techniques can now accomplish impressive results even if the theory which guides their employment is little more than common sense. But this is a minor fraction of the undertanding they promise if they can be genuinely integrated with a really technical and generalized theoretical scheme.

It is the promise of the fruitfulness of developments in such directions as these which motivates the author not to undertake a thorough revision of *The Structure of Social Action* at this time. Indeed, such a revision does not seem to be really necessary. Whatever theoretical progress the author has been able to make

---

* For a fuller account of this focus and what it involves, see Talcott Parsons, *Essays in Sociological Therapy* (The Free Press, 1949), Chapters I and II.

since its original publication* has been built solidly on the foundations it provides, starting, of course, with the insights provided by studying the great theorists whose works it analyzes. There seems to be substantial reason to believe that this is not merely of idiosyncratic significance. Further dissemination of these contributions, even in their present form, should help to elevate the general level of theoretical understanding and competence in our profession and to stimulate other contributors to develop the most fruitful lines of theoretical advance of social science to a level so much higher as to fulfill the promise in the work of their great predecessors of the turn of the century.

TALCOTT PARSONS.

CAMBRIDGE, MASSACHUSETTS
March, 1949

---

* See Talcott Parsons, *Essays in Sociological Theory* (The Free Press, 1949).

PREFACE

In a sense the present work is to be regarded as a secondary study of the work of a group of writers in the field of social theory. But the genus "secondary study" comprises several species; of these an example of only one, and that perhaps not the best known, is to be found in these pages.

The primary aim of the study is not to determine and state in summary form what these writers said or believed about the subjects they wrote about. Nor is it to inquire directly with reference to each proposition of their "theories" whether what they have said is tenable in the light of present sociological and related knowledge. Both these questions must be asked repeatedly, but what is important is not so much the fact that they are asked, or even answered, but the context in which this takes place.

The keynote to be emphasized is perhaps given in the subtitle of the book; it is a study in social *theory*, not *theories*. Its interest is not in the separate and discrete propositions to be found in the works of these men, but in a *single* body of systematic theoretical reasoning the development of which can be traced through a critical analysis of the writings of this group, and of certain of their predecessors. The unity which justifies treating them together between the same covers is not that they constitute a "school" in the usual sense, or that they exemplify an epoch or a period in the history of social theory, but that they have all, in different respects, made important contributions to this single coherent body of theory, and the analysis of their works constitutes a convenient way of elucidating the structure and empirical usefulness of the system of theory itself.

This body of theory, the "theory of social action" is not simply a group of concepts with their logical interrelations. It is a theory of empirical science the concepts of which refer to something beyond themselves. It would lead to the worst kind of dialectic sterility to treat the development of a system of theory without reference to the empirical problems in relation to

xxi

which it has been built up and used. True scientific theory is not the product of idle "speculation," of spinning out the logical implications of assumptions, but of observation, reasoning and verification, starting with the facts and continually returning to the facts. Hence at every crucial point explicit treatment of the empirical problems which occupied the writers concerned is included. Only by treating theory in this close interrelation with empirical problems and facts is any kind of an adequate understanding either of how the theory came to develop, or of its significance to science, possible.

Indeed though this volume is published as a study in theory in the sense just outlined, the tracing of the development of a theoretical system through the works of these four men was not the original intention of the author in embarking on intensive study of their works. It could not have been, for neither he nor any other secondary writer on them was aware that there was a single coherent theoretical system to be found there. The basis on which the four writers were brought together for study was rather empirical. It was the fact that all of them in different ways were concerned with the range of empirical problems involved in the interpretation of some of the main features of the modern economic order, of "capitalism," "free enterprise," "economic individualism," as it has been variously called. Only very gradually did it become evident that in the treatment of these problems, even from such diverse points of view, there was involved a common conceptual scheme, and so the focus of interest was gradually shifted to the working out of the scheme for its own sake.

Many of the author's debts, in the long history of the study, which in continuity of problems extends back into undergraduate days, defy acknowledgment, because they are so numerous and often so indefinite. An attempt will be made to acknowledge only those of most important direct relevance to the study as it now stands.

Of these immediately relevant debts four are of outstanding significance. The least definite, but perhaps the most important, is to Professor Edwin F. Gay, who over a period of years has taken an active interest in the study, has been a source of encouragement at many points in the long and sometimes discouraging process of its development, and has consistently stimulated the author to the highest quality of work of which he was capable. Secondly, the author's colleague Professor Overton H. Taylor has contributed, in ways which would defy identification, at innumerable points, largely through a long series of personal discussions of the problems, particularly those associated more directly with the status of economic theory. Both have also read parts of the manuscript and made valuable suggestions. Third, Professor Lawrence J. Henderson has subjected the manuscript to a most unusually thorough critical examination, which led to important revision at many points, particularly in relation to general scientific methodology and to the interpretation of Pareto's work. Finally, much is owed to the changing group of students, especially graduate, with whom the author has carried on discussions of problems of social theory throughout much of the period of incubation of the study. In the lively give and take of these discussions many a fruitful idea has emerged and many an obscure point has been clarified.

Two other critics have been particularly helpful through the suggestions and criticisms they have given after reading the manuscript, Professor A. D. Nock, especially in the parts dealing with religion, and Dr. Robert K. Merton. Various others have read the manuscript or proof in whole or in part, and have made valuable suggestions and criticisms. They include Professor P. A. Sorokin, Professor Josef Schumpeter, Professor Frank H. Knight, Dr. Alexander von Schelting, Professor C. K. M. Kluckhohn, Professor N. B. DeNood, Miss Elizabeth Nottingham, Mr. Emile B. Smullyan and Mr. Edward Shils. To Mr. Smullyan and Dr. Benjamin Halpern, I am also indebted for research assistance.

The foregoing have aided this study in relation to the technical subject matter as such. But this is by no means all there is to the completion of such a work. In other respects two other debts are particularly important. One is to the Harvard University Committee on Research in the Social Sciences, which made possible by its grants some valuable research assistance in bibliography and the secondary literature, and stenographic assistance in preparation of the manuscript. The other is to my father, President Emeritus Edward S. Parsons of Marietta College, who took upon himself the heavy burden of going through the whole manuscript in an attempt to improve its English style.

Whatever of readability an unavoidably difficult work may possess is largely to be credited to him.

For secretarial assistance in typing the manuscript I am much indebted to Miss Elizabeth Wolfe, Miss Agnes Hannay and Mrs. Marion B. Billings, and for assistance in preparation of the bibliography to Miss Elaine Ogden.

TALCOTT PARSONS.

CAMBRIDGE, MASS.,
October, 1937.

CONTENTS

PART I

THE POSITIVISTIC THEORY OF ACTION

PART II

THE EMERGENCE OF A VOLUNTARISTIC THEORY OF ACTION FROM THE POSITIVISTIC TRADITION

End of Volume I

PART III

THE EMERGENCE OF A VOLUNTARISTIC THEORY OF ACTION FROM THE IDEALISTIC TRADITION

PART IV

CONCLUSION

*Jede denkende Besinnung auf die
letzten Elemente sinnvollen mensch-
lichen Handelns ist zunächst gebunden
an die Kategorien "Zweck" und "Mittel."*

Max Weber, Gesammelte Aufsätze
zur Wissenschaftslehre, p. 149.

PART III

THE EMERGENCE OF A VOLUNTARISTIC THEORY OF ACTION FROM THE IDEALISTIC TRADITION

CHAPTER XIII

THE IDEALISTIC TRADITION

METHODOLOGICAL BACKGROUND

Like every other great tradition of thought, the idealistic is highly complex, composed of many interwoven strands. As in the earlier case of the positivistic tradition the present sketch does not and cannot pretend to render an exhaustive historical account, even in outline. It must, rather, content itself with selecting, by the ideal-type method, a few major strands which are particularly relevant to the problems of this study.[1]

For the purposes of this study, it is unnecessary to trace the idealistic tradition back to a period earlier than that of Kant. Few thinkers have ever displayed so many facets to a variety of interpreters. It is proposed here only to call attention to a few salient points. In England and the United States it is customary to regard as Kant's principal contribution his solution of the dilemma presented by Hume's epistemological skepticism. This is one major element and a few words must be said about it by way of introduction to the others, which are of more immediate concern.

The empirical knowledge with the validity of which the epistemological discussion of modern philosophy, at least down to relatively recent times, has been primarily concerned, has been that of the physical world, embodied in the classical system of physical theory. It was its validity which Hume's skepticism attacked and in which Kant restored confidence. Kant quite definitely shares this preoccupation with the physical world. Perhaps the clearest indication of this is his inclusion of space, by which he clearly meant the physical space of the classical

[1] For purposes of this study the two most useful general accounts are in H. Freyer, *Soziologie als Wirklichkeitswissenschaft* and E. Troeltsch, *Der Historismus und seine Probleme*. The recent work of Friedrich Meinecke, *Die Entstehung des Historismus* may also be mentioned, though it has appeared too late to influence the formulations of the present chapter.

mechanics, as an indispensable schema of intuition, a logical prerequisite of empirical knowledge of any sort. Phenomena for Kant are things or events *in space*.[1]

Kant's answer to Hume involved, however, the repudiation of the naïve empiricist realism which had characterized the earlier physical scientists, the "simple faith" of which Professor Whitehead speaks,[2] which had been broken down by the epistemological criticism culminating in Hume. Kant did not, of course, return to this but reestablished the validity of physical science by reducing physical bodies and events to the status of "phenomena," depriving them of their more substantial metaphysical reality by making them relative to another order of being, the "ideal."

But in this process of "relativizing," the classical physical system remained intact, and remained, for the phenomenal world, an empirically closed system. Man, to be sure, participated in this phenomenal world, not only as knowing subject but also as object, as a physical body. But this did not exhaust man; he also participated in the world of ideas and of freedom. The tendency of Kantian thought was thus toward a radical dualism reaching its most acute point of focus in relation to man—at the same time a physical body and a spiritual being. Hence the Kantian scheme favored the reduction of all phenomenal aspects of man, especially the biological, to a "materialistic" basis, and produced a radical hiatus between this and his spiritual life—a hiatus which still persists in the rigidity of the line customarily drawn between the natural sciences and the sciences of culture or of mind (*Geist*) in Germany.

[1] There are really two issues involved in this Kantian position. One is whether there are in human experience of the empircial world *concrete* entities which do not exist in space or have a spatial aspect. The negative Kantian position on this issue is probably acceptable; certainly it produces no difficulties in the present context. It is rather the second issue which is here important, which is whether theoretical systems analytically applicable to the empirical world, tò phenomena in the Kantian sense, must always be couched in terms of a spatial frame of reference. Since in Kant's time the view of analytical abstraction here put forward was not known, his view that all phenomena are observed "in space" strongly tends to be combined with the view that theories which analyze them must involve also spatial categories. It is this latter tendency which creates the dichotomy at present under discussion.

[2] A. N. WHITEHEAD, *Science and the Modern World*, pp. 27–28.

For Kant the Practical Reason fell definitely on the noumenal, not the phenomenal side of the line. This meant that man as an active, purposive being, an actor, was not to be dealt with by the sciences of the phenomenal world nor even by their analytical, generalizing methods. In this sphere man was not subject to law in the physical sense but was free. An intellectual apprehension of his life and action could be attained only by the speculative methods of philosophy, especially by a process of the intuition of total wholes (*Gestalten*) which it was illegitimate to break down by "atomistic" analysis.

In the post-Kantian development of idealism it was this element which was in the center of philosophical attention. By the time of Hegel the phenomenal world was not merely made relative to, and to a high degree dependent on, the ideal—it was practically absorbed. Since what to the idealistic philosopher was interesting about man, his action and his culture, was radically excluded from the phenomenal sphere, interest in man was guided away from general theorizing on the model of the physical sciences, but it was by no means extinguished. If one was forbidden to analyze, one could at least record human acts and their effects in their concrete wholeness. One could also philosophize about these actions and events in terms of their significance for the totality of human development.[1] Hence the tendency for the idealistic interest in human action to issue in two main directions—detailed, concrete history on the one hand, the philosophy of history on the other— which have undoubtedly been the main lines of social thinking and research in Germany since the great days of idealistic philosophy.

The two lines have, of course, been by no means completely distinct. And they have shared with each other several fundamentally important characteristics. In the first place the common filiation from the idealistic horn of the Kantian dilemma has resulted in a common opposition to positivistic trends of thought, to anything in the nature of a "reduction" of the facts of human life and destiny to terms of the physical world or to biological terms. This tendency has, as has been remarked, found its clearest expression in the sharp methodological distinctions drawn

[1] That both these procedures in the end involve analysis is a fact which may be neglected for the moment.

between the "natural sciences" and the disciplines concerned with human action and culture.[1]

Secondly, *general* analytical theory has been associated with these objectionable positivistic views—hence the tendency to repudiate it for purposes of the nonnatural sciences. Perhaps the clearest expression of this was the almost universal German hostility, throughout the nineteenth century, to the classical economics, *Smithianismus*, as it was frequently called.

What is perhaps the deepest methodological basis of this conflict has lain in the empiricism common to both great traditions of thought. As long as this persists, the two are, indeed, irreconcilable if any attempt is made to apply them to the same concrete subject matter. The only way to avoid conflict is to keep the fields of their application rigidly distinct, as is done in the usual German distinction between the natural and the sociocultural sciences.

Though empiricism is common to both traditions, it is important to realize that it is not the same thing in the two cases. Positivistic empiricism has been predominantly a matter of the "reification" of theoretical systems, to use Professor Cohen's phrase,[2] or of the "fallacy of misplaced concreteness," to use Professor Whitehead's. Its starting point has been the possession of a general analytical scheme which, for a certain body of fact, works. This circumstance has been interpreted to mean. methodologically, that the concrete reality was "reflected" in the conceptual scheme, adequately for all scientific purposes. It has carried with it, inevitably, the implication of determinism. The logically closed system of theory becomes, in an empiricist interpretation, an empirically closed system. This is true regardless of its content, whether it is the system of the classical mechanics or of the classical economics.

The question of determinism has been, understandably enough in terms of the Kantian background, one of the focal points of the conflict. From the idealistic side the determinist implication has not been taken to indicate a methodologically unsound way of relating the general analytical scheme to concrete reality which could be overcome by correcting the fallacy of misplaced

---

[1] The most prominent names in this connection are W. Windelband, H. Rickert and W. Dilthey.

[2] *Cf.* MORRIS R. COHEN, *Reason and Nature*, pp. 224–228, 386–392.

concreteness. On the contrary, the empiricist interpretation has been accepted without question. Then since it was equally accepted as a fundamental fact that human action could not be mechanistically determined in this sense, the inference drawn was that no general analytical system of theory was applicable to this concrete subject matter at all. A corollary of human freedom was the unique individuality of all human events, in so far as they are "spiritual."

Hence "idealistic empiricism" has not been a deterministic reification of systems of analytical theory, but has involved a repudiation of all such theory in favor of the concrete uniqueness and individuality of all things human. It is in this sense that "historicism" has been the predominant tendency of German social thought on an idealistic basis. Since the general analytical level of scientific comprehension is a priori excluded, things human can be understood only in terms of the concrete individuality of the specific historical case. It is a corollary that all the important things cannot be known from a limited number of cases, but each must be known by and for itself. History is the indispensable road to fullness of knowledge.

It has previously been noted that this tendency has worked out in two main directions. One is the interest in the concrete detail of historical processes for its own sake. This is a persistent strain of German nineteenth century thought, receiving perhaps its most striking methodological formulation in Ranke's famous dictum, that the business of the historian is to render the past *wie es eigentlich gewesen ist,* that is, in all its concrete detail. It has constituted a major element of almost all the monumental works of German historical scholarship in many different fields, and has been thus a major motive in the production of one of the great intellectual movements of the nineteenth century. Methodologically, however, it can scarcely be said to have created a school of theory in social matters—it rather issued in a negation of theory in general.[1]

But there were excellent reasons why this could not remain the sole, or even the predominant, trend of idealistic social thought. Kant himself had, in spite of his idealism, certain strong "individualistic" elements, particularly in the ethical aspects of his

---

[1] As brought out with especial vividness in the famous *Methodenstreit* between Schmoller and Carl Menger.

thought. It may be surmised that this, with its emphasis on freedom in its relatively individualistic Kantian sense, predisposed Kantians to a certain "particularistic" mode of treatment of human action, emphasizing the uniqueness of the particular human individual, and the freedom from determination by circumstances of his particular acts.

While perhaps Fichte in one phase of his thought represented the culmination of this branch of idealism, the Hegelian branch, which was much more influential, went in a different direction. Its emphasis was on the element of "objectivism" in idealistic philosophy[1] as against the greater "subjectivism" of Kant. In application to human affairs this led to a kind of "emanation" theory. Instead of being treated by and for itself an individual human act or complex of action tended to be interpreted as a mode of expression of a "spirit" (*Geist*) sharing this quality with multitudinous other acts of the same and other individuals. Thus to Hegel human history was the process of "objectification" of the single unitary *Weltgeist*.

The result of this tendency was to arrange human activities in relation to comprehensive "collective" or "totality patterns." Historical attention was focused not on individual events or acts but on the *Geist*, which constituted their unity.

Under these conditions the "historical" trend of thinking was, however, preserved intact. The unifying concept under which discrete empirical data were subsumed was not that of a general "law" or analytical element, as in the positivistic tradition, but rather a particular, unique *Geist*, a specific cultural totality clearly distinct from and incommensurable with all others. It is in this emphasis on the importance of historically unique cultural systems, and the tendency to treat all empirical data in relation to such systems that the main trend of German social *theory* on an idealistic basis is to be found.

The various fields in which this tendency has worked out are too numerous and complex to detail here. Perhaps the first prominent one, outside of history proper, was that of jurisprudence, where the famous historical school starting with Savigny applied this historical method to the analysis of systems of law, above all, Roman law. Instead of treating it as the Roman

---

[1] *Objektiver Geist* is the German term. This element was present in Kant but in a position of different relative emphasis.

jurists themselves did, in relation to a universal natural "reason," they saw it as a self-contained system expressing a certain *Geist* which could be formulated in terms of a limited number of principles.[1] But this system was radically distinct from other legal systems, for instance, that of Germanic law.[2]

There was a similar movement in the German historical school of economics[3] especially in its earlier phase. They held that the classical economics did not constitute, as its proponents claimed, a set of universally applicable principles of economic life, but was rather the expression of a particular *Geist*, that of liberalism, individualism, commercialism, *Manchestertum*. Hence its usefulness is confined to the social circumstances where the particular "spirit" in question is predominant; it is not of general application. Hence the attempt to work out in contradistinction other alternative economic systems, such as that of the Middle Ages.

In the Hegelian form the background of this "historicism" was a rigidly monistic idealism which in historical application required a unified conception of human life and history as a whole. The bridge between this final unity and the historical uniqueness of particular historical epochs and cultures was provided by the "dialectic" which left room for qualitative differences in the stages of "self-realization" of the *Weltgeist*, each stage standing in certain respects in antithesis to the preceding one.

This movement, however, has also gone through what was, in a certain sense, a "positivistic," critical stage. This has taken the form of a skeptical attitude toward great speculative constructions on the Hegelian model. As is usually the case, however, such criticism has attacked only certain elements of the thought system, leaving others intact. In this particular instance it was mainly the continuity of structural principle as between cultures which was attacked. But the underlying mode of thinking, the attempt to organize data about the concept of a *Geist* and the unique "system" associated with it, was left undisturbed. The result is that the particular historical epochs or their "spirits"

---

[1] *Cf.* as an explicit recognition of this the title of Jhering's work: *Der Geist des römischen Rechts.*

[2] See for instance Gierke's great work, *Das deutsche Genossenschaftsrecht.*

[3] This school, under Schmoller's influence, tended strongly in the direction of a complete empiricism.

remained in a state of disconnection, a *Nebeneinander*. The dogma of individual uniqueness is pushed to the point of breaking all theoretical continuity with others. So in place of a theory of dialectic evolution on the Hegelian model there emerges a complete historical relativism. History becomes a succession of such unique and essentially unconnected systems. On the empirical plane one of the first radical representatives of this relativistic view is Dilthey.[1] Since his time the same tendency has been carried still farther onto the epistemological plane by the recent movement known as *Wissenssoziologie*.[2]

As has already been noted, this emphasis on the whole, the totality of a cultural system, has involved a repudiation of the type of analytical theory inherent in the conceptual structures of the positivistic tradition. The prevailingly empiricist temper which has characterized both parties to the controversy has only served to intensify this repudiation, since it is unquestionably true both that these theories, of the classical economics for instance, have failed to do justice to certain of the concrete facts, and that an important and valid correction of them could be arrived at by viewing the phenomena concerned from the point of view of cultural totality.[3] Thus the prevailing German view has been very far from completely lacking its own empirical justification.

At the same time this repudiation of general analytical concepts and the corresponding emphasis on organic totality has forced German theory into methodological paths which were highly dubious from the point of view of those interested in analytical theory. For, on the one hand, science could not be limited to the isolated observation of discrete individual facts and phenomena—particular acts and events—as one branch of German empiricism would require. At the same time, there was no general analytical theory in terms of which to organize particular discrete observations, and to evaluate their scientific significance. Hence the

---

[1] Spengler also gives one of the more radical instances of this view.

[2] Perhaps the best-known representative is Karl Mannheim. *Cf.* his *Ideologie und Utopie*, translated by Louis Wirth & Edward Shils as *Ideology and Utopia*.   For a general sketch of the literature of the movement, see E. Grünwald, *Das Problem der Soziologie des Wissens*.

[3] From the above analysis it will be clear that one main reason for this is the fact that the phenomena are in fact "organic," a fact obscured by the "atomistic" tendencies of utilitarian and positivistic social theories.

necessity for recognizing a source of knowledge with little place in the repertoire of science as generally understood—a kind of "intuition" for the peculiar structures of wholes which could neither be "observed" in the usual operational sense, nor constructed by the ordinary theoretical processes.[1]

The methodological conflict has been the more irreconcilable the more definitely positivistic thought has been "mechanistic" and "atomistic," and, indeed, throughout a good deal of its history these characteristics have been strongly marked. The stock German criticism of the ideas of the "enlightenment," of utilitarianism, positivism, rationalism, has run in these terms. Over against this has been set some version or other of an "organic" view. Germany has been preeminently the home of "organic" social theory all through the nineteenth century and up to the present.

The dichotomy of "mechanistic," "atomistic" or "individualistic" and "organic" is stated, however, in exceedingly general and formal terms. It denotes scarcely more than the most formal general relations of parts or units to a whole. In the course of the development of German thought a more specific account of what is involved has gradually emerged.

The issues between German idealism and Western European positivism have been more than merely methodological in the above formal sense. They have concerned differences over the substantive factors invoked in explanation of human action. The original Kantian dualism laid down a sharp distinction between the sphere of "nature," of phenomena, of determinism, on the one hand, and that of freedom, of ideas, of *Geist*, on the other. The main line of German social thought has been concerned with the latter sphere. This means that its "organicism" has not been mainly a matter of the biological analogy, though this has sometimes appeared, but has lain in this sense in the ideal sphere.

The essential "reality" then, the determining factors in human life and action, has tended to be found on this level. There is, however, a radical distinction between this order of reality and that dealt with by positivistic thought, or given in Kant's world of phenomena. The latter is a complex of elements func-

---

[1] Hence the tendency for the "hard-boiled scientific" wing to run off into the historical particularism noted above. Schmoller is a conspicuous example.

tionally or causally related to each other. This conception involves at least the postulate of process *in time*—for underlying every conception of causal relationship is that of variation. Two entities are causally related if, and in so far as, a *change* in one will result in a change in the other. Change in this context certainly implies temporal process.

An "ideal reality," on the other hand, implies a complex of elements mutually related to one another—constituting hence a "system"—but this mode of relationship is of a radically different character from the causal—it is a "complex of meanings."[1] Thus a scientific theory is a complex or system of propositions *logically* related to one another.[2] Similarly an artistic "form" constitutes a structure of elements, in the case of a symphony, for example, of sound combinations, related to each other, not logically, but still "meaningfully." There is, to use Professor Köhler's[3] term, a certain mutual "requiredness" such that it is quite evident when a "false" note is struck, as it is possible to detect, in a theory, a logical fallacy.

Whatever else they may be, these meaningful relations of the elements of a system are not causal relations. Two circumstances may be noted to bring this out. In the first place, the relation to time is fundamentally different. Logical relations are timeless as is the form of a work of art. This is not to say that such systems do not have an origin in time in one sense—of the time of their creation.[4] Nor does it mean that time is irrelevant to the form of concrete symbolic expression, as in music or poetry. What it means is that the system of meanings "in itself" is atemporal. The relations between the elements of the system are not relations in a temporal process but are of a radically different order.[5]

---

[1] *Sinnzusammenhang*, in the expressive German term.

[2] In discussing these things it is both important and difficult to keep two levels of discourse distinct, that of the ideal system "in itself" and its relations to action. Thus in the first sense a change in one proposition of a system of scientific theory results in changes in other propositions of the same system. But though there are in the logical sense "inevitable" implications, it is not in the real world inevitable that they should be drawn. To the actor correct logic states a norm conformity with which is problematical.

[3] WOLFGANG KÖHLER, in William James lectures at Harvard University (unpublished).

[4] That is, in their relation to action.

[5] This is brought out by the fact that the "same" meanings may be

Secondly, the relation to action is entirely different. As has been shown at great length, causal relations are relevant to rational action in the role of conditions and means. In so far as causal relations subsist between elements of his situation the actor is thereby "conditioned" in the sense that attainment of an end in the given situation depends on his "taking account of" these relations. Meaningful relations, on the other hand, condition action[1] in one sense, but not in the same sense. Their role is normative—they express relations between various elements and aspects of an ideal toward which action is oriented. In elaborating a theory for instance, there is nothing in the conditions of his situation to prevent the theorist from making a logical error—what prevents him is, rather, his effort to conform his action to the norm of logical correctness. Similarly, in playing a musical theme it is perfectly "possible" objectively for a pianist to strike a "wrong" note. He avoids doing it because it would contravene the normative requiredness of the musical form.

It has already appeared in the course of the present analysis of action that at least two modes of relation of "ideal" elements to the spatial and temporal aspects of experience are significant to action, whatever others further analysis might disclose. Normative elements may, that is, be related to action and thought, first, in an intrinsic context and, second, as one term of a symbolic relation.

The first relation is that which lies closest to positivistic modes of thought, since for thought processes the elements of scientific methodology constitute such a norm, especially the logical, and in so far as action is rational, in the sense employed throughout this study, the same elements are normative not only to thought but also to action. Or, better, thought, considered as a process of attaining knowledge, is one case of a much larger category of actions oriented to logical norms. In this context the meaningful elements of action become, in the terms of a voluntaristic theory of action, of causal significance, for it is only in terms of orientation to such norms that a measure

---

expressed in two different symbolic media, one of which does and the other does not require temporal order. Thus Euripides' plays and Phidias' sculpture may be said to express roughly the same things.

[1] That is "make a difference" in it.

of independence of the processes of action from their conditions is conceivable.

The second mode of relation, the symbolic, has come into prominence especially in connection with Durkheim's treatment of religion. At the polar extreme there ceases to be any intrinsic relation between the particular symbol and its meaning; certainly the relation is not that between the non-normative elements of a situation and a norm. In this context spatiotemporal phenomena of all sorts are capable of interpretation, not in terms of their intrinsic properties and their causal relations, but as symbolic expressions of meanings or systems of meanings. In so far as phenomena are interpreted in this context, it means dispensing with the causal explanation of the natural sciences altogether.

For the connection between a particular symbol and its meaning is in the causal sense always arbitrary. It can be known only when a key is provided to open the door, when the "language" is known. The only intrinsic element common to symbols and their meanings is that of order. And this can never be grasped by the isolated study of particular symbols, but only in terms of their mutual relations in systems.[1] This fact undoubtedly constitutes one of the basic reasons for the "organicism" of German social thought, its hostility to any attempt to break down the concrete whole analytically.   Both modes of relation of the ideal or meaningful to the spatiotemporal play a prominent part in idealistic social thought, with, however, a tendency for the symbolic to take precedence over the normative.

In the course of time this basic distinction between causal and meaningful relationships has come to be embodied in methodological terms. As distinct from the analytical methods of the natural sciences, that of the sciences of "Culture" has been given the particular name *Verstehen*. Under this somewhat difficult concept, which owes more perhaps to Dilthey than to anyone else, the most important meaning for present purposes is its reference to

---

[1] That the "key" is necessary even here is brought out vividly by the experience of archaeologists with inscriptions. Before the discovery of the Rosetta stone Egyptian hieroglyphs had been known for a long time. There was no mystery about their physical properties: nothing significant has been added to our knowledge in this respect. What was needed was their meaning, which was provided by a translation of these symbols into a known language—Greek. For lack of such a key many inscriptions such as the Minoan and the Mayan can still not be deciphered.

the grasp of symbolic relationships. An entity is *verstanden* when it is given a place in a system of meaningful relationships, by which it acquires *Sinn*. If it is itself an ideal entity, for instance, a proposition, this takes place directly. If not, if it is rather a spatiotemporal object or event, the method of *Verstehen* involves a further step—this entity must by symbolic interpretation be assigned a meaning which makes it congruent to such an ideal system.

As will be seen these considerations by no means exhaust the concept of *Verstehen*, particularly as employed by Weber. Another fundamental aspect is its reference to "subjective" phenomena. In so far as "meanings" may be said to have an empirical spatiotemporal "existence" at all it is "in the mind."[1] There is unquestionably an exceedingly close connection between the apprehension of meaningful relations as such, on the one hand, and the study of the subjective aspect of action, on the other. Here only a reference is made to the relation. It will have to be discussed at considerable length in connection with Weber.

If, however, the above interpretation of the main line of German idealistic social thought is correct, the chronic conflict of that thought with that on a positivistic basis is not surprising. Against mechanism, individualism, atomism, it has placed organicism, the subordination of the unit, including the human individual, to the whole. Against essential continuity in its field of study, which has looked upon particular cases as instances of a general law or principle, it has emphasized the irreducible qualitative individuality of the phenomena it was studying and has issued in a far-reaching historical relativism.

But underlying these differences is a still more fundamental one. Positivistic thought has always directed its efforts to the uncovering of intrinsic causal relationships in the phenomena; idealistic thought to the discovery of relations of meaning, of *Sinnzusammenhang*. With this difference has gone that of method—on the one hand, causal theoretical explanation, on the other, interpretation of meaning, *Sinndeutung*, which has seen in the concrete facts of its field symbols, the meanings of

---

[1] Or "embodied in symbols" which, since they have a meaning, imply an understanding mind. Still another aspect is the subjective understanding of action and its motivation in relation to normative elements. See below, Chap. XVI, pp. 635 *ff*.

which are to be interpreted. The order and system of social phenomena has been a meaningful,[1] not a causal order at all.

Given the empiricist bias characteristic of both traditions, a mutual aggressiveness was inevitable. The positivist has persistently tried to "reduce" ostensibly meaningful systems to a causal basis, to make his causal analysis cover all intellectually apprehensible relationships; the idealist, on the other hand, has with equal insistence tried to absorb causal relationships into meaningful systems. Both have been imperialistic in the sense of attempting to make their own methodological principles cover the whole field of things knowable, at least in relation to human beings.

Earlier in this study the attempt has been made in the course of a long analysis to bring out certain fundamental difficulties of a completely positivistic version of the theory of action, and to demonstrate to what extent the positivistic theory of action has itself become involved in these difficulties and in so doing has transcended the rigidly positivistic basis, developing at least partly in an idealistic direction. The task of the present section will be to follow the reverse process and show some of the inherent difficulties of a completely idealistic position, and how positivistic elements have come into the idealistic tradition. It will not, however, do merely to say that both the positivistic and the idealistic positions have certain justifications and there is a sphere in which each should be recognized. It is necessary, rather, to go beyond such eclecticism, to attempt, at least in outline, an account of the specific modes of interrelation between the two. It is in this connection that the voluntaristic theory of action assumes a place of central importance. It provides a bridge between the apparently irreconcilable differences of the two traditions, making it possible, in a certain sense, to "make the best of both worlds."[2]

It should almost go without saying that the category "systems of meaning," or "meaningful complexes," is not homogeneous

---

[1] The term sounds somewhat awkward in English but seems to be the best available translation of the German *sinnvoll* and its various related words.

[2] It should be clear to the reader that in the view put forward here action is precisely the point of articulation in human experience between the causal-functional and the symbolic-meaningful elements. Hence a dogmatism which assigns exclusive validity to either one is unsuitable in this field.

but covers a number of different types. It is not intended anywhere in this work to attempt thoroughgoing analysis which could issue in an exhaustive classification. Certain distinctions will, however, naturally emerge from the general theoretical framework of the discussion to be more precisely formulated later on. At the present juncture, however, one fact should be noted and its significance suggested. One such type of meaning complex has been of paramount importance in relation to the positivistic tradition, namely scientific theory. A most important result of the above analysis of Pareto's work was to develop a clear distinction between it and another type which is also highly significant for action, that is, value ideas.

It is not fortuitous that in so far as the idealistic tradition has been concerned with human action it has been upon the latter that the principal stress has been laid. If the *Volksgeist* or other *Geist* has been held by various schools to be the central determinant of a concrete system of action or relationships to be analyzed, its content will generally be found to consist in normative value ideas, a set of conceptions of what human actions and relationships *should* be. Furthermore the actual treatment of historical cases will be found to bring out the close affinity of these value systems to other meaning systems such as religious and metaphysical ideas and artistic styles, all of which stand in sharp contrast to scientific theories.

In the discussion of Durkheim the significance of this basic distinction has already been commented upon. Scientific theories constitute the closest connecting link between the causal and the meaningful elements of reality because, while the theories as such are systems of meaning, the symbolic references involved are to systems of intrinsic causal relationship. This is not in the same sense true of the other types of meaning system—they can, in fact, be arranged in a series extending from purely scientific theories at one end to what are "pure forms of expression" at the other, in which intrinsic elements are of *only* symbolic significance. Certain types of art form constitute the clearest example of the second category.

The Problem of Capitalism

So far the discussion of the idealistic tradition has been confined to a bare logical outline with only sporadic references to particular developments of thought in specific fields. Before closing this chapter the main stages of development of one particular historicotheoretical problem—capitalism—will be sketched both to illustrate the way in which the logical distinctions of the foregoing discussion are involved in a particular subject matter, and because it forms the central empirical focus of Weber's work, which will be taken up in detail in the two following chapters.

The disposition to consider the modern economic order as a historically unique system of relationships expressing a particular *Geist* was already strong in the earlier historical school of economics. As has been noted, the classical economics was thought of as an expression of this *Geist* and hence as applicable only to this particular set of relationships, those of an "individualistic" order. But by far the most important thinker to work out a *theory* of the modern economic order on a historical basis was Marx.[1] It is the Marxian system which has formed the central focus of the German discussion of capitalism.

Marx

Marx is not generally considered as belonging to the historical school of economics as such. He is, in the respects of importance here, a direct descendant of Hegel. Whatever may be the conflict involved in the difference between Hegelian idealism and Marxian materialism, in certain essential respects Marx took over a Hegelian mode of thought. Like Hegel he worked out a philosophy of history conceiving human development as a single process toward a determinate goal, though both the goal and the character of the process differed from Hegel's account. But also like Hegel and unlike the positivistic evolutionists he conceived the process not as continuous in a single line, each stage constituting in certain respects a quantitative increase over the previous stage, but as dialectical. That is, while there is continuity in the process as a whole, each stage forms a well-marked "system" distinct in principle of organization from the others, and arising in direct conflict with its predecessor in the series. While in a

---

[1] For purposes of the present discussion it is not necessary to attempt to distinguish in Marxian thought the specific contributions of Marx from those of Engels. The reader may, if he prefers, substitute "Marx-Engels" for "Marx" in the following pages.

continuous process the delimitation of stages is arbitrary, this is not the case in a dialectic process.

As has been noted,[1] for his own purposes Marx took over the main framework of the classical economic theory. But, characteristically, he turned it from an analytical theory of the economic aspect of social phenomena in general into a historical theory of the functioning and development of a particular economic system, the capitalistic. There is relatively little light to be found in Marx on what economic theory would be required by other systems, such as the feudal or the socialistic. But in spite of this it is entirely clear that the capitalistic system is definitely distinct, not merely as a stage, but in principle, from both its predecessor and its putative successor in the dialectic process.

The classical economic theory had been put forward on an empiricist basis—which Marx did not question. Hence it necessarily involved elements of social organization—what some modern writers would call "institutional" elements. But in those he chose to emphasize, Marx differed strikingly from the principal classical theorists. Their main concern was with the phenomena of division of labor and exchange as between discrete individuals, each producing a complete commodity for the consumers' market; this was at least the main institutional starting point. Marx, to be sure, took over the conception of a plurality of competing productive units, but centered an attention which, in spite of strong suggestions in Malthus and Ricardo, was new in its intensity and emphasis on the theoretical consequences, on the internal structure of the productive unit.

Here, of course, what mainly interested him was what Malthus had referred to as the "division of society into classes of employers and laborers." There was thus an internal conflict of interest within the basic unit of the system, the capitalistic enterprise. This was the class conflict, involving a power relationship between the classes.

Thus it was its class structure based, in turn, upon the organization of the unit of production, which primarily characterized the capitalistic system for Marx, and it was this element which he generalized beyond the capitalistic system to make the systematic unifying principle of the whole evolutionary process. It was, on the one hand, its specific class structure which char-

[1] See Chap. III, pp. 107 *ff.*

acterized each social system, this class structure in each case being founded in the "conditions of production." Each system is dominated by a class but at the same time requires, and in its own development creates, another class which, in turn, destroys it. Thus, on the other hand, it is class conflict which constitutes the dynamic element of the evolutionary process and forms the contradiction between any one system and its predecessor or successor as the case may be. It is this element, a form of the power element of the previous discussion, which gives the Marxian theory its dynamic cast as against the equilibrating tendency of "orthodox" economic theory.

It is now possible to approach the question of what can be meant by *materialism* in the Marxian sense. The experience of this study has certainly been that it is always helpful to attempt to understand a writer in terms of the polemical oppositions of the thought of his time. Marx's own polemics were aimed mainly in two directions, against Hegelian idealism and against the Utopian socialists. But before taking up the implications of this double polemic it is well to eliminate one possible and rather frequent misapprehension. Marx did not use the word materialism in the familiar positivistic sense of reducing social phenomena causally to terms of the nonhuman environment, as natural resources, or of biological heredity or some combination of both. This interpretation is definitely precluded by the historical features of the Marxian theory. To be sure, natural resources are of fundamental importance in it, as is also nationalism with whatever racial basis may underly it, but in both cases the importance derives from the relation of these elements to a particular form of social organization. They cannot, however, account for the social organization itself, since these factors have not *changed* in the process of development of the capitalistic system. There is a fundamental element in capitalism independent of men's biological needs, their other biologically inherited traits or their external environment. Marxism is a social doctrine.

Marx made the famous remark that Hegel was standing on his head and he, Marx, set him right side up. What does this mean? Only that the dynamic forces of history are not to be found in the immanent self-development of a *Geist* in the Hegelian sense, but in a different sphere, that of men's "interests." Materialism is here to be understood by contrast with the specific Hegelian sense of idealism. It is as such a residual category and not to be identified with the prevailing Western sense of the same term in the common phrase scientific materialism.

The other related epithet most frequently applied to Marx, *determinism*, acquires its meaning largely by contrast with Utopian socialism. The Utopians, of whom Owen and Fourier may serve as examples, belong mainly to a phase of the movement of thought discussed above[1] as radical rationalistic positivism. In relation to the irrationalities of contemporary social conditions they were characterized by a belief in the overwhelming power of reason to show men the "true" conditions of their happiness, independently of the particular situation a given individual happened to be in. Then all that would be necessary to change a social system would be to appeal to the "reason" of individuals, above all of those in positions of responsibility, to show them the irrationality of the present order and the reasonableness of the alternative proposed.

To this Marx opposed his view of "interests." There is, in Marx, no suggestion of a radical anti-intellectualism of the positivistic variety. Indeed, he could not have accepted classical economic theory had he taken this position. Men acted rationally for him, even if in a somewhat limited sense more suggestive of Hobbes than of Locke or Condorcet. But they acted rationally within a given concrete situation and within such a situation the rational norm itself necessitates certain lines of action, precluding others. Men, precisely because they do act rationally, will follow their "interests" as defined for them by the situations in which they are placed.

It was inherent in the conceptual framework of the classical economics that strong emphasis should be thrown on the positive advantages of the division of labor. By comparison with the state of nature it was a more efficient way of securing means to want satisfaction. The mechanism of competition was thought of more in this light and less as a mechanism of control; and even when it was considered as the latter, it was thought of more as a check on possible abuses than on anything else.

Marx, through his doctrine of interests, elevated not only competition but the whole structure of the economic order into a

[1] Chap. III, p. 119–121.

great control mechanism, a compulsive system. This is the essential meaning of Marx's conception of economic determinism. It is not a matter of psychological antirationalism, but of the total consequences of a multitude of rational acts. On the one hand, the system itself is the resultant of the myriad of individual acts but, on the other, it creates for each acting individual a specific situation which compels him to act in certain ways if he is not to go contrary to his interest. Thus for Marx exploitation was to be blamed on neither the unreasonableness nor the plain selfishness of the individual employer, but the employer was placed in a situation where he must act as he did, or be eliminated in the competitive struggle.[1]

Thus, while "liberal" theory focused its main attention on the superior efficiency of an individualistic order, Marx stressed its compulsive aspect and through this the total structure of the system. The system itself would be thought of as self-acting. Once the individuals involved in it are placed in the situations that are given, their actions are "determined" so as to maintain the system as a whole, or rather to drive it forward on the evolutionary course, to end at last in its self-destruction.

The peculiar forms of compulsion found in the capitalistic system are not universal, but are limited to its particular conditions, to its specific combination of the "conditions of production." Under feudalism, exploitation of labor in the capitalistic enterprise was not the dominant feature of society, and with the advent of socialism it will cease to be. The essential question of Marxism, then, is, what are the factors accounting for this situation which results in capitalistic determinism? This raises again the question of materialism.

The materialistic view, in the Marxian sense of the term, is that the compulsive discipline in one system, the capitalistic for instance, is a development from the similarly compulsive conditions of the preceding system. History constitutes from this point of view an unbroken chain of such deterministic systems. Whatever the degree of their incommensurability with each other, and of the importance of class conflict as the propulsive dynamic force in the dialectic process, the causal link is unbroken and each system by the process of its own "immanent "breakdown

---

[1] An excellent discussion of this aspect of Marx is to be found in Sombart's *Der proletarische Sozialismus.*

inevitably gives birth to its successor in the series. Naturally this conception implies an original historical element in the sense of an originally deterministic set of conditions of production out of which the whole thing flows.

It should be emphasized again that the determinism of the theory lies not on an individual-psychological, but on a social, level. It is the situation which dictates a given course of action; in a different situation all would be changed. Many Western critics of Marx have thought to detect an insoluble contradiction between the determinism of his historical materialism and the advocacy of an active revolutionary policy. Indeed, if his materialism were of the positivistic variety this would be the case—but it is not. It arises out of the *resultant* of innumerable rational acts, each act presupposing a given situation. Marx's difference from the classical economists is merely this: In the first place he threw his attention from the rational process itself back to the situation which dictated its course. Secondly, with the aid of the dynamic element supplied by the conception of class conflict[1] he saw what the classical economists did not see, that the fundamental character of these situations was subject to historical change. He thus introduced an element of historical relativism of the first importance.

But his conception of social causation remained essentially that of the classical economists; it was, in the terminology of the previous discussion, essentially utilitarian, with the addition of the historical element. It shares with them the complete preoccupation with means and conditions of action, hence the corresponding implicit assumption of the randomness of ultimate ends.

Marx took over the main "economic" elements of the classical theory, including the conception of a self-regulating competitive system. But, as has been stated, he differs in his emphasis on a particular form of social organization. Hence he invoked for the dynamic part of the theory, elements *not* central to the main framework of classical theory. It is interesting to note what these are: One is industrial technology, the development of which is to be thought of as a continuous linear process. Of course the orthodox economists were by no means oblivious of this, but they thought of it only in its bearing on productivity, while for Marx

[1] In combination with technological advance.

its main significance lay in its relation to social organization, starting with the structure of the productive unit. Thus there is one dynamic factor of a linear character.

The other is, of course, the class struggle. This it is which, in its particular combination with the technological and the economic, characterizes a given economic system and constitutes the element of discontinuity; because the class structure of each is different, the different systems cannot be compared. This is, however, at bottom a type of power element in the above sense,[1] a power relation on the basis of a given situation.

Thus Marxian economic determinism is a matter not of economic causation alone in the specific sense arrived at in the previous discussion but of the total intermediate sector of the intrinsic means-end chain, a combination of technological, economic and political determinism. It is materialistic only as *opposed* to idealistic in the Hegelian sense. It has no necessary implication of materialism in the usual positivistic sense.[2]

It is true that there is also another element in Marx—that expressed in his revolutionary side. The proletariat is characterized, in the first place, by a particular interest in the capitalistic order. But there is a fundamental difference between the case where this interest is dormant, expressed only in attitudes to immediate situations, and the case of class consciousness. At the class-conscious level another factor enters the situation, the organized concerted action of the proletariat to overthrow the existing order and establish socialism. This looks very much like a common value element. Why does it not play a part in Marx's general view of history instead of entering only at this one point?

In the first place Marx was after all an evolutionist. In such a context there is nothing inherently unreasonable in thinking of a given phenomenon as emergent at a fairly well-defined point in the process. And his view of human nature did not logically preclude the possibility of this *Sprung in die Freiheit*. But, secondly, Marx himself undoubtedly shared to a large extent the rationalistic-anarchistic philosophy of the Utopian socialists whom he criticized. He differed from them in possessing a far

---

[1] *Cf.* Chapter III, p. 109.

[2] Modified of course by the instability of the utilitarian position which has been analyzed.

greater degree of realism about the process by which the goal could be reached. The appeal to reason could not be effective regardless of social conditions, but only when it corresponded to an interest. And only at this stage of the total evolutionary process did the particular basis of interest exist.

But there is one and only one goal. Marx was in a sense a sociological relativist—but by no means an ethical relativist. And his ethical absolutism unquestionably meant the focusing of his whole system of thought, in its pragmatic aspect, on the conditions for the realization of his own ideal. In this respect it is logically the exact counterpart of the Hegelian system, with different content.[1]

SOMBART

As has already been noted, the Marxian theory in the broader aspects which have been under discussion here[2] has formed the focus of the discussion of capitalism in Germany. In closing this chapter a brief outline may be presented of one prominent issue of the discussion, the theory of Werner Sombart, which may be said in a sense to have assimilated the main content of Marx into the framework of orthodox historicoidealistic thought. Then in the next chapter Weber's treatment of the same set of problems will be taken up in more detail. It differs in important respects from that of both Marx and Sombart.

The subject of Sombart's life work has been the study of a single, historically unique economic system—modern capitalism.[3] In the process, however, Sombart has not considered himself merely as a historian but quite definitely as an economic theorist. But in his view there is no such thing as general economic theory applicable to the facts of any time or place, but only the theory of an indefinite plurality of economic systems, each separate from the others. Sombart himself gives us only the theory of one particular economic system, capitalism, in all its ramifications, and to throw it into relief, a sketch of two pre-

[1] On this aspect of Marx *cf.* Troeltsch, *Hiztorizmus*, pp. 314 *ff.*

[2] It is noteworthy that in Germany only the socialists have been much preoccupied with the technicalities of Marxian economic theory. His broader influence has been exerted almost entirely in such fields as the problems of capitalism and historical materialism.

[3] Documented mainly in Sombart's massive work, *Der moderne Kapitalismus,* 2d ed.

capitalistic systems, self-sufficient economy and the handicraft system.

The economic system is not for Sombart a historical phenomenon which he merely describes, but an "ideal type"[1] which he employs for the understanding of the concrete historical process. For him the radical discontinuity of economic systems applies only to the type. The concrete process itself is continuous, representing a gradual shading off of systems into each other.

But however much Sombart may emphasize the abstract theoretical character of his concepts, the fact remains that their reference is individual and historical and not analytical and general.[2] The economic system capitalism is useful not in general but in the analysis of the facts of only one historical epoch. In this respect Sombart has drawn the radical conclusion appropriate to following the historical-idealistic tradition.

He is equally radical in the other main aspect of his work—his theory of causation, which is a direct polemical answer to Marxian historical materialism. There are, he says, three aspects of an economic system: a form of organization, a "spirit" (*Geist*) and a technique. With one notable exception he takes over the Marxian description of the system (that is, its ideal type) but he differs profoundly in his interpretation of the relations of its elements, giving definite priority to the spirit, which, he says, has created the form of organization for itself. It is worth while to outline briefly the particular concepts in order to illuminate the general theoretical issue.

On the organization side the system is characterized, on the one hand, by the character of the unit which makes it up, the capitalistic enterprise, and, on the other, by the kind of relations between these units. The enterprise is internally organized by division into two main classes, the owner-managers on the one hand, the propertyless wageworkers on the other. Their relations to each other are typical competitive-market relations. The total complex of enterprises forms a closed, self-sustaining system.

---

[1] See below Chap. XVI for a more extended discussion of the ideal type in connection with Weber.

[2] Here, of the two elements of Marxian thought, he has self-consciously taken over one. Marx took over classical economic concepts when they were useful to him without bothering too much about their methodological status.

The immediate end of each enterprise must above all be profit making, whatever the private motives of the individual participants may be, for the competitive process focuses all capitalistic activities on profit and makes its attainment the measure of success and the condition of survival.

Thus Sombart agrees with Marx on the compulsive character of the system. Its competitiveness and acquisitiveness are not matters of the private motives of individuals but of the inexorable conditions of the situations in which individuals are placed.[1] Moreover he also agrees that this has not always been characteristic of all economic systems; it was not true, for instance, of the handicraft system.

But this compulsiveness applies only to the fully developed system where its *Geist* has become "objectified" or "institutionalized." But Sombart differs radically from Marx in his interpretation of how this has come about. Instead of this objective form of organization being a resultant from previous similar forms, it is the creation of a *Geist*. The principles of this *Geist* are acquisitiveness, competition and rationality.

For Sombart this *Geist* has two aspects, the spirit of enterprise and the bourgeois spirit.[2] The former accounts for the first two principles. Its principles are by no means confined to the economic sphere but its working there is a phase of the great movement of the Renaissance. Its distinguishing characteristics are individuality, initiative, energy and a struggle for power. It is the same spirit which has created the modern state, science and exploration.

Economic enterprise, however, is a peculiarly favorable field for this spirit, because acquisitive activities once loosed from the bonds of traditionalism do not contain, on the one hand, any inherent limit; on the other, are inherently competitive. And only in this field has the Renaissance spirit created so tightly knit an institutional system.

Another interesting difference from Marx is the way Sombart pushes his thesis of system discontinuity into the field of tech-

---

[1] It is instructive to note the similarity of this to Durkheim's approach to the problem of constraint.

[2] See *Der Bourgeois*, trans. by M. Epstein as *The Quintessence of Capitalism;* see also Talcott Parsons, "Recent German Literature on Capitalism, I, Werner Sombart," *Journal of Political Economy*, December, 1928.

nology, the central stronghold of positivistic, linear evolutionism. The technology of developed capitalism is not, he holds, merely more "advanced" than that of the precapitalistic era; it rests on radically different principles. Where the latter was traditional, it is rational; where the latter was empirical, it is scientific. Handicraft technique rested on empirical rules, that is, rules embodying particular experiences traditionally handed down without reference to general principles. Capitalistic technique, on the other hand, consists mainly in the application of theoretical scientific knowledge to particular problems without reference to tradition.

Finally, the class struggle is far less prominent in Sombart than in Marx. This is not essentially because Sombart fails to recognize its organizational basis in the structure of the capitalistic enterprise—on the contrary, he does so quite explicitly—but because he has a quite different conception of the process of the development of capitalism. For Marx it was the progressive emergence of the contradictions inherent in the material basis; for Sombart, on the other hand, it represents the progressive objectification of the *Geist*, that is, the gradual transformation of subjective attitudes into a compulsive institutionalized system. This is the process which forms the central theme of Sombart's treatment. Moreover, his work is not oriented "forward" to the emergence of the successors of capitalism, but is concentrated rather on the system itself; ethically he looks backward, if anything.

This brief sketch of Sombart's theory of capitalism should serve to bring out certain points. In concrete subject matter, and most of the descriptive characteristics of the system, the origin of the theory lies in Marx. But not only does it agree with Marx in emphasizing the historical character of the system; it goes far beyond him both in eliminating everything but its historical character and in bringing the interpretation of the latter away from Marx's materialism back into the main line of German historicoidealistic methodological thought.

This is accomplished principally by the role he assigns to the "spirit of capitalism." This entity is given the sole creative role except for certain limiting conditions. The concrete activities of men in the system are "expressions" of this *Geist*, not, as in orthodox economic theory, means of want satisfaction. More-

over, this *Geist* is not thought of as one element in a process
of complex interaction with several others; it acts alone.

Indeed, Sombart is still in a certain sense an empiricist. His
theory is not, to be sure, a direct description of the total concrete
phenomenon of capitalism; it is an ideal type. But it is not
analytical in the sense of the previous discussion; it states the
"essence" of the concrete facts. Apart from the fact that more
than one system can be identified in the same situation, what is
omitted is contingent in the sense of not being significant for
any social science theory whatever. It is an "economic" theory
but not, like Pareto's, abstract in the sense that for concrete
adequacy it requires supplementing by other theories dealing
with other elements in the same concrete phenomena. That is
why Sombart is under the logical necessity of including in his
system even such an apparently foreign element as technology.

Thus in the Marx-Sombart conflict is to be found for this
study the statement of a fundamental issue. As far as it is
possible to read a factor theory into Marx's materialism, it
involves essentially the elements dominant in the utilitarian
tradition. Sombart, however, attacks Marx on the ground of his
not being able to account for the facts of the objective compulsive
system which was Marx's own empirical starting point. The
outcome of the above analysis of the internal difficulties of the
utilitarian tradition is a position empirically favorable to Sombart's criticism.

Moreover, in Sombart an element has emerged which fits
in with the previous analysis of his study. His *Geist* is unquestionably a common value element. But the methodological
framework in terms of which he treats it is "imperialistic"
as are all empiricisms. It makes the total concrete phenomenon
of capitalism, so far as it can become an object of the social
sciences at all, a "manifestation" of this *Geist*. It thereby
altogether eliminates the utilitarian factors. Hence Sombart's
perfectly logical and definite repudiation of orthodox economic
theory.

Weber, on the other hand, was a thinker steeped both in the
idealistic tradition of thought and in the particular empirical
problems of Marx and Sombart. He transcended, however, the
Marx-Sombart dilemma in a way consonant with the general
scheme of analysis developed in this study. To him, then, it will
now turn for more intensive consideration.

Chapter XIV

MAX WEBER I: RELIGION AND MODERN CAPITALISM

A. Protestantism and Capitalism

The peculiar circumstances under which Weber's work on the relations of Protestantism and capitalism has come to the attention of English scholarship have given rise to a widespread but erroneous impression of his intellectual character. His association with what has been widely interpreted as a dramatic and radical thesis in historical interpretation has favored the view that he was the type that takes a simple idea and drives it to extremes, concerned only with bold outlines and showing a sovereign disdain of meticulous detailed factual study. He has often been interpreted as a "philosopher" or "theorist" in the derogatory sense of one who makes the facts fit his theories rather than the reverse.

It is true that Weber could on occasion formulate his views very sharply, particularly where a polemical element was present in the situation. But this by no means exhausts his character. Anyone who attempts to understand his sociological work in its completeness to any degree cannot fail to be impressed, and to a great extent bewildered, by the enormous mass of detailed historical material which Weber commanded. Indeed so vast is this mass, and much of it so highly technical in the various fields from which it is drawn, that an ordinary human being is under very serious difficulties in any sort of critical analysis, since a real factual check on Weber's work as a whole would probably be well beyond the powers of any single living scholar. Weber's was, what is exceedingly rare in the modern age, an encyclopedic mind.[1]

[1] While obviously the main interest at present is in Weber's central sociological theory and methodology, which transcends any particular concrete field, in the case of a man who covered such a vast range of factual material, the opinion of his work on the part of specialists in these fields is particularly important. Three opinions, given orally to the author by eminent scholars in different fields, all of whom hold a high opinion of

Without accepting the common adverse evaluation, it may well be held that Durkheim's mind was of the type Weber has often been held to have.[1] The above treatment of his work shows that he was always concerned, on the theoretical plane, with relatively simple bold outlines and clear-cut alternatives. The incisiveness of his thinking in this sense is a rare quality. This is not a criticism, but high praise. Durkheim's was almost the pure type of theoretical mind. This is not, of course, to say that he misused facts or was lacking in empirical insight—the above discussion should disprove any such misconception. But given the starting points of certain empirical problems, his central interest was theoretical. Like most great theorists his subsequent factual interest was mainly intensive rather than extensive, of the order of the crucial experiment.

Weber's was a very different type of mind. Its theoretical component, important as it was, coexisted with an omnivorous appetite for detail and for piling up masses of fact. It is only at certain crucial points that the bold outlines of a theoretical system stand out clearly above the mass of detail—and they must be brought out by following his interest from a clearly defined starting point step by step. That is what will be attempted here. But in doing so, it will be necessary to emphasize the theoretical as distinct from the historical aspect of his work. The element of abstraction, even "construction," in this is the more

---

Weber's competence in the respective fields with which they deal, may be quoted. Professor E. F. Gay, a specialist in Economic History, regards Weber as "one of the few most stimulating and fruitful minds of the past generation in the field of economic history." Professor W. E. Clark, a specialist in Indic Philology, holds Weber's treatment of Hinduism and Buddhism to be "the most satisfactory existing attempt to treat the Indian religio-social system as a whole." Finally, Professor A. D. Nock, whose field is the History of Religions, speaks of Weber's work in that field as "not merely work of great ability, but of genius."

Against these views is to be set the adverse opinion of a number of historians on the capitalism-Protestantism issue. As the present author has already attempted to show (*Journal of Political Economy*, October, 1935) at least one—not atypical—case of this criticism (see H. M. Robertson, *The Rise of Economic Individualism*) is based on a serious misunderstanding of Weber's work.

[1] Durkheim did not disregard facts but was intensively concerned with a small body of crucial facts rather than extensively with a vast body of information.

unavoidable because, like Durkheim's, Weber's work was left unfinished. It is not a rounded system, logically perfected and finished, but a great pioneer work. Therein, as also in the cases of Pareto and Durkheim, lies much of its interest.

The historical aspect of Weber's work is indeed understandable not only from whatever hereditary proclivities he may have had, but also from his intellectual background. His main formal training was in jurisprudence under the aegis of the historical school, particularly Goldschmidt and Mommsen. Probably his original interest in economics was largely dictated by dissatisfaction with the "formalism" of the Neo-Kantian *Rechtsphilosophie*.[1] Preoccupation with the details of legal history opened his eyes to the importance of economic and other nonformal-juridical factors in the development of legal systems. Moreover, his shift from jurisprudence to economics came at the time of the definite ascendancy in Germany of the historical school in the latter discipline, especially the particularistic empiricism of Schmoller. And, at Heidelberg, he succeeded an eminent historical economist, Knies.

Thus his primary background of training and interest lay in the detailed, empirical tradition of German historical thought, a subject discussed in the last chapter. From it doubtless more than any other source he derived his rigorous standards of objectivity in historical research. But, as has been seen, it was difficult to avoid all theory, and the most eminent members of the historical schools had always gone beyond mere observation and recording of detailed fact to the organization of facts under concepts. But in the historical tradition this took place largely in terms of the total system of a given cultural epoch, as for instance in Mommsen's *Römisches Staatsrecht*. Weber's was too actively theoretical a mind to remain indefinitely immersed in detailed historical research for its own sake. His own theorizing started, however, from the basis of the historical tradition, though it was eventually to transcend it.

As has been noted, his early studies in the field of legal history became more and more preoccupied with the "material" factors involved in legal development—material in the Marxian sense.

---

[1] Which may well help to explain the sharpness of his attack on Stammler. *Cf. Gesammelte Aufsätze zur Wissenschaftslehre*, pp. 291 *ff*. Cited below as *Wissenschaftslehre*.

His doctor's thesis already had an economic slant, as the subject, "Trading Companies in the Middle Ages,"[1] shows. Perhaps the culmination of this earlier phase of his work lay in the essay *Agrarverhältnisse im Altertum*[2] which stressed the material factors, but mainly those of military organization rather than the economic in a narrower sense.

Already in this period a strong trend of historical relativity was evidenced in his work, as for instance by his attack on Eduard Meyer's use of "modern" economic categories such as "factory" to describe the economic conditions of the ancient world.[3] But with these general trends the earlier period remained on the whole one of disconnected historical studies with a rather definite materialistic bias. A changed orientation came in rather dramatic fashion with Weber's recovery from the nervous breakdown which forced his retirement from all scientific work for about four years and from university teaching until almost the end of his life. This new orientation[4] resulted in the investigations which will occupy this discussion. It took three main directions: first an empirical concentration on a particular historical-social phenomenon—"modern capitalism"; second a new anti-Marxian interpretation of it and its genesis, which ultimately issued in an analytical sociological theory; and third a methodological basis for the latter which developed parallel with it. All three will be extensively treated. The first of the three, the problem of capitalism, descriptive and explanatory, will be treated in the present chapter and the next, the methodological basis of the studies of capitalism in Chap. XVI and, finally, in Chap. XVII, the broader theoretical system involved in, and emerging out of both.

The Principal Characteristics of Capitalism

Under the influence of the historical tradition of thought it was only natural that the systematization of the results of detailed historical studies from various epochs should be directed

---

[1] Reprinted in *Gesammelte Aufsätze zur Sozial und Wirtschaftsgeschichte.*

[2] Originally written for the 3d edition of the *Handwörterbuch der Staatswissenschaften,* but reprinted in the above volume.

[3] *Aufsätze zur Sozial und Wirtschaftsgeschichte,* p. 8.

[4] For the biographical aspect in this as in other connections see **Marianne Weber's** distinguished and charming *Max Weber, Ein Lebensbild.*

in the first instance to the working out descriptively of concrete systems of social structure and relationships. Thus Weber's empirical interest following his earlier economic bent came to be focused on the phenomena of the modern economic order considered as a socioeconomic system.[1] Like Marx and Sombart, he insisted upon its uniqueness in history, that nothing like this system had been seen at any other time or place.

Undoubtedly the main starting point of Weber's descriptive treatment was Marx. Marx's writings and the discussions of capitalism and socialism revolving about them were making a profound impression in Germany in Weber's formative period, but typically enough it was the "historical" Marx and not the Marx who was most closely related to the classical economic theory. In many of the descriptive categories applied to the capitalistic system, Weber concurs with Marx.

Thus he certainly thought of an organized capitalistic enterprise as its basic unit, an enterprise which, whatever the diversity of technological and organizational elements involved, was primarily oriented to the attainment of profit, to the exploitation of opportunities of acquisition in a system of market relationships. To at least a certain degree this fact alone justifies calling the system as a whole "acquisitive" in that the competitive element inherent in a system of market relationships was such as to make profit not only the immediate end but also the measure of success, indeed, in the last analysis, of the ability of an enterprise to survive. Thus *in* the system once established profit had to be an end, in fact the ruling end of action within the system of capitalistic relationships as such no matter what the ultimate individual motive above might be. The system then is not merely acquisitive; it is compulsive and "objective" in much the same sense that it was for both Marx and Sombart.

So much follows from this most general and formal concept of "capitalism" as a system of profit-making enterprises bound together in market relationships. Such enterprises or even systems of enterprises are by no means peculiar to modern Western society. Indeed Weber does not hesitate to speak of "capitalism" as existing at many times and places, and, according to the source of the opportunities for profits, as of many different

[1] *Cf.* TALCOTT PARSONS, "Capitalism in Recent German Literature, II, Max Weber," *Journal of Political Economy*, February, 1929.

kinds. In this respect the difference of the modern West from other societies is only a difference of degree, though a highly significant one. It is probably only here that Weber held there had been anything approaching the "capitalistic organization of society as a whole"[1] which is necessary for the compulsory acquisitiveness of the system to emerge in its full consequences. But this by no means exhausts the matter.

In the first place, Weber is careful to distinguish capitalistic "acquisitiveness" in general from that which is merely an expression of greed or psychological instinct of acquisition. The latter is by no means peculiar to modern society or even to societies with a high development of any kind of capitalism. What characterizes capitalistic acquisition is rather its "rationality."[2] It is acquisition, the pursuit of gain in a "continuous, rationally conducted enterprise."[3] This may well involve a high degree of disciplining and tempering of the acquisitive impulse.

But furthermore modern capitalism has certain specific traits which distinguish it clearly from that of other times. As an identifying characteristic Weber definitely excludes the "capitalistic adventurers," men who, however continuous and rational their enterprise, conduct it on an adventurous, speculative basis without ethical restraint. These have existed at all times and places wherever the opportunity has presented itself. What is characteristic of the modern West is rather what Weber calls "rational bourgeois capitalism." In what does this consist?

Weber like Marx started from the conception of an organized productive unit, the enterprise rather than the isolated individual of the early economists. But in his interpretation of the important features of this unit he made an important departure from Marx. In his conception of the role of the wage-earning laborer he agrees with Marx that only modern Western capitalism has "centered on a [formally] free wage-earning class separated from ownership of the means of production."[4] And the existence and situation

[1] *Gesammelte Aufsätze zur Religionssoziologie*, Vol. I, p. 4. Cited below as *Religionssoziologie*.

[2] In a specific sense to be worked out in the course of the discussion. Weber is very careful not to oversimplify on this point.

[3] *Religionssoziologie*, Vol. I, p. 4.

[4] *The Protestant Ethic and the Spirit of Capitalism* trans. by Talcott Parsons, p. 21. Cited below as *Protestant Ethic*.

of this class, the proletariat, accounts for the peculiarities of the modern socialist movement, expresses a class conflict unlike those of any other times.[1]

But though there is this agreement the center of interest of the two economists is different. For Marx it lay in the conflict of interest of the two classes as such; for Weber in the specific social type of organization as such.[2] The central feature of rational bourgeois capitalism is the "rational organization of free labor." This is, in turn, an example of a more general, fundamentally important type of social organization which Weber calls in a special sense of the term "bureaucracy."

Bureaucracy, as Weber uses the word, is a rather complicated phenomenon.[3] It involves an organization devoted to what is from the point of view of the participants an impersonal end. It is based on a type of division of labor which involves specialization in terms of clearly differentiated functions, divided according to technical criteria, with a corresponding division of authority hierarchically organized, heading up to a central organ, and specialized technical qualifications on the part of the participants. The role of each participant is conceived as an "office" where he acts by virtue of the authority vested in the office and not of his personal influence. This involves a clear-cut distinction in many different respects between his acts and relationships in his official and his personal capacity. It in general involves separation of office and home, of business funds and property from personal property, above all of authority in official matters from personal influence outside the official sphere.

The office is conceived of as a profession or calling (*Beruf*)[4] which involves a certain impersonal devotion to the tasks of the office imposing obligations on the incumbent. The typical form of remuneration is salary which is looked to not so much as a "reward" or as the equivalent of "sacrifice" as it is a guarantee of a scale of living consonant with the social position of the official

[1] *Ibid.*, p. 23.

[2] This difference of emphasis cannot be due to Weber's general lack of appreciation of the class struggle or more generally of the power factor. The later treatment will show that Weber gave much attention to these phenomena.

[3] See *Wirtschaft und Gesellschaft, Grundriss der Sozialoekonomik*, Vol. III, pp. 650 *ff.* Cited below as *Wirtsch. u. Ges.*

[4] *Ibid.*, p. 651.

according to his rank. Above all bureaucracy involves discipline. A bureaucracy is, Weber says, "a mechanism founded on discipline."[1] It is the fitting of individual actions into a complicated pattern in such a way that the character of each and its relations to the rest can be accurately controlled in the interest of the end to which the whole is devoted. The importance of discipline lies in being able to count on the individual doing the right thing at the right time and place.

Bureaucracy is by far the most efficient known method of organization of large numbers of persons for the performance of complicated tasks of administration, and its spread is to a considerable extent accounted for by this sheer superior efficiency.[2] But at the same time it is dependent on the existence of rather special social conditions,[3] the absence of which may constitute a very serious barrier to its development, no matter how great the objective need.

The occurence of bureaucracy even on a large scale is, of course, by no means confined to modern capitalism. Weber notes[4] six conspicuous historical cases: Egypt of the New Kingdom, the later Roman Empire, the Chinese Empire,[5] the Roman Catholic Church, the modern European state and the modern large-scale capitalistic enterprise. Of these the last two are, technically speaking, distinctly the most highly developed cases, above all, in differentiation of specialized training and in independence of method of remuneration (money salary) of all nonbureaucratic influences.

A conspicuous fact about modern capitalistic bureaucracy is its relative independence of that of the state. The large firm has not had its mode of organization imposed on it from without by the state, nor has it to any conspicuous extent grown up in imitation of state bureaucracy. The latter everywhere owes much to military influences, since the modern army is of a pronounced bureaucratic character as opposed, for instance, to the armies of feudalism. But it is a conspicuous fact that two of the most

---

[1] *Ibid.*, p. 651.

[2] *Ibid.*, pp. 128, 660.

[3] Which cannot be treated in detail here except at one or two points.

[4] *Wirtsch. u. Ges.*, p. 655.

[5] As will be seen below, this case involves certain elements differentiating it very sharply from Western capitalistic bureaucracy. See Chap. XV.

pronouncedly capitalistic countries, including the earliest, England and the United States, are precisely those among all modern great powers in which the armies have had the least influence on social structure, as compared with the principal continental European states. These facts definitely point to capitalistic bureaucracy as essentially an independent growth.

It is, of course, true that a relatively highly developed state structure has existed wherever capitalistic bureaucracy on a large scale has appeared, and appears to be a necessary condition of it, for the latter requires internal peace and order, mobility and other circumstances. But these may be present wherever capitalism develops at all in modern times without any strong bureaucratic component.

A certain amount of division of labor and specialization of function is possible on an "individualistic" basis without highly organized productive units. This was broadly true of the stage of handicraft industry and of the putting-out system. Moreover the sheer objective requirements of efficiency have constituted an important factor in the more stringent organization of the productive unit which has in general meant its approach to bureaucratic forms.

But at the moment the question of the explanation of capitalistic bureaucracy is not at issue. The present concern is, rather, to point out that under the more general category of capitalism, the subtype in which Weber is primarily interested is "rational bourgeois capitalism" and the principal characteristic of the latter is "bureaucratic organization" in the service of pecuniary profit in a system of market relations. It is this, highly developed and quantitatively widespread, which Weber considers to be the principal distinguishing feature of the modern Western economic order. It is the center about which other elements are grouped and from their relation to which they derive their main significance.

This is by no means to say that he denies the existence or even the importance of many other features of this order which are much discussed. Technology is obviously most intimately related to bureaucratic organization since it is responsible for much of the elaborate division of functions. The enterprise is oriented to a market which in the absence of control is competitive; hence the role of the price mechanism is definitely included in Weber's concept of capitalism. The high development of technical means of facilitating exchange such as money, credit, banking, organized speculation, finance is there, though by no means stressed. Finally there is no attempt to deny the importance of class relations. What characterizes Weber's treatment is rather a relative shift of emphasis brought about by bringing into the center of attention phenomena which had previously been left on the periphery and hence considered of relatively little theoretical significance. Roughly, for Weber, bureaucracy plays the part that the class struggle played for Marx and competition for Sombart.

This shift has one most important concrete result: in contradistinction to Marx and most "liberal" theories, it strongly minimizes the differences between capitalism and socialism, emphasizing rather their continuity. Not only would socialistic organization leave the central fact of bureaucracy untouched, it would greatly accentuate its importance. This important difference of perspective is, indeed, closely connected with Weber's attempt to appraise the modern order in terms of a very broad comparative framework.

In concluding this preliminary discussion, it should be pointed out that Weber has thus far been treated only on the descriptive level. The very difference of his descriptive terms from those used by Marshall in talking about free enterprise or even by Marx and Sombart, indicates that description is not simply a matter of "letting the facts speak for themselves." It involves rather an element of selection and emphasis among the facts which amounts to a judgment of their theoretical importance. But nevertheless both capitalism and bureaucracy are for Weber concrete phenomena. To be sure, they are stated in the form of "ideal types," which involves a certain form of abstraction, but even though "ideal" they are none the less concrete within the frame of reference.[1]

The main point to be noted is that there are "bureaucratic" organizations even though they do not fully conform to the type, and that these are typical of capitalism. One misunderstanding must, however, be warned against. The distinction between "rational bourgeois" and "adventurers'" capitalism is not to be taken to apply to economic systems as a whole, but only to elements of such systems. It is not even a distinction of classes of

[1] See Chap. XVI for an extended discussion of the concept "ideal type."

concrete enterprise, but rather of types of action and relationship within the enterprise. A brokerage house, for instance, which is engaged, for its members and its clients, in the wildest speculation on the stock exchange, may well have, on the part of the clerical force who execute the orders, a highly developed rational bureaucratic organization. The "rationality" which is so prominent a feature of bureaucracy to Weber applies mainly to the internal functioning of the enterprise rather than to its market relations, though it may be extended to the latter sphere.

In this descriptive aspect of his treatment of capitalism Weber, allowing for the difference of "accent," is in rather close agreement with Marx. His emphasis on the "compulsive" aspect of the system implies agreement beyond mere description; it involves a thesis concerning the determination of individual action within the system, namely that the course of action is determined in the first instance by the character of the situation in which the individual is placed, in Marxian terminology, by the "conditions of production." This implication Weber recognizes quite explicitly.[1] The system, once fully developed, is self-sustaining by virtue of its compulsive power over individuals. Whether it is going on to self-destruction by virtue of any specific laws of its own development as Marx held, Weber omits to say; on this point he is agnostic.

But here the agreement between them stops. While in a certain sense a "materialistic" view was adequate to the description of the fully developed capitalistic system, it was not, Weber held, adequate to the explanation of its genesis. For this purpose entirely different forces must be invoked. At the opening of the new period of his thinking Weber came quite decisively to the view that an indispensable (though by no means the only) element in the explanation of the system lay in a system of ultimate values and value attitudes, in turn anchored in and in part dependent upon a definite metaphysical system of ideas. This constituted, for the particular case in hand, a direct polemical challenge to the Marxian type of explanation.

The remainder of the present chapter and, more indirectly the next, will be concerned with the attempt to outline Weber's proof of the above thesis. But first it may be useful briefly to indicate the main steps in the process, following the line of logical rather

[1] *Religionssoziologie*, Vol. I, pp. 203–204; *Protestant Ethic*, pp. 54–55, 72.

than temporal continuity, though here the two correspond fairly closely.

Weber nowhere attempts to deny the importance of what Marx called the "material" factors of social change. Hence for his critical purposes it is not necessary to discard them, but only to refute exaggerated claims of their sole adequacy. Scattered throughout his whole work there are critical remarks to this effect on a number of particular points. Yet his main line of proof is not critical but positively inductive. The principal steps may be outlined as follows:

1. Having established his descriptive account of the phenomenon "modern capitalism," he proceeds to point out that there is empirically associated with it a set of values (in Pareto's terms, part of a "state of mind") which may be approached through the study of linguistic expressions. This Weber attempts to formulate systematically, but descriptively, as the "spirit" (*Geist*) of capitalism. This is taken as a set of mental attitudes directed toward economic activities as such.

2. A hint as to deeper connections of these particular attitudes is given by certain statistical facts bearing upon the relation between religious adherence and occupational grouping in parts of Germany, which brought out the tendency of Protestants to outnumber Catholics in the ownership and leadership of capitalistic enterprise, and in the branches of higher education leading to scientific, technical and business careers as compared with the "humanistic" branches. These facts constitute too small a sample to furnish "proof" but furnish rather guiding lines for further inquiry. Weber took them as such; his own further attempt at proof took another course. Subsequent studies of this character have, however, confirmed his views.[1]

3. This is followed up by establishing a close relationship, a "congruence" on the "meaningful" level, between the mental attitudes in question, the spirit of capitalism, and the ethics of the ascetic branches of Protestantism, as well as a relative lack of relationship with Catholic ethics and those of Lutheran Protestantism. This involves demonstrating the "correspondence"

---

[1] See the additional facts, which strongly confirm Weber's position, summarized in the forthcoming study by R. K. Merton, "Science, Technology and Society in Seventeenth Century England," to be published in *Osiris, History of Science Monographs*, Vol. IV.

or mutual congruence of two rather complicated systems of value attitudes. In view of this complexity the number of distinguishable elements in a rather specific relation to each other is so great that, on grounds of probability, sheer chance in effecting congruence is practically excluded and hence a close functional relationship becomes highly probable. This says nothing about causal priority, but the fact of temporal relations strongly indicates a preponderant causal role of the system of religious attitudes, since it existed prior both to any high degree of development of the spirit of capitalism as such and to any high development of the actual socioeconomic organization. Hence on these grounds alone there is a strong case for imputing to the ethical values of Protestantism an important, though not exclusive, causal role.

4. Weber not only establishes this congruence in general terms. He also shows, by analysis of Protestant writings, that there is a gradual process of transition from a religious position which though showing certain important similarities with the spirit of capitalism yet certainly would not have sanctioned it, to one which yielded direct ethical justification of acquisitive activities without limit so long as they were "righteous." Moreover, not only is the process of transition itself traced, but an understandable motivation for it is provided through Weber's analysis of the relation of Protestant theological ideas to the religious interests of believers. So long as there is no direct demonstration of the derivability of these religious attitudes and ideas from "material" factors this yields a further strong presumption in favor of the view that they constitute an important independent element in the process of modern economic development. That is, the actual system of economic activities is of a character which one would expect to develop on the hypothesis that it had been importantly influenced by the Protestant ethic by the process that Weber traces. This is where Weber stops in his essay on *The Protestant Ethic and the Spirit of Capitalism.*

5. But he is not satisfied with this. His inductive study turns from the method of agreement to that of difference. This takes the form of an ambitious series of comparative studies all directed to the question, why did modern rational bourgeois capitalism appear as a dominant phenomenon *only* in the modern West? What are the differentiating factors that account for its failure to appear in other cultures? The comparative study is couched

mainly in terms of the Marxian dichotomy of "material" and
"ideal" factors. The general upshot is the thesis that at the
relevant stages in the development of cultures the material conditions in China, India, Judea compared favorably, from the point
of view of capitalistic-bureaucratic potentialities, with those of
our own medieval and early modern times, while in each culture
the "economic ethic" of the dominant religious tradition concerned was directly antagonistic to such a development. On the
other hand, in Protestantism (to a less extent in Christianity as
a whole) the economic ethic was directly favorable. This conclusion confirms the functional relationship between Protestantism and capitalism. Furthermore, on the one hand, it decreases
the probability that the spirit of capitalism is merely a reflection
of the material conditions, in other words, is a dependent variable
and, on the other hand, it increases the probability that a main
differentiating element lies on the value plane. This is a perfectly
valid scientific method provided, of course, that Weber's allegations of fact are correct. A closer approach to "proof" is probably
not attainable in a field of empirical theses of similar dimensions.
But closer consideration of the methodological question involved
must be postponed to Chap. XVI. The present task is to sketch
the main outline of Weber's empirical argument.

THE SPIRIT OF CAPITALISM

What Weber calls the "spirit of capitalism" is a set of attitudes
toward the acquisition of money and the activities involved in
it. It is, of course, an attitude which strongly endorses such
acquisitive activities but not in any and every form; among
positive attitudes it is a quite specific one. In the first place, the
capitalistic attitude is clearly distinguished from all attitudes
toward acquisition as a necessary evil, which is justified because
it is an indispensable means to something else. There is a great
range of the latter type of attitudes all the way from condemnation of such severity as to leave little room except for the barest
necessities, to a relatively complete "worldliness" that, giving
free reign to enjoyment and the gratification of the appetites,
cannot but approve the necessary means to these ends. This
qualified sanction of worldly activities has, of course, been variously motivated, sometimes as in the case of medieval Catholicism
by otherworldly religious interests; at other times, in the classical
Greek ethics for instance, by a humanistic theory of harmony.

In contrast with all these, the spirit of capitalism looks upon such activities not as a means or a necessary evil, but as an ethically enjoined end in itself. To earn money is an ethical obligation for its own sake.[1]

Secondly, this ethical sanction is not applied to acquisition only within certain quantitative limits, until "enough" has been earned—there is no standard of satiety—but, rather, the pursuit of gain is enjoined without limit. This characteristic sharply marks off the spirit of capitalism from the attitude of "traditionalism" which Weber regards as in certain respects its principal antithesis. He emphatically denies that an endlessly expanding bundle of concrete wants is the normal situation for mankind. The normal situation is rather that rationally acquisitive activities are oriented to a traditionally fixed standard of living. The "economic principle" normally takes the form of satisfaction of these traditional needs with the least possible exertion. For example, the normal reaction to a rise in piece rates is not a desire by harder work to earn more but, rather, by less work to earn the same amount as before.[2] It is only in capitalistic areas that this kind of traditionalism has been to any marked extent broken down. The result is that to this extent acquisition has been freed from any definite limit and becomes an endless process. This attitude toward acquisition is "rationalized," in the form in which Weber is interested in it, by holding it to be an ethical duty for its own sake.

Another way in which the spirit of capitalism forms an antithesis to traditionalism is in its relation to the actual processes of acquisitive activities. Here instead of accepting ways of doing things as handed down, the capitalistic attitude is at every point to reorganize its procedures systematically in terms of the total task. Only the ultimate end, maximization of money, is "sacred"; the particular means are not, but are chosen anew according to the exigencies of each particular situation.[3] This double antithesis to traditionalism gives the spirit of capitalism, so far as it may be assigned causal influence at all, a strongly dynamic character which is highly important for Weber's purposes.

[1] Sanctioned beyond this only by transcendental considerations.

[2] See *Protestant Ethic*, pp. 59–60; in general on the concept of the spirit of capitalism, Chap. II therein.

[3] *Cf. Protestant Ethic*, pp. 67–69.

This attitude toward acquisition is correlated with a particular attitude toward labor, whether its immediate end be acquisitive or not. Labor also is not looked upon as a necessary evil, whether because of its traditional origin in the curse of Adam or for any other reason. It is carried out with the same sense of positive ethical obligation, as a field for directly realizing the highest ethical aims of man. The capitalistic attitude toward labor is what Veblen calls the spirit of "workmanship." One of its most conspicuous symptoms is the *ethical* feeling against early retirement from active work. A man who does not "produce" as long as he has health and strength, no matter how well he can afford to retire, is somehow neglecting his ethical responsibilities.

Finally, the "spirit of capitalism," although devoted to unlimited acquisition and emancipation from traditionalism both in goal and in process, still by no means implies emancipation from discipline and control. On the contrary, it gives approval to acquisitive activities only under a very stringent discipline and control. It is here that the line between Weber's spirit of capitalism and the "adventurers'" spirit (the undisciplined impulsive greed of gain) is to be drawn.[1] As against this the spirit of capitalism enjoins systematic, continuous rational honest work in the service of economic acquisition. Such work is necessarily subjected to a strict discipline which is quite incompatible with giving free rein to impulse.

The relation of all this to bureaucracy should be evident. Bureaucratic organization requires a "disinterested" impersonal devotion to a specialized task and a readiness to fit into the rational requirements of a complicated scheme of coordinated specialized activities regardless of tradition. This equally involves a rigid submission to discipline within the limits of the task. The spirit of capitalism is for Weber a special case of the "professional spirit" (*Berufsgeist*) which is the specific attitude required for the efficient functioning of bureaucracy. It is that special case where the impersonal task, to which disinterested ethical devotion is directed, contains the unlimited acquisition of money as a basic component.[2]

[1] *Ibid.*, pp. 56–58, 69.
[2] Directly as for managers of a business, or indirectly as for most of its employees. Typically in the latter case it is not their own financial interest but that of the firm which is decisive.

In all this treatment, Weber's historical approach comes out strongly in his insistence on the uniqueness of the attitudes concerned. While they are so well known to us that we tend to take them for granted as simply "natural," such is by no means the case. In all the essential respects discussed Weber maintains that the capitalistic attitude is highly exceptional. Most ethical teachers, religious and otherwise, have sanctioned acquisition, if at all, only as a means to an end or as a necessary evil, never as an end in itself. The rule in fact as well as in theory has been traditionalism, broken through to a greater or less extent by an amoral, undisciplined greed for gain, the basis of adventurers' capitalism. The theoretical importance of this thesis of historical uniqueness lies in making the origin of the spirit of capitalism itself problematical. If it were the rule at most times and places it might be explained simply as "human nature." To such an interpretation Weber's whole treatment is directly opposed.

CALVINISM AND THE SPIRIT OF CAPITALISM

Having established a set of descriptive categories by which to distinguish the spirit of capitalism from other related attitudes, Weber is finally faced with the theoretical problem of its origin.[1] He readily admits that a fully developed capitalistic system is to a large degree capable itself of generating these attitudes in the people living in it—through selection and direct influence.

What he doubts is its capability to generate itself out of markedly different conditions without an independent, widely spread mental attitude favorable to capitalism. For this doubt he gives, among others, two general critical grounds: (1) While, given the "conditions," the standards of selection, the theory of selection can account for the particular types of individuals attaining a given position, it cannot account for the origin of the standards themselves.[2] (2) A "form of organization" alone is not enough to create the attitudes concerned. It is possible for a definitely capitalistic form of organization to be administered in a thoroughly traditionalistic spirit.[3] Only when it is combined with a

---

[1] The problem is essentially causal rather than historical. The methodological problem of the relation of the two will be discussed in Chap. XVI.

[2] *Protestant Ethic*, p. 55.

[3] *Ibid.*, p. 63 *ff.*

capitalistic spirit can a completely capitalistic situation be spoken of.[1]

But these critical considerations serve only to open the door to Weber's positive proof that the "spirit" forms a fundamental causal factor in the genesis of the concrete capitalistic order and is not merely a "reflection" of its "material" elements. The first step in this proof is the establishment of the congruence of this set of attitudes with those deriving from a set of ideas which were widespread prior to the large-scale development of rational bourgeois capitalism. This he finds in the religious ethic of what he calls the "ascetic" branches of Protestantism.

The starting point is the consideration of the attitudes toward worldly activities of the various branches of Christian ethics, in particular activities largely oriented to economic acquisition.

Catholic ethics, at least from the Middle Ages on, was by no means completely hostile to the things of this world. Its dualism was by no means so radical as that of the Christianity of antiquity. The society of Christendom was, at least to a relative degree, blest with a religious sanction, was a *res publica christiana*.[2] There are, however, two fundamental reasons why this relative sanction was not a powerful stimulant to the spirit of capitalism. In the first place, the medieval view considered "callings" in relation to their religious value in terms of a hierarchy, the apex of which was the religious life as lived in the monastery. Acquisitive activities, on the other hand, were not far from the bottom of the list of those approved at all, and precisely in proportion as they tended to become capitalistic they were more and more under suspicion. This suspicion tended strongly to press capitalistic activities in the amoral, "adventurous" direction.[3]

Secondly, and largely explaining this suspicious attitude, the whole burden of medieval religious pressure was thrown on the side of traditionalism in relation to worldly callings. The medieval "organic" social ideal thought of society as a hierarchy of classes,

---

[1] Thus for Weber's descriptive concept, at least of *modern* capitalism, the form of organization, with which his general concept starts, is not enough. The total concrete phenomenon includes a given concrete set of attitudes.

[2] *Cf.* especially E. Troeltsch, *Social Teaching of the Christian Churches*, Vol. I, Chap. III.

[3] As, above all, in the Italian Renaissance.

each in its proper divinely ordained place, each with its function for the whole. The duty of each individual was to live according to his station and to perform his traditional tasks. To such a view any break in tradition was ethically dubious. Moreover, capitalistic activities also ran counter to the strongly personal type of social relations which received the main religious approval. Related to this, in turn, was the universal sanction of charity, an attitude definitely antagonistic to the formal contractual "justice" under which capitalism thrives most.[1]

In one field, however, Catholic ethics achieved something approaching the modern conception of the "calling," namely in the place it gave to labor in the monastic discipline. As distinguished from mortification, contemplation and purely ritual devotions, Western monasticism has always been conspicuous for the role of rational labor as an ascetic exercise, and as such was distinguished from any sort of oriental counterpart. This attitude toward labor, though, of course, not generally devoted to acquisition or, if at all, certainly not for the benefit of the individual monk, was indeed in the line of "bureaucratic" development. But the very fact that it was a phenomenon of monasticism and that the way of life of the monk was so sharply distinguished from that of the laity prevented it from being generalized.

One of the fundamental results of the Reformation was to eliminate the monastery from the sphere of Protestant influence. And with this went an increase in the stringency of ethical discipline expected of the lay Christian in his daily life. The extent of this and its practical implications, however, varied greatly with the different branches of the Protestant movement.

For Weber's purposes the important distinction is that between Lutheranism, on the one hand, and what he refers to as the ascetic branches of Protestantism, on the other. The essential limitation on the capitalistic implications of the Lutheran ethic lies in the fact that it failed to break through the limitations of traditionalism.[2] This was due in the last analysis to the peculiar combination of Luther's basic doctrine of salvation by faith alone, which made any ascetic valuation of worldly activity smack suspiciously

---

[1] Other relevant features of Catholic ethics will be brought out by contrast with those associated with the doctrine of predestination (see below).

[2] *Protestant Ethic*, Chap. III.

of salvation by works, with his version of the conception of Divine Providence which placed a powerful sanction on the established traditional order of things in this world. The general result was the injunction to remain in the calling and station in which you are placed and faithfully to perform the traditional duties appertaining to it.

This is not, of course, to say that the Lutheran doctrine did not contain an important departure from the Catholic position in the general direction of an attitude to worldly activities more favorable to capitalistic bureaucracy. It did so above all by erasing the religiously privileged position of the monk and transferring religious approval to all "legitimate" worldly occupations essentially on an equal footing with each other. This may be considered the common basis of all Protestant attitudes. But the traditionalistic[1] tendency of Lutheran ethics prevented its developing further in a direction more favorable to capitalistic bureaucracy.

Among the ascetic branches Weber rested his theory mainly though not exclusively on Calvinism and for the sake of brevity the present discussion will be confined to it.[2] The discussion of the relation of Calvinism to the spirit of capitalism will throw light upon the Lutheran position and make clear the ethical differences between the two.

It is perhaps well at the outset, however, to state specifically the general relations in which Weber tried to place the three entities, the spirit of capitalism, the concept of "calling" of a given religious movement and the basic religious ideas and attitudes of that movement. The spirit of capitalism has already been outlined. The concept of the calling is one manifestation in a particular context of the typical attitudes associated with a religious movement toward the participation of its adherents in worldly activities. The spirit of capitalism, as Weber formulates it, involves a particular kind of calling attitude toward a certain

[1] And also its closely related authoritarianism. It may be argued that this favored a set of attitudes more favorable to *state* bureaucracy than to that of independent capitalistic enterprise. This may well have something to do with the peculiarities of German capitalism and the fact that it developed later than in England.

[2] In this respect the Calvinist position is to be regarded as the extreme polar type, the other ascetic movements are in various respects mitigations of its rigor.

class of such activities, those involving economic acquisition. This is the principal point of articulation for Weber's purposes between the spirit of capitalism and the system of religious ideas in question.

It would, however, be a serious misinterpretation to suppose that Weber's argument for a causal relation between the spirit of capitalism and the ethics of ascetic Protestantism rested on the concept of the calling as such, especially if the latter is taken to mean, in turn, the explicit statements made by adherents of this movement of the desirable attitude toward worldly activities. Such statements form one body of evidence but only one. The concept of the calling Weber sees, in turn, as a manifestation in one direction of a set of attitudes in which the structure of the system of religious ideas in question *taken as a whole* forms a central element. As Weber puts the position in the most general terms:[1] it is "interests" not "ideas" that in conjunction with the conditions of the situation in which they are placed determine immediately the conduct of men. Among these interests are those concerned with the religious status of the individual, in Protestant terms, the "state of grace." The importance of religious ideas lies in the fact that in particular ways they canalize these interests, and hence relevant action in pursuit of them. According to the conception of the universe held, the interests in grace or salvation will be or can be pursued in very different ways. Weber's concern with religious ideas is based on this fact. He is interested in the practical attitudes that large masses of men take toward their everyday activities. These attitudes, so far as religion is concerned, he tries to see in the perspective of the religious ideas with which they are associated. But it is not the mere verbal injunction to certain kinds of conduct, delivered by representatives or leaders of religious bodies, to which these masses of men adhere, on which Weber's argument depends.[2] It is, rather, the structure of the total system of religious ideas *in its relation* to men's religious interests. Both the injunctions of religious leaders and the practical attitudes of the masses are to be understood in relation

---

[1] *Religionssoziologie*, Vol. I, pp. 252–253.

[2] A conspicuous example of this misinterpretation is the book of H. M. Robertson, *The Rise of Economic Individualism*. See the critical note, TALCOTT PARSONS, "H. M. Robertson on Max Weber and His School," *Journal of Political Economy*, October, 1935.

to this system. It is by no means necessary for Weber's purposes to assume it is the personal or institutional authority of these leaders as such which is the decisive factor.[1] These considerations have unfortunately often been neglected in discussing Weber's work.

Furthermore, with this is closely associated another highly important point. Weber's interest is by no means confined to the *logical* consequences of the initial system of religious ideas, or to the directly expressed wishes of religious leaders for practical conduct based on them. He is, rather, concerned with the *total consequences* of the religious system. This involves two important points: First, the relevant consequences are, as he puts it, "psychological" rather than purely logical. The logical consequences operate, but not alone; they must be taken in conjunction with the constellation of interests involved, which may, as between two equally possible logical alternatives, bias action in the direction of one, or even inhibit the development of the full logical consequences in certain other directions.

Secondly, the influence of a system of religious ideas on practical attitudes is to be regarded as a real process in time, not a static logical deduction. In the course of it the system of ideas itself may also undergo change. In fact, as will be pointed out, the Protestant attitude toward economic acquisition underwent a steady process of change, and it was only in the later stages that the full consequences relevant in the present context emerged. Above all Weber insists that the original Reformers themselves were by no means filled with the spirit of capitalism.[2] Their concern was solely religious and they would have sharply repudiated the attitudes taken by their successors. But this does not in the least disprove that these later attitudes were in an important degree the consequence of the religious ideas put forward by the Reformers.

With these general considerations in mind the discussion may now proceed to the specific Calvinistic[3] system of ideas and its

---

[1] He explicitly states he is not mainly concerned with *church* discipline but with the *direct* religious motivation of the individual (see *Protestant Ethic*, p. 97).

[2] *Protestant Ethic*, p. 91.

[3] Weber defines "ascetic" Protestantism as including (1) Calvinism, (2) Pietism, (3) the sects growing out of the Baptist movement, (4) Methodism. For lack of space the present discussion is confined to Calvinism.

relation to economic activities. For present purposes the Calvinistic theology may be said to consist of a body of five logically
independent yet empirically interdependent propositions. They
are independent in that they do not directly imply one another;
any one of them could be fitted into other theological systems. But
they are logically compatible with each other, mutually limiting
the inferences which can be drawn from any one while the others
are adhered to, and taken together they cover all the main metaphysical problems of a theology; they constitute a meaningful
system.

The propositions are, schematically, as follows: (1) There is a
single, absolutely transcendental God, creator and governor of
the world, whose attributes and grounds of action are, apart from
Revelation, completely beyond the reach of finite human understanding. (2) This God has predestined all human souls, for
reasons totally beyond possible human comprehension, either
to eternal salvation or to "eternal sin and death." This decree
stands from and for eternity and human will or faith can have
no influence on it. (3) God for His own inscrutable reasons has
created the world and placed man in it solely for the increase of
His glory. (4) To this end He has decreed that man, regardless
of whether predestined to salvation or damnation, shall labor to
establish the Kingdom of God on Earth, and shall be subject to
His revealed law in doing so. (5) The things of this world, human
nature and the flesh, are, left to themselves, irreparably lost in "sin
and death" from which there is no escape except by divine grace.

All these elements play a prominent part elsewhere in Christian
thought and history; only their specific combination and the
rigorous consistency in drawing their theological consequences
are specifically Calvinistic. This system of theology yields one
of the few logically consistent solutions of the problem of evil in
history,[1] by declaring it beyond the reach of finite human intelli-
gence, hence relegated to the inscrutable will of God. Logically
the elements need not be thus combined. A transcendental God
might conceivably have made grace dependent on good works
rather than deciding it by predestination; he could let sinners
go their own way to perdition on this earth rather than subjecting
them to His law. He could have created the world for man's
happiness rather than His glory.

---

[1] *Religionssoziologie*, Vol. I, pp. 246–247.

But given this system what are its implications for practical conduct?

In the first place, the complete transcendence of God and the hiatus between fleshly and divine things exclude the mystical attitude of union with the divine spirit, absorption in it. This fact is, in turn, reinforced by the conception of submission to the *law*[1] for the glory of God, and the corresponding interpretation of predestination in relation to the things of this world as assigning to the elect the task of building and maintaining the Kingdom of God on Earth in accordance with divine will. God's main relation to man becomes that of will, and man is above all an instrument, obedient or recalcitrant as the case may be, of the divine will. The net effect in Weber's view is to direct religious energies in the active, ascetic rather than the passive, mystical direction.[2] God cannot be approached at all; He can only be served. And, on account of the fundamental dualism, this service cannot be in the direction of indulgence in the things of the flesh, or of adaptation to it; it must lie in that of *control* over the flesh, in its subjection to a discipline for the glory of God. This is what Weber means by asceticism.

One further consequence of the transcendence of God and the resultant dualism is highly important. Since the finite world is a creation of God and a manifestation of His will, the best way to know Him is to study His works. Just as He wishes to submit man to a law, so in a different but related sense is order the keynote of His nonhuman works. His decisions stand for eternity; He does not continually alter them and interfere with the order of nature. At the same time nature is nature and God is God. Hence sanctification of natural things is idolatry.

This belief in divine order has two corollaries—a faith in the order of nature, which is undoubtedly a highly important motive in the development of modern science,[3] and a strong hostility to ritual as involving superstition and idolatry. God is too completely transcendent to be adequately embodied in concrete

---

[1] Of course the revealed divine law, not that of earthly authorities. The two may on occasion be held to be in acute conflict with each other.

[2] See below Chap. XV, pp. 570 *ff.*, for a discussion of the more general bearings of this distinction, which is fundamental to Weber's sociology of religion.

[3] See the study of R. K. Merton, cited above, p. 511.

sacred things or acts. Only in the specific ways revealed by Him does He intervene in the order of this world—primarily through the action of His predestined saints. Thus ascetic activity in the service of God's will is diverted away from ritual channels of expression into active control over the intrinsic relations of the world.

Thus the believing Calvinist would tend to regard himself as an instrument of God's will called to act in accordance with it in the great task of increasing the glory of God by living according to His law and helping to establish the Kingdom of God on Earth. This action could not, moreover, consist primarily in ritual observances but rather in ethical control over the world in the service of an ideal. Thus already there was a general orientation in the direction of practical worldly activity. This was, of course, reinforced by the general Protestant repudiation of monasticism with its consequent subjection of all to the same law and the same ethical standards, and the necessity of doing the will of God in the ordinary occupations of everyday life, not withdrawn from them in the monastery.[1] Moreover the strict construction of the doctrine of predestination was that election was to be recognized by no external signs whatever. Hence conviction of damnation was no ground for failure to live up to the highest standards, since one did not know his fate, and furthermore God's will demanded the subjection of all alike to His law.

This problem of knowing one's state of grace brings out the more specific consequences of predestination for conduct. The authentic Calvinistic position was, as just noted, that election could not be recognized by external signs. But even more important was the implication of the tenet that the acts of the individual could have no influence on his state of grace since the latter had already been determined from eternity. Then precisely in so far as the whole religious question was taken seriously, as the *interest* in salvation was strong, the individual was placed in a terrific position. His acts could not influence his eternal fate; hence the whole pressure of his religious interest was to *know* whether he was saved or damned.

[1] What Weber calls worldly asceticism (*innerweltliche Askese*) as distinguished from the otherworldly asceticism of the monastery (*ausserweltliche*). "Otherworldly" here does not imply so much orientation to the "hereafter" as refusal to participate in the ordinary daily life of the average, not especially religious person.

It is here that for Weber the "psychological" as distinct from the purely logical consequences appear. Given a serious interest, he holds the pressure was too great for the mass of men. Under this pressure it was the first doctrine which gradually gave way. It gradually came to be held[1] that good works, while they could not influence salvation, could be interpreted as *signs* of grace. A good tree could not bear evil fruit. Then gradually the elect came to be identified with the "righteous," those who did the will of God, and the damned with "sinners," those who failed to obey His will.

Before following this line of development further, however, certain other fundamental consequences of the doctrine of predestination in its Calvinistic context should be noted. As has been stated elsewhere,[2] a certain "individualistic" character has been fundamental to Christianity from the beginning and this was greatly strengthened by the Reformation. Calvinism represents the extreme of the development of this individualistic element in one particular direction.

For, in the first place, its extreme antiritualism cut off the individual far more drastically than Luther ever did from the protecting, guiding hand of church and priest, which was felt especially in the confessional. According to predestination there was no help for him; no earthly agency whatever could have any influence on the state of his soul. But at the same time the *one* fundamentally important interest to him, deprived of this comforting intermediary, was his eternal fate and the one important relation, that to his God. But this relationship to his God in the "secret places of his heart" had to be separated from relationships to any human being. Moreover, in this situation other human beings were not merely useless to him, they might be positively dangerous, since however virtuous his outward conduct, any other human being, even the closest relative or friend, might be one of the damned. The net result was, as Weber puts it, an unheard-of "inner isolation of the individual,"[3] which placed him squarely on his own responsibility in all things, and involved a radical devaluation, not to say mistrust, of even the closest human ties. God always came first.

[1] From Beza on.
[2] Chap. II.
[3] *Protestant Ethic*, p. 108.

Secondly, this inner isolation in combination with the other aspects of the doctrine of predestination, had an extremely important implication for the rationalization of conduct. Conduct acceptable to God had to be in direct obedience to His will, and could not be the result of any human motivation or interest. But since individual good works could not affect grace, and outward conduct could at most be a sign of grace, the conduct enjoined could be judged only as a *total coherent system*, as the expression of the *kind of man* one was, not as a plurality of disconnected acts. The Catholic could receive absolution for particular sins, and receive credit for particular good deeds. For the Calvinist there was possible no such release from pressure, and hence there was an incomparably greater drive to the rational systematization of conduct.

The following are a few of the more specific practical implications of these convictions: The inner isolation, the suspicion of all things merely human and worldly, the abhorrence of "idolatry"[1] turned the energy of the Calvinist into the service of impersonal ends. They also made him share the general ascetic suspicion of the rich and mighty of this world, and even sometimes made the Calvinistic movement dangerous to established authority when the latter involved a personal homage which suggested idolatry. At least the strong tendency was to "mind his own business" and to hold aloof from the struggle for worldly power, except when it was a matter of fighting God's battles directly—as in the case of Cromwell's army.

The Calvinist turned rather to pursuits where he could labor, soberly and rationally, in a calling acceptable to God. Independent, solid, honest business was a particularly suitable field.

One cannot say that the Calvinistic ethic or any of its legitimate derivatives ever approved money-making for its own sake or as a means to self-indulgence, which was, indeed, one of the cardinal sins. What it did approve was rational, systematic labor in a useful calling which could be interpreted as acceptable to God Money was, certainly in the beginning, regarded as a by-product and one by no means without its dangers.[2] The attitude was, that is, an ascetic one. But even this served capitalistic

---

[1] A fundamental Puritan concept.

[2] See the many examples Weber brings forward in *Protestant Ethic*, Chap. V, especially the quotation from John Wesley, p. 175.

interests since, on the one hand, work in economic callings would serve to increase earnings but, on the other, the fear of self-indulgence would prevent their full expenditure for consumption. It was, as Weber says,[1] a case of "ascetic compulsion to save." Acquisition was not only promoted, but was "freed from the bonds of traditionalistic ethics."[2] After all, traditions themselves were only human; to respect them where they stood in the way of the work of God was idolatry.

Moreover, it is clear that the changed attitude to labor noted in connection with the spirit of capitalism here receives an adequate motivation. No longer is the necessity to labor the curse of Adam, a punishment for original sin. Nor is it merely an ascetic technique in the sense of a means of combating the temptations of the flesh. All these are negative motivations. The Puritan ethic added a positive one of basic importance. Labor in a calling, with no other earthly aim than "doing a good job" according to the intrinsic requirements of the situation, was a positive command of God, the first duty of one who was eager to do His will. It was a God-given opportunity to take part in the great task for which God has placed man in this vale of tears, the building of the Kingdom of God on Earth. For the true believer such work was not an unpleasant necessity to which he must grudgingly submit. It was the highest fulfillment of his own deep religious interests.

However, the more extreme asceticism of the position was gradually weakened by the results of the "psychological" process noted above. From the admission that righteous conduct was a legitimate sign of grace (since a good tree would not bear evil fruit) it was not a very long step to the view that success in a worldly calling could be regarded also as a sign of grace so long as it was righteous success and not attained by means at variance with the law. For would not God bless His chosen ones in this world as well as the next?[3] In its economic context this doctrine could supply an excellent justification for the successful man,

---

[1] *Protestant Ethic*, p. 172.

[2] *Ibid.*, p. 171.

[3] At approximately this point it may be said that there enters in an element of "secularization" which is a different thing from the direct religious influence. See below, Chap. XVII, p. 685, for a brief discussion of the place of this element in Weber's thought.

giving him a good conscience about his gain and being one important source of a kind of conspicuous self-righteousness on the part of circles with a Puritan background.

Finally the doctrine of predestination performed another signal service to the consciences of successful businessmen. They did not need to worry too much about the lot of the unfortunate in this world, since it might well be interpreted as a sign of God's displeasure with their conduct, especially if the misfortunes of the unfortunate could in any way be attributed to idleness[1] and failure to work. Puritanism had no place for the easy Catholic attitude toward charity. It organized what charity it allowed to remain as a severe discipline on a rational basis.

There can be no doubt that in his treatment of the ethics of ascetic Protestantism Weber has in general succeeded in his task of finding a system of ultimate-value ideas "adequate" to the spirit of capitalism as he himself formulated the latter conception. All its leading traits find their counterpart in the Protestant attitude properly interpreted. Above all the "irrational" element in which the peculiar capitalistic "rationalism" is centered,[2] so incomprehensible from any hedonistic point of view, has found a meaning. What other explanation of it has accomplished this fundamental thing?[3]

The effect of the juxtaposition of the two attitude systems is to bring into even sharper relief than in his original formulation the "ascetic" aspect of capitalism in Weber's theory. It is, indeed, very largely on the empirical significance of this element as a fact that the importance of Weber's theory rests. Some critics go so far as to hold in effect[4] that it is entirely an invention of Weber's. This view is not justifiable, but naturally it cannot be disproved without an elaborate argument. Attention may, however, be called to the fact that Weber is by no means alone among recent writers in noting the *concrete* importance of this element, however much they may differ from him in their explanation of it.

[1] "Sloth" is a very common Puritan term.

[2] *Protestant Ethic*, pp. 76–78.

[3] For a general theoretical discussion of the status of this explanation and the role of religious ideas in it see the note appended to this chapter.

[4] Thus H. M. ROBERTSON, *op. cit.*

It has already been pointed out[1] that Marshall's emphasis on "activities" has very similar connotations. There is no other explanation of the prominence of the concept in Marshall's work than his conviction that an ethical element radically distinct from hedonistic want satisfaction is essential to free enterprise. Durkheim also, though in a somewhat different connection, thought ethical discipline essential to the working of an individualistic economic order. Besides these, two others may be mentioned. Professor Carver[2] lays great stress on the importance of what he calls the "workbench philosophy," the devotion to work for its own sake, including "business." To him pure "economic individualism" in Dr. Robertson's sense certainly implies the "pig-trough philosophy" which he so sharply combats. Finally, in Veblen, who, on the one hand, strongly depreciated hedonism and, on the other, elevated to a position of central importance what he called the "instinct of workmanship,"[3] there is at least an implied recognition of the same fundamental facts. In his emphasis on the importance of "technology" evidently there lies more than the "technological element" of the previous analysis.[4] It involves also a specific attitude toward the task, an attitude of "workmanship," to use his term. Is not that regarding the task as a "calling" in Weber's sense? These four cases seem to be the more significant because they come from very different intellectual backgrounds and have no direct relation to one another nor to Weber. Is such an agreement simply fortuitous?

The establishment of "congruence" between the Protestant ethic and the spirit of capitalism does not, however, in itself constitute proof that the religious system is an important factor in the genesis of the capitalistic attitude and through it of concrete rational bourgeois capitalism. Nor does it demonstrate the quantitative order of this importance. This is the more true, in view of the fact that Weber himself not merely grants, but emphasizes the importance of, other quite distinct factors,

[1] Chap. IV.

[2] T. N. CARVER, especially in *The Religion Worth Having*.

[3] *Cf.* T. VEBLEN, *The Instinct of Workmanship*, and Talcott Parsons, "Sociological Elements in Economic Thought, I, Historical," *Quarterly Journal of Economics*, May, 1935.

[4] Chap. VI, above.

for instance, modern science, a rationalized legal system, rational bureaucratic administration in the state. None of these factors were, he holds, primarily creations of ascetic Protestantism though they may have been helped by it.

There are a number of ways in which Weber attempted to prove the causal relation of Protestantism and capitalism. After very briefly reviewing the rest, however, the main attention will be devoted to one, by means of the *comparative* sociology of religion, both because it is methodologically the most important and because, in spite of the fact that Weber himself laid by far the greatest stress on it, it has been almost completely overlooked in the English discussion of Weber's theory.[1]

First, as has been noted, there is a small amount of statistical evidence available concerning the correlation between religious affiliation and position in the social structure. This on the whole confirms Weber's hypothesis. What he used, however, was not derived from his own researches,[2] and his own work did not take this direction. He used this material more as a pointer to the significant problems than as proof. Secondly, the temporal relations of the Protestant ethic, on the one hand, and the spirit of capitalism, on the other, are such as strongly to suggest a causal relationship. That is, the Protestant ethic on the whole mainly preceded the spirit of capitalism in the same areas and social classes. Indeed in so far as the causal factors are on the "ideal"

[1] In part no doubt because the material has not been translated into English, but mostly for deeper reasons, because most of the participants in the controversy have not clearly seen the nature of Weber's problems. In general, more space and care have been devoted to Weber's theory of capitalism than to the empirical theories of the other writers treated in this study, because it has been the object of sharp controversy, involving very serious misunderstanding of Weber's work. It is necessary to set all this right in order not to obscure the theoretical and methodological significance of Weber's work, which will occupy Chaps. XVI and XVII. In general, it is only fair to evaluate Weber's treatment of the relations of Protestantism and capitalism in the light of his sociological work as a whole, including both the comparative sociology of religion and his general theory and methodology. Similarly, the reader should evaluate the attitude of this study toward Weber's theory in terms of its relation to the total methodological and theoretical framework of the study as a whole, and not *alone* in terms of *ad hoc* factual considerations.

[2] The study which he used most is M. Offenbacher, *Konfession und soziale Schichtung*, Tübingen, 1901. It was suggested by himself.

side this conclusion seems inevitable. But a materialistic case can be made against it on the ground that they might both be creations of the same set of material conditions at different stages of their development. It is also possible, though extremely improbable, that the congruence was purely fortuitous.

But in the most important of these three methods of proof, Weber goes beyond demonstrating the congruence of the two sets of attitudes. He builds an empirical bridge between them by tracing in the writings of Puritan leaders the internal development of the Protestant ethic itself. In the beginning the Protestant ethic was so exclusively interested in religious problems as to be strikingly otherworldly. In Calvin's own Geneva the result was a highly theocratic state of an almost socialistic type, characterized by an extremely stringent church discipline. From this point, partly no doubt under the influence of material conditions—Calvinists in a minority, for instance—the development was in a more and more individualistic direction. Instead of an immediate authoritarian, if necessary forcible,[1] introduction of the Kingdom of God on Earth, the emphasis was more and more on the duty of the individual to do God's will in his calling.

Moreover the tendency was increasingly to a direct approval of acquisitive activities under the proper conditions. Then action in a business calling, so long as it was sober, honest, rational, "useful" work, came to be looked upon as one of the most righteous things a man could do, and its fruits, "honestly" acquired riches, as the direct sign of God's blessing.

Weber not merely traces this evolution, but maintains (indeed, demonstrates) that it is not solely a process of "accommodation" to the necessities of a world recalcitrant to religious control. On the contrary, a major factor is a genuine "dynamic" of the Protestant ethic itself, the result of following *religious* interests in the situation in which the men of that time were placed. This is brought out above all by two circumstances. Devotion to a capitalistic calling was enjoined for *positive religious motives.*[2]

[1] As Cromwell attempted to carry out.

[2] This is so important it may be pointed out again. It is *not* Weber's thesis that Protestantism influenced capitalism through religious *approval* of acquisitive activities, expressed by preachers or otherwise, but because the religious *interests* of the believing individual directed his action in that direction. The distinction is highly important, both empirically and method-

The attitude was not permissive. Second, the later Puritan doctrine was not one of approval of any and every form of acquisitive activity under any conditions, but only under a very strict discipline. The original ascetic element, the main element for Weber, had by no means disappeared but remained intact in the somewhat altered context. This result no ethic of accommodation could have achieved.[1]

The articulation between the two was thus fully established. The development did not, however, stop here but proceeded still farther on the path of secularization.

In the line of development with which Weber is concerned this is not altogether a matter of relaxation of discipline, of concession to "moral laxity,"[2] but of gradual dropping out of the religious background of the attitudes concerned and in place of the religious substituting a utilitarian[3] motivation. It is only here that the "pure" spirit of capitalism, as Weber illustrated it from the writings of Benjamin Franklin[4] is to be found. But even here the central ethical element, the ascetic devotion to impersonal tasks for their own sake, is intact.

The gist of Weber's *causal* argument here may be put as follows: The empirical material (the writings of Protestant leaders down through the seventeenth century) shows a process of development toward the stronger and stronger sanction of individualistic acquisitive activities. Is this accommodation or is it an independent development of the religious ethic for *religious* reasons? Weber argues for the importance of the latter element on the ground that such a development is meaningful within the framework of the system of religious ideas; it is not

---

ologically. The two have generally been confused by Weber's critics. Dr. H. M. Robertson (*op cit.*) is an excellent example.

[1] This is not to say either (a) that no attitude of disinterested devotion to a calling is conceivable apart from the influence of the Protestant ethic or (b) that accommodation had played no part in the development of the spirit of capitalism. But Weber seems to have shown, with a high degree of probability (1) that the Protestant ethic played an important part in the development of *this* particular set of disinterested attitudes and (2) that they *could not* have been *exclusively* the products of "capalistic interests." That they were, is Robertson's central thesis.

[2] Though this no doubt also happened. See Chap. XVII.

[3] Not necessarily in the technical sense of the above discussion. See pp. 51 *ff.*

[4] *Protestant Ethic*, pp. 48–50.

only possible in the sense of not conflicting with essential elements of it, but it is in accord with strong religious motives inherent in the system of religious ideas itself in relation to the world. Furthermore the element of concrete capitalism in which Weber is interested is not at odds with this later ethic; it may on the contrary to a large extent be interpreted as the direct expression of these motives in practical conduct.[1]

But this, as Weber himself clearly states,[2] is "only one side of the causal chain." His book on the *Protestant Ethic and the Spirit of Capitalism* was expressly concerned only with this side. In spite of many scattered suggestions which, if all brought together, would form quite a respectable theory, Weber does not there, nor anywhere else in his work, attempt any systematic analysis of the other side with respect to this specific empirical subject matter. This would have to be done to exhaust the possibilities of empirical proof. But, instead, he turns to another line of investigation. He turns from the "method of agreement" to the "method of difference," to use Mill's term. Instead of continuing to ask directly what specific forces account for the appearance of rational bourgeois capitalism in the modern West, he asks inversely, why did anything like it *fail* to appear in any of the other great civilizations of the world?

NOTE ON THE ROLE OF IDEAS

At a number of points in the preceding chapter and below there is raised the general theoretical question of the role of ideas with particular reference to whether Weber's treatment is vitiated by any bias in the direction of rationalism. It is therefore well to insert at this point a general statement of the problem as it appears up to this point in the study, in particular attempting to relate Weber's approach to it to the previous discussion of Pareto.[3]

Weber's attention is focused on religious ideas in their relation to the motivation of action in what is ordinarily thought of as the secular sphere. The starting point of the analysis is the allegation of fact that, in the groups

[1] That is, in more general terms, there is a high degree of correspondence between the kind of socioeconomic organization that would be expected on the hypothesis that the development of the system had been importantly influenced by the Protestant ethic and the actual state of affairs. This certainly puts the burden of proof on the one who would radically deny its influence.

[2] *Protestant Ethic*, p. 23.

[3] Chap. VII, pp. 269 *ff.*

under consideration, the adherents of the Calvinist movement in the six-teenth and seventeenth centuries, there was, generally, a strong religious interest in salvation. Assuming, then, that these Calvinists were to an appre-ciable extent motivated by their interest in salvation, that they may be thought of as trying to attain it or to make certain of it, the question arises as to what bearing this fact will have on their actions in the secular sphere, particularly the economic. The comparison of the three religious groups, the Catholic, Lutheran and Calvinistic, shows that the interest in salvation, which may be attributed to all three groups, does not suffice to account for the differences in the direction of secular activities in which Weber has become interested. It is, rather, necessary to take into account other elements in the religious context. Weber sets about doing this by asking the question, what kind of action can, to the adherent of such a movement, be appropriate as a means of attaining or proving salvation? This depends upon the "situa-tion" in which the believer is placed, and in particular on certain features of this situation, namely the structure of religious ideas in relation to which the interest in salvation is carried out in action. For the Catholic whose interest in salvation is strongest the indicated course is to renounce the world and enter a monastery. For the one whose interest is less intense, it is to be faithful to tradition in the station in life in which he is placed, and to lay up merit for himself by an accumulation of discrete good works, particu-larly of ritual devotion and charity. For the Lutheran the monastery is excluded; for him the line of action is faithful performance of the traditional duties of his station in life and obedience to the duly constituted authorities. The Christian is held to be placed in a world of sin which he cannot, in general, hope to reform. Sin, which is inevitable, is to be expiated by sincere penitence and the pious resolve to do better next time. The Calvinist, finally, is exhorted to labor in a calling, soberly and rationally, in order to bring about the Kingdom of God on Earth. He is neither to renounce the world and retire to a monastery nor to accept the traditional order, but, so far as it falls within his calling, to attempt to make over the world accord-ing to the dictates of righteousness.

These differences of attitude are also matters of fact. Weber contends that he has demonstrated that they are, respectively, the typical attitudes toward secular activity, particularly economic, of members of the three religious groups. Weber then proceeds, sketchily for the Catholic and Lutheran reli-gions, in detail for the Calvinistic, to show that, given the initial interest in salvation, each of these attitudes becomes meaningful on the hypothesis that the actor to whom it is attributed is a believer in the system of religious ideas associated with the attitude. Thus according to the Calvinistic posi-tion: Good works cannot be a means of attaining salvation, but only a sign of election; predestination precludes the former. Meritorious conduct, furthermore, cannot consist mainly in ritual devotions since these would involve the sanctification of worldly things, in other words, idolatry. Tradi-tion cannot be sacred since that also would be idolatry. Mysticism is ex-cluded by the absolute transcendentality of God. Finally, the sinfulness of the flesh excludes a hedonistic attitude. Activity in the world should be directed toward rational mastery of the flesh in the interest of the glory of God, not use of the things of this world for self-indulgence and hedonistic gratification. The Calvinist works *in* the world, but neither *of* nor *for* the world.

Finally Weber's analysis not only establishes the meaningfulness of the attitude which he describes as worldly asceticism in terms of the Calvinistic theology, but he also demonstrates the congruence of this attitude with that of the spirit of capitalism with relatively minor alterations. The conspicuous thing about the spirit of capitalism is that it is a set of attitudes not clearly related to a developed system of religious or metaphysical ideas. The transition between these Weber has traced genetically, showing the existence of many connecting links.

But for the moment the genetic aspect of the question may be left aside. Granting his statements of fact are correct, it can be definitely held that Weber has demonstrated that there is a mutual relation on the meaningful level between (1) the particular form that the interest in salvation took predominantly among Calvinists, (2) the system of religious ideas summed up above as the Calvinistic theology and (3) the ascetic element in the system of attitudes which he described as the spirit of capitalism. Apart from genetic considerations what light, if any, does his analysis throw on their causal relations?

At this point it may be illuminating to try to state the relation of this problem to Pareto's conceptual scheme. Weber, being unacquainted with Pareto's work, did not carry through formally any residue-derivation analysis of his material. He is, however, interested in trying to understand what certain people do by analyzing what they say, and since their "theories" are largely nonscientific it seems an excellent case to which to apply the Paretian analysis.

It should be remembered that the residue is an operational concept. A residue is that which is arrived at by following the particular procedure that has been described in Chap. V. It is a relatively constant element of the linguistic expressions associated with action so far as they have no place in a scientific theory. In these terms if the linguistic expressions of Calvinists so far as they bear upon secular activities are analyzed they will yield not one, but several residues. One will be the residue of salvation, the manifestation of the "sentiment that men should act in such a way as to further the attainment and ascertainment of the state of grace." Associated with this among Calvinists, to form a "complex," will be certain other residues, namely the five major premises of Calvinistic theology discussed above. Since these are metaphysical propositions, not statements of empirical fact, they are nonlogical and may in the present context be treated as residues.

Now the Paretian operation as such contains no specific theorem relative to the role of ideas in general. It contains only the negative theorem that in so far as the residues constitute an important independent variable in a social system, changes in that system cannot be held to be determined by scientifically verifiable theories alone. But it has been shown above[1] that a residue, which is a verbal proposition, may vary all the way from a logically precise statement of a meaning which may stand in the same causal relation

---

[1] *Supra*, p. 212 *ff.*

to action as a scientifically verifiable theory to the case at the opposite pole, where it is an index of other forces, and its reciprocal influence on them is as negligible as is that of a thermometer, generally, on the system the temperature of which it indicates. The fact, then, that by the Paretian operation it is possible to arrive at the principal elements of Weber's analysis of Calvinism as residues proves nothing as to whether or how far the religious ideas are causal factors or merely "manifestations" of something else. That remains a question to be answered by further analysis of the particular facts.

It is, however, possible to extend the Paretian analysis in a manner which at first sight would seem to throw doubt on Weber's thesis of the causal role of the religious ideas. That is, it is possible to include the verbal expressions not only of Calvinists, but of those that fit Weber's description of the spirit of capitalism, in terms which do not involve any explicit religious motivation. Then some, at least, of the residues of the previous phase of the analysis, those with a specifically "religious" content, turn out, for the material being considered, to be less fundamental than others—those involved in the worldly ascetic attitude. That is, they become, in the wider context, derivations. Their place from the time of Benjamin Franklin on tends to be taken by other secular derivations, like that of the usefulness to social survival of the "workbench philosophy," or of the value of "activities" and the like. It must be remembered that the distinction between residues and derivations is a relative one and that what is in a narrower context a residue may in a broader become a derivation. This is, indeed, quite sufficient to disprove a naive "emanationist" view of the mechanisms of the influence of nonscientific ideas. The residues of worldly asceticism are clearly not simply "tied" to the Calvinistic theology in such a way that given the one the other can be inferred without further investigation. This, however, in no way disproves a significant functional relation between them. But to get farther with the problem it is necessary to bring still further considerations into the discussion. In Weber's work there are two different lines of analysis which serve to carry the argument beyond this point.

The one which fits most closely into the Paretian analysis will be discussed in some detail in the next chapter. This will broaden the comparative basis of the analysis still farther. On the basis of his comparative study of religions Weber comes to the broad conclusion that certain types of religious ideas are associated with certain types of attitudes toward secular activities. The most pronounced development of worldly asceticism is to be found in the culture which has or has had, a system of religious ideas emphasizing the transcendentality of God, the sinfulness of the flesh, etc. The farther attitudes depart from this type in the direction of either indifference to the things of this world or uncritical acceptance of tradition, the more they are associated with such religious ideas as the immanence of God, and the absence of a radical dualism of divine and worldly. Attitude and idea are, then, in all probability in close functional relation with each other, though perhaps also they may both be manifestations of sentiments lying still deeper. But this line of argument could injure Weber's position only by proving that it had not carried analysis so far as it could be carried, not by demonstrating positive error in Weber's work so far as it has gone.

The other line of analysis is one with which Pareto himself did not deal. It is that of introducing genetic considerations into analysis of the particular case. In genetic terms it may be possible to demonstrate causal connections which, in the then state of general theory could not be demonstrated in terms of such a general analytical framework as Pareto's.

The main points to be kept in mind are the following: The Calvinist theology, with its related ethical attitudes, existed in Western Europe prior to an extensive development of rational bourgeois capitalism. The theological ideas in question give, from the actor's point of view, an adequate meaning to these attitudes, and to the actions of which they constitute the residues. Not only is this the case, but Weber has traced historically, and made motivationally understandable, a process in the course of which, though certain central ascetic residues have remained essentially unchanged, they have moved in their direct relations to action steadily farther in the direction of closer congruence with the spirit of capitalism. Furthermore, he has traced a process of secularization by which the religious elements have gradually lost their importance, and he has made the probable motives for this understandable. The result of this genetic analysis is greatly to strengthen the probability that the system of religious ideas has had an important influence.

Finally there is a set of very general considerations which will be discussed in the following chapter and in Chap. XVII. Though for certain proximate purposes the attitude manifested in a residue may be taken as an explanatory factor, it is always possible to attempt to push beyond this to inquire into the forces at work in its genesis. In so far as value elements are involved it is relevant to ask whether such an attitude is, to the actor, meaningful in terms of his total conception of the world. The general tendency to rational integration of systems of action, discussed above,[1] is sufficient basis for this. Then in so far as a given system of ideas has existed for a long time in a society at strategic points, it is a reasonable hypothesis that it exerts a steady influence in the direction of canalizing attitudes in such a way that they will become, in terms of such a system, meaningful. This is the more true, the more the society in question is one characterized by the persistence of aggregates, by strength of "belief."

The question of the role of religious ideas, which is involved in so acute a form in Weber's work, is in part a phase of the broader question, which is of central interest to this study, of that of value elements. The clear distinction made by both Pareto and Weber between scientific and nonscientific ideas has cleared the way considerably. Part, at least, of the latter form a cognitive element in the value complex. The status of such ideas has been clarified by the above discussion of Durkheim's treatment of religion. Weber goes still further in clarifying it. But it seems quite apparent that the cognitive constitute only one group of elements in the value complex. Knowing, or believing, is not, as such, doing. In addition an element of effort of some sort is needed. The actor does not take toward his ideas the emotionally neutral attitude of the scientist which has played such an important part in the

[1] *Supra*, p. 21.

discussion of Durkheim. But while the ideas of the value complex are concretely bound up with other, noncognitive elements, there is no reason why they should not be analytically distinguished from them. Moreover, Weber has brought a great deal of evidence to show that while believing is not, *ipso facto*, doing, what one believes has much to do with what one does.

CHAPTER XV

MAX WEBER II: RELIGION AND MODERN CAPITALISM (*Continued*)

B. THE COMPARATIVE STUDIES

The vehicle of Weber's comparative investigation is the series of studies on the "Economic Ethics of the World Religions."[1] Weber declared his intention[2] of including Confucianism, Buddhism, Hinduism, Judaism, early Christianity and Islam. Unfortunately it was left unfinished at his death and only four were in a condition to be published in any form. Owing to limitations of space, attention will be confined to the results of two of them, the studies of Confucianism and Hinduism, since they strikingly illustrate what are theoretically the most important types.

But before entering upon a discussion of them it is necessary to say a word about the character of the whole series. Here, as distinct from the essay on the *Protestant Ethic*, Weber deals with both sides of the causal chain. But the series is not to be understood as a general "sociology of religion" if by that is meant a systematic study of all the interrelations of religion and society. Nor is it even a general study in the correlation of religious and economic phenomena, as has sometimes been maintained. Both these interpretations would contravene one of Weber's fundamental methodological principles, which will be discussed in the next chapter.[3] It is, on the contrary, definitely oriented[4] to

---

[1] "Die Wirtschaftsethik der Weltreligionen," *Gesammelte Aufsätze zur Religionssoziologie* (cited below as *Religionssoziologie*), Vol. I, pp. 237 *ff.*, Vol. II and Vol. III.

[2] *Religionssoziologie*, Vol. I, pp. 237–238. Many of the results are systematically put together in the section "Religionssoziologie," Part II, Chap. IV, pp. 227–356 of *Wirtschaft und Gesellschaft* (cited below as *Wirtsch. u. Ges.*).

[3] *Wertbeziehung.*

[4] That is, in the central argument. About this are gathered all manner of subsidiary problems partially independent of the main one. See A. von Schelting, *Max Webers Wissenschaftslehre*, pp. 283–284.

the problem of modern capitalism in the above sense. It is primarily a comparative study of the ethics of other religions in respects relevant to the spirit of capitalism and the ethics of ascetic Protestantism. This is equally true whether the relevance is by agreement or by contrast. It is this fact which justifies dealing with it in the present context.

As Dr. von Schelting points out,[1] methodologically the "ideal" procedure for Weber would have been to work out cases of social development where *only* the element of religious ethic differed from the situation in Western Europe. Unfortunately that is not to be found in concrete fact and would involve a degree of positive[2] construction of which Weber was highly suspicious.[3] What Weber does is to sacrifice methodological precision in favor of the concreteness to be gained by dealing with actual historical instead of hypothetical events.

In general terms, then, the situation is approximately as follows: In the cases which will be discussed Weber succeeds in demonstrating that the economic ethic associated with the religion in question is fundamentally different from that of ascetic Protestantism in its implications for economic activities. This fact is correlated with the further one that in the areas in which the ethic in question has been predominant, no development has taken place which is at all comparable with that of Western rational bourgeois capitalism. Thus there is established a prima-facie connection between the lack of capitalistic development and the character of the religious ethics in question since, as compared with that of ascetic Protestantism, they must, so far as they influence action at all, be held to constitute directly inhibitory forces.

The principal methodological difficulties in approximating an accurate estimate of the concrete importance of the religious ethic in the development of types of economic system, arise at two points. In the first place, the "observable" economic ethic of a religion is a concrete entity. Weber is perfectly frank to admit that in the course of its development such an economic ethic is certainly[4] influenced both in its character and in the fact

---

[1] von SCHELTING, *op. cit.*, pp. 285–286.
[2] The methodological issue will be discussed in the next chapter.
[3] See von SCHELTING, *op. cit.*, p. 267.
[4] See *Religionssoziologie*, Vol. I, p. 238.

of attaining ascendancy by "material" factors, above all by the social character of the class who constitute its bearers, but also by other factors. The differentiation of these from the *Eigengesetzlichkeit* of the religious system can never be arrived at historically since that would lead to a regress beyond the point where historical evidence is available. The only recourse is to analysis.

Secondly, the elements in the concrete social system other than the religious ethic which may be considered as favorable or unfavorable to capitalistic development do not, in any two cases which can be compared, directly correspond. China lacked some of the important hindrances present in the West while, on the other hand, the West had certain nonreligious favorable elements not present in China.

The practical limitations are such that certainly no quantitatively exact proof is empirically possible. Weber attempts an approach to it in the form of estimates of probability in terms of the known laws governing the behavior of each element. Thus, on the one hand, he attempts to estimate whether the concrete economic ethic could have resulted from the operation of nonreligious factors, above all whether it could be a reflection of "material interests."[1] In this it should be remembered that evidence for *Eigengesetzlichkeit* in the religious sphere is just as much entitled to be considered seriously as is evidence from the other side.[2] On the other hand, judgments must be made of the probability that in the modern West the favorable factors could have overcome the unfavorable without the intervention of the religious ethic, while in China and India the opposite would have happened. Here it is Weber's judgment that in both China and India the *combination* of nonreligious factors was at the crucial time at least as favorable to capitalistic development as in the Western situation. Hence the strong probability that in this respect a principal *differentiating* factor with respect to

[1] As noted above Weber does not attempt this systematically. For a collection of the main arguments he deals with at various points, see von Schelting, *op. cit.*, pp. 291 *ff.*

[2] On the question whether the Protestant ethic can be considered a product of "accommodation," see above, and Talcott Parsons, "H. M. Robertson on Max Weber and His School," *Journal of Political Economy*, October, 1935.

capitalism lay in the religious element of the economic ethic. It should be noted particularly that the reliability of these admittedly complex estimates of probability increases greatly with the broadening of the comparative perspective and hence the clarification of the different elements and of their possible relations to each other. Therefore the total result of Weber's comparative study becomes much more reliable than the judgment of any one particular case can be from its own data, taken alone. This is a well-recognized methodological principle.

CHINA

The "classical" Chinese social system[1] when compared with our own presents a curious combination of similarities and dissimilarities. On the side of social structure as such, there are two fundamental aspects—what is often called the "familistic" organization and the "political" superstructure. As is widely known, the mass of the Chinese people has been closely organized in kinship groups, to the modern sociologist strongly reminiscent of many primitive societies. The basic unit is the patrilineal exogamous clan[2] which is broadly coterminous with the local village group. It is, in turn, subdivided into smaller household groups. In general these familistic groups stand in the closest connection with the soil, and are religiously sanctioned by the highly developed system of ancestor worship.

The Chinese family system stands in perhaps the sharpest contrast with that which has been progressively developing in the United States, interestingly enough a country of typically "Puritan" background. The Chinese family group exhibits an exceptionally high degree of collective solidarity; the principle of parental authority and "filial piety" is exceedingly strict, requiring both obedience on the part of children and a high degree of ritual respect. Finally it is the extreme antithesis to the modern American independence of women. The family, not the individual, is the unit of Chinese society.

While there is a relatively high degree of differentiation of wealth among family groups, there has been since the imperial time in China no rigidly hierarchical class system as in medieval

[1] Roughly since the consolidation of the Empire down to quite recent times.

[2] For Weber's discussion, see *Religionssoziologie*, Vol. I, pp. 373 *ff.*

Europe, above all nothing even approaching a caste system.[1]
There has been at least a formal equality of opportunity in
choice of occupation,[2] in fact in practically all relations outside
the familistic ties. In this respect the Chinese situation has
resembled that of Western capitalistic countries[3] with the same
order of limitation on substantial equality of opportunity—
through the effective privileges of wealth and superior social
status. In all this the striking difference from the modern West
is the position of the familistic groups.

The Chinese imperial "state"[4] had two main aspects. On the
one hand, it was a theocracy, in a sense differentiating it radically
from any Christian political structure. The emperor was the
"Son of Heaven" and was conceived of as the principal intermediary between the divine order of things and that of human
society. A break in the harmony of the latter could be laid to
his ritual inadequacy. Thus the emperor formed the center
of the ritual interests of China.[5]

But this religious aspect did not lead, as it might have, to
the placing of political power in the hands of a hereditary priesthood of which he was the head. Under the emperor stood a special
class of bureaucratic administrators, the mandarins. In certain
respects the Chinese political system carried bureaucratic principles through to a point scarcely reached anywhere else, but in
others it differed radically from the type important for bourgeois
capitalism.

The mandarins were a class of men with literary training whose
eligibility for appointment to office was based on the passing of a
series of examinations. Thus in spite of the extent to which fac-
tually personal favor and other modifying elements entered in,
there was definitely an impersonal objective standard of qualification. Favoritism was confined largely to the matter of selection
among available candidates, since the number of eligibles was
always much larger than the number of offices to be filled. Moreover, certain other highly important bureaucratic principles
were radically carried through. The official could not be stationed

---

[1] *Ibid.*, p. 389.
[2] *Ibid.*, p. 390.
[3] Though developed much later in Western countries.
[4] See *Religionssoziologie*, Vol. I, pp. 314 *ff.*
[5] The mandarin as his local representative also had ritual functions.

in the province where his family was resident and his term in the same office was rigidly restricted to three years. Thus in spite of a high degree of independence of control from above, offices never became hereditary or politically dangerous to the central authority. Feudalization was effectively prevented. The mandarins as a class, but no few great families among them, monopolized offices. The class was never closed and each new accession to office depended on appointment from above.

At the same time there were fundamental limitations to a full bureaucratic development. In the first place, the bureaucratic principle was confined to a small group of high officials. The much larger number of subordinates necessary to carry out effective administration were not subjected to general bureaucratic discipline but their appointment, payment and control were left to the individual mandarin. He was naturally highly dependent on these subordinates with their knowledge of local conditions. They in turn were likely to be in league with local interests, such as the prominent familistic groups, gilds and village organizations. Hence the administrative system was not in a position to put through radical policies against powerful local interests and was forced to leave an extraordinary amount of autonomy to the local groups. The bureaucracy remained a superstructure and did not penetrate deeply into the social structure to achieve a direct control of the individual as the modern Western state bureaucracy has done.

Secondly, the mode of payment of officials under the tax-collection system was a limitation. The mandarin was obligated to turn over to the central government a certain quota of taxes. But the costs of his local administration, including his own remuneration, were met from taxes he himself set and collected. This fact and his limited term of office led him to get as much as possible out of his position while there was time.

Finally, it was not a *specialized* bureaucracy: there were no special technical qualifications for particular offices and the necessary training was not at all specialized or technical. A knowledge of the classics was required, the same for everyone. The object was not to fit a candidate for the particular technical requirements of a given office but to insure that he was a sufficiently highly cultivated gentleman to be worthy of the exalted position of a mandarin. This circumstance obviously increased the official's dependence upon subordinates and was an important hindrance to the extension of the bureaucratic principle into the details of routine administration. It remained what Weber calls a patrimonial bureaucracy.

Between the mandarin class and the familistic group there was room for the development of a considerable amount of specifically economic enterprise. With variations at different periods craftsmanship developed highly and a large amount of mercantile trade, often on a considerable scale, and in each case with powerful craft gilds. But in spite of the occasional large scale of enterprise nothing approaching the modern Western industrial capitalism was ever developed. In spite of a great deal of technological invention, techniques remained traditional and industrial production was mainly on a handicraft basis. The large-scale organization of trade was not associated with a corresponding organization of production as in the West.[1]

At a very early time China had permanent peace over a wide area. It had relatively few restrictions on internal mobility and trade.[2] It had an unusual degree of equality of opportunity and freedom in the choice of occupation. It was practically free from such restrictions on economic development as the Catholic prohibition of usury.[3] Finally the state recognized and left a very high degree of autonomy to organizations of economic interest such as the gilds. If, as is often thought, absence of restricting circumstances alone could bring about a modern capitalistic development, surely it should have happened in China long before the modern era.[4]

When the economic ethic is considered the paradox becomes even more striking. For probably there is no ethic in the world

---

[1] There were, Weber says, three main sources of accumulation of private wealth: (1) the political exploitation of office and tax collection, (2) government contracts and tax farming, (3) commerce. See *Religionssoziologie*, Vol. I, p. 393.

[2] *Ibid.*, p. 390.

[3] *Ibid.*

[4] The principal hindering circumstances of not *directly* religious origin Weber mentions were (1) the absence of a solid, formal legal structure, (2) the absence of corporate autonomy of towns, (3) defective monetary development. See especially *Religionssoziologie*, Vol. I, pp. 391 *ff.* Transportation facilities were always primitive, though probably no more so than in medieval Europe.

which has any pretense to religious status which is more definitely utilitarian and worldly than that of China. Above all, nowhere else in the world has there been a more strikingly positive valuation of wealth among all classes of society. In prudent care for the interests of this world and lack of interest in any other, perhaps no people has ever surpassed the Chinese. Moreover this worldliness or utilitarianism is combined with a kind of rationalism. It involves a far-reaching repudiation of the irrational aspects of religion, above all orgiastic and transcendental elements. Wherein then lies the difference from the utilitarian rationalism of the Protestant ethic?

The predominant[1] ethical system of China which gives a definite clear-cut attitude toward the world is the Confucian orthodoxy.[2] It is important to recognize that this came to be the specific ethic of the mandarin class—that of the polished, educated gentleman. Confucianism is conspicuous for the fact that it is almost purely an ethical doctrine, a collection of practical precepts without any explicit metaphysical foundation. Confucius would have nothing to do with metaphysical speculations; they were to him useless and vain. There is no definite interest in a future life, and no concept of salvation. The doctrine is concerned with conduct in this life for its own sake with no concern beyond that except for a good name.

Its worldliness does not, however, sanction a lack of discipline. On the contrary its rationalism involves a particular kind of discipline. The central underlying conception is that of a harmony or order. The universe itself constitutes such an order ruled by "Heaven" and human society is a microcosm of the world order. The higher, educated man seeks to live in accordance with this order. To do so involves abstention from any kind of loss of self-control which might endanger his equilibrium.

There is no such thing as a radically evil principle; there is no "sin"—only error, the failure to become the most perfect "gentleman" possible with one's inheritance and opportunities. The rational man will avoid display of emotion, will be always self-controlled, dignified, polite. He will always observe the proprieties of any situation most punctiliously. His basic aim

---

[1] On the whole becoming increasingly so with time. See *Religionssoziologie*, Vol. I, p. 454.

[2] *Religionssoziologie*, Vol. I, pp. 430 *ff.*

is to live in harmony with a social order which is generally accepted and to be an ornament to it.

His duty is not to shoulder other people's responsibilities, not to be concerned with the state of society generally, but to attend to his own concerns. These include two main elements—his self-development as an educated gentleman and his relations to others. In the latter connection the primary emphasis is on certain specific personal relations, above all those of piety.[1] The central Chinese virtue is filial piety, and the attitude of the official to his superior should be as that of a son to his father. In fact Confucius conceived the whole of society as a network of such personal relationships and his injunction to each was to see that his conduct was right in his *own* relationships. He should not set up to be his brother's keeper. The contrast with the Puritan concern for the conduct of all is striking.

The order with which the Confucian gentleman sought to live in harmony was a definite concrete order. In the Confucian ethics no motive is given for an attempt to alter its main outline. This fact is the source of one fundamentally important set of attitudes, those toward the "religious" practices and beliefs of the society. They fall into two categories.

On the one hand, the state structure itself, of which the mandarin was a part, was a "sacral" structure. The emperor and his officials were the carriers of the state cult and, as in classical antiquity, religious duties of a ritual character were part of the accepted duties of public office. Confucianism simply accepted these things as a matter of course. One did not combat them but neither did one inquire into their meaning—that would be fruitless metaphysical speculation. They were part of the order. There was, in spite of its rationalism, as Weber says, not the slightest Confucian tendency to rationalize these things in an ethical sense. Similarly, to the duties of filial piety so strongly stressed there belonged an elaborate ritual aspect which was also simply accepted without any attempt at ethical rationalization.[2]

On the other hand, there has always been in China, as elsewhere, an enormous amount of popular magic and superstition. This also the Confucian gentleman accepted but in a different way. He did not himself participate in it because it was beneath

[1] *Ibid.*, pp. 445–446.
[2] *Ibid.*, p. 453.

his dignity, but at the same time there was not the slightest attempt to drive it out. It belonged to the life of the uneducated mass.[1]

The conception of the means to perfection expressed the same idea—acceptance of the given. Perfection was attained by a study of the classics.[2] What marked off the gentleman from the vulgar mass was not birth or wealth but classical learning. It is important to see how different this conception of learning was from the modern Western. It never occurred to anyone that the classics could be improved upon. Learning was not dynamic but static according to a constant norm.

This combination of circumstances could not but foster traditionalism. The rationalism of the Confucian ethic was genuine enough. It was also a rationalism of this world; it would have nothing to do with transcendental things. Within the framework of the Chinese society it placed an unquestioned value on the good things of this world, above all on wealth, long life and a good name. But its rationalism was limited by the fundamental traditional acceptance of an existing order, above all of the traditional religio-magical elements of it, whether state cult, ancestor worship or popular magic. Moreover, the ideal of the Confucian gentleman was a traditional static ideal, the basis of which was assimilation of a traditionally fixed body of literary culture, the classics. Confucian learning entirely lacked the dynamic quality of Western science. Finally, the dominant ethical value of Confucianism, as Weber says, its only absolute duty, "piety,"[3] was itself a traditionalistic virtue. It enjoined *acceptance* of the order of the fathers and the duly constituted authorities and proprieties. There was no sanction of rebellion against this order in the name of an abstract ideal. Confucian rationalism was that of dignified adaptation to a traditional order. Its discipline was the avoidance of all disorderliness and the self-discipline of the dignified gentleman. It was, as Professor Sorokin says,[4] "a prudent policy of sound conservatism."

But this is precisely what the ethic of ascetic Protestantism was not, as should be abundantly evident from the above dis-

[1] *Ibid.*, p. 443.
[2] *Ibid.*, pp. 451 *ff.*
[3] *Ibid.*, p. 445.
[4] P. A. SOROKIN, *Contemporary Sociological Theories*, p. 695.

cussion. It was rather a distinctly revolutionary force. Its animus
was not adaptation of the individual to a social world uncritically
accepted. It was an injunction to make over his world, as far
as lay within his power, in the name of a transcendental ideal—
to establish the Kingdom of God on Earth. It was, as Weber
succinctly puts it,[1] not a doctrine, like Confucianism, of rational
adaptation *to* the world, but of rational mastery *over* the world.
Archimedes is reputed to have said, "Give me a place to stand
and I will move the world." The Confucian ethic failed to move
the world precisely because its worldliness denied it a place to
stand outside the world. The Protestant ethic, on the other hand,
had such a place to stand, its transcendental God and its conception of salvation. In precisely the *ascetic* aspect of its ethic
lay its driving force.

From this basic difference follow a number of more special
differences. On one hand, from the worldliness of Confucianism
followed its acceptance of tradition, even more its sanctification
of it. On the other hand, from the transcendental basis of the
Puritan ethic followed the absolute unsanctity of tradition.[2] To
the Puritan, Chinese filial piety would be a sheer case of idolatry
of the flesh; the state cult, pure "superstition." The only sanction
of earthly things was their conformity with the will of God.
Puritanism carried out one of the most radical possible extremes
of elimination of magic from the world;[3] Confucianism left the
deep-rooted popular magic untouched. This difference is, in
turn, part of one of Weber's most fundamental theses, that
everywhere traditionalism is the rule in the earlier stages of a
given social development.[4] It is so powerful that it requires forces
of exceptional strength to break through it even appreciably, and
only when that has happened are certain kinds of social
development, like that of rational bourgeois capitalism, possible.
Not only did the Confucian ethic, in spite of its worldly rationalism, entirely fail to do this; on the contrary it provided a
direct and powerful sanction of the traditional order.

Without any pretense of exhaustive treatment two other
important differences may be pointed out. One of the fundamental

[1] *Religionssoziologie*, Vol. I, p. 534.
[2] *Ibid.*, p. 527.
[3] "Entzauberung der Welt," *Religionssoziologie*, Vol. I, p. 513.
[4] The general theoretical issue will be taken up below (see Chap. XVII).

requirements of modern bureaucratic structure is specialization of function and, with it, specialized technical knowledge, legal or scientific. This is one of the features of modern Western bureaucracy that the mandarin bureaucracy conspicuously failed to develop. Such specialization inevitably involves renunciation of a completely rounded personality. With us specialization has been bitterly attacked in the name of humanistic ideals. The Puritan ethic went far to break through this barrier by its conception of man as the instrument of God's will. His own highest self-fulfillment lay in playing his part, even though it be a highly specialized part, in a calling. The Confucian gentleman, on the other hand, was no "instrument" in any sense,[1] but an end in himself, a fully rounded, harmonious "work of art." Far from there being positive motives to specialization there was strong inhibition against it. Moreover, for the Confucian the only personally valuable knowledge was that of the classics, not of technical specialties. The Confucian was a humanist.

Secondly, another of the fundamentals of our modern Western social order is its ethical "universalism." To a very high degree both in theory and in practice our highest ethical duties apply "impersonally" to all men, or to large categories of them irrespective of any specific personal relation involved. For instance, the duties of honesty and fair treatment are held to apply to business dealings with everyone, not only with one's relatives and personal friends. Indeed, without this universalism, as Weber repeatedly points out, it is difficult to see how the modern economic system could function, for on it rests the essential confidence which must underlie such business relationships as the maintenance of contracts and quality of goods.[2]

In this respect the Puritan ethic represents an intensification of the general Christian tendency. It has an extremely powerful animus against nepotism and favoritism.[3] To this the Confucian ethic stands in sharp contrast. Its ethical sanction was given to an individual's *personal* relations to particular persons—and with any strong ethical emphasis *only* to these.[4] The whole Chinese

---

[1] See *Religionssoziologie*, Vol. I, p. 532.
[2] See above, Durkheim's treatment of the conditions of a contractual system, Chap. VIII.
[3] *Religionssoziologie*, Vol. I, p. 531.
[4] *Ibid.*, p. 527.

social structure accepted and sanctioned by the Confucian ethics was a predominantly "particularistic" structure of relationships.[1] This left relationships outside this category in a realm of ethical indifference, with a general unwillingness to assume ethical obligations. Since most economic relationships in a market system are of this outside character the tendency for any break in traditionalism was to take the form of emancipation from ethical limitations, of "adventurers' capitalism," not the ethically disciplined acquisition typical of rational bourgeois capitalism.

Finally, while it is in general true that Confucianism rejects metaphysical speculation, there is a predominant current of Chinese thought, within which it belongs, which shows a strong contrast to the Western, and is relevant to the general question of the basis of religious ethics. The Confucian philosophy implied the presence of principles of order in the universe; the social order is but an aspect of a cosmic order. But unlike the predominant Western view the basis of this order is immanent and, in the last analysis, impersonal. There is no analogue to the Judaeo-Christian transcendental, personal God, the creator and ruler of the world. In Chinese thought this order came to be formulated in terms of the conception of Tao which was common to the Confucian and most of the other schools.

This fact is connected with another to which Weber attributes the greatest importance, namely, the complete failure of a class of prophets like the Jewish to arise in China, whose "mission" it was to impose an ethical obligation to a transcendental ideal in the name of such a transcendental God.[2] Such prophecy he held to be a main source of the break in traditionalism in the West in favor of an ethical rationalization of the world. Indeed this prophetic attitude was incompatible with a pantheistic system of ideas. It is true that Confucian orthodoxy does not stand by any means alone in Chinese religious thought. But its principal competitor, Taoism, did not lead in the Western direction of ethical rationalization, but rather, farther away. Taoism[3] embraced two main tendencies. On a high level of intellectual sophistication it was a mystical, contemplative doctrine. Instead

---

[1] We shall come back to these problems below (see Chap. XVII, appended note).

[2] *Religionssoziologie*, Vol. I, p. 516.

[3] *Ibid.*, pp. 458 *ff.*

of seeking to uphold the ideal of a polished, worldly gentleman, like the Confucian, the Taoist held that the highest activity of man was the contemplative grasp of the essence of the universe— a path obviously leading directly away from any sort of active ascetic mastery over the world. Indeed, given the pantheistic background of Chinese thought, Weber held, there are only these two possibilities of a rationalization of the "knowing" man's attitudes toward the universe—either the Confucian worldly "adaptation" to the world order within society, or the Taoist mystical, contemplative, asocial attitude. On the other hand, the vulgarization of Taoism resulted in a tremendous proliferation of magical superstition. There is a close parallel to these two tendencies of Taoism in Buddhism. This suggests a similar metaphysical basis and may well help to explain the receptivity to Buddhism in China.[1]

India

Indian society and religion may be treated somewhat more briefly than the Chinese since in both respects the contrast with

[1] In view of this discussion it is impossible to agree with Professor Sorokin's contention that Weber failed to establish an adequate distinction between Puritan and Confucian rationalism in respects relevant to rational bourgeois capitalism. The reasons he advances in his very brief discussion are inadequate to the conclusion and only take account of a small part of Weber's treatment. They have all been met in the above discussion. See P. A. Sorokin, *Contemporary Sociological Theories*, pp. 694–695.

Professor Sorokin also holds (*ibid.*, p. 696) the Japanese reception of Western economic organization in the later nineteenth century to be important empirical evidence against Weber's position. While Weber did not deal with Japan at all thoroughly (in any way comparably to his treatment of China) he was by no means unaware of the problem. Professor Sorokin's point does not seem conclusive for two reasons: In the first place, he attributes to Weber a view he did not hold—that modern capitalism could not *exist* or be adopted without the Puritan ethic. Weber's thesis is that it could not have been *developed spontaneously* without the assistance of these religious forces. There is a great difference between the possibility of a non-Protestant culture being able to assimilate rational bourgeois capitalistic forms from without, and its producing them spontaneously. The former is exemplified by Japan, and there is no statement in Weber that such a thing is impossible (see passage quoted below from *Religionssoziologie*, Vol. II, p. 300). Professor Sorokin gives no specific reference to support his imputation of that view to Weber.

Secondly, among different non-Protestant cultures there may be a great variation in the formidability of the obstacles to reception of such capitalistic

the Western situation is much more obvious and there is little danger of failing to distinguish the religious ethic of Hinduism from that of Protestantism. India is the proverbial home of otherworldliness in the everyday sense of the term.

To the Westerner the most striking feature of the Indian social system is caste.[1] While some are perhaps inclined to regard caste as primitive, nothing could be farther from the truth. To any degree such as its development in India it is an absolutely unique phenomenon. Moreover, in its full state of crystallization it does not belong to the early stages of Indian history but definitely to the later. It is a product of a long process of development.[2]

Though in some respects in its recent form, as revealed by the Indian Census Reports, caste presents an extraordinarily

---

forms. Without having investigated the question thoroughly the opinion may be ventured that in certain important respects these obstacles have been distinctly less formidable in Japan than in either China or India (*ibid.* p. 359). For instance, an able distinction thesis at Harvard University (E. C. Devereux, Jr., *"Gemeinschaft and Gesellschaft in Tokugawa Japan"* [1934, unpublished]) has maintained the presence of important indigenous religious elements in Japan of a "universalistic" as against a "particularistic" character [in the sense used above, p. 550] which probably went far to neutralize the imported Confucian elements. Weber also notes the presence in Japan of a political structure of quite a different character from that of the Chinese. "A population in which a class of the Samurai type played the predominant role could not—apart from all other circumstances—evolve a rational economic ethic *from its own resources.* Nevertheless the terminable relation of fealty, which created firm contractual relations in law, provided a far more favorable basis for 'individualism' in the occidental sense than for instance the Chinese theocracy. Japan could adopt capitalism as a completed thing with relative ease, even though it could not itself produce its *Geist.*" (*Religionssoziologie,* Vol. II, p. 300. Italics mine.) See also *ibid.,* p. 376 (compare the last sentence with Professor Sorokin's "According to Weber this is impossible." *Op. cit.,* p. 696).

Hence in the absence of supporting evidence, which he fails to provide, it seems that Professor Sorokin's categorical statement of the seriousness of the Japanese case as against Weber's position cannot be accepted. The Chinese and Japanese cases are the only empirical points he raises against the comparative parts of Weber's sociology of religion. His methodological objection will be discussed in the following chapter.

[1] The general problem of India is treated by Weber in *Religionssoziologie,* Vol. II, caste and the other features of the social system in Vol. II, Sec. I.

[2] According to the best contemporary opinion the full crystallization cannot be placed before A.D. 700 and possibly took place as late as A.D. 1300. *Cf.* E. A. H. Blunt, *The Caste System of Northern India.*

heterogeneous picture, there is in it an element of order which definitely entitles it to be called a system.[1] It is composed of a very large number of rigidly endogamous, generally local, hereditary groups arranged in a hierarchy of relative inferiority and superiority. The ultimate endogamous units are the subcastes but these are for the most part grouped in larger, more or less well-defined units, the castes proper, those in the same caste maintaining at least the fiction of equal social status with each other.

Though by no means without exception, the caste groups are usually characterized by a hereditary occupation so that the division of society into castes is roughly a functional division of labor on a hereditary basis. A great many of the caste names, though by no means all, designate this occupation.

Furthermore the castes are conspicuously characterized by ritual barriers. The prohibition of *connubium* itself has a prominent ritual aspect as does, perhaps even more, the other most prominent single criterion, the prohibition of commensality. There is an extraordinarily elaborate system of ritual rules governing the preparation and consumption of food and personal contacts. On the whole these rules are sharply differentiated according to caste and are different for the members of any one caste according to what other castes are involved in a given situation. There are only a few all-Hindu ritual elements such as the sacredness of the cow; for the rest the ubiquity of ritual serves to make the castes a congeries of ritually watertight compartments.

In the hierarchical aspect there is a certain element of vagueness, in the sense that it is not always possible to place every single caste or subcaste in relation to all others, but the general outline of the hierarchy is clear enough. The apex is the Brahman caste and the main criterion of caste status is that of the relation of the particular caste to the Brahmans. And the criteria are on the whole of a special type—ritual relations. The status of a caste is primarily determined[2] by such considerations as what things and under what circumstances (food for instance), a Brahman of good standing will take from a member of that caste, what kinds of contact will occasion purification rites on the part

[1] Which will be sketched as an "ideal type," many of the details being neglected.

[2] In the sense of criterion, not the causal sense.

of the Brahman and what kinds of ritual services the Brahman will perform for members of the caste in question.

As has been stated, this caste structure in its present or recent form is not an inheritance from ancient India but has developed into its present form in the course of a long, slow process. At various times it has been affected by a number of different elements. As the oldest literary sources reveal, a class division into conquerors and conquered created and repeatedly reemphasized a color line. There were also differentiation of occupation and of organized occupational groups; differentiation of wealth; reception into the single system of many different ethnic groups with differing cultures, sometimes with, sometimes without, special occupations. These and, no doubt, many other circumstances have played a part.

One dominant fact, however, requires explanation. The pivot of the specific hierarchical form seems to lie in the undoubted and unchallenged social supremacy of the Brahman caste—a priestly caste. Not only are they the top, but other castes are ranked with reference to them and *on their terms*, ritual terms, which are the professional concern of the Brahman. This has happened in spite of the fact that the Brahmans did not at any historical period command an organized religious association in any way comparable, for instance, with the medieval church. In fact explicit caste organization varies in inverse relation to the rank of the caste—the panchayat or caste council is most highly developed among the lower castes.[1] Moreover, though many Brahmans have acted as ministers and advisers of princes in both lay and spiritual matters, they have never as a caste held political authority in their own right, but only as individuals by appointment of others. Finally, though often wealthy, their position certainly does not rest upon wealth as such independently of the prestige of their religious position and services. And they have by no means uniformly been the wealthiest caste. No other priesthood in history has such an achievement to its credit.

Other aspects of the social structure may be briefly noted. India has always been primarily an agricultural society[2] and the typical local unit is the village. It is, however, unlike the Chinese village, not made up of a group of blood relations but in any

---

[1] See BLUNT, *op. cit.*

[2] *Religionssoziologie*, Vol. II, p. 1.

given village a number of different caste groups are typically represented. But in spite of caste barriers the village organization has in general been highly integrated and stable with, as in China, a large amount of self-government as against superior political authority.

This points to a highly important contrast between both India and China, on the one hand, and the modern West, on the other. India like China produced imposing political structures, though not nearly so stable over long periods. They both developed patrimonial bureaucracies and disciplined armies, but never a full modern Western bureaucracy. China approached nearer to such an organization than India. And—a most important fact— in India, as in China and in the same sense, the state remained a "superstructure." It did not penetrate in its administrative functions directly to the individual[1] but, rather, stopped at the caste, village and other groups, leaving them essentially intact with a large degree of self-government.[2]

As in China, in India there developed craft and merchant gilds, at one time very powerful, a very considerable trade even over long distances, and high skill in craftsmanship. There was a considerable capitalistic development in trade, in war supplies, tax farming, and considerable accumulation of wealth through these and other channels. But at no time did this development approach the rational bourgeois capitalism of the West.

It is quite clear that the caste system, with its extreme of both vertical and territorial immobility and its ritually sanc- tioned hierarchy of traditionally stereotyped occupations, con- stitutes an almost insuperable barrier to such a development, certainly to a spontaneous development from indigenous sources. And such capitalism of this character as exists in India today is clearly a European importation.

But clearly the problem is not the incompatibility of caste with modern capitalism. It is, rather, why the Indian develop- ment took this direction. For not only has a rigid caste system not always existed there, but especially in the time of the growth of the great religious systems there was in India a great deal of

---

[1] As Weber puts it, administration was "extensive" rather than "inten- sive."

[2] It may be noted that an opposite development was a striking feature of both the polis of antiquity and the modern Western state.

social flexibility, certainly comparing favorably with medieval
Europe. The question of Brahman supremacy was at that time
by no means settled, least of all in the Buddhistic period. Furthermore there were a number of elements hostile to a traditional
crystallization of castes; apart from the economic elements
mentioned Buddhism was at least indifferent to caste. Warfare
with its unsettling effects was rife at almost all periods. Moreover,
India was repeatedly subject to foreign conquest with impacts
on the class structure even more unsettling than internal
war.[1]

The dominant religious system of India in recent times is generally referred to as Hinduism. It is necessary, however, to
exercise care not to read into it our own Western ideas of what
constitutes a religion. In the first place, there is no Hindu
"church" one may join. The only way to become a Hindu is to
be born into a caste which is recognized as Hindu. This recognition is not based upon any dogmatic propositions of belief but
primarily on ritual practices. Above all a caste must observe
the sacredness of the cow and avoid eating beef and recognize, in
general, the religious authority of the Brahmans, which is above
all ritual. India has its sacred books, especially the Vedas, and a
good Hindu would never think of questioning their sanctity, but
his attitude is one of general, undefined respect, not of subscription
to any specific articles of faith contained in them or deduced from
them.

The Hindu has, to be sure, religious duties for failure in which
sanctions may be visited upon him. But these lie in the realm not
of doctrine, but of *dharma*. Dharma can perhaps best be translated as duty. It consists essentially in the traditional obligations
of everyday life, including above all ritual obligations. Some
dharma such as not eating beef and respecting Brahmans is
common to all Hindus, but for the most part it consists in the
traditional duties of one's station in life, above all one's caste.
So long as one does not violate these, he may think as he pleases.
But for such an offense as marrying outside one's caste one may
be "excommunicated," that is, expelled from the caste.[2]

[1] For a summary of circumstances favorable to capitalism in India see
Religionssoziologie, Vol. II, pp. 2–4.

[2] A very serious penalty indeed when the caste system is intact. It is then
nothing less than "social death."

What the Hindu is bound to by his feelings of religious duty then is the traditional social order, above all in its caste structure. Hinduism as a "religion" is but an aspect of this order with no independent status apart from it.

As has been said, there is no binding dogma in the Christian sense. More than that there is a bewildering variety of religious ideas and practices, of gods and cults, and means to salvation recognized as Hindu. But underlying all are certain definable elements. In the first place, there is a fundamental religious relativity. There is no way of life alone religiously acceptable, and no one exclusively valid approach to the divine. No Indian cult would think of the Western *extra ecclesiam nulla salus*. On the contrary, there are in principle many ways suitable for different kinds and classes of persons, adapted to their abilities and needs, which all lead ultimately to the same goal. In this religious sense India presents probably the most radically individualistic situation known to history.

But there is a more specific content of ideas, those of transmigration and karma.[1] Each soul has existed from eternity, is definitely not the creation of a god and passes through an unending series of rebirths. Karma, on the other hand, is the doctrine that each act of such an entity has permanent indestructible effects on the fate of the actor's soul which can never be evaded. The two combined yield a completely closed rationalization of the problem of evil—one of the three most consistent, Weber says, in history.[2] These doctrines are, to be sure, not dogmas in the sense that they are enforced by a church, but they are religious ideas common to the whole Hindu community, nowhere seriously attacked within it. As such they have stood intact for many centuries.[3]

The relation to practical motivation emerges with one further element, the association of karma and transmigration with dharma and through it with the place of the individual in the

---

[1] "These and only these are really 'dogmatic' beliefs of all Hindus." *Religionssoziologie*, Vol. II, pp. 117 *ff*.

[2] *Religionssoziologie*, Vol. II, p. 120. The others are that of Calvinism and the dualism of Zoroastrianism.

[3] As already noted (Chap. VII, p. 286) this is an interesting case for Pareto's thesis of the inherent instability of "nonlogical" theories. The reason certainly does not lie in restrictions on intellectual freedom.

caste structure.[1] According to the good or bad acts of the individual in past incarnations the causality of karma will determine
the place of his rebirth in the caste hierarchy. For purposes of the
theory this hierarchy is extended below human society into the
animal world, and above it so that one may be reborn a god—
with the implication that the gods are not immortal but are
really only superhuman. Finally in this context good and bad
can have only one meaning. Good is the faithful performance of
dharma, of the traditionally stereotyped duties of one's caste
position; bad, failure in this.[2]

Once this connection was made, in so far as the motives of action
were religious at all, it was effectively turned in the direction of
the traditional performance of caste obligations and hence the
maintenance of the caste structure. The religious interest of
the individual could never be in the upsetting of the system but
only in the improvement of his chances of a better incarnation
within the system. And the sole means to ensure this lay in complete conformity with the system in all its details of traditionally
prescribed conduct. It was in a sense a conception of "calling"
but with the utmost possible stress on traditionalism.[3] Indeed
a more completely watertight and effective[4] sanction of traditionalism could scarcely be devised.

This whole conception of the individual's religious duty
implied, and to a considerable extent doubtless had its origin
in, the still deeper character of Indian religious thought. The
latter was, along with caste, totally unknown to the classic Vedic
literature which gave a religious outlook closely related to the
Greek. But in the course of development the Vedic gods themselves tended to lose importance as compared with the objective
efficacy of the ritual of sacrifice. This tendency seems to have
centered attention on the objective impersonal order of the
ritual forces, and philosophic speculation adumbrated the meaning of this ritual.

Whatever the historical process may have been, there is no
doubt that by the period of Brahmanism[5] the doctrines of karma

[1] *Religionssoziologie*, Vol. II, p. 118. A product, as Weber here says, of
Brahman intellectualism.

[2] There is thus, as in China, no concept of a radically evil principle.

[3] The Lutheran case raised to the *n*th power.

[4] In so far as religious "interests" operate at all, of course.

[5] Historians habitually divide Indian religious development into **three**

and transmigration had appeared and were bound up with an impersonal pantheistic conception of the principle of order in the universe, which excluded any possibility of a personal, transcendental creator-god. The ultimate order including souls was eternal and uncreated, the gods themselves of only subordinate significance. "God" was to be found within the order, not outside and above it. The Western conceptions both of creation and of grace[1] were radically excluded. In the orthodox Vedanta school of Brahmanism only this impersonal unity was recognized as real; everything else was "maya," illusion.

The process by which this extraordinary Brahmanic rationalization of the universe came to fit so perfectly a peculiar social system was certainly not a simple one. The theory was the creation of a highly cultivated intellectual class and its dissemination on the purely ideal level to the point at which its basic doctrines become the common property of a vast population, the majority illiterate, must have been a slow process. And this dissemination is the necessary condition of its serving as the canalizing framework of the religious interests of the masses.

A number of suggestions have been advanced by different writers to explain the caste system, the most important emphasizing the roles of occupational differentiation and of the racial difference between conquerors and conquered. The latter is especially notable because it involved a color line. Both undoubtedly contributed, but both are common enough elsewhere without having given rise to caste. The color line, however, could not fail to accentuate the hereditary principle and to gather about it magical and ritual elements in the culture, emphasizing what Weber calls the principle of *Gentilcharisma*.[2]

Another central element, Brahman supremacy, was by no means original. In the feudal period the Brahmans were often held inferior to the highly cultivated Ksatriya aristocracy. Their

---

main periods: (1) the Vedic period, from the Aryan invasions to about 1000 B.C., (2) Brahmanism, from 1000 B.C. to about the beginning of the Christian era, and (3) since that time Hinduism. Professor W. E. Clark, in lectures at Harvard University.

[1] The idea of such "arbitrary" interference with the cosmic order would shock the Indian mind.

[2] *Religionssoziologie*, Vol. II, p. 125. The concept of charisma will be discussed below.

supremacy was a result of various complicated changes in the social balance of power. Among these were the tendency of the patrimonial rulers to ally with the Brahmans against the feudal forces. The position of the Ksatriya was deeply shaken by the long series of foreign invasions, of which they, as warriors, bore the brunt. The Brahman literature was stereotyped and given influence by the Mohammedan conquests.[1] Patrimonial administration, especially fiscal, tended to strengthen the solidarity of existing groups.[2]

One force which conceivably might have broken through the whole traditionalistic system and which, indeed, played a very large part in the West, the influence of the urban trading and handicraft classes, failed to do so. To be sure, they became organized in gilds and were at times powerful and prosperous. But, on the one hand, they never succeeded in making the towns independent corporate units with an independent military basis, as in the West during the Middle Ages. And, on the other hand, they were crushed by the growing patrimonial states to which their power became dangerous.[3]

The Brahman theory was an incomparably fine bulwark of authority, especially for a regime of foreign conquerors. Once the Brahmans were in the saddle of power and influence, without which there would have been no caste development,[4] the Brahmanic religious philosophy had the opportunity to do its work. The other elements adapted to it were already there, and the dangerous competition of the old Ksatriyas and the gilds, was broken, so that a long slow process of pressure of ideas in a constant direction leading to the formation of a caste system could go on. Without many nonreligious conditions the Brahmanic religious ideas could not have had their influence.[5] But equally, without this peculiar system of ideas, none of these conditions,

[1] On all these points, see *Religionssoziologie*, Vol. II, p. 125.

[2] *Ibid.*, p. 127.

[3] *Religionssoziologie*, Vol. II, pp. 127–128. Weber lays great stress on this independent corporate character of the Western city, a trait common to the polis and the medieval town, but unknown in the Orient. See especially the extremely interesting study, "Die Stadt," *Wirtschaft und Gesellschaft*, Part II, Chap. VIII.

[4] *Religionssoziologie*, Vol. II, p. 131.

[5] On the general theoretical issue of the role of ideas involved here see above, note appended to Chap. XIV.

nor even the whole combination of them including the supremacy of a hereditary priesthood, would have produced the caste system. And this system of ideas is to be explained "as a product of rational ethical thought, not of any sort of economic conditions."[1]

While the general pantheistic basis and the doctrines of karma and transmigration formed the common foundation of all the main movements of Indian religious philosophy, religious interests were by no means confined to the means of bettering an individual's prospects in the cycle of rebirths. On the contrary, while this was the preoccupation of the mass, the elect have for many centuries been concerned with the problem of "salvation" in a much more radical sense. But what salvation could mean, what one was to be saved from and for is understandable only in terms of the underlying metaphysical position.[2]

As has been noted, the immanent pantheistic conception of divinity precluded that of a radically evil principle. There could be only "imperfection." It precluded equally eternal rewards and punishments for finite merits or faults. Such Christian ideas would appear to the Indian mind nonsensical. Salvation could not be from "sin" in the Christian sense, nor for eternal bliss. Salvation was rather radically different, from karma. Indian pessimism is founded on the conviction of the senselessness and transiency of all things worldly. Even the most meritorious conduct could only result eventually in rebirth as a god, and that too was transient, fated to death and the repetition of the whole process. Permanence, essential stability, "eternal life" could be attained only by escape from the whole thing, not only from this life but from all other conceivable "lives."

In India there have been many paths to salvation but they have only one goal. In so far as they lead to "higher" religious aims than merely better prospects of rebirth, they are all directed to escape from involvement in this world altogether, they are all otherworldly in this specific sense.[3]

The means employed have been many, but may be divided into the two great categories, the ascetic and the mystical. The latter is the predominant trend and, finding its highest value in

---

[1] *Religionssoziologie*, Vol. II, p. 131.

[2] The general treatment of these doctrines of salvation is to be found in *Religionssoziologie*, Vol. II, Sec. II.

[3] *Religionssoziologie*, Vol. I, p. 359.

contemplation, its attitude to the things of this world is, in principle, one of indifference. The importance of this world is so radically devalued that from this source there is no possible motive for a remaking of the world in the name of an ideal. The world is not combated as dangerous except as a source of diversion from true interests. But no more positive relation to it is possible than that of the passive acceptance of things as they are.

India is known as a classic land of asceticism. But this asceticism is always and necessarily on this basis what Weber calls otherworldly. Its combat with the flesh is in the interest of destroying its power to divert the soul from contact with the absolute. The flesh is to be mastered, not that it may be used as an instrument, but that it may be rendered harmless. There is, in the basic Indian position, no motive for the active "worldly" asceticism which is the essence of the Protestant ethic.[1]

Buddhism was in a sense an anti-Brahman and anticaste movement. Its opposition, however, does not lie in its departure from the basic Indian religious position in the Western direction, but in carrying it to still more radical conclusions than the Brahmanic philosophy. It represented the contemplative type par excellence. In its extreme of indifference to the world, and in its prohibition for the fully qualified person, the monk, to become involved in it in almost any way, it supplied no direct sanction of any social system but was specifically asocial. But for just this reason it could not serve as a basis of a rational economic ethic.[2]

The Systematic Typology of Religion

Weber's comparative sociology of religion did not consist only of a series of separate studies of "cases" which serve to bring out religious elements inhibiting the development of capitalism elsewhere than in the modern West. It is mainly preoccupied with the problem of capitalism and its main theoretical framework focuses upon it. But out of it emerges a general system of religious typology which gives the final breadth to the perspective of the religious aspect of the problem of capitalism. It is possible to

[1] *Ibid.*, Vol. II, p. 360.

[2] For lack of space no treatment is included here of the later popular developments of Hindu cult-religion. They do not in any fundamental way affect the general relation to capitalism. For Weber's treatment see *Religionssoziologie*, Vol. II, Sec. III, pp. 316 *ff.* The same is true of the popularization of Buddhism, see *ibid.*, pp. 251 *ff.*

give here to complete the preceding presentation only a bare sketch of some of the major concepts.[1]

Even a sketchy presentation of this systematic typology is not possible without some reference to Weber's general conception of historical development which will be treated more fully below.[2] It was his view that in what is relevant to his analysis there is something like a point of common origin for processes of religious development, a general "primitive religion." The various possible types of "developed"[3] religious system are then to be thought of as arising by a process of differentiation from the common starting point. They represent possibilities which are to a large extent mutually exclusive. The present concern is not, however, with the historical applications, but with the logical relations of the different type elements.

For the "primitive" type it is not, Weber thinks, possible to differentiate religious and nonreligious elements on the basis of rationality as such or of the character of "ends." The ends are in general worldly and a certain relative rationality applies to religious and magical actions as well as to secular techniques. The distinction in such terms is rather one brought in from the point of view of modern views of nature and not to be found in the primitive material itself.[4] The fruitful starting point is rather the observation that religious as distinct from secular actions involve qualities, forces, etc. which are exceptional, removed from the ordinary (*ausseralltäglich*), to which a special attitude is taken and a special virtue attributed. This exceptional quality Weber calls *charisma*.[5] It is exemplified in such conceptions as mana.

---

[1] The places where this is most systematically set forth are the "Zwischenbetrachtung," *Religionssoziologie*, Vol. I, pp. 536–573, and the section "Religionssoziologie," *Wirtsch. u. Ges.*, Part II, Chap. IV. See also on the Asiatic religions, *Religionssoziologie*, Vol. II, pp. 363–378 and in general the "Einleitung," *ibid.*, Vol. I, pp. 237–275.

[2] Chap. XVII.

[3] These terms are purposely put in quotation marks. They are here relevant only to the process in which Weber is interested.

[4] But see the view of Malinowski quoted above, p. 425.

[5] *Wirtsch. u. Ges.*, p. 227. A term coined by himself. The similarity of this concept to Durkheim's *sacré* is striking, as is that of the general approach of the two men to these problems. The theoretical significance of this similarity will be fully discussed below (see Chap. XVII).

From this conception of things "set apart" can easily arise that of a "world" of entities different from that involved in the ordinary affairs of everyday life—in this sense and only this, a "supernatural" world. The ways in which these entities may be conceived and the character of their relations to the "natural" world are most various. They may, for example, be distinguished as "personal" and "impersonal," but Weber does not for present purposes lay great stress on these distinctions; the important thing is the difference of attitude toward these entities, however conceived, from that toward everyday things. They tend to issue in two types of entity; in so far as this supernatural world is involved in the individual personality itself, it becomes the "soul," or if outside the individual, "gods" or "demons." Whether or not the conceptions are anthropomorphic is of secondary importance. The ordering of the relations of these entities to men is what Weber designates as the realm of religious action.[1]

One further element of this complex is important. This quality of special apartness, charisma, is often attributed to objects, acts, human beings, which in other respects belong to the everyday world or are closely related to it. This quality is in some sense a manifestation of these supernatural forces or entities. Some distinction between the natural and the supernatural elements in these concrete things is imperative. Among the possible interpretations of the relation of the two elements is that the former symbolizes the latter. As Weber says, "Now not only do things play a part in life which are merely there and happen, but also which have a 'meaning' and are there because of this meaning. With this, magic, from the direct action of forces, becomes symbolism."[2] However different the "native" interpretation of this may be from our own self-conscious symbolism, here is an element of fundamental importance.

From this basal idea Weber draws one of his fundamental theses, that the first effect of "religious ideas" on action including economic action—an effect everywhere present—is to sanction the stereotyping of tradition.[3] "Every magical procedure which has been 'proved' efficacious is naturally repeated strictly in the successful form. That is extended to the whole realm of sym-

[1] *Wirtsch. u. Ges.*, p. 229.
[2] *Ibid.*, p. 230.
[3] *Ibid.*, p. 231.

bolically meaningful actions. The slightest departure from the
approved norm may vitiate the action. All branches of human
activity get drawn into this circle of symbolic magic."[1] While
there are specific acts and complexes of action which are in Durkheim's term typically "profane," that is not true of any of the
great spheres of conduct, economic or political activity, love or
war. In so far as these are brought into relation with charismatic
forces they become traditionalized. As Weber says, "The sacred
is that which is specifically unalterable."[2]

The above characterization is that of only a very broad basis
of "primitive" religion. In a large number of different respects
there can, on this general basis, be variations of different types
and developments in different directions. Weber treats them at
considerable length and with at least the beginnings of a systematic classification. There is no space here to follow through
these complexities. There may be, however, great variations in
the character of the supernatural entities involved, their relations
to each other, to men of different classes and to the nonhuman
world. There may be variations in the ways in which these sacred
traditions are maintained and transmitted, by word of mouth or
in written form, in the degree of specialization as between those
who do and do not have especially intimate relations with sacred
things and the relations of specialists such as the magician and
the priest to other classes in the community.

However important these differences may be in other connections, they do not touch what is for Weber the central question
of the way out of traditionalism. Religion remains on this level
an aspect of the general social community and on the whole
sanctions the general structure of this community and its practices, including ritual.[3] What is lacking is a rationally systematized attitude toward the religiously significant aspects of
life.

Once the level of symbolism is reached the question arises of
the "meaning" of things and events of this world. Rationalization

---

[1] *Ibid.*, p. 230.

[2] *Ibid.*, p. 231. Points bearing on the theoretical explanation of this have
already been discussed above (Chap. XI) and will be further elaborated
below.

[3] This is a type closely resembling what Professor A. D. Nock calls
"cultural" religion.

of these discrete meanings into a coherent system, an inclusive interpretation of the world as a whole and man's place in it, is an "immanent" need of the intellect once the question of meaning is raised. It is as one of the points where this question is most acutely raised that Weber lays such great stress on the problem of suffering, more broadly that of evil.[1] This leads up, by the process of rationalization, to the great theodicy conceptions.[2] But this rationalization is deeply inhibited by traditionalism. For the traditionalistic situation will inevitably have assimilated and given its traditional sanction to very diverse elements which cannot all be accepted in *any* single rational system.[3]

Hence a carrying of the rationalization process beyond a certain point involves a break with traditionalism and, conversely, every sharp break with traditionalism involves rationalization —for the breaker of tradition is by his very act forced to define his attitudes toward that with which he has broken. When such breaks with tradition involve religious elements, that is, when the breaker claims charismatic authority, Weber calls the process "prophecy" and the personal agent of it a "prophet."[4] It is with prophecy and its implications and effects that the main body of his sociology of religion is concerned. The prophet is significant as the initiator of a great process of rationalization in the interpretation of the "meaning" of the world and the attitudes men should take toward it. The possible attitudes they can take Weber holds to be conditioned by the structure of ideas which results from this process.

As has been pointed out, Weber is interested in systems of religious ideas as *differentiating* elements in social development. Underlying this interest is his basic thesis that the process of religious rationalization is not predetermined by its immanent nature in *one* particular direction, but that it can proceed in a limited number of possible directions according to various circumstances. Though the subtypes are numerous, the major directions can be reduced to two—a dualism, which runs through all of Weber's work on this subject.

[1] *Religionssoziologie*, Vol. I, pp. 241 *ff*.
[2] *Wirtsch. u. Ges.*, pp. 246 *ff*.
[3] This is a theorem which Weber maintains is proved by a vast body of factual evidence.
[4] *Ibid.*, pp. 250 *ff*.

Weber defines the prophet as "a purely personal[1] bearer of *charisma* who by virtue of his 'mission' preaches a religious doctrine or a divine command."[2] He is always one who has a mission, who feels himself in particularly close connection with a "supernatural" entity or order. And he undertakes his mission without authorization by any human agency, in fact in conscious opposition to all such agencies. Jesus' words, "It is written . . . , but *I* say unto you . . . ," the opposite, are typical. Of the two forms of mission, a command, if it is to make sense, implies a doctrine but a doctrine need not imply any commands.

It is on this basis that Weber distinguishes his two fundamental types of prophecy. Either the prophet feels himself to be the instrument of a divine will, bringing in the latter's name a concrete command or a norm with which people should comply as an ethical duty. This is ethical prophecy[3] (Mohammed, Jesus). Or he is one who by his personal example shows others the way to religious salvation (Buddha), what Weber calls exemplary prophecy. But whichever type is involved, prophecy always implies "first for the prophet, then for his followers a unified attitude toward life gained by a deliberate meaningful stand taken toward it."[4] Human action must, to realize religious interests, be in conformity with the coherent meaning of the world implied in such a stand.

The ethical prophet feels himself to be the instrument of a divine will. As such a part of his mission is to give men ethical norms with which they are expected to conform. And by definition these norms are different from the existing traditional state of affairs. The rationalization of this situation leads in a particular direction. The will of which the prophet is an instrument, the source of the new norms, cannot be merely a manifestation of the immanent order of the world as it is. Only the conception of a transcendental personal God,[3] concerned with, but not in his essence involved in, the existing cosmic and human order, can be adequate to ethical prophecy. This is not to say that such a conception of God arose only as a "rationalization"[5] of ethical

---

[1] He is not "legitimized" by any human authority, especially neither by tradition nor an "office."

[2] *Wirtsch. u. Ges.*, p. 250.

[3] *Ibid.*, p. 255.

[4] *Ibid.*, p. 257.

[5] In the derogatory sense.

prophets, or vice versa, but that they are phenomena mutually interdependent. Thus Weber holds that the pantheistic conceptions of India and China, once firmly established,[1] were enough to prevent the development of ethical prophecy.

On the other hand, such a pantheistic conception of the divine as an immanent principle of order is related to the emergence of the exemplary prophet. A norm or command to change the world is out of the question, but not an attempt to live in harmony with it. And there is no inherent reason why traditional modes of achieving this "harmony" should be beyond criticism; indeed they certainly are not. In the sense of a path to salvation, an exemplary prophet may well have a new doctrine that is not traditional, and others may follow his example and his teaching of the doctrine.

There is one immediate social implication of the appearance of a prophet. If his prophecying is efficacious he gathers about him a community[2] of disciples. The fact that prophecy itself involves a break with traditionalism means that the relation of both the prophet and his followers to the society in which they appear is highly problematical, especially to the bearers of its religious tradition, but also to other elements. Moreover, in the course of its own development, this community or *Gemeinde* inevitably undergoes changes within itself, particularly the change of leadership from the founder to his successors. In all these matters a large number of different possibilities are open according to the character of the prophet and his doctrine and to the circumstances. But the main fact is that prophetic religion is a source of social organization independent of the immanent development of the traditional order. It may also itself become retraditionalized, but not necessarily so. Religion thus becomes not merely an aspect of a social community, but the basis of one.

The social implications of a prophetic movement, both within its *Gemeinde* and without, depend, in relation to the character of the prophecy and the system of ideas it involves, on the means it takes to the realization of its religious interests. These again fall into a dichotomy of two main types which Weber calls asceticism and mysticism. Their significance, however, only becomes

---

[1] "Established" may, in Paretian terms, be taken to mean "turned into residues."

[2] "Gemeinde," *Wirtsch. u. Ges.*, pp. 257 *ff.*

understandable on the basis of Weber's view, already noted, that
no traditional order can be made to conform completely to the
requirements of *any* fully rationalized conception of the meaning
of the world. Hence it is inevitable that certain elements at least
of the worldly order will come into conflict with religious values.[1]
It is this conflict that indeed forms the basis of the need for
"salvation."

In this conflict there are in principle two generally possible
attitudes compatible with a consistent rational view. It is obvious
that the world cannot be simply "accepted." Then worldly
things can, so far as possible, be controlled, mastered in the
interest of the religious idea. Or, on the other hand, they may be
radically devalued and become indifferent. In Weber's terminology the former course is the ascetic, the latter the mystical.[2]
Each may, in turn, be subdivided into worldly[3] and otherworldly
types.

Both are carried through in a radical form only by a minority
of religious virtuosos.[4] The unequal religious qualification of men
is a fact on which Weber lays great stress.[5] The ascetic type of
salvation is associated with ethical prophecy. The individual feels
himself to be an instrument of God's will. He must hence, in
terms of the latter, subject the traditional ethical code to a radical
criticism, and set for himself ideals far above those of the mass
even of "good" men. The "world" becomes sinful, in the extreme
case radically evil, something to be combated and, if possible,
controlled.

According to circumstances this may take one of two directions.
The "world" to be fought and mastered may be only within
oneself—for such a person there are no positive duties beyond
that. Then the ascetic will flee the world, as hermit or monk. Or,
where this retirement from the world is excluded as it was in
Protestantism, the only recourse is to control, not only oneself,
but also the rest of the world, which still, however, remains

---

[1] *Wirtsch. u. Ges.*, pp. 330 *ff.; Religionssoziologie*, Vol. I, "Zwischenbetrachtung."

[2] *Wirtsch. u. Ges.*, pp. 310 *ff.*

[3] "Worldly" here means remaining within the order of society, not an
inner attachment to "worldly" goods. "Otherworldly" involves, on the
other hand, a break with the everyday social order.

[4] A term Weber frequently uses.

[5] *Wirtsch. u. Ges.*, p. 310.

sinful. Otherworldly asceticism is also compatible with the pantheistic background as a means of mastering the interfering desires and interests of the flesh, thus rendering them harmless.

On the other hand, the end of salvation may be the attainment of an exceptional higher "state," through "mystical experience." This is attained only by a minority, using a systematic technique, that of "contemplation." The interests of the world can appear only as disturbances. To one with such an experience there can be no positive relation to such interests; they can only be avoided. The result is indifference to the world, attained either by avoiding it as far as possible—"otherworldly mysticism"—or living in it but not of it, allowing no inner attachment to it—"worldly mysticism." The connection of this attitude with the immanent, impersonal conception of the divine is evident.

The relations of these different roads to salvation to the different elements of social life are by no means simple and cannot be analyzed here. But in general it can be said that the farther over on the mystical side the position is, the more difficult it is for a stable social organization to grow up on a religious basis, even a *Gemeinde*, without a reversion to traditionalism, and the less influence the system of religious ideas will have on the life of the society except indirectly in stereotyping tradition. Buddhism represents the extreme in this direction.[1]

On the other hand, the farther over the position is in the ascetic direction, the more the opposite is true under certain conditions. Otherworldly asceticism may become radically antisocial, but the worldly asceticism of Protestantism represents the extreme of possible religious interest in shaping the organization of life in this world in the image of a rationalized religious ideal.

Weber sharply rejects the view that these rationalized systems of religious ideas can be understood as the creation of any "material" conditions.[2] They are, on the contrary, the outcome of the immanent *Eigengesetzlichkeit* of solving the problem of the meaning of the world from different starting points. He does, however, allow a very considerable role for nonreligious factors in the concrete processes by which they develop and in the particular

---

[1] That is, in its asocial character. It did not provide so strong a sanction of "lay" traditionalism as did Brahmanic Hinduism.

[2] This statement is made many times.

directions the development takes. A few of the main relations may be noted.

In the first place, the emergence of prophecy itself, and hence the start of the whole process, is to be attributed in a large degree to social situations. Above all, where the traditional values have been shaken and overt conflicts arisen, a strong stimulus is given to "taking a stand." In fact prophets have often been related to social conflicts. Secondly, when a society is differentiated, the problems of the meaning of the world will not be entirely the same for all classes of society. Just as the social significance of a system of religious ideas lies in its canalization of interests, so the kinds of ideas one will turn to will depend on the kind of problems one is faced with. Not in the sense that class interests determine religious ideas, but that some types of class situation make its members more receptive to a given line of religious thought than to another—or to the idea of salvation at all.[1] Third, the chances for a given religious doctrine to gain a predominant position in a culture are bound up with the position in the social "balance of power" of the class who are its principal bearers. This has been illustrated above in the case of the Brahmans.

On the other side it must again be made clear what is Weber's conception of the mode of influence of systems of religious ideas on practical life and through that on social structure. Society is not in any sense merely an "emanation" product of the religious idea. The process is, on the contrary, highly complex. The central theoretical concept is that of religious "interest." Ideas are effective in action because they determine the directions of practical activity in which the interests can be pursued.

But the very conception of interest implies another factor. Human action is subject not only to "ideal" but to real conditions. Moreover the rationalization that is the characteristic of these religious systems involves sacrifice of many potential values which are more or less embodied in social institutions. The process is, then, one of highly complex interaction between these various elements. In the process a selective influence at least may be exercised on the course of the development of the religious system itself. Finally, the elements of potential conflict, especially between religious interests and the "world," which are absolutely

---

[1] See *Wirtsch. u. Ges.*, pp. 267 *ff*.

fundamental to Weber, ensure that the process shall be highly dynamic. Nothing is more unjust than to accuse Weber, because he insisted on the social importance of religious ideas, of a naïve monistic "emanation" theory of the mode of their influence.

The Protestant ethic can now be set in the broad perspective of Weber's comparative treatment of religion. Certain fundamental features were common to the religious developments of both China and India, however much these two may differ from each other. Rationalization of religious thought in both cases went in the immanent, impersonal, pantheistic direction, starting from the conception of an impersonal order of ritual forces, tao and rita. Connected with this is the fact that in neither development did there appear a movement of *ethical* prophecy, setting up ethical standards in opposition to the traditional order.

Another circumstance on which Weber lays great stress was that the rationalized religious ideas in both areas were the creation of cultivated intellectual classes.[1] In both the status of the class and its highest religious good were bound up with "knowledge," not the empirical knowledge of modern Western science but knowledge of a totally different order. It was either the knowledge of a literary tradition, as in China predominantly, or a mystic gnosis.[2] In either case faith, in the Christian sense, was excluded. And since this knowledge was accessible only to the cultivated few there was a great chasm between the sophisticated religion of the elite and the religion of the masses. The latter was not shaken out of its state of magical traditionalism; it remained "primitive."

In China, in keeping with the character of the mandarin class who were the bearers of the Confucian tradition, the rationalization process took an entirely worldly direction. All metaphysical speculation was rigidly avoided. But precisely on this account a radical rationalization of the meaning of the world did not arise at all. Rationalization remained confined to adaptation to a given order of things. This order itself, including its ritual and magical elements, was left unquestioned. There was hence no motive for salvation by escape from it, and equally no Archimedean point from which to undertake its radical reconstruction. Confucian rationality is that of prudent conservatism, adaptation

[1] In contrast to Christianity.
[2] *Religionssoziologie*, Vol. II, pp. 364 *ff.*

to a given order. In so far as sophisticated minds departed from this worldliness it was not in the direction of worldly asceticism but of Taoist mysticism, the counterpart of the Indian movements.

In India, on the other hand, the radical rationalization did take place in the hands of the cultivated intellectuals. This process yielded the doctrines of karma and transmigration. For the masses, linked with the caste hierarchy, there resulted only the sanction of an extreme of traditionalized immobility; as Weber says, "the one completely logically consistent form of an 'organic' theory of society which has ever arisen."[1] For the elite, on the other hand, salvation could lie only in turning away from the things of this world in mystical contemplation and other-worldly asceticism. The traditional order was either left untouched as in Buddhism or radically sanctioned as in Hinduism. In both religions, to use Weber's words,

. . . the layman [in China the man without literary schooling] to whom the gnosis and hence the highest religious goal is denied, or who repudiates it for himself, acts ritualistically and traditionally in the pursuit of his everyday interests. Everywhere the unlimited acquisitiveness of the Asiatic is famous as unequalled, and on the whole rightly. But it is an "acquisitive impulse" which is served with all possible means of deception and with the help of the ubiquitous recourse to magic. There was lacking precisely what was decisive for the economic life of the West—the rational disciplining of this impulsive character of acquisition and its incorporation into a system of rational ethical conduct in the world. This was brought about by the "wordly asceticism" of Protestantism carrying the beginnings of a few related predecessors to completion. For such a development the necessary elements were lacking in the Asiatic religions.[2]

The differences of the ethic of ascetic Protestantism from the religious ethics of both China and India should now be clear. In Weber's typology it is the extreme logical antithesis of the Buddhistic, more generally that of Indian mysticism. China lies between. In its radical Calvinistic form the Protestant rationalization of the world combines the following elements: (1) the transcendental God, (2) predestination, involving the complete cutting off of the individual from salvation by his own efforts including the gnosis of mystical contemplation, (3) the sinfulness

[1] *Ibid.*, p. 367.
[2] *Ibid.*, p. 372.

of the flesh leading to the most radical possible tension between ideal and real, (4) the conception of man as the instrument of God's will in building the Kingdom of God on Earth with its tendency to guide religious interests in the direction of active ascetic mastery over the world in the interest of an ideal, finally (5) the complete corruption of the world which implied the absolute devaluation of traditionalism, especially magical, ritual or symbolic. If *any* system of religious ideas could constitute an active social force, surely it was this.[1]

Protestantism and Capitalism: Schematic Summary

In conclusion, the question may again be raised of the sense in which Weber may be said to have "proved" his original thesis that the Protestant ethic was one basic factor in the development of Western rational bourgeois capitalism, and though not standing alone, an indispensable one. As a result of the above unavoidably long discussion the following conclusions as to Weber's position seem to be justified:[2]

1. By contrast with other civilizations, rational bureaucratic organization and closely related forms are major elements in the distinctive social structure of the modern West.

2. There is a congruence of the ethic of ascetic Protestantism with the bureaucratic rational bourgeois element of modern Western capitalism and its *Geist*.

3. There is a lack of congruence with the spirit of capitalism of the ethical implications of the major Asiatic religions. In so far as they have had an influence on secular social life it *could not* have been in a rational bourgeois capitalistic direction. In the thesis that the Protestant ethic was the only religious ethic which could have had such an influence, there is a gap left in the present presentation, which has not taken up the ethics of Judaism, Islam and the non-Protestant branches of Christianity. This gap was by no means left completely unfilled by Weber himself

[1] Calvinism and Buddhism represent the antithetical polar extremes of Weber's classification so far as his empirical material goes. Whether they are maxima in any more general theoretical sense need not be discussed.

[2] Compare with the formulation of von Schelting, *Max Webers Wissenschaftslehre*, pp. 287 ff. Though the position stated here was arrived at for the most part independently of Dr. von Schelting, its formulation was aided by his work and the agreement in the general interpretation of what Weber had and claimed to have proved is most gratifying.

though just this part of his work was left unfinished at his death. He unquestionably planned to fill it completely. In general, it may be said without presenting supporting evidence that all these three religious ethics are less unfavorable to capitalistic development than the Asiatic religions, especially since the conception of a transcendental God was common to them. But also each of them contained serious obstacles to the full force of the Protestant type of thought. But, after all, Protestantism was the product of a long process of development continuous from early Judaism.

4. In general there is a high degree of correspondence between what, on the basis of "ideal-typical" construction, the concrete social influence of the three religious ethics treated here would be expected to be, and the actual empirical state of affairs. This is strong prima-facie evidence for the reality of such influence, placing the burden of proof on anyone who would question it.

5. In a considerable part of the field, though not in all, Weber has been able to trace the unfolding of the actual processes and mechanisms by which this influence has probably been exerted. This greatly strengthens the prima-facie case referred to in point four.

6. Weber has not established and never meant to establish that other than religious elements have not to a highly important degree been involved both in the concrete process of development of a religious ethic itself, and in that of its influence on concrete social affairs.[1] On the contrary, such an interpretation is directly opposed to Weber's whole fundamental position in sociology, which as will be seen is a voluntaristic theory of action and not an idealistic theory of emanation. The attempt has been made to set forth typical examples of the different ways in which he held nonreligious elements to be involved. But this is only a sample. Anyone who reads his work carefully can be easily convinced that Weber was anything but a naïve oversimplifier.

7. On the matter of quantitative imputation of the religious as against other factors Weber has not arrived at any conclusion (such as that the causation of modern capitalism was 47 per cent Protestant) nor did he claim to have done so. Indeed on methodological grounds such a claim could, in problems like those Weber

---

[1] Even if he does not say so explicitly, Professor Sorokin's language is often such as strongly to suggest this erroneous interpretation. See, for instance, *Contemporary Sociological Theories*, pp. 678, 680, 682.

was dealing with, have no meaning. A phenomenon is not "compounded" in a given proportion of the "variables" which are used to explain it. And even the values of these variables are like most in the social field reduced not to quantitative terms but, like Pareto's residues, to a classification.

But this does not mean that Weber's work has not increased our scientific knowledge of the relations between religious ideas, action and social structure. For, the above points combined with his estimates of the net favorableness and unfavorableness of the constellations of nonreligious elements justify the conclusion that the Protestant ethic was a major factor in the capitalistic development, that it was a necessary though not sufficient condition, and more generally that religious ethics constitute a major factor in the differentiation of the characters of the great civilizations from each other.

That these judgments of the favorableness and unfavorableness of the *total* nonreligious situation are estimates, not rigorous proofs, Weber would be the first to admit. But so must any empirical judgment of such scope arrived at by such an analytical procedure be.[1] Weber has left us, by his interpretation of the evidence, with a balance of capitalistic predisposition on the whole in favor of the oriental countries, especially China. In order seriously to damage his general position it would be necessary to turn the balance a long way in the other direction. In any event this can be done only by a detailed critical examination of the empirical evidence on which Weber's judgments were based, and whatever additional relevant evidence may now be available. This is entirely beyond the scope of the present study, but the opinion may be ventured that none of the critics of Weber's general position has done it. The burden of proof rests upon them.

On this basis, then, it seems justified to accept Weber's theory of the relations of Protestantism and capitalism, in the only sense in which it is ever justified to accept a scientific theory. Within the limits of its own claims, it is in conformity with all the facts with which the present author is acquainted. The facts brought against it in the critical literature will not stand examination with respect both to their factual correctness as such and to their relevance to and importance for Weber's problems. Aside

[1] Weber certainly did not exhaust the analytical possibilities. The methodological question will be discussed in the next chapter.

from those brought forward explicitly by critics, none have been advanced that are, in the present writer's opinion, damaging to his position. This, of course, does not mean that Weber's, any more than any other scientific theory, should be held immune from continual retesting in terms of any new facts that may come to light. The attempt to discover these would, however, be clearly outside the present scope. The present discussion has been concerned with the status of the theory on empirical grounds. In the latter part of the next chapter will be brought forward methodological considerations that do affect the theory, not in the validity of its central thesis, but in its form of statement and in certain implications.

This discussion of Weber's treatment of religion and capitalism, prolonged though it is, is at best a poor substitute for the extraordinary richness of the original work. The attempt has been made to state the main outline of Weber's position. But of necessity most of the supporting evidence and many relevant considerations have been left aside. This discussion is the "ideal type" of an "ideal type." Its inadequacies, many of which are inherent in the nature of the enterprise, should not be blamed upon Weber. The discussion now turns to the methodological position that lies at the basis of Weber's empirical research.

Chapter XVI

MAX WEBER, III: METHODOLOGY[1]

Weber devoted even more explicit attention to methodological problems than did Pareto and much more than Durkheim, a circumstance which is fortunate since it brings out explicitly many things important for the present context which would otherwise have to be elicited by analysis. No more than with respect to the other thinkers will there be attempted here a critical estimate of Weber's *total* significance to the social sciences either on the methodological side or on any other. But a good share of his methodological work is of peculiar relevance.

Like the other principal figures of this study, indeed like the work of most creative minds[2] in science, a good deal of Weber's methodological work has a distinctly polemical element. But it is perhaps even more prominent in his case than in that of the others; so that most of his methodological views were developed in directly polemical essays. Indeed he never wrote a general statement of his methodological position except in very brief form,[3] apart from an immediately polemical context. This fact makes understanding it as a whole difficult and in the absence, until

---

[1] It is indeed fortunate that there is available for the purposes of this chapter the excellent secondary study, already referred to, by Dr. Alexander von Schelting, *Max Webers Wissenschaftslehre*. Secondary work of such quality is distressingly rare in the field this study has covered. The present writer is greatly indebted to Dr. von Schelting's treatment at many points and will follow him closely, especially in the first part of the chapter. Although in general there is close agreement with Dr. von Schelting as far as he goes, it seems, as will appear, that he neglects certain of the limits of Weber's "methodological self-interpretation" which are vital for present purposes. See also the present writer's review of Dr. von Schelting's book in *American Sociological Review*, August, 1936.

[2] Scientific "prophets," as it were.

[3] The most important is in Chapter I of *Wirtschaft und Gesellschaft*, reprinted in *Gesammelte Aufsätze zur Wissenschaftslehre* (hereafter cited as *Wissenschaftslehre*), pp. 503–523.

quite recently,[1] of really authoritative secondary interpretation helps to explain the large amount of misunderstanding and controversy that has arisen over it.

The justification for dealing with Weber in connection with the "idealistic" tradition lies in the fact that, though his own position does not fall there, his polemical starting point is in opposition to some of the commonest methodological doctrines of that school.[2] The doctrines which he attacks may be classified roughly under two headings, which, following Dr. von Schelting, may be called objectivism and intuitionism.[3]

Underlying the whole discussion is the common German distinction, remarked upon above,[4] between the "natural" sciences and the sciences dealing with human action and culture, which can be traced back to the Kantian dualism. In terms of positive influence, Weber's own position owes most to Rickert.[5] It will not, however, be necessary here to investigate in detail the question of its genesis, but only to state its main outline. Hence its antecedents are relevant only as a means to the understanding in general of the situation from which he started.

In the above discussion of the background of the idealistic tradition the tendency was noted for idealistic social thought to run in two main directions.[6] The two sets of methodological doctrines within the group of social sciences which Weber attacks correspond roughly to these two. Common ground for both is the denial that the sociocultural sciences can make use of "general laws"[7] of the logical character of those occupying unquestioned status in the natural sciences. The difference of the two schools is over what they consider to be the reasons for this alleged fact. Weber's quarrel with both is essentially over this issue. He still holds to the distinction of the natural and social sciences, but

---

[1] Dr. von Schelting's book was published in 1934.

[2] Just as the polemical starting point of Durkheim is the "utilitarian" position.

[3] Weber's polemic in this context is documented mainly in the series of essays on *Roscher und Knies und die logischen Probleme der historischen Nationaloekonomie*, reprinted in *Wissenschaftslehre*, pp. 1–145.

[4] Chap. XIII.

[5] HEINRICH RICKERT, especially *Über die Grenzen der naturwissenschaftlichen Begriffsbildung*.

[6] Chap. XIII, pp. 475 *ff*.

[7] Called by Rickert "nomological" knowledge.

radically denies that it can rest on the exclusion from the latter of general explanatory concepts.

OBJECTIVISM

One of the two main idealistic trends was in the direction of historical "particularism." This view is that the historical and social sciences should concern themselves only with the detailed facts of particular human acts and not attempt to build up *any* general theories. Weber, of course, denied neither the desirability of detailed historical research[1] nor the possibility of legitimate empirical criticisms of particular systems of systematic theory which had been set up in the social sciences, for instance, that of the classical economics. What he attacked was, rather, the elevation of this "tendency" into the methodological dogma that systematic theoretical thinking could not legitimately be used in the social field. Indeed he went a step farther than criticism of this view, to maintain that every demonstrable judgment of historical explanation rested implicitly if not explicitly on such general, theoretical concepts.

The search for a basis for this dogma led to the view that it was founded in the fact that the objective nature of the subject matter of the social sciences was such as to make generalization about it impossible. Human action was held not to be subject to regularities in the sense that the phenomena of nature are. Since general concepts formulate such regularities they cannot be applicable to such a subject matter. Hence the necessity for research being confined to particular description, and explanation, if attempted at all, involving only the specific temporal antecedents of a given event, without reference to general principles.[2]

This position was put in the form that historical reality is "irrational."[3] General concepts, on the other hand, are rational, and the two cannot meet. Weber, in the first place, accepts the proposition that the completely concrete historical reality is of infinite diversity and complexity so that in the full richness of its concreteness and individuality it cannot be grasped in terms of any system of abstract concepts. But he denies both that this constitutes a ground of difference from the natural sciences and

[1] He himself was a distinguished contributor to it.

[2] This is the necessary implication of radical empiricism in the one direction, as is "intuitionism" in the other. See below.

[3] See *Wissenschaftslehre*, pp. 64 *ff.*; von Schelting, *op. cit.*, pp. 182 *ff.*

that it is in any way relevant to the problems of the *logical* nature of scientific categories. All "raw" experience is of this character. What we formulate as scientific laws about "nature" is not the total concrete reality even as humanly "experienceable" but certain particular aspects, which can be expressed in abstract concepts.[1] Precisely the same is true of the subject matter of human action. Whatever the basis of difference between the two groups of sciences (and Weber believes there is one) it does not lie on this plane. It must lie in the principles according to which, among "experienceable" elements of reality, "facts" are to be selected which are significant for a given scientific purpose. This lies, in Weber's opinion, in its logically relevant respects; not in the objective nature of the "reality" a science deals with, but in the "subjective" direction of interest of the scientist.

With this are connected two other important points. First the goal of "adequate" knowledge in a given field can never be to know "all the facts," that is, the total concrete reality; such a goal is impossible.[2] A standard of adequacy of knowledge must be relative to the scientific purpose in hand. Whatever it is, it falls short of "all the facts." Secondly, it follows from these considerations that *logically* the natural and social sciences are in the same situation with respect to the standard so often applied, predictability. In neither case is it ever possible to predict future states of affairs in all their concrete fullness of detail. Weber uses the example of the distribution of fragments of a boulder shattered by falling in a storm.[3] No science known to man is capable of predicting the exact size, shape and position of every fragment after a storm from data available before the storm. Nor does anyone want to know. Predictability in the natural sciences seems to be high because our *interest* is predominantly in the aspects of natural events formulable in terms of known abstract laws. Our interest in human affairs is generally on a different level. In any case predictability is always relative to the extent of abstract generalization, and where this exists predictability follows. Weber is careful to point out how much of actual social

[1] In this antiempiricist interpretation of the logical nature of natural laws Weber, writing about thirty years ago, was a pioneer in a movement which has since become predominant.

[2] Pareto, it will be remembered, expressed the same view. See Chap. V, p. 183.

[3] *Wissenschaftslehre*, pp. 65, 67.

life is completely dependent on the ability to predict with reasonable accuracy the reaction of others to a given stimulus. For example, how much "militarism" would be possible if officers could not depend on obedience to commands, that is, predict the behavior of their soldiers after the commands had been issued? Indeed it was in just this predictable aspect of social life that Weber had a peculiar interest.

But driven from this position the objectivist may fall back on another and say that there is a certain mystery about men and their actions. Nature has no secrets to the scientist; there is nothing mysterious about her; but human action is not "understandable";[1] it is in that sense "irrational."

To this Weber replies by turning the tables. Far from the natural sciences having the advantage in understandability, in principle the reverse is true. For in nature we can only observe the external course of events and discover elements of uniformity. This is equally possible for human behavior but *in addition* the scientist is able to impute motives to men, to "interpret" their actions and words as expressions of these motives. That is, we have access to the subjective aspect of action. In so far as the facts of human action give access to this, they carry a peculiar quality of their own (*Evidenz*).[2] This is the first appearance in Weber's methodology of the fundamentally important concept of *Verstehen*.[3]

This fact constitutes an objective difference between the subject matters of the two groups of sciences, and one of central importance. Weber does not, to be sure, make it an absolutely rigid difference in the sense that such elements are included in one concrete subject matter and rigidly excluded from the other, a position that would involve an empiricism quite foreign to his thought. There is, on the contrary, a gradual shading off toward teleological elements as in biological and perhaps even physico-

---

[1] *Wissenschaftslehre*, pp. 67 ff.; von Schelting, *op. cit.*, pp. 185–187.

[2] This is because they admit of interpretation as symbols. More of this later. It is to be noted that here also Weber's position is very similar to Pareto's.

[3] The impossibility of finding immediately understandable motivation for action in this sense is one of our main standards of mental abnormality (see *Wissenschaftslehre*, p. 67). It may, however, be possible to discover understandable motives of abnormal behavior on a deeper level of analysis, as by psychoanalysis.

chemical phenomena.[1] But the analytical distinction is none the less fundamental.

At the same time Weber insists that for the questions at issue this difference does not constitute the basis of a *logical* distinction of the two sets of sciences. In the field of *Verstehen* as well as of *Begreifen*,[2] general concepts have a real place, and valid empirical proof is dependent on their use, implicitly or explicitly. This raises an issue to which we shall return later.

Finally, the "irrationality"[3] of human action may be attributed to the freedom of the will—an argument of good Kantian origin, used particularly by Knies.[4] This Weber answers by again turning the tables, and in the process he uses a very interesting argument. If this were true, he says, we should expect the sense of freedom to be associated primarily with "irrational" actions, those involving emotional outbreaks and the like. On the contrary, however, the reverse is much more nearly true. It is when we act most rationally that we feel most free, and the curious thing is that, given the end, rational action is to an eminent degree both predictable and subject to analysis in terms of general concepts. The sense of freedom[5] in this case is a feeling of the absence of constraint by emotional elements.

There can be no doubt about the correctness of Weber's point and its significance is far-reaching. For the general concepts involved in the analysis of rational action in this sense (*Zweck-rational*, as Weber calls it) formulate general relations of means and ends. And these concepts are of a logical nature strictly comparable to the general laws of the physical sciences, indeed to a large extent, in such fields as technology, they involve the direct application of such laws. Thus at this early critical stage of Weber's methodological work has appeared the concept with

---

[1] *Wissenschaftslehre*, p. 91.

[2] In German *Verstehen* has come to be applied to the situation where a subjective motivational or symbolic reference is involved, while *Begreifen* is employed for the "external" grasp of uniformities where no such additional evidence is available.

[3] See *Wissenschaftslehre*, pp. 64 *ff.*; von Schelting, pp. 189 *ff.*

[4] It is as Dr. von Schelting points out not the only type with which a sense of freedom is associated.

[5] The good old term passion expresses this—it is something to which we "succumb," in the presence of which we feel helplessly carried along by forces beyond control.

which this whole study started, that of the type of rational action which involves the means-end relationship as verifiable in terms of scientific generalizations. For him, also, rationality in this sense plays a central role, methodologically as well as substantively. And it is especially interesting that its methodological role comes out in critical opposition to an idealistic theory.

By thus emphasizing the susceptibility of rational action to general causal analysis, Weber by no means intends to convey the impression that "irrational" action is not understandable (*verstehbar*) or is not also subject to such analysis. On the contrary, he most emphatically states that it is. Rational action is used primarily because of its peculiar relevance to the freedom argument.[1] Nor is Weber in the least concerned to deny that freedom of the will exists—only that it can be the basis of a *logical* difference between the natural and the social sciences, more specifically a basis for excluding general concepts from the latter.[2]

Out of the critical discussion of "objectivism"[3] has arisen not only a defense of the use of general concepts in the social sciences,[4] but a number of the important elements of Weber's own methodological theory of the latter. First through his attack on the radical empiricist position (in the terminology of this study), he has insisted upon the abstract nature of these general concepts and hence the necessity for another term of reference in their formation than the sheer "reflection" of the experienced reality. This Weber finds to be of the general order of a "subjective" direction of interest of the scientist.[5] Secondly, the subjective aspect of action as the object of *Verstehen* has made its appearance, and third, the central role of the concept of rationality of action involving a relation of means and ends. This last is particularly

[1] Rational and irrational here clearly have a narrower meaning than in the other two contexts.

[2] It is a metaphysical problem which Weber thus shows is not important to his methodological context.

[3] Not Weber's term, but one introduced by Dr. von Schelting first in his earlier study.

[4] One of the most striking statements is "So ist eine gültige Zurechung irgend eines individuellen Erfolges ohne die Verwendung 'nomologischer' Kenntnis der Regelmässigkeiten der Kausalen Zusämmenhänge, überhaupt nicht möglich." *Wissenschaftslehre*, p. 179.

[5] Involving a choice of variables.

important in that Weber shows its relevance to be not merely substantive but to go down into the deepest methodological roots of social science. Rationality of action and systematic scientific theory are inseparably linked. The development of science is a process of action, and action is in part an application of science.

INTUITIONISM

Under the term intuitionism a highly diverse group of methodological doctrines may, following Dr. von Schelting,[1] be grouped together. The present sketch, like his own analysis, in no way pretends to do justice to the great philosophical systems which in one way or another stand back of these doctrines. It is, rather, concerned with a single fundamental methodological point— whether these doctrines may claim to have established the possibility of valid scientific knowledge of the phenomena of human action without reference to general concepts. It is this claim which Weber attacks.[2]

In their predominant trend the intuitionist theories may be held in the main to constitute the methodological rationalization of the collectivist branch of German historical thought.[3] This, it will be remembered, was concerned with the grasp of total cultural *Gestalten* as wholes in their unique individuality. Moreover, in the cultural-social field it has been linked with the theory of *Verstehen*. The essence of these cultural totalities has been found in some kind of "meaningful" system of which the concrete facts constitute an expression or a manifestation. The elevation of this tendency into a methodological dogma has involved two main propositions which are not inseparably linked in logic. One is that "generalization" in the field of human affairs can only mean the grasp of these cultural totalities in all their uniqueness and individuality. The other is that this grasp takes the form of an immediate "intuition"[4]—a direct grasp of meaning without the intervention of concepts in any form. It is this latter, more radical proposition which Weber directly attacks. His relation to the other is more complex.

---

[1] von Schelting, *op. cit.*, pp. 195 *ff.*
[2] The principal names Weber himself deals with are Wundt, Münsterberg, Lipps, Simmel, Croce.
[3] See Chap. XIII, pp. 478 *ff.*
[4] *Einfühlung* is one of the commonest German terms, *Nacherleben* another.

In this connection there are a number of arguments brought forward by Weber. Three are important to this discussion. First, he maintains that the intuitionists confuse two distinct things: (1) the processes by which valid knowledge is arrived at and (2) the logical grounds of its validity.[1] He fully grants that our knowledge of important historical relationships is not arrived at exclusively, or even predominantly, by logical deduction from known facts, but that "flashes of insight" play an important part. But, in the first place, this fact is by no means confined to the genesis of knowledge of human action or phenomena to which the method of *Verstehen* is applicable; it is true generally. Secondly, the psychological (rather the subjective) mode of origin of a piece of knowledge is logically quite heterogeneous from the grounds of its validity. The latter need become explicit only when it is necessary to demonstrate the truth of a proposition.[2] And this last will always be found to involve general concepts.

Secondly, the intuitionists confuse the "raw data of experience" with "knowledge."[3] This point brings the argument back to the previous discussion of objectivism. In this particular context the important thing is that the "whole" which is picked out and set forth is never a simple reproduction of immediately given experience. It involves selection and systematization of the elements of this experience.[4] And this selection and systematization involves relating experience to concepts, including general concepts which serve as the basis of judging what *elements* of the raw experience are significant to the whole. This is as true of the social as of the natural sciences.

It is interesting to note that there is one type of phenomenon which can apparently be grasped with an immediacy approaching that which the intuitionist claims—that of the rationality of

---

[1] *Wissenschaftslehre*, p. 96; von Schelting, *op. cit.*, p. 200. The formulations in this part of the discussion follow mainly Dr. von Schelting, who has in certain respects gone beyond Weber's own in classification and systematization, though without essential alteration of meaning.

[2] *Wissenschaftslehre*, p. 111.

[3] *Erleben* and *Erkennen*. *Wissenschaftslehre*, pp. 105 *ff.*; von Schelting, *op. cit.*, p. 201.

[4] Weber might well have gone a step farther and pointed out that experience itself is never "raw" in that sense but is itself "in terms of a conceptual scheme." Raw experience is itself an abstraction of an *element* of knowledge.

action. But this is precisely because the conceptual element is already contained *explicitly* in the object of intuition itself.[1]

One thing Weber grants, that in our statements about human affairs the conceptual element often remains implicit, and the statements take a form suggesting immediate intuition.[2] This, Weber says, is owing to the fact that common knowledge in this field reaches so far, and above all covers so many of the aspects of interest to the social scientist, that to make them explicit would be superfluous; they are omitted on grounds of "economy." But this does not imply that they are logically irrelevant to the validity of the statements.

The fundamental point is that "immediate experience" is diffuse and not capable of precise formulation. It is only through concepts that such precision can be gained. Weber suggests here a principle in terms of which selection and systematization can be and is made—that of "relevance to value" (*Wertbeziehung*).[3]

Finally, Weber returns to his own treatment of *Verstehen*. It will be remembered that there he granted or, rather, maintained that experience with meaningful content had a special quality of immediate certainty (*Evidenz*). It is something not present in the sense data of natural events. Very obviously the intuitionist theories lay great stress on this fact. Here, however, Weber charges them with another confusion. The immediate certainty of perception of meaning is at most only *one* element in the proof of the validity of knowledge and cannot by itself be trusted. It must be checked by reference to a rationally consistent system of concepts.[4] Without this check one immediately certain intuition may give rise to an endless succession of "intuitional judgments" which depart farther and farther from reality.

This situation also is no different from that existing in the physical sciences. There immediate sense impressions cannot be trusted without theoretical, conceptual criticism. When a stick is thrust into a pool of still water there can be no doubt that the

---

[1] This case is a strong point against the "fiction" view of the nature of concepts (see below).

[2] This, again, is Dr. von Schelting's formulation which is more explicit than Weber's own.

[3] *Wissenschaftslehre*, p. 124; von Schelting, *op. cit.*, p. 204.

[4] *Wissenschaftslehre*, pp. 67 *ff*., 88 *ff*. and many other passages; von Schelting, *op. cit.*, pp. 211 *ff*.

observer "sees" that the stick is bent at the water line; his sense impression is that of a "bent stick." When he judges that the stick is not "really" bent, but that the impression is an optical illusion, it does not mean that he does not really *see* what he describes, but that the description is corrected by reference to a general system of theoretical knowledge.[1]

Similarly in the field of *Verstehen*. Our immediate intuitions of meaning may be real and, as such, correct. But their interpretation cannot dispense with a rationally consistent system of theoretical concepts. Only in so far as they measure up to such criticism can intuitions constitute knowledge. And without such criticism the door is opened to any number of uncontrolled and unverifiable allegations. Weber had a very deep and strong ethical feeling on this point; to him the intuitionist position made possible the evasion of responsibility for scientific judgments.

Weber again, however, does not discard everything in the positions criticized. On the one hand, it is a fact that the social sciences have an interest in human action and its motivation from the subjective point of view and, on the other hand, that there is a specific quality of immediacy in the understanding of the subjective.[2] It is with the elaboration of the consequences of these facts, and their relation to systematic theoretical thinking that most of the rest of Weber's methodological work is concerned.

Before proceeding to this development it is well to stop a moment to point out the relevance of Weber's critical position to the methodological problems which have mainly occupied the general study thus far. It may be said that Weber's attack has been for the most part upon the methodology of radical empiricism.[3] It was because of the particular features of his own intellectual milieu that he attacked two particular forms of it and not the third. As has already been noted,[4] on a positivistic basis empiricism has generally involved "reification" of particular theoretical systems, such as that of the classical physics or of the classical economics—as Professor Whitehead calls it, the "fallacy of misplaced concreteness."

[1] Indeed if he did not see a bend in the stick, although it is not "really" there, there would be something wrong with his eyesight.

[2] *Wissenschaftslehre*, pp. 89, 126; von Schelting, *op. cit.*, p. 213.

[3] In the two idealistic forms discussed in Chap. XIII, not that of reification, though this also has been incidentally criticized.

[4] Chap. XIII.

The Kantian dualism and its consequences precluded this form of empiricism from playing an important role in the social sciences in Germany, since they were predominantly in the idealistic tradition. Hence Weber's immediate concern was with the two forms of radical empiricism possible on that basis—particularistic and collectivistic *Historismus*. In his critique he has on the whole left the natural sciences and the natural science model for the social on one side.

His critique has, however, had one very important result—it went a very long way toward bridging the hiatus which the idealistic methodology had created between the natural and the social sciences in a *logical* context. He concludes that both must involve systems of general theoretical concepts, for without them anything approaching logical proof is out of the question. But in neither case can this system of concepts possibly be conceived of as a literal representation of the total concrete reality of raw experience. Hence his critical position *did* react on the methodology of the natural sciences. It is interesting to note here a definite convergence on a common *logical* meeting ground with the movement of methodology from a positivistic basis, which has been seen most explicitly among the subjects of this study in Pareto. Pareto, it will be remembered, laid down a general methodological outline common to all empirical explanatory science, natural and social. But to make natural science methodology applicable to social subject matter it was necessary for him to divest it of certain positivistic-empiricist implications of earlier methodologies. Weber has come to the same result from the other side, and has seen the same implications for the natural sciences.

In fact the radical methodological hiatus between natural and social sciences in the idealistic tradition was primarily a result of its predominant empiricism with regard to *both* branches. The intuitionist theories, it must not be forgotten, however vague and metaphysical they may appear to those with positivistic leanings, are strictly *empiricist* theories.[1] And that there is perception of meaningful wholes can hardly be denied.[2]

---

[1] My colleague Professor O. H. Taylor has called this view, very aptly, "romantic empiricism."

[2] See the immense amount of work on perception by Gestaltists. The material is summarized in K. Koffka, *Principles of Gestalt Psychology.*

Given this empiricism on both sides, the fundamental reason for the hiatus is evident—there are basic substantive differences between concrete phenomena involved in the behavior of stars and of human beings. The attempt to fit the latter into a positivistic formula has uniformly failed. Weber's achievement has been to separate out these substantive differences of the order of fact from considerations of the logical character of scientific theory. While the former differ fundamentally, the latter remain fundamentally the same.

The fact that German methodological thought has been dominated by the Kantian-idealistic dualism and our own by positivistic monism has not been without its historical benefits. Certain fundamental elements of the theory of action have emerged from the positivistic tradition only by virtue of a painful process. But in the idealistic tradition these elements have been from the start in the center of the stage. Weber's task was not to vindicate their legitimacy, but to clarify their methodological status and relation to the logical structure of scientific theory.[1] *Verstehen*, value and the means-end schema are the fundamental elements peculiar to human action which for Weber are left over from his critical analysis. The question is, what did he do with them? It is clear he did not attain a fully satisfactory position. Two main difficulties arose.

NATURAL AND SOCIAL SCIENCE

The first important question is that of the standards Weber would lay down for the selection out of the total flux of raw experience of elements which are significant for the concepts of the social sciences, since such selection is the necessary logical prerequisite of *knowledge* as distinguished from raw experience. The starting point is Weber's statement that these standards are to be found in the subjective "direction of interest" of the scientist. In interpreting what are in turn the determinants of this direction of interest in the two groups of sciences, Weber's position is not altogether clear and consistent, and hence it is here that the first serious methodological difficulty of his position arises.

[1] For this he was very widely called a positivist in Germany.

He holds that our interest in natural phenomena so far as it is a scientific interest[1] is centered in their aspects of abstract generality, not of concrete individuality. Hence the aim of the natural sciences is the formulation of a system of universally applicable general laws. For the natural sciences general concepts constitute an end in themselves. With the social sciences, on the other hand, this is not so. Our interest in human beings and their cultural achievements is not that of abstract generality but of individual uniqueness. They are not to us "cases" of general laws.[2] A man does not love "woman" but a particular woman; he is not fond of "pictures" but of particular paintings. Since in the social field interest is in the aspect of concrete individuality, general concepts cannot stand in the same relation to this interest; their formulation and verification cannot be an end in itself for the scientist's labor; they are only means to the elucidation and understanding of the particular, unique and individual phenomena. This is the formula Weber advances to cover the basic methodological distinction of the two groups of sciences. Can its grounds of justification be analyzed still farther?

In Weber's view, as far as it seems clear on this point, there is a common human basis for the interest in natural phenomena, that is, control. It is through the aspects formulable in terms of abstract general concepts that this is possible; in the application of science to technology, the forces of nature are subjected to the service of human ends. Hence the interest in them is in the general aspect, and is a uniform interest which can have, for all times and places, a common aim. Apart from this interest in control, natural phenomena are, as an object of science, indifferent to human values.

But this is just where the difference lies between natural phenomena and the social case. Human beings, their actions and cultural achievements are the embodiments of value toward which we must, in some degree, take a value attitude. Hence our interest in them is directly determined by their relevance to the values which either the scientist himself shares or which are significant to him by agreement with his own values or conflict with them.

---

[1] We may have others, such as an aesthetic interest, in natural phenomena, thus in the individuality of a sunset.

[2] *Wissenschaftslehre*, pp. 175–176, 178–179, 193. This is Weber's position, not the present writer's (see below, pp. 597 *ff*.).

It is this "relevance to value" (*Wertbeziehung*)[1] which constitutes the[2] selective organizing principle for the empirical material of the social sciences.

Even in this case, it is important to note, the concrete individuality in which our interest is centered is not that of "raw experience." There is no reason to deny such individuality to our experience of natural phenomena. It is rather a constructed, selected individuality. From the elements given in experience are selected a limited number which are important from the point of view of relevance to value. This process results in a constructed concrete phenomenon, what Weber calls the historical individual.

Now, unlike the natural science case, the important elements of the direction of interest are not here common to all humanity. For it is one of Weber's basic theorems that value systems are diverse; there is a plurality of different possible systems. In so far then, as the selection of material is determined by relevance to such systems the same concrete materials will give rise not to one historical individual but to as many as there are, in this sense, points of view from which to study it. It is, in turn, in the process of analysis of the historical individual and comparison of it with others that general concepts are built up. It follows, then, that the process will not issue in one ultimately uniform system of general concepts but in as many systems as there are value points of view or others significant to knowledge. There can be no one universally valid system of general theory in the social sciences.[3] This is one of the main routes by which Weber arrives at his view of the "fictional" nature of social science concepts, so important to his doctrine of the ideal type.[4]

Before discussing this, however, it is necessary to prepare the ground by clarifying a number of related issues. In the first place, the principle of value relevance combined with that of the relativity of value systems introduces an element of relativity into the social sciences which raises in an acute form the question of their claim to objectivity. Does it not reduce their structures of so-called knowledge to mere "manifestations of sentiments?"

[1] *Wissenschaftslehre*, p. 178.
[2] For Weber. There are certainly others.
[3] *Wissenschaftslehre*, p. 184.
[4] Others will be discussed below, pp. 602–603.

In the first place, Weber distinguishes carefully between determination of scientific interest, through value relevance (and thus of the immediate objects of scientific study, the historical individuals) and the exercise of value judgments. Value judgments (*Wertungen*) cannot claim the objective validity of science, and science must, as a methodological ideal, be kept free from them. Even though a value element enters into the selection of the material of science, once this material is given it is possible to come to objectively valid conclusions about the causes and consequences of given phenomena free of value judgments and hence binding on anyone who wishes to attain truth, regardless of what other subjective values he may hold.

This is possible first because even though in describing a concrete phenomenon what is made the subject of scientific analysis is not the full totality of experienceable fact about it, but a selection, the facts included in the historical individual as it is constructed are objective, verifiable facts. The question whether a statement of fact is true is clearly distinguishable from that of its significance to value. The relativity of *Wertbeziehung* touches only the latter, not the former, question. Secondly, once a phenomenon is descriptively given, the establishment of causal relations between it and either its antecedents or its consequences is possible only through the application, explicitly or implicitly, of a formal schema of proof that is independent of any value system, except the value of scientific truth.[1] This formal schema is basic to all empirical science, and only in so far as they conform with it can scientific judgments that pretend to assert causal relationships be valid. It may be remarked in passing that this scheme involves the use of general concepts transcending the historical individual.[2] Thus in spite of the relativity introduced by the concept of *Wertbeziehung* Weber maintains both that it is possible to keep value judgments logically distinct from those claiming objective scientific validity, and that the latter judgments can be made with confidence, escaping the subjectivity inherent in all value judgments.

So far Weber's position is acceptable. It is not, however, possible to accept his view of the methodological relations of the

[1] See von Schelting, *op. cit.*, pp. 255 *ff.*

[2] Weber's historical individual is clearly simply a unit or combination adequately described for theoretical purposes within a frame of reference.

natural and the social sciences. It has been pointed out that his critique of the objectivist and intuitionist methodologies has gone a long way to bridge the gap between the two groups of disciplines created by the Kantian dualism. There are two main criticisms of this methodological position. The first is that he did not go far enough, but that in following Rickert in this distinction he attempted to stop at an unstable halfway point.[1] He should have gone all the way to the view that in a purely *logical* aspect there is no difference whatever. The differences all lie on a substantive level.

The first source of difficulty seems to lie in Weber's attempt to draw too rigid a distinction between the subjective directions of interest of the scientist in each of the two groups of sciences. There seems to be no reason to doubt the importance of the motive of control with reference to the phenomena of nature. But it is possible to doubt both the extent to which that is the exclusive or even dominant motive of interest in the natural science field and that it is as unimportant as Weber maintains by implication in the sociocultural field. Indeed in the latter case it is curious that Weber took the position that he did, for one of his major theses throughout his work was that of the importance of scientifically verifiable knowledge of human affairs as a guide to rational action. Moreover in just this connection he strongly emphasized the need for general, theoretical knowledge. In so far as this is the context in which social studies are considered it would seem that, on the cognitive level, the ultimate aim of research was the building up of one or more systems of valid general theory, which would be equally applicable to any concrete situations that might arise.

Indeed, with reference both to nature and to action and culture two main types of nonscientific motives of cognitive interest may be differentiated. One is the "instrumental" interest. This is manifested whenever the question arises of using elements of the situation of action as means, or adapting action to them as conditions. But surely in rational action generally the social environment looms at least as large as does the natural. Particularly in the field Weber had primarily in mind, that of political action, this seems to be the case. The other main type of nonscientific motive of cognitive interest is what may be called a "disinter-

[1] The second will be taken up below (see pp. 606 *ff*).

ested" value attitude. This is not a matter of using things, but of defining one's attitude toward them in themselves. It is here that the element of concrete individuality becomes most prominent and that the principle of value relevance as formulated by Weber is applicable. There is no reason to deny that this element is quantitatively much more important in the social situation. But even if this is true it is not sufficient ground to justify its being made the basis of a radical methodological distinction between the two groups of sciences.

There is indeed no reason to exclude radically a value interest in this sense from the field of the natural sciences. In so far as value relevance is made the basis for an element of relativism in the theoretical systems of science, it may well be suspected that this relativism enters into the natural science field to a much greater extent than Weber intimated. Indeed a comprehensive comparative study of the interpretations of nature to be found in different civilizations with widely differing value systems would almost certainly reveal that this relativity existed to a surprising extent.[1]

Moreover, there is no reason to believe that a value interest as distinguished from a control interest is always necessarily one which concentrates on the aspect of concrete individuality. Indeed Weber himself, in the *Protestant Ethic,* gives several hints of the existence of religious motivation in the promotion of natural science in the Puritan era, a view which has been substantiated by later studies.[2] This urge, to know God through his works, was directed to the element of order in the physical world, and thus to those aspects of it that could be formulated in abstract and general terms. Indeed it may be suspected that Weber's distinction, in the rigid form in which he advanced it, is itself the manifestation of a particular value attitude of its author. It has been held to be a protest against the bureaucratic tendency to fit human beings as cogs into a machine, in which their place is defined by impersonal capabilities and functions rather than by their unique personality. In addition it is probable that Weber

---

[1] For an important study of this character see M. Granet, *La pensée chinoise.*

[2] See especially the study of R. K. Merton on *Science, Technology and Society in Seventeenth Century England.*

was misled into an exaggerated view of the unity of all natural science by lingering vestiges in his thought of Kantian empiricism, which blinded him to the elements of relativism to be found there.

A further element seems not to have received sufficient consideration on Weber's part. It is that, whatever the motives of original interest may be, there is an inherent tendency for the theoretical structures of all science in whatever field to become logically closed systems. Then, in so far as there is an instrumental interest in the social field, the general conceptual products of this interest will tend to become integrated in the same systems as those issuing from the value aspect. Once this has happened to an appreciable degree there will exist, as has been emphasized throughout this study, a secondary basis of interest in concrete phenomena—that derived from the structure of the theoretical system itself. The interest to this extent will be directed to those aspects of concrete phenomena which are important to the theoretical system.

Indeed, throughout, Weber seems not to have laid sufficient emphasis on the fact that scientific knowledge involves not only the fact that a selection is made from the possible data of "raw experience," but that what is experienced is itself determined, in part, by what scientific knowledge we have and, above all, by the general conceptual schemes that have been developed. Observation is always in terms of a conceptual scheme.

In all these respects, then, there seems to be no basis for a radical distinction in principle between the natural and the social sciences with regard to the roles of individuality and generality. Quantitative differences of degree there may be, but these are not sufficient to justify such a distinction.

The principle of value relevance helps to explain the element of relativism, in scientific methodology, but it is applicable to both groups of sciences, not to one alone.

For the classification of the sciences the methodological arguments Weber has developed seem to indicate a basic division into two groups, substantially on the lines he has suggested, with a dominant direction of interest, on the one hand, toward the concrete individuality of one or a class of historical individuals and, on the other hand, toward a system of abstract general principles and laws. But this division does not coincide with that between the natural and the sociocultural sciences.[1] There are, rather, examples of both in each field. The first group may be called the historical sciences, which concentrate their attention on particular concrete phenomena, attempting as full an understanding of their causes and consequences as is possible. In doing this they seek conceptual aid wherever it may be found. Examples in the natural science field are geology and meteorology; in the social field, history, above all, but also anthropology as it has generally been conceived. The other group, the "analytical," sciences, is concerned primarily with building up systems of general theory verifiable in terms of and applicable to a wide range of concrete phenomena. To them the individual phenomenon is a "case." In the natural science field theoretical physics is the leading example, but chemistry and general biology may also be included; in the social sciences theoretical economics is by far the most highly developed, but it is to be hoped that theoretical sociology and certain others will find a place by its side.[2]

These two types of sciences cut across each other in their application to fields of concrete phenomena. The same historical science will necessarily draw theoretical aid from a number of different analytical sciences, for example geology from physics, from chemistry and, in explaining the origin of organic deposits like coal, from biology. Similarly history should draw on biology,

[1] Weber himself partially recognized this, but went much too far in identifying the two groups of sciences.

[2] Then for the historical sciences theoretical concepts are means to understanding the concrete historical individual. For the analytical sciences, on the other hand, the reverse is true; concrete historical individuals are means, "cases" in terms of which the validity of the theoretical system may be tested by "verification."

From this it follows that there are two different possible meanings of the term "theory" which are often confused. On the one hand, we speak of the total explanation of a given concrete phenomenon, a historical individual or class of them, as a "theory," thus a "theory of eclipses" or Weber's own "theory of modern capitalism." On the other hand, we may apply the term to systems of general concepts as such, thus the "Newtonian physics" or the "classical economics." Weber points out quite correctly that a theory in the second sense cannot *by itself* explain a *single* empirical fact. It requires *data* which are always empirically unique, are part of a concrete historical individual, for any concrete explanation or prediction. See *Wissenschaftslehre*, pp. 171–172.

psychology, economics, sociology and other sciences. On the other hand, the theoretical system developed by an analytical science will normally be applicable to a number of different classes of concrete phenomena, for example physics to celestial bodies and the behavior of terrestial objects; economics to human actions in the market place and, in a less crucial role, to the church and the state. A distinction between the natural and the social sciences is possible on both levels. Historically considered the latter group is confined to the concrete phenomena of human life in social groups, analytically to those conceptual elements which are applicable only to this concrete subject matter.

But the basic distinction between historical and analytical is not to be identified with that between the natural and the social sciences. Indeed on no account is it possible to identify the distinction with any classification of concrete phenomena, for the analytical sciences of necessity cut across all such classifications. From this point of view it may be said that to make this identification is the basic fallacy of all of what has here been called empiricism, common to all three of the varieties discussed above. The result is invariably a dilemma. On one hand, the class of concrete phenomena in question may be treated by the method of an analytical science. Then the result is "reification," the fallacy of misplaced concreteness, with all its consequences. Or, on the other hand it may be treated by the method of a historical science alone, in which case the result is, theoretically considered, irrationalism, the denial of the validity of general conceptualization at all. On an empiricist basis there is no escape from this dilemma. Weber made his way out of it to a great extent, failing only to take the final step.[1]

Before concluding this phase of the discussion it should be remarked that Weber's methodological work has succeeded to a notable degree in synthesizing, on the methodological plane, elements which are central to science and to action, indeed in establishing a very close solidarity between the two. The traditional methodology of science has tended to think of it in complete abstraction from action. Hence, whenever the close factual interdependence of the two has been brought to attention it has tended to result in a wave of scientific skepticism. Weber has

---

[1] It is true that he was in it in the first place because of his inherited philosophical preconceptions.

succeeded in bringing a much needed element of relativity into his methodology thus relieving it of the necessity of making claims to an empiricist absolutism which would place it in a vulnerable position. At the same time he has vindicated its claims, properly qualified, to objectivity. Above all he has established the logical independence of the standards of objectivity, the schema of proof, from the relativistic elements.

Finally, among the principal elements of relativity in science prove to be elements that are of central importance to the analysis of action—the value elements. Scientific investigation, then, takes its place as a mode of action to be analyzed in the same terms as any other, rather than as a class of actions set apart. At the same time not only is it possible to place the development of science in the context of action without destroying its claim to objectivity but also verifiable knowledge itself is seen, with great clarity, to be an indispensable element of action itself. For the norm of intrinsic rationality in relation to the means-end relationship is devoid of meaning unless there is valid knowledge as a guide to action. Thus the two are elements of the same fundamental complex; a knowledge of action and its elements is indispensable to ground the methodology of science and, vice versa, scientific knowledge itself constitutes an element indispensable to the analysis of action. This insight is basic to the analytical system that has been emerging in the course of the present study.

It is well to emphasize again just what the element of relativism introduced by Weber means for the objectivity of scientific knowledge. In the first place, it means that scientific interest in any given action setting is not in the full totality of knowable facts, even about the concrete phenomena studied, but in certain selected elements of the latter. Hence at any given time even the total body of knowledge is not a complete reflection of humanly knowable reality. But to counterbalance this relativism, once the direction of interest is given and the relevant historical individuals constructed and correctly described, the system of propositions is, so far as it meets the requirements of the logical schema of proof, verifiable and objective. It follows that even though values change and with them the direction of scientific interest, in so far as past investigation has yielded valid knowledge, it remains valid, a permanently valid precipitate of the process.[1]

---

[1] The fact that a later age may completely lose interest in parts of it does not make it any less true.

And however different from each other the conceptual schemes are, in terms of which such knowledge has been formulated, they must if valid be "translatable" into terms of each other or of a wider scheme. This implication is necessary to avoid a completely relativistic consequence that would overthrow the whole position.

Furthermore, it is one of Weber's basic theorems that while there is a plurality of possible ultimate value systems, their number is, in fact, limited. From this it follows that on Weber's own principles there is a limited number of possible constructions of historical individuals from the same concrete objects of experience, on the one hand, and of systems of theoretical concepts, on the other. From this it follows further that there is in principle a finite totality of humanly possible scientific knowledge. Even this totality would not by any means be a complete reflection of the totality of conceivable objective reality[1] but would stand, like all objective knowledge, as Weber often puts it, in a functional relation to it. That is, the development of scientific knowledge is to be regarded as a process of asymptotic approach to a limit. The concrete impossibility of actual attainment at any given time or at any predictable future time does not affect the principle. Thus Weber's principle of value relevance, while it does introduce an element of relativity into scientific methodology (and a much-needed one by comparison with all empiricist views), does not involve the skepticism that is the inevitable consequence of any really radical relativity.[2]

The Ideal Type and Generalized Analytical Theory

But this still leaves certain questions of the relation of scientific concepts to reality highly problematical. They can best be discussed in relation to Weber's theory of the ideal type.

Dr. von Schelting in an earlier study,[3] has shown that Weber's own treatment of this subject was not altogether satisfactory, and that he failed to distinguish several different kinds of con-

---

[1] Which is, however, precisely on this account not itself an object of experience in the sense of scientific knowledge but an abstraction arrived at by implication. It has logical affinities with the Kantian *Ding an sich*.

[2] Involved equally in Durkheim's sociological epistemology, Mannheim's *Wissenssoziologie* and many other trends of thought.

[3] "Die logische Theorie der historischen Kulturwissenschaften von Max Weber . . . ," *Archiv für Sozialwissenschaft und Sozialpolitik*, Vol. 49, summarized in *Max Webers Wissenschaftslehre*, pp. 329 ff.

cepts that he included under the same term. This fact is not without significance here. It is important to distinguish some of these different possible types of concepts, to relate them to each other and to explain certain unsatisfying features of Weber's treatment.[1]

The most fruitful way to get at Weber's approach to the concept of ideal type is to do so in terms of the polemical situation in which he was placed. From this it will appear that, like other categories that have been discussed,[2] this type is defined negatively, by contrast with other things, and is hence a residual category. It is then not surprising that further analysis should reveal a lack of homogeneity. The elements most relevant to this discussion are the following:

1. Weber throughout emphasized that scientific concepts do not exhaust concrete reality but involve selection and are hence in this sense unreal.

2. In his insistence on the logical distinction of the natural and social sciences this was strongly accentuated for social science concepts. For if the end of its study is always and exclusively the understanding of concrete historical individuals, such concepts can only be means. And the relativity inherent in the principle of value relevance prevents their being considered as final concepts even within the logically possible limits of science.[3]

3. Weber's general polemical animus was directed at methodological views derived from idealistic philosophy, above all, the intuitionist theories. At the same time he made *Verstehen* a basic methodological postulate of the social sciences. This involved dealing with the subjective aspect of action, above all, ideas, norms and value concepts. In this polemical situation the most immediate danger was that of having his position confused with an idealistic one which identified these value elements with the totality of concrete reality as scientifically knowable, or regarded the latter as an emanation of such ideas. This circumstance drove him strongly in the direction of insisting upon the unreality of the concepts in terms of which such elements were formulated.[4] Weber was right in this polemical context; but in another context

---

[1] Without full textual criticism, for lack of space.

[2] Notably Pareto's nonlogical action.

[3] *Wissenschaftslehre*, p. 207.

[4] *Cf.* Chap. X, *supra*, p. 396.

his formulations might lead to unfortunate impressions of his position.

4. Finally, a more general point has already been noted. In his polemics, especially against the "objectivist" position, Weber again rightly, laid powerful stress on the fact that scientific concepts, particularly in the social sciences, did not reflect the totality of "raw experience," which was of infinite diversity and complexity. In this situation he was led to minimize the other side of the picture, that all concrete observation of empirical fact, above all rigorous scientific observation, takes place in terms of a conceptual scheme. "Raw experience" in Weber's sense is not a concrete actuality at all but a methodological abstraction. Hence again the emphasis on the unreality of concepts.

The combination of these four elements could not but have the effect of driving Weber strongly in the direction of a fiction theory of the logical nature and function of social science concepts, and of as strongly inhibiting him from any sort of realism that ran a risk of confusion with any or all of the empiricist positions against which he was fighting. Hence, besides the fact that it contains elements which have a subjective reference, the only positive characterization of the ideal type that Weber gives[1] is that it is a construction of elements abstracted from the concrete, and put together to form a unified conceptual pattern. This involves a one-sided exaggeration (*Steigerung*) of certain aspects of the concrete reality, but is not to be found in it, that is, concretely existing, except in a few very special cases, such as purely rational action. It is a Utopia.[2] On the other hand, Weber is quite clear what it is not: (1) It is not a hypothesis,[3] in the sense that it is a proposition about concrete reality which is concretely verifiable, and to be accepted in this sense as true if verified. In contrast to this sense of concreteness, it is abstract. (2) It is not a description of reality if by this is meant a concretely existing thing or process to which it corresponds. In this sense also it is abstract. (3) It is not an average[4] (*Gat-*

---

[1] The main discussion of the ideal type which Weber gives is in the essay "Die Objektivität sozialwissenschaftlicher Erkenntnis," *Wissenschaftslehre*, pp. 146 *ff.*, but especially pp. 185 *ff.* See also pp. 505 *ff.* reprinted from *Wirtsch. u. Ges.*, Chap. I.

[2] On all this see especially *Wissenschaftslehre*, p. 190.

[3] *Wissenschaftslehre*, p. 190.

[4] *Ibid.*, p. 201.

tungsbegriff, in one meaning) in the sense that we can say the average man weighs 150 pounds. This average man is not an ideal type. (4) Nor, finally, is it a formulation of the concrete traits *common* to a class of concrete things, for instance in the sense that having beards is a trait common to men as distinct from women—this is a *Gattungsbegriff* in a second meaning.

Dr. von Schelting[1] was the first to point out that under the term ideal type Weber included the two quite heterogeneous categories of generalizing and individualizing concepts. In his later work[2] Dr. von Schelting has also worked out the fundamental distinction between two subcategories of the latter. On the one hand are the concrete historical individuals which constitute the *objects* of causal analysis, such as, among the phenomena discussed in the previous two chapters—modern rational bourgeois capitalism, the Indian caste system, Chinese patrimonial bureaucracy. Here, it may be said that the element of abstract "unreality" is essentially a consequence of the selectiveness of scientific interest. It is precisely the statement in outline form of the aspects of the concrete situation which are *of interest* for explanatory purposes. If the historical individual is to be capable of causal analysis it must be oversimplified; it must be reduced to what is essential, omitting the unimportant. Thus in Indian caste the complex details of the hierarchical aspect of the caste structure are disregarded and only the fact of hierarchical relation to the Brahmans is kept in view. But though simplified, and in the sense involved in value relevance one-sided, such a concept is still definitely *individual;* there is one and only one Indian caste system. The construction of such historical individuals has the function of preparing and organizing the concrete material for causal analysis. While it is not descriptive in the sense of fully reproducing reality it is so in the sense that its application to the concrete reality *explains* nothing as such, but only states what is to be explained. Explanation, on the other hand, involves general concepts.

---

[1] VON SCHELTING, "Die logische Theorie der historischen Kulturwissenschaften von Max Weber, "*Archiv für Sozialwissenshaft und Sozialpolitik*, Vol. 49, summarized in *Max Webers Wissenschaftslehre*, pp. 329 *ff.;* see also pp. 333 *ff.*

[2] VON SCHELTING, *Max Webers Wissenschaftslehre*, final chapter. This distinction was not contained in the earlier study.

The second category of individual concept is very similar in its logical function but different in its content. The first contained at least elements of real phenomena—things and events in time— elements of social fact. The other contains another order of object—ideas. Such are for example, the Calvinistic theology, the Brahmanic philosophy of karma and transmigration. These are, of course, relevant to real process—otherwise this study would have no interest in them—but short of Hegelianism they cannot be identified with it. Indeed the problem of their relations is precisely the central problem of Weber's concrete sociological work.

But neither are they the actual concrete contents of the minds of all Calvinists or all Brahmans, to say nothing of all members of all castes not explicitly rejecting Brahmanic authority. On the contrary, these two are exaggerations, they are developments into the most clear-cut and consistent form of the general tendencies of religious thought to be found in the circles in question. Here the ideal type may actually concretely exist in the sense that the system of ideas is explicit in some one document, Calvin's *Institutes*, for instance.[1] But this is not methodologically necessary, and above all it is certain that, for instance, the mass influence of the Calvinistic theology cannot be limited to those persons who have had a completely clear intellectual grasp of the logical structure of the theological system in Calvin's statement. Such concepts are, in their sociological application at least, in a sense unreal.

At the present stage of the discussion it is the other kind of "ideal type," the generalizing concept, which is important. Quoting Dr. von Schelting[2] it may be said, "The causal explanation of an individual event requires an answer to the question what would, under certain hypothetical, hence unreal, but nevertheless 'possible'[3] assumptions, have happened." A general ideal type is such a construction of a hypothetical course of events with two other characteristics: (1) abstract generality and (2) the ideal-typical exaggeration of empirical reality. Without the first of these last two elements, the concept might be applicable

[1] For essentially the same reason that a purely rational act may be intuitively apprehended. See above, p. 588.

[2] *Max Webers Wissenschaftslehre*, pp. 329–330.

[3] Weber's conception of "objective possibility" will be discussed below, pp. 610 ff.

only to a single historical situation;[1] without the second it might be merely a common trait or a statistical average. It is neither of these, but is an ideal construction of a *typical* course of action, or form of relationship which is applicable to the analysis of an indefinite plurality of concrete cases, and which formulates in pure, logically consistent form certain elements that are relevant to the understanding of the several concrete situations. Since *these* are the general concepts necessarily involved in the logic of empirical proof, their methodological status is vital.

Weber himself was fond of using the general concepts of orthodox economic theory as an example. Since this is an example that has concerned this study already[2] and since it contains in clear-cut form all the elements of the problem except one, it will be used as the main basis for discussion. The main point[3] is that neither Weber nor Dr. von Schelting seems to see a central problem in the methodological status of these concepts of economic theory.[4]

This example is taken from the field of the social sciences and involves *Verstehen*, which Weber regarded as essential to the ideal type; its relation to natural science concepts is another matter. On this basis the concepts of economic theory all involve a normative element—what is usually referred to as the postulate of economic rationality. There is general agreement[5] on the proposition that action can only be explained in terms of economic principles in so far as it *in fact* approaches the expectations in terms of this norm. Departures from it must be due to other than economic factors. All this is common ground. The problem arises here: the concepts of economic theory may be held to state a type of action fully conforming to the norm, to state a course not of concretely observed action but of *hypothetical*[6] concrete action. That this

[1] See VON SCHELTING, *op. cit.*, footnote page 330. Indeed Weber referred to certain constructions of this character as ideal types.

[2] See above, especially Chap. IV, V, VI.

[3] To this study.

[4] This has been developed at some length in Talcott Parsons, "Some Reflections on the Nature and Significance of Economics," *Quarterly Journal of Economics*, May, 1934.

[5] In orthodox circles.

[6] Hypothetical not in the sense that a concrete course of events is expected which will exactly correspond to the construction but negatively in the sense that it describes a course of events which has not actually been observed exactly as described.

norm has perhaps never been fully attained,[1] may in fact be unattainable and is in that sense unreal, is not the point. It makes sense as a limiting case—in much the same way as the physical concept of a frictionless machine which would involve no transformation of mechanical energy into heat. On the other hand, these concepts may state certain *analytical elements* in a generalized system of action.[2]

If analysis is confined to the first kind of concept it leads, when applied to situations which are not ideal experimental conditions for the theory, to the dilemma: either an illegitimate reification of a *single* theoretical system, or a "fiction" theory of the role of concepts in science which does not really get away from the empiricist irrationalism of the objectivist and intuitionist positions. More specifically in the case of Professor Robbins analyzed in the above article,[3] it leads to reification.[4] Weber, since most of his general ideal types are of this character, is caught in the same dilemma, but because of his much greater methodological sophistication and empirical knowledge and insight his is a much subtler case. He is no naïve monist like Robbins. But his "pluralism" tends, by hypostatization of ideal types, to break up, in a sense not inherent in analysis as such, the organic unity both of concrete historical individuals and of the historic process. In its reification phase it issues in what may be called a "mosaic" theory of culture and society, conceiving them to be made up of disparate atoms.[5] This, with his use of the rational norm, is the source of what has often been referred to as his objectionable "rationalism" and of the iron-bound character of the process of rationalization that is such a prominent feature of his empirical work. It is the central methodological difficulty of Weber's position, and far more than any factual mistakes underlies whatever serious difficulties there may be in his empirical theories.

The difference of the two types of concepts and, above all, the consequences of their respective employment have already been shown. There can be no doubt that the norm of free enterprise

---

[1] In a total action system.

[2] The two may overlap in concrete content. *Cf.* Chap. I, p. 35, note 1.

[3] *Supra*, footnote 4, p. 606.

[4] Most evident in his deep laissez-faire bias. See Lionel Robbins, *An Essay on the Nature and Significance of Economic Science.*

[5] Defined as ideal-type units.

as used by Marshall, with all its main subsidiary concepts, corresponds to the above postulate of economic rationality. Free enterprise is, for Marshall, a hypothetical state where men actually would live up to this norm. But it is equally clear that in this hypothetical state as conceived by Marshall more than one analytical element[1] is involved. *Two* are important here— utility and activities[2]—but neither of these two is conceivable even hypothetically as a concrete type of action. The whole analysis has shown that the economic concept of utility makes sense only in terms of a *given* system of ultimate ends, on the one hand, and, on the other, of elements of a given situation as well as certain other elements. It is possible to speak even of hypothetical action as "determined by considerations of maximum utility," only in so far as the values of these other elements are given independently of utility considerations; that is, the utility element must be considered as independent of these others. But the same is true of the activities element.[3] It is quite clear that it is analytically separable from that of utility as any comparison with a distinctly different concrete situation from that which Marshall had in mind will show. For instance, the case that Weber deals with[4] under the heading of traditionalism, in which a rise in rate of pay leads to *less* work so that the same total amount as before is earned, is in no respect less an example of maximization of utility than that which Marshall had in mind. Put a little differently, the concept of maximization of utility is completely meaningless by itself. It simply cannot be reified without bringing in logically distinct elements, such as the nature of ultimate wants.[5] But the fact that in a plurality of different hypothetical (ideal-type) cases, for example Weber's traditionalism and Marshall's free enterprise, the same funda-

---

[1] In the sense of the previous discussion.

[2] This is not to be taken to mean that for all purposes these two variables are the only ones that it is significant to distinguish in these phenomena. Another choice of variables might cut across this. The present concern is merely to illustrate the *logical* distinction between elements and units.

[3] However inadequately defined it may be by Marshall for present purposes.

[4] *Supra*, Chap. XIV, p. 514.

[5] Hence the role in the utilitarian position of the conception of random ends. The value of an element *may* be capable of separate existence as a unit. The argument is directed against the implicit assumption that it *must* be.

mental element of rational maximization of utility is involved, and *logically indispensable* to the concept, proves that this element of utility is an independent variable relative to traditionalism and to activities. The two elements simply are not reducible to terms of one another in the sense that maximization of utility logically implies either maximization of traditionalism (in Weber's sense) or of activities (in Marshall's sense).

This is brought out clearly by considering the relation of Marshall's case to Pareto. Essentially the same elements which Marshall dealt with as the utility elements appear in Pareto's generalized system as at least part of the "interests." But it is quite clear that Pareto treats the interests as variable independently of the residues and the sentiments they manifest. For example these interests may operate as well in a system characterized by the predominance of the residues of persistence as in one where the residues of combination are particularly strong, but the concrete outcome will be very different in the two systems. Marshall suppresses this independence of variation by relating maximization of economic rationality to a particular class of residues, those involved in activities. This involves an implicit theorem which, as the work of all three others, Pareto, Weber and Durkheim, has shown, is not in harmony with the facts.

But either this or another theorem of corresponding rigidity is the inevitable logical outcome of the implicit methodological view that *all* the analytical concepts of a theoretical system must correspond to units of concrete systems the independent existence of which is conceivable. What has, in the previous discussion, been dissected out of the structure of systems of action as the economic element cannot be thought of as such a unit. It is a mode of relation of units in systems beyond a certain minimum degree of complexity by virtue of which they have certain emergent properties. Yet the foregoing example demonstrated that it is independently variable relative to certain other elements of the same system, namely the value elements. Robbins' course is, by postulating that it is adequately descriptive of a concrete type of action, to push the value element out of the concrete system altogether; ends become random. Thus the interdependence of the economic and value elements *cannot* be taken account of. Marshall, on the other hand, bound economic rationality to a particular value of the value complex. Weber tends to be guilty of still a third fallacy, the "mosaic" atomism discussed above. None of these courses is satisfactory.

That Weber should not have arrived explicitly at the distinction of these types of concept is not at all surprising in view of the fact that the positions from which he started were of a thoroughly empiricist character and that his main task was to vindicate the logical necessity of the use *at all* of general concepts in explanatory science. It was not unnatural, above all in view of his polemical relation to idealist methodologies, that he should in his explicit formulations stop at the type of general concept which was nearest an empirically descriptive one, namely the hypothetically concrete type of action or relationship.

THE LOGIC OF EMPIRICAL PROOF

The logic of the situation in Weber's thought can best be followed through in terms of his treatment of the conditions of objective proof of empirical propositions, for which he developed the categories of objective possibility and adequate explanation.

At the outset it must be remembered that Weber's discussions of proof and causal imputation concerned immediately the question, how is it possible to prove the existence of a causal relation between certain features of a given historical individual and certain empirical facts which have existed prior to it? It is as a result of following up the logic of this problem that he is led to analyze the role of general concepts.

Dr. von Schelting gives a convenient summary of the logical steps involved in the procedure of causal imputation.[1] It presupposes the construction and verification descriptively of a historical individual—the thing to be explained. Then the indispensable[2] steps are as follows: (1) Analysis of this complex phenomenon (or process) in such a way that it is broken down into elements of such a character that each of them may be subsumed under a general law (*Regel des Geschehens*). (2) There is presupposed previous knowledge of such general laws. (3) Hypothetical elimination or alteration of one or more factors of the process, concerning which it is wished to raise the question of its (or

[1] VON SCHELTING, *op. cit.*, p. 262.
[2] Dr. von Schelting adds four others which *may* be taken; for the sake of brevity they may be negelected here.

their) causal significance for the result. (4) Hypothetical construction of what would *then* (after the elimination or alteration) be the expected course of events (application of the category of objective possibility). (5) Comparison of the hypothetical conception of a possible development (really that which would *have been* possible had certain things happened differently) with the actual course of events. (6) On the basis of this comparison, the drawing of causal conclusions. The general principle is that, in so far as the two, the actual and the possible, courses of events differ, the difference may be causally imputed to the factors "thought away" or considered as changed. If, on the other hand, this hypothetical change fails to make a difference, the judgment is justified that the factors in question were not causally important.

This schema[1] contains all the main elements of the problem. The main questions that arise lie in interpreting: What is a factor, in the sense of an element of the problem which may be thought of as eliminated or altered for purposes of the hypothetical construction? What are the general laws under which it is to be subsumed (*Generelle Erfahrungsregeln* or *generelle Regeln des Geschehens*)? And finally what is the character of the general relations of these two apparently equally indispensable elements of scientific knowledge to each other?

The first statement to be made is that, for purposes of this schema a factor is an entity involving statements of concrete fact. The question of causality is that of the consequences for the ensuing course of events arising from the existence of these facts at the time and place that they existed, in the given total circumstances. Thus in the examples that Dr. von Schelting takes from Weber the factors are (*a*) the *fact that* the Persian advance was held up at Marathon for a certain time, (*b*) the *fact that* the young mother had had a dispute with her cook,[2] and (*c*) the *fact that* there existed in Western Europe at a given time among large numbers of people the complex of attitudes Weber called the ethic of ascetic Protestantism.[3] These are the factors the causal significance of which is to be tested. In each

---

[1] It is a perfectly valid statement of Weber's position in a form more convenient than any of his own.

[2] von Schelting, *op. cit.*, p. 280.

[3] *Ibid.*, p. 281 *ff.*

instance they refer to concrete specific states of affairs or events.

But each of these in turn forms "part" of a historical individual. It would be nonsense to attribute the freedom of Hellenic culture from religious-priestly, traditionalistic rigidity to the outcome of the battle of Marathon had the social situation in Greece at the time of the battle been that of contemporary Egypt, or to attribute a part in the development of capitalism to the Protestant ethic had the social situation in Western Europe been that of India during the same period.

Both the factor to which causal importance is to be attributed (or denied) and the situation in which it occurs are concrete phenomena. The phenomena with which the causal analysis is concerned constitute a "real process." The problem is that of the part played in the determination of the concrete individuality of a later stage by the fact that the factor in question happened or existed at an earlier one. This question can only have a definite meaning if the factor is thought of as operating in terms of a given concrete situation. Moreover, the only way in which to arrive at a judgment of the causal significance of a factor is to ask what would have happened if the factor in question had not been present or had been altered, *e.g.*, if the Persians had not been stopped at Marathon at all. It is clear that this is nothing, in principle, but the logic of experiment. Where practical difficulties make it impossible actually to reproduce the initial situation, and alter the factor in question, and then see what would happen, recourse must be had to a mental experiment, the construction of an objectively possible course of events.

But any such historical individual, including the factor in which interest is centered, is an organic unity and can only be observed as such (in the absence of possible experimentation). Hence anything with which to compare it must be[1] a "construction." In so far as the whole was in any sense determined the process *had* to result as it actually did. The construction of what would have happened under different circumstances therefore requires knowledge of how certain elements of the situation would have developed. This involves, then, as stated in the schema, both analysis of the phenomenon into elements and, with respect to each element, ability to predict with more or less

[1] With one exception, to be noted, that of analogy.

accuracy its trends of development. It is as logically necessary prerequisites of this latter prediction of tendencies that general laws become involved.

But, what are the other elements into which the historical individual in question is to be analyzed? In the Marathon[1] example it is certain features of the social structure and situation at the time in Greece, on the one hand; of Persian interests and probable policy on the other. They may be stated as follows: In the religious situation of Greece, beyond the family cults, there were at the time two main structural elements: (1) the civic cults, administration of which was assimilated to ordinary public office, a situation definitely incompatible with the dominance of a hereditary professional priestly class; (2) a professional element, especially in the oracles such as Delphi but *outside* the structure of the polis. The central question was whether the first element should continue to develop in its secularizing direction or whether this tendency should be counteracted and suppressed by a shift in the balance of religious power to the other element. Weber, with Eduard Meyer, argues that a Persian victory would with a high degree of probability have brought about this latter outcome. The main reasons are (1) it would have destroyed the political autonomy of the polis and with it the whole development of citizenship with which the "state-religion" was bound up; (2) the professional religious element would have been very useful to a Persian regime as a means of domestication and hence the latter would have done everything to promote the former's influence (this happened in Judea).

The historical question cannot be pursued further. The present issue is what is meant by the elements and the general laws that are necessary to the schema of logical proof. Only one thing can be definitely gathered from Weber's treatment: they are *general* concepts or categories. When a factor in a given historical individual or its temporal antecedent is thought of as altered or eliminated, it can only be the specific facts which change. The elements referred to must be in some sense general categories, forms of which the facts in question constitute the particular

---

[1] Weber regarded the battle of Marathon as decisive in the first place because it gave the Athenians time to get together a fleet and withdraw it to Salamis. The real point here, however, is the failure of the Persians to gain permanent political control over Greece.

content. The alteration must be one of content within the same form. The question is, then, what, in the terminology of logic, is the universal, of which the specific facts in question constitute a particular?

This is where the dichotomy that has been discussed above becomes relevant. In the relation of a universal to the particular facts of a concrete situation can stand not one type of general category but two. Weber fails to make the distinction, to specify which of the two is meant or the relations the two bear to each other. It is here that it is necessary, in order to clarify the implications of his position, to go beyond Weber's own analysis.

One type of universal is logically related to the particulars of a class[1] of objects as the concept of man is related to the individual human being. In one sense man is an abstraction—there is, empirically, no such thing as man, but only particular men and aggregates of them. But in the concept man are brought together a certain number of criteria such that any concrete entity in relation to which all of them can be identified may be placed in the class man in common with all other concrete entities sharing, within certain limits of variation, the same features. As Weber's analysis has shown, there are a number of different possible ways in which general concepts of this class character may be related to the totality of concrete entities included within the class. The class may be formulated as an average, with a certain range of variation, such that particulars falling within the range may still be said to belong to the class. Thus man may be defined with reference to such a feature as average stature or body weight. Or, secondly, the class may be defined with reference to traits common to the particulars, as when man is defined with reference to a certain type of brain structure, erect posture, opposable thumb and the like, but not with reference to hair or skin color, cephalic index, etc. Finally, it may be defined as an ideal type.

There can be no doubt that the elements that play the principal part in Weber's schema of proof as the universals into which the particular facts of the alterable factor fit, are class concepts in this sense. The ideal-type mode of formulation is chosen rather than one of the others mentioned above mainly for two reasons: First, their scientific function lies in connection with

[1] In the logical sense.

understanding the normative orientation of action. For this purpose it is convenient to take the case where the norm in question is conceived as completely realized; in this way, as Weber often notes, it is easiest to determine the role of other factors in terms of departure of the concrete case from the state of realization of the norm. Second, the concrete historical individuals to which these concepts are to be applied are organic phenomena. The isolation of parts, or units, of them is thus attended with the abstraction always involved in such a procedure. Since they must be abstract anyway because the class concept cannot be adequately descriptive of the concrete phenomena, the ideal-type concept is more suitable than either of the other kinds.

Weber himself frequently lays down as a principal criterion of the correct formulation of an ideal type that the combination of features used to characterize it should be such as taken together are meaningful, make sense. What this means is clear—that they must adequately describe, in terms of a frame of reference, a potentially concrete entity, an objectively possible entity in Weber's sense. Not, to be sure, in the sense that a concrete entity exactly corresponding to the type must be demonstrable as actually existing, but that all the essential properties of a concrete entity are included.[1] Thus, in mechanics it would not make sense to describe a body that had mass and velocity but no location in space. Similarly an action system which has means and ends but no norm governing the means-end relationship is nonsensical. The ideal type as relevant to this context is, then, a hypothetically concrete entity, a state of affairs or a process or a unit in one of these. It is ideal only in the sense of being a construction with a fictitious simplification and exaggeration of certain features. Examples which Weber employs frequently are "handicraft," "bureaucracy," "feudalism," "church," "sect."

It is clear that this kind of ideal type is not necessarily an analytical element in the sense in which the term has been used in this study. An element is also a universal or combination of them of which the facts descriptive of a concrete entity or state of affairs may be the particulars. But it need not be a class universal at all. It may be what might be called a universal of

---

[1] Essential, as defined by the requirements of the frame of reference employed.

predication. It may refer to general properties or qualities of concrete phenomena the values of which are facts descriptive of the phenomena. Thus in mechanics mass is an element in this sense. Its concrete counterpart is not, however, any unit of a mechanical system, but the mass *of* a particular body. Both the class concept and the universal of predication are abstractions. Both are so in part because they are universals and not particulars. But it is clear that the abstraction involved is of a different sort in the two concepts. The particular corresponding to the one is a concrete entity, George Washington *was* a man. The particular corresponding to the other need not be a concrete entity but may be the concrete property or quality *of* such an entity. The sun *has* (not *is*) a given mass. The two only coincide when the latter includes the universals involved in all the facts necessary for an adequate description of a unit.

A concrete entity is always capable of description in terms of a certain number of predications about it. What and how many these are will be determined by the frame of reference in terms of which it is described. There is always, for such a frame of reference, a group of general properties, the values of which, taken together, constitute an adequate description of a concrete unit or entity. Thus, in the classical mechanics, to describe a particle or body adequately it is necessary to state its mass, velocity, position in space and direction of motion. The omission of one or more of these makes the description indeterminate.

These considerations make it possible to designate certain general relations between the ideal-type universal and the analytical-element universal. The former is a true universal and is thus applicable to an indefinite plurality of particular cases. It cannot, therefore, include in its formulation a set of specific values of the elements relevant to the description of particulars of the class. It contains no concrete facts.

What it does contain is a fixed set of relations (possibly including variation within certain limits) of these values of elements. Only in so far as these relations are maintained can the type in question be said to exist or be relevant to the concrete situation being analyzed.

This may best be brought out by reverting to the previous illustration. Economic rationality may be regarded as such a

general property of action systems. It is a property of the type
of action Weber has described as traditionalism. Indeed this
type involves, as one essential predication, the maximization of
economic rationality. But the maximization of economic rationality alone is not an adequate description of the type of action
Weber has in mind. It is action which is economically rational
relative to a traditionally fixed standard of living, that is, not
relative to *any* given ends whatever but relative to a system of
ends in which the property of traditional fixity is maximized.
It is the *combination* of these two specific properties which
defines the type. But so long as this condition is given there is
room for wide variation in the concrete instances in other respects,
as in the concrete content of the ends and the particular features
of the situations. The example of the Silesian mowers is only
one of the many possible examples of this type of action. The
type is equally applicable to American miners whose consumption
habits and whose situations, in so far as they are relevant to
securing a fixed income, are widely different.

This is what was meant when it was stated above that in the
ideal type the elements are related to each other in a particular
combination. Traditionalism[1] exists only in so far as, if economic
rationality is maximized, the fixity of the standard of living is
also maximized at the same time. The *relations* between the
values of the analytical elements which are important to the
formulation of the type are always the same whatever may
be their particular values and those of other elements. Ideal-
type analysis provides no means of breaking down the rigidity
of these fixed relations.[2]

There would be no objection to this were it true that in fact
the relations in question always subsisted in concrete reality,
but this is not necessarily so. This is vividly brought out by comparison with the case from Marshall already discussed, of wants
adjusted to activities. There the property of economic rationality

---

[1] It should be noted that Weber also uses this term in a much broader
sense. For a discussion of it, see next chapter.

[2] Whether or not it should be broken down is a question of scientific con-
venience, of fact. If the combination is best treated as a unit, ignoring the
possibility of independent variation of its elements, the type concept may
also serve as an element. It may, on the other hand, be convenient to break
it down.

is maximized, but its maximization is not combined with fixity in the standard of living, of wants; on the contrary, it is correlated with a progressively rising standard of living. Thus Marshall's free enterprise is characterized by another action type in which the maximization of economic rationality is combined with that of the activities discussed at length above, one aspect of which is an increasing want scale.

There is no difference whatever in the element of economic rationality in the two types of action; the difference between the types is a matter of the way in which this element is related to others, in these examples to elements of the ultimate value complex. This fact is of fundamental methodological significance. The formulation of class concepts, including ideal types in Weber's sense, is an indispensable procedure. But it is not usually possible for scientific analysis to stop there. To do so would result in a type atomism—each type concept would be a unit of analysis by itself. But in reality these units are systematically related to one another. This is true because they are formulated in terms of combinations of relations between the values of a more limited number of properties, each property being predicable of a number of different type concepts.

Above all, the values of the general elements concerned are not always combined in the particular way that any one type concept involves; they are independently variable over a wider range. This has just been demonstrated for one case. Maximization of economic rationality is not rigidly bound to fixity of wants but is doubtless in various ways empirically compatible with their flexibility also. To employ only the type concept in analysis is to obscure these possibilities of independent variation.

Furthermore, such a use of the type concept is a violation of the basic methodological canon of scientific economy. For on the type basis it is necessary to have a separate general concept for every possible combination of relations between the values of the relevant elements, while in terms of an element analysis it is possible to derive all these types from a much more limited number of element concepts.

Indeed, it is impossible to work out a systematic classification of ideal types without developing at the same time, at least implicitly, a more general theoretical system. For the relations between the types in the classification can only be stated by employing the categories that comprise such a generalized system. Thus, by virtue of the fact that maximization of economic rationality is common to them, traditionalism and free enterprise belong, for certain purposes, in the same class.

But this more generalized theoretical systematization involves, as has been seen, two different kinds of possible conceptualization. The one with which this study has been mainly concerned is a generalized system of structural categories applicable to any system of social action. The other is a system of variables. Even ideal types in Weber's sense may sometimes be treated as variable elements, since they are genuine universals. The same is true of the structural categories with which this discussion has been occupied. But elements need not be identifiable with either of these—for instance, Pareto's category of residues is not.

An ideal type, as Weber uses the term, is always a generalized unit of a social system. But it is usually of a more specific and concrete character than any of the categories of our generalized system of structure. For example, a rational unit act might be more likely to be treated by Weber as an ideal type than the unit act as such. But the unit act in this sense *may* be an ideal type. The same is not, however, true of certain other structural categories. These describe modes of relation of the units and their elements in complex systems of action and are not even conceivable as independently existing apart from the other structural elements. They constitute what may be called structural aspects of concrete systems, and the properties of the systems dependent on them are emergent properties. In common with the element that is a universal of predication short of adequate description of a unit, these have the fact that they cannot be conceived as corresponding to a class of objectively possible entities. The economic sector of the intrinsic means-end chain is such a structural aspect.

Before leaving this phase of the discussion, it may be remarked that the employment of ideal-type concepts in place of more general analytical concepts, with the rigidity of combinations of relations between the values of the latter which this entails, is one of the principal sources of bias in empirical interpretation. Two conspicuous examples may be mentioned. In the first place, Marshall was right in interpreting increasing economic rationality as an inherent tendency of human action. But he failed to see that this trend need not lead to free enterprise; it is not in the least incompatible, for instance, with an Indian caste system. The latter may well differ from free enterprise in the scope of considerations brought within the range of economic calculation, but not necessarily in the degree to which the typical individual attains a norm of economic rationality within the scope of its application to him at all.[1] What Marshall does is to relate the value of economic rationality to the whole complex of other elements which he sums up as the progressive development of character. This is the ultimate logical basis of his linear evolutionism, culminating in free enterprise, and it is responsible for his view of the inevitability of the latter. The result is an empirical error of the first magnitude.

A somewhat different situation is to be found in another school of economic theory of which the views of Professor Robbins[2] furnish a convenient example. There the professed aim is to construct an abstract science of economics. But by merely refusing to discuss them, it is not possible to evade the questions of the relations of the elements formulated in economic theory to the other elements of a system of action. Ignoring these relations altogether amounts to the implicit assumption that they are random relative to the economic. With reference to ultimate ends this consequence puts Professor Robbins squarely in the utilitarian position. Since the problem of order in the Hobbesian sense is not faced, there enters the further implicit assumption of a natural identity of interests. The result is a profound laissez-faire bias which appears conspicuously in Professor Robbins' other works.[3]

To sum up: The factor which the schema of proof requires to be eliminated or altered is always a set of concrete facts descriptive of concrete historical individuals. The concrete historical

---

[1] For instance, for Westerners choice of occupation is included within that scope. In India, so far as castes have a hereditary occupation, it is necessarily excluded. In one sense, but not the present one, this is ground for attributing greater economic rationality to Westerners.

[2] L. ROBBINS, *op. cit.* See also Talcott Parsons, "Some Reflections on 'The Nature and Significance of Economics,'" *Quarterly Journal of Economics*, May, 1934.

[3] *Cf.* L. ROBBINS, *The Great Depression.* Here the thesis is maintained that the depression is entirely due to arbitrary outside interference with the working of the competitive system.

individual is thought of as capable of analysis into different concrete elements in such a way that it is possible to think of one of them as altered in value independently of the others.

But for this procedure to lead to proof of causal relationship, it must be possible to subsume these facts under general concepts. It is there that the difficulty arises. These general elements are not all of one kind; three kinds are possible. Weber's ideal type belongs to one: it is a hypothetically concrete unit or part of the historical individual in question, the combination of general features of which is shared with an indefinite plurality of other concrete historical individuals.

This is an abstraction like any class concept because it is a logical universal, not a particular. It is also abstract because it is an ideal type, not an average or a bundle of common traits. The other kinds of concept are on a more generalized analytical plane. They need not be units at all. The corresponding particulars may describe a concrete separate entity but may also be limited to the predication of a single property to one or more such entities, or designate a structural aspect of a system. Such concepts also are abstract in the sense of being universals, but not in the same sense as the ideal type.

All concrete phenomena, including the particulars corresponding to ideal types, are capable of description only in terms of a specific combination of the values of analytical elements. The ideal type, being a universal, does not involve a combination of specific values, but it does involve a fixed set of relations between the values of the analytical elements. These elements are, however, often independently variable beyond the range permitted by the definition of the types. Hence confining general conceptualization to ideal types introduces an element of rigidity that may issue in a methodological atomism. In so far as these types are reified the result is either a "mosaic" theory of history, or a rigid evolutionary scheme.[1] On this basis the only defense against both implications is to insist on the fictional character of the type concepts.[2]

The meaning of the general laws under which the factors are to be subsumed may be different in the different cases. Ideal-type

---

[1] Weber leaned to the former alternative, however, with an evolutionary element present in his process of rationalization.

[2] This does not really help, as it involves equally serious difficulties.

elements may, as units, be supposed to have typical modes of behavior under given circumstances. In this case the laws in question are generalizations about these modes of behavior. They are "empirical generalizations" in the sense of the previous discussion,[1] qualified only by the element of fictional abstraction inherent in the ideal-type concept. They are not general statements of what actually happens, but of what would happen were the actual facts in complete conformity with the ideal type. Thus, in an example Weber cites, Gresham's law is a generalization about the concrete behavior of men relative to two monetary elements of differing value.[2] In this case the actual course of events generally conforms closely to the law, a proof of the empirical importance of economic rationality since the law is formulated on the assumption of its maximization.

An analytical law, on the other hand, states a uniform mode of relationship between the values of two or more analytical elements. It is thus likely to be applicable beyond the range of any one ideal type.[3] At the same time the kind of generalization about the behavior of the ideal-type units just discussed cannot usually be arrived at by the application of any one analytical law, but only by the application of the combination of several.

The principal exception to this statement is that where there exist what have been called ideal experimental conditions. These are present when a given change in the concrete phenomena in question can be attributed to variation in the value of the one element or the small group of elements explicitly under consideration at the time. This is true only when the values of all others concretely relevant can be treated as constants throughout the process being studied, or when their values remain within a certain limited range. Thus the law of falling bodies applies without qualification when air resistance or friction is constant at zero.

The fundamental distinctions which the foregoing discussion has attempted to clarify have nothing to do with that between the natural and the social sciences. They belong to the strict logic of empirical science in general in which, as it has already been maintained, the two groups of sciences do not differ at all.

[1] *Supra*, p. 33.
[2] "The overvalued currency will disappear from circulation."
[3] Whenever the elements are not identical with the types.

Weber's failure to clarify the distinctions and their consequences for general theory and its empirical application seems to have been largely due to the rigidity of the methodological line that he attempted to draw between the two groups. It is in the natural sciences that generalized theory in the present sense has been most highly developed in the past, and his rigid separation prevented him from making the fullest possible use of the methodological achievements in that field. In this respect Pareto had a distinct advantage over Weber.

In these fundamental *logical* respects there is no difference between the physical and the social sciences. They differ as far as seems relevant to the present study in only three respects, none of them logical, all substantive. (1) The elements, both structural and variable, differ from each other in specific character, and hence the laws do also. To speak of an act as having mass is as meaningless as to speak of a star as rational. Indeed a theoretical system in the analytical sense may be defined as a unit when it involves such a body of interrelated elements as, with their relations, cannot be expressed in terms of another set, and refers to a concrete system of the corresponding generalized structure. (2) They differ in the character of empirical evidence for their application. The subjective point of view is a source of evidence for the one but not for the other. It makes possible a set of definable operations. (3) They differ in the degree of organicism of the concrete historical individuals with which they have to deal.[1] Even this, however, is more a matter of adequacy in relation to a concrete aim of knowledge than of intrinsic difference.[2]

A concrete, even a hypothetically concrete act or complex of action, may involve *all* the elements of action.[3] This is why the analytical sciences cut across the historical sciences as noted above. But another point should be emphasized. Any concrete type of act may involve all the elements of action, but in a speci-

---

[1] That is, in the possibility of isolating concrete type elements from their context without doing violence to their essential properties. *Cf.* Aristotle on the sense in which a hand separated from the living body is a hand only in an equivocal sense.

[2] See final chapter.

[3] Qualified by the distinction between elementary and emergent properties. The unit act involves only the former. See Chap. XIX, p. 738 *ff.*

fic combination of relations of their values. But precisely in so far
as the values of these elements can vary independently of each
other—and there is no other reason for distinguishing them as
elements—this independent variation is inhibited by the particular combination involved in the type.

The key to the overcoming of the rigidity, involved in the
"ties" of ideal-type theory, is given in the statement that
several elements of action are involved in every concrete act
on the one hand, that they may vary independently of each
other on the other. Variation in this context has a specific meaning. A complete scientific theory is not attained until all possible
concrete types of a class of historical individuals (or concretely
thinkable type-parts[1] of them) can be thought of as exemplifying
different combinations according to laws, of the same analytical
and structural elements. Independent variation here means that
the value of one element can change while the values of the others
do not in the same way and proportion.[2] The only road, then,
to the development of generalized theory on either plane is the
comparative study of different actions and complexes of action,
differing in respect to their observable properties. By a sufficiently
long and laborious process of such comparison, taking cases
similar in some respects, differing in others, it is possible to
formulate the variable elements. In the case of activities versus
traditionalism, it is clear that the rational allocation of means
to ends is a property *common* to the two cases, while the specific
character of the ends is not. Once such an element is formulated
it is possible to construct the concrete results of its operation in
various possible combinations with others.

Adequacy of Explanation

With this reference to construction, the discussion comes back
to Weber's treatment of "adequate explanation" with its bearing on the relation of empirical generalization to analytical law.
The thesis may be advanced (1) that the degree to which it is

[1] In the sense in which professional priesthood was an element of Greek
society.

[2] The variables in a system are in functional relations to each other. Hence
a change in one will have repercussions on the others defined by the laws of
the system. But they are not simply "tied" to each other. They are both
independent and interdependent.

necessary to push forward from empirical generalization to analytical law in order to attain adequate explanation is relative to the given empirical problem, and (2) that if it is necessary the "empirical abstraction" of Weber's ideal types is a necessary stage[1] in the process of attaining a definition of the elements, both analytical and structural, of a generalized system.

To revert to an example employed above:[2] A housewife boils a potato only fifteen minutes and then serves it to her husband. He declares it is hard and adds, "It was not cooked long enough." This is a perfectly adequate causal imputation for the purpose. His interest in the potato is only in its relative hardness or softness in relation to palatability. It is "generally known" that to make a potato soft it must be boiled about forty-five minutes. The point is that for this purpose it is not necessary to know the explanation of the complex chemical changes which go on within a potato in the process of being boiled, or the laws these follow. The one law is quite sufficient to make the explanation valid and adequate. It can be verified. Similarly in the field of action an inquirer may be told that the quickest way to get from Harvard Square in Cambridge to the South Station in Boston is to take the subway. All the elements of this statement can be verified in terms of generally known laws about everyday experience (to Bostonians). Without such general laws, indeed, all rational action itself would be unthinkable. Moreover, they are strictly comparable to scientific laws, are indeed themselves entirely adequate scientific laws *for the purposes for which they are used*.

From this pole of common sense there is a very gradual transition to such conceptions at the other end of the scale as the second law of thermodynamics. The transition is a matter of (1) the increasing complexity of the data which must be taken into account in arriving at a judgment of adequate explanation, (2) of the extent to which the hypothetical constructions involved in arriving at such a judgment transcend common sense and what is generally known and become judgments of probability involving highly technical formulations of elements, and rigorous deduction of the involved logical consequences of certain facts. In arriving at concrete judgments of probability the point is

[1] Where the subject matter is markedly organic in the above sense.
[2] Footnote, p. 65.

soon reached where the elements of a problem are so many that concrete certainty is impossible.

As the complexity of problems increases in this way explicit conceptual aid becomes necessary. First the number of possible data is so great, and the question of their relevance so difficult that it is necessary deliberately to construct a historical individual, which becomes the thing to be explained. Second, in describing it we must be able to refer parts of it to type concepts of a range of applicability beyond the particular case. Thus in describing modern capitalism, Weber uses the concept of bureaucracy. Finally, in our judgments of objective possibility we must attempt to formulate typical lines of development for these elements. All these three kinds of ideal-typical construction are prominent in Weber's work, and entirely proper and necessary.

But this cannot be all. If it is, the unfortunate result is to hold all explanatory concepts to be mere fictions which, since they are not empirically true, do not explain anything. Then against this skepticism and the fact that it fails to do justice to the actual situation, comes the reaction, their hypostatization, with the resulting "mosaic" theory of concrete society. This is due to the rigidity of the "ties" which bind the elements of action together, in specific combinations, in the ideal types. History then becomes a process of shuffling ideal types, as *units*. It comes to be held that instead of being a useful fiction the ideal type exists as a constant concrete unit through a long process. The only means of breaking this mosaic rigidity without recourse to skepticism is generalized theory which breaks down the particular element combinations in the ideal types, but by seeing in them a manifestation of common elements in constant modes of relationship with each other, transfers knowledge to a more flexible, yet at the same time more realistic basis.

It has already been noted that Weber did not really confine himself to ideal-type theory. Indeed he could not without leaving his types entirely unrelated to each other. The attempt, which constitutes the principal theoretical aspect of his work, to construct a systematic classification of ideal types, really involved him by implication in generalized analytical theory. His sociological theory is neither the one nor the other but a mixture of both.

The reasons for this mixture should be clear. General concepts were for Weber, methodologically, a residual category—because his polemical animus was against those who would deny their role altogether. Of possible general concepts there are the three main categories, hypothetical concrete types, generalized structural categories and variable elements.[1] The first may be types either of action or of relationship. Given Weber's *Historismus,* his strong sense of the individuality of cultures and culture phenomena,[2] it is not surprising that he concentrated on relationships. Hence one body of systematic theory, the most conspicuous in his work, is a classification of possible types of social relationship. It is probably the most complete and systematic in the literature, and an indispensable aid to concrete research. But the main interest of this study is not in it but rather in the generalized account of systems of action which is, for the most part implicitly, interwoven with it and, as would be expected, to a large extent forms its logical foundation.

The present discussion of the logical nature of general theory has become involved in some difficult questions. No claim is advanced that they have been all cleared up—very far from it. Nor is it proposed in this study even to attempt to push them farther. The justification of this lies in the general starting point of the study. The procedure throughout has been one of cautious advance from well-known and clearly formulable "islands" of theoretical knowledge—above all the conception of science in its relation to the rationality of action—bit by bit into the unknown. The guiding principles have been two: never to refuse to face unsolved methodological problems (on such a plea as that they are metaphysical) if their solution promised to be important to the study, and never to go farther than necessary. The conclusion cannot be evaded that the scheme of the structural elements of action, which has formed the principal subject matter of this study, makes logical sense *only* when it is conceived of as the framework in one aspect of a generalized system of theory. Hence it has been necessary to go into the method-

---

[1] Which may, in specific content, overlap.

[2] As distinct from the anhistorical classical economists, for instance. He does this because it is in the aspect of structure rather than function that concrete individuality is most prominent. Social relationship is above all a structural category.

ological status of general theory far enough to establish what relation it holds to empirical causal explanation and to the other types of theoretical concept relevant in this same context. For present purposes it is not necessary to go further than this. Before turning to the outline of Weber's scheme of the structure of action systems, however, it will be helpful to remark on a few special points in order to prevent misunderstandings and to point certain directions of analysis.

In the first place, the discussion may revert to the schema of causal imputation. It will be remembered that among the indispensable requirements of that schema were cited (1) the analysis of a historical individual into elements each of which could be subsumed under a general law and (2) knowledge of such laws. The upshot of the foregoing analysis is to force the recognition that the concepts element and law really conceal different things, which need to be distinguished. There are, on the one hand, type-units—such as bureaucracy, priesthood, handicraft, etc. On the other hand, there are generalized theoretical categories such as rationality of action. Correspondingly, the laws may be empirical generalizations, which are judgments of the probable behavior under certain given circumstances of these concrete type elements, or they may be analytical laws which are statements of the general modes of interrelation of the values of the analytical elements, independently of the particular values of the latter.

It is perfectly possible for adequate judgments of causal imputation to be arrived at in terms of concrete type-units and empirical generalizations alone. The decisive question is whether, as in most common-sense judgments, our empirical knowledge of the behavior of the type-units under the relevant circumstances is adequate to the scientific interest in question. This is so not only in everyday life, but in a very large number of cases of historical imputation. As the cases become more complex, however, it is necessary to resort to more and more sharp and explicit formulation of these types—as ideal types— and to explicit construction of lines of their development. Finally, when this does not alone serve the needs of adequacy the resort to more generalized concepts and laws becomes necessary. This does not, however, compel one to dispense with the other kind of concept. They are often indispensable preparatory measures in terms of which to formulate clearly and accurately the points of articulation between the generalized theoretical system and the concrete reality. In turn, however, analytical theory naturally serves as a most important check on the formulations of general empirical type concepts. And for concrete causal imputation these analytically corrected empirical concepts must be reemployed.

Closely related to the question of adequacy in causal imputation is the role of another important methodological concept of Weber's to which brief mention should be given, that of probability (*Chance*). When it is necessary to make a very complex judgment of causal imputation, as in the relation of the Protestant ethic to modern capitalism, the historical individual concerned must be analyzed into a larger number of type-units.[1] Each of these must be subjected to judgments of probability as to its line of development under the relevant circumstances. These judgments rest on construction. Hence the predictability of a hypothetical objectively possible concrete state is naturally subject to error, in the case of the construction of each element, to say nothing of the totality of elements.[2] Hence objective empirical certainty is out of the question; the judgment can be only one of probability. In this sense Weber speaks of adequacy when the great majority of the causally relevant type-units that *might* have influenced a given historical individual are favorable to the particular thesis. When this is the situation those few which are not favorable may be regarded as in this sense contingent[3] and may be disregarded.

---

[1] Bureaucracy, rational law, state, science, etc.

[2] Of course positive construction (that of the total concrete situation) is by no means always necessary. A negative construction of the *difference* made by a change in the element in question is often enough. See *Wissenschaftslehre*, p. 286; von Schelting, *op. cit.*, p. 267.

[3] *Zufällig.* See *Wissenschaftslehre*, p. 286; von Schelting, *op. cit.*, pp. 312 *ff.* This formulation of Weber's clearly shows the embarrassment growing out of the imperfect development of his analytical theory. It rests on the assumption of an equal causal value of all the elements thus formulated. In the absence of any positive criterion of importance this is safer than any other assumption. But it is unsatisfactory. Such positive criteria may in fact be derived from analytical theory. Thus economic theory tells us beyond doubt that under present conditions the decisions of those in control of central banking policy are more important to the functioning of the economic order than are those of a group of businessmen whose operations are purely local. Both are elements in Weber's sense.

Thus in the case of modern capitalism, the positive relations between the Protestant ethic and the spirit of capitalism were established, as were the negative relations of the latter to other religious ethics. The construction of the influence of the Protestant ethic, backed up on the way by evidence of intermediate stages, corresponded to the observed facts. Then comes the application of the category of objective possibility. This Weber does in the case in point mainly by the aid of analogies.[1] The thinking away of the Protestant-ethic factor is done by analyzing situations where it does not exist.[2] This involves a judgment on the probability that the remaining constellation of factors (the material factors) would be on the whole not much less favorable to the historical individual in question (modern Western capitalism) in the analogical cases, especially China and India, than it was in the West. Weber's judgment of probability that it was not markedly less favorable, confirms his historical imputation of an important positive role to the Protestant ethic.

"Probability" here means only an expression of our failure to attain completely accurate empirical knowledge. "Contingency" of a factor is not to be confused with absolute chance in the sense of the mathematical theory of probability.[3] It is entirely relative to the concrete problem in hand.

This concept of probability[4] Weber carries over into the definitions of his type concepts. Thus in *Wirtschaft und Gesellschaft* he defines most of them as a "social relationship in so far as there is a probability that . . . " a certain abstractly defined norm of behavior or relationship will be adhered to. This is a consequence of the peculiar kind of abstraction involved in the ideal-type concept. For, on the one hand, it is descriptive in the sense that it states a hypothetical concrete unit or part; on the other hand, it is abstract or unreal in that this unit does not, in its

[1] Point 10 of Dr. von Schelting's list. *Op. cit.*, p. 262.

[2] That is, where the type-form economic ethic of religion has a different factual content.

[3] *Wissenschaftslehre*, p. 204.

[4] It seems to me that Professor Abel (*Systematic Sociology in Germany*, Chap. IV) distinctly exaggerates the importance of this concept of probability in regarding it as Weber's *principal* contribution to the methodology of the social sciences. He thereby gives Weber's position a positivistic twist which is distinctly misleading and accentuates the fictional character of his concepts.

theoretical purity, really exist. The gap between it and the facts is bridged by the concept of probability. It is a measure of the fact that such concepts are always *empirically* lacking in precision and protects Weber against the danger of reification. On the other hand, it is to be noted that analytical concepts, in their strict theoretical formulation, do not require this qualification; they are not fictional in the same sense.

At this point a few words should be said about the application of the foregoing analysis to Weber's treatment of capitalism. Weber's failure to recognize explicitly the role of a generalized theoretical system is responsible for a certain atomism in this treatment. The most important point at which this is evident is in the rigidity of the separation, as *concrete* type-units, between rational bourgeois capitalism, on the one hand, adventurers' capitalism, on the other. Weber's distinction is undoubtedly the result of entirely sound insight and, above all by contrast with the complete reification of the latter element in most Anglo-American criticisms of Weber,[1] of the greatest usefulness in understanding the problems he raised.

Yet there is almost certainly a more intimate fusion of the two in concrete fact than Weber's conceptual scheme recognizes. And this fusion could be better accounted for if, instead of concrete *types* of capitalism, the distinction were made in terms of the relative values of the different elements of action in concrete capitalistic activities. Thus in adventurers' capitalism the element of *Zweckrationalität* has a high value relative to that of disinterested moral obligation,[2] while in the main in rational bourgeois capitalism the reverse is true. The essential point is that modern capitalism is one socioeconomic system, not two. Unfortunately it is not possible to discuss the question further here. It may, however, again be emphasized that this criticism does not touch the main empirical thesis of Weber's theory, the role in the modern economic order of the disinterested ascetic sense of moral obligation to an impersonal task.

Essentially the same considerations give a certain element of justification to Professor Sorokin's methodological criticism of Weber's general sociology of religion. Its substance is as fol-

---

[1] *Cf.* Robertson's economic individualism.

[2] This distinction of elements is formulated *ad hoc* for the immediate purpose. It is not a final one. Weber's concept of *Zweckrationalität* is discussed in the next chapter.

lows:[1] The economic ethic of a religion is a concrete phenomenon (in ideal-typical formulation). The religious factor in the genesis of it is only one of several possible ones—there will also, for instance, be economic influences. Hence the effects of the economic ethic on concrete economic life are not exclusively the product of religion. From this Professor Sorokin concludes:[2] "Weber's analysis does not show even tentatively what the share of the religious factor is in molding the *Wirtschaftsethik* and correspondingly, its share in conditioning the effects of the latter in the field of economic phenomena. Thus, after Weber's work we are as ignorant about the degree of efficiency of the religious factor as we were before."

The substance of the methodological point is correct—as Weber himself fully recognized. This does not, however, justify the conclusions. In the first place, on the level of analysis by means of concrete type-units Weber certainly accomplished a great deal.[3] Suffice it to say that Weber has immensely clarified the question of the kind of influence on concrete economic life it may reasonably be expected that religion will have; this question is clarified particularly with respect to his doctrine of religious interests and their relation to ideas. This is a necessary preliminary to any sort of general theory of the influence of a religious factor. Secondly, in the only case for which he claimed it (the case of the influence of Protestanism on capitalism) Weber has arrived at a judgment of historical imputation with a high degree of adequacy which is in no way shaken by the criticism. It is not a judgment of exact quantitative importance in percentage terms—such a judgment would be absurd. It does, however, say a great deal about the degree of efficiency of this factor— that without it the historical development would certainly have been radically different.

In fact, in making this a criticism Professor Sorokin measures Weber's work by a standard inapplicable to it. In principle it is impossible, except in a limiting case, for any concrete phenomenon to be explicable in terms of the empirical laws governing any one concrete type-unit such as the Protestant ethic. It is in principle

---

[1] P. A. SOROKIN, *Contemporary Sociological Theories*, pp. 690–691.

[2] *Ibid.*, p. 691.

[3] It has been summarized at the end of Chap. XV and need not be repeated here.

impossible by Weber's method to assess its exact quantitative importance. Weber was fully aware of this logical situation and met it by judgments of adequacy, of imputation in terms of probability. On this level no other procedure is possible. It would, however, be possible on an analytical level to remedy some of these defects and hence arrive at a more accurate judgment. This would take the form of analyzing Weber's hypothetically concrete religious and economic factor-types in terms of their elements, and applying the results of this analysis. There is no space here to go into this further, though certain suggestions will be given in the next chapter.

It is interesting to point out one aspect of the question of why Weber did not bring analytical concepts and their role explicitly into his range of methodological self-consciousness. The primary explanation is that his approach to the question of the role of general concepts was that of their vindication against a radical empiricist attack, and that his attention focused so nearly exclusively on this issue that they remained for him a residual category, not adequately analyzed. Closely related to this is the circumstance that his mistaken contrast of the role of general concepts in the natural and the social sciences led him to lay the principal stress in connection with the latter on those concepts which were fictional constructions. This was, in turn, closely related to the importance, in his approach, of scientific knowledge as a means of practical action—and hence a strong feeling against pushing abstraction too far.[1]

But his failure self-consciously to develop a generalized theoretical system was not entirely due to an unwillingness to go to impractical extremes of abstraction. On the contrary, there is, in connection with his conception of the role of individuality in the social sciences, a definite misconception of certain aspects of the question of abstraction. That is, he held, in Dr. von Schelting's formulation, that[2] "Generalizing knowledge of historical-cultural reality cannot seek *without limit* for more and more general concepts and laws. For it cannot except in a relatively limited degree allow the 'de-individualization' and 'atomization' of concretely qualitative reality which that involves." That

---

[1] See VON SCHELTING, *op. cit.*, Section I. Weber's ethical position was what he called *Verantwortungsethik*.

[2] VON SCHELTING, *op. cit.*, p. 339.

is, the interest in individuality implied in *Wertbeziehung* and the generality of laws and elements are logically incompatible if generalization is pushed too far.

This appears to be a misconception based on a failure to distinguish the different levels of generalization. It arises from thinking of general concepts as always *type*[1] concepts. It is true that the broader these are—that is, the more individual cases they can include—the more abstract and empty they become.[2] Hence pushing generalization indefinitely in this direction would lead to more and more abstract concepts that are out of touch with the concrete individuality of real phenomena. This would be atomization.

But this argument fails to note that both of the other types of general concepts do not necessarily constitute simply a farther step in abstraction beyond the type-part concept in the same direction, but that they are abstract in a different sense. In this, the direction of a general system of elements into which concrete phenomena are broken up, abstraction is on a different level —the elements need not be parts. Moreover, when given concrete phenomena are seen from a specific focus of attention there is a definite limit to the extent to which analytical abstraction can be pushed without doing violence to the phenomena. That is, according to our focus of attention, our interest will be in the aspects of a concrete phenomenon relevant to a given theoretical *system*.[3] In the case of motivated human action this is the system which has concerned this study, that of the "theory of action." Dr. von Schelting has hit upon this fact without, apparently, fully appreciating its significance when he notes that the limit to generalizing abstraction in the social sciences is set by the postulate of *Verstehen*.[4] Without the subjective point of view

---

[1] The term type itself suggests the hypothetically concrete, not the analytical element.

[2] VON SCHELTING, *op. cit.*, p. 241.

[3] Or, stated a little differently, the unit subdivision of concrete phenomena is limited by the frame of reference. Unit analysis beyond the point where the unit can as a concrete entity be located in terms of the frame of reference is meaningless for purposes of the theory in question. In the action frame of reference it is an element (means, end, condition, norm) of a unit act which is the ultimate meaningful unit. It may be further subdivided into atoms and the like, but these are not, as such, units of an action system.

[4] VON SCHELTING, *op. cit.*, p. 342.

the theory of action becomes meaningless. The ununderstandable may be analyzed in terms of (one or more) other systems of categories, but not of *this* system.

Failure to see this involves an empiricist-monistic fallacy—that there "is" a single system of ultimate elements of concrete reality which would be reached by pushing abstraction far enough, and which somehow is held to express its ultimate reality. In this argument of Weber's, the reification which he seemed to have exorcised so thoroughly comes creeping back by an inconspicuous back door. His failure to bring the role of a general theoretical system clearly into the limelight of methodology is really a failure completely to overcome the empiricist fallacy. Once this is done, however, there need be no fear of analytical abstraction on the score of its incompatibility with the concept of individuality. For the inherent nature of the frame of reference of a theoretical system sets a limit to the extent of abstraction which is possible or in any way admissible within the range of any given type of focus of interest. The structure of such systems is most intimately related to *Wertbeziehung.*

ACTION AND COMPLEXES OF MEANING

Dr. von Schelting in the final section of his book[1] analyzes another limit to Weber's own methodological self-interpretation which calls for brief comment here because of its relevance to certain points that will be taken up in the next chapter. It concerns the concept of *Verstehen* which as he says, was essentially unproblematical to Weber. It was a basic postulate of the social sciences and that was all.

Weber dealt with it almost entirely in the context of the causal analysis of action. Hence to him it meant essentially the accessibility of the subjective aspect of other people's action as a real process in time. The object of this *Verstehen* is to uncover motivations.

Weber did, to be sure, attempt in a few places to make a distinction between two kinds of *Verstehen.* The most notable is the distinction[2] between *aktuelles* and *motivationsmässiges Verstehen.* When he brings in the understanding of the meaning

[1] *Ibid.,* pp. 353 *ff.*
[2] *Wissenschaftslehre,* pp. 504 *ff.*

of a mathematical proposition (2 × 2 = 4) under the first heading it would seem that he had reference to an atemporal world of meanings in abstraction from concrete motivations. But this line of distinction is quickly lost again when Weber includes under the same category understanding of "what he is doing" when we see a man chopping wood. The latter case certainly involves elements of concrete motivation—it is impossible to interpret the movements observed without reference to an end to which they are related as means.

In fact analysis of this distinction shows that Weber apparently conceived it as a pragmatic one. We understand things *aktuell* in so far as, in terms of ordinary everyday experience, they are evident through the mere fact of being observed. Just as to one with a grammar school knowledge of arithmetic the meaning of the symbol combination 2 × 2 = 4 is evident, so is it evident when we see a man wielding an object that we call an ax in a certain way that he is chopping wood. On the other hand, it is not evident from these immediate facts either why the proposition 2 × 2 = 4 was enunciated at that time and place (whether it was a school demonstration, a figuring of accounts or something else) or why the man was chopping wood (for exercise or to earn a living). *Motivationsmässiges Verstehen* is understanding of the elements of motivation that are not evident in the particular concrete observation but remain problematical.

Thus Weber just missed the important distinction. It is between motivation considered as a real process in time and atemporal complexes of meanings as such (*irreale Sinngebilde*). As Dr. von Schelting shows, Rickert held *only* the latter to be capable of *Verstehen*. But without going to his extreme the distinction is none the less vital and Dr. von Schelting has done a great service in emphasizing it.

This distinction may be restated in a form that will bring out more vividly its relations to the problems of this study. Concrete motivation involves an intrinsic relation between the meaningful elements and the others in the action complex. One meaning system involved in rational action is scientifically valid knowledge which expresses at least hypothetical intrinsic relations between end, means and conditions. In motivation, considered as a real process in time, meanings cannot be divorced from intrinsic relationships of this, or an analogous character.

On the other hand, the real things or events that may be observed may be significant *only* as symbols with no intrinsic significance of their concrete properties. In this case *Verstehen* is necessarily limited to the meanings of the symbols as such without reference to any intrinsic relationships in the real world.

These two are polar types and in concrete reality naturally shade off into one another. But the distinction is analytically important. Complexes of meanings as such are significant for the analysis of action mainly at two points. Dr. von Schelting clearly shows that understanding of them in abstraction from motivation plays an important part in Weber's own empirical research at both points.

Attention has already been called to the way in which Weber's work necessitated the ideal-typical formulation of systems of ideas which are relevant to concrete motivation, those of Calvinist theology, Brahmanic philosophy, etc. These are systems of interrelated propositions, and must be understood as such. Only when they have been so understood can their relation to concrete motivation in the form of the canalization of religious interests be understood, in turn.

Secondly, a subtler point, to a certain degree Weber also treated complexes of concrete actions as such as meaningful systems. That is, concrete acts are not treated as intrinsically significant in a means-end context but as symbolic of a system of meanings. No attempt will be made to go into examples here. Its connection with the role of symbolism in Durkheim's later work is, however, evident. In the next chapter certain relations of this type of symbolic expression to a system of the structural elements of action will be shown. Here it was only necessary to note its point of articulation with the general methodological basis of the study.

Two consequences may be suggested of the solidarity of science and action which Weber's methodological work has done so much to clarify on the scientific side. The first involves the problem of the relativity of scientific knowledge, arising from the principle of *Wertbeziehung*. This relativity cannot be pushed to an extreme which would involve dispensing with the formal schema of logical, objective proof. This is the nonrelative point of reference which is needed to bring order into the mass of relative specific propositions that constitute concrete scientific knowledge.

Now does not the solidarity of scientific knowledge with rational action imply the existence of a formal schema of elements of action which is in a similar sense exempt from the relativity of concrete knowledge? This seems to be a legitimate interpretation of the passage from Weber placed at the head of this study.[1] At least the main formal outline of the means-end schema is *inseparable* from the conception of action. Relativity can only apply to the specific modes of its application and framework of values, etc., not to the formal scheme itself, so long as the conceptual scheme of action is employed at all.

Secondly, Weber laid very great stress on the freedom of science from value judgments, a position that has been violently attacked. It seems to the present author Weber was entirely right. The fundamental logical distinction between value judgments and judgments of objective fact is basic both to science and to the theory of action. Without it science cannot be distinguished from the manifestation of sentiments nor can the rationality of means-end relationships be established. But the solidarity of science and action here goes even farther. Schematically stated, on a positivistic basis which, as has been shown, eliminates the normative aspect of action, such a distinction is impossible, for all meaningful judgments become scientific. On an idealistic basis, on the other hand, the distinction is equally eliminated—all judgments become those of value. Of the three systems considered here, only a voluntaristic theory of action can make the distinction significant—but also necessary.

Like the above treatment of his theory of capitalism and sociology of religion, this discussion of Weber's methodology has done scant justice to the manifold problems raised by his thought. It has, however, brought out certain basically important points for present purposes. Above all Weber, almost alone in Germany, came near to completely overcoming the predominant idealistic empiricism in the social sciences. He definitely succeeded in vindicating the logical necessity of general concepts for valid empirical knowledge. Beside this great achievement even his failure to appreciate the role of a generalized system of theory

[1] *Wissenschaftslehre*, p. 179.

is a minor matter. And his critical reaction against idealism finally led him in a direction which is of basic importance here—toward a voluntaristic theory of action. With the development of the outline of its structural aspect in the next chapter the main task of this study will be complete. The process of convergence will have been demonstrated.

Chapter XVII

MAX WEBER, IV: SYSTEMATIC THEORY

Chapter XVI has shown that Weber's central methodological concern was to vindicate the necessity for general theoretical concepts in the sociohistorical sciences. But the only kind of general concept for which he provided an explicit methodological clarification was his general ideal type. This, it has been shown, is a hypothetically concrete type which could serve as a unit of a system of action or social relationships. But it was not, on a methodological plane, explicitly related to a generalized theoretical system in either of its two main aspects, as a structural outline of systems of action or as a system of elements. Weber did, however, attempt to build up a systematic classification of ideal types[1] starting from a conception of action closely similar to that dealt with throughout this study. It is a reasonable hypothesis that in so far as these types are empirically verified and their classification is logically coherent, the general framework of concepts underlying the classification should be closely related to a generalized theoretical system, even though its methodological status as such is not explicitly worked out. It will be the task of the present chapter to test this hypothesis by systematically analyzing the logical framework of Weber's classification with the general scheme of the structure of systems of action, which has already been developed, in mind.

The Types of Social Action

Weber's logical starting point is the concept of action: "We shall call 'action' (*Handeln*) any human attitude or activity (*Verhalten*) (no matter whether involving external or internal

---

[1] The system is all to be found in Part I of *Wirtschaft und Gesellschaft*. To appreciate its significance, however, it is necessary not only to read the abstract formulations but to see them in the context of both his methodological and his empirical work. Of the latter there is a vast mass in the other parts of *Wirtschaft und Gesellschaft* as well as in *Gesammelte Aufsätze zur Religionssoziologie*.

acts, failure to act or passive acquiescence) if and in so far as the actor or actors associate a subjective meaning (*Sinn*) with it."[1] *Social* action is "such action as, according to its subjective meaning to the actor or actors, involves the attitudes and actions of others and is oriented to them in its course."[2] Sociology, finally, is "a science which attempts the interpretive understanding (*deutend Verstehen*) of social action in order thereby to arrive at a causal explanation of its course and effects."[3]

These famous and fundamental definitions of Weber's call for brief comment. It is clear that Weber directly associates the concept of action with an accessible subjective aspect, with the postulate of *Verstehen*. In so far as human "behavior"[4] is not accessible to such understanding through the subjective point of view of the actor, it is not action and does not concern the formulation of Weber's systematic sociological theory. With this negative limitation the present study has no quarrel. The second point is that Weber's interest is in understandable aspects of behavior, that is in action, only in so far as it is relevant to the causal explanation of its course and effects. The concepts Weber is concerned with are thus those of an empirical explanatory science, not of any normative[5] or other related kind of discipline. Finally, it is quite clear from the discussion of the previous chapter that he did not consider *Verstehen* restricted to the rational case. The latter plays, as will be seen, a basically important part in his scheme but not the only part. The *Evidenz* of *Verstehen* may be, he says,[6] either rational or emotional (he sometimes says *affektuell*). For instance we can understand an outburst of anger, even though when seen in terms of the situation of the actor it be strictly irrational.

[1] *Wirtsch. u. Ges.*, p. 1. The "in so far as" suggests that he is dealing with an abstract system and not a class of phenomena.

[2] *Ibid.*

[3] *Ibid.* This chapter will not be concerned with Weber's particular concept of the scope of sociology. See Chapter XIX. Translations of Weber's text quoted in this chapter are by the author.

[4] "Action" is much to be preferred as a translation of Weber's *Handeln* because it fits Pareto's usage, and because it does not have the behavioristic connotations of the term behavior, which Professor Abel (*op. cit.*) uses. Behavior here may be taken to be the broader category.

[5] Which, for instance, he interpreted systematic jurisprudence to be.

[6] *Wirtsch. u. Ges.*, p. 2.

For any science of action nonsubjective processes and objects are not altogether excluded from consideration, but have a place as occasion, condition, result, favoring or hindering circumstance of human action.[1] It is possible that things which appear to a given investigator as explicable in subjective terms will in the end turn out to be the product of the laws of nonsubjective systems,[1] that is, the meaningful aspect may be epiphenomenal. Where a subjective explanation, *e.g.*, adequate motivation, cannot be discovered it may be possible to fall back on regularities which, however great their probabilities of correctness, still remain *unverstehbar*. A motive is "a meaningful complex (*Sinnzusammenhang*), which appears to the actor himself or to the observer to be an adequate (*Sinnvoll*) ground for his attitudes or acts."[2] A correct causal interpretation of concrete action implies "that the outward course and the motive are each correctly grasped and that their relation to each other is 'understandable.' "[3]

It is unnecessary for present purposes to go further into Weber's explicit methodological basis for the concept of action since the foregoing is sufficient to show it is substantially the concept dealt with all through this study. He proceeds immediately to give a classification of social as of other action which is the starting point of his systematic differentiation of types. The relevant passage[4] in full is as follows:

Like all action, that which is social may be determined: (1) *Zweckrational*[5]—by expectations of the behavior of objects of the external environment and of other persons, and through use of these expectations as "conditions" or as "means" for rational ends, rationally weighed and pursued. (2) *Wertrational*[5]—through conscious belief in the *absolute value in itself*—whether to be interpreted as ethical, aesthetic, religious or otherwise—of a given line of conduct purely for its own sake, quite independently of results. (3) "Affectual"[6]—especially

---

[1] *Ibid.*, p. 3.

[2] *Ibid.*, p. 5.

[3] *Ibid.* Error and/or other modes of lack of correspondence between the subjective and objective aspects of action are of course often understandable.

[4] *Ibid.*, p. 12.

[5] These two terms are purposely left untranslated. It is hoped that their meaning will become clear in the course of the discussion.

[6] *Affektuell.*

emotional, through given affects and states of feeling. (4) Traditional—through the habituation of long practice.

Weber introduces these four concepts as ways in which action may be determined, leaving the question of their methodological status undecided. The way in which he uses these concepts leads to the general conclusion that in definition they are primarily ideal types of concrete action, but their later use tends to set them in a different context. This situation is the source of much confusion.

In the first place, the distinction between the first two as stated in the passage quoted seems definitely to refer to types of concrete action. At first sight it might look as if *Zweckrationalität* referred to the intermediate sector of the intrinsic means-end chain of the previous analysis; *Wertrationalität*, on the other hand, to the element of ultimate ends. This will not, however, meet Weber's definitions, since in them each describes a complete type of action including both means-end relationships and ultimate ends. Both are ideal-type concepts.

The key to Weber's meaning is given in the distinction that Dr. von Schelting discusses[1] between the two possible "formal" types of ethical attitude which Weber calls *Verantwortungsethik* and *Gesinnungsethik*.[2] *Zweckrationalität* is the normative type of action logically implied by the former position, and *Wertrationalität* by the latter. The distinction is essentially as follows: The actor either recognizes a plurality of legitimate directions of value achievement, though perhaps all are not equally important, or he orients his total action to a single specific value, *e.g.*, salvation, which is absolute in the sense that all other potential values become significant only as means and conditions, possible aids or hindrances, to the attainment of this central value.[3]

In the first case one must not only be concerned with the choice of means to a particular end—this is common to both—

[1] VON SCHELTING, *Max Webers Wissenschaftslehre*, Part I. It is taken from Weber. See "Politik als Beruf" in *Gesammelte Politische Schriften*.

[2] These terms are difficult to translate; perhaps tentatively they may be translated as "ethics of responsibility" and "ethics of absolute value."

[3] Another relation to other values is possible: they may be incompatible with the supreme value, directly antagonistic to it, so that the indicated attitude is one of disinterested moral hostility. Thus to a dogmatic religion it is a duty to combat heresy.

but also with the weighing of values, *i.e.*, ultimate ends, against
each other, and the possible effects of a given course of action,
not only in relation to the achievement of its own immediate, or
ultimate end in a direct chain, but also directly or through indirect channels on other values.[1] Hence the urge of the man in
this position for objective knowledge is particularly strong, for
only by possessing this can he make such judgments rationally.
His action must be directed to the achievement of a harmony, a
maximization of value achievement in a number of fields according to their relative urgency. In this connection Weber was
very far indeed from believing in a preestablished harmony
with no real conflicts between different possible values. On the
contrary, he took a tragic view of the situation, maintaining the
existence of very deep conflicts between the different possible
value spheres[2] and especially emphasizing the tragic effect of
the unanticipated indirect effects of action (*Schicksal, die
Paradoxie der Folgen*).

The other position is concerned, as has been said, with the
conditions of action only as means and conditions to attainment
of the particular absolute value. Of course the actor is obligated
to pursue such an absolute value with every possible effort,
but he is not concerned with the success (*Erfolg*) of his action.
Whether he can succeed or not has no relation to whether he
should try—for there is no other value to compete or to com-
pensate for lack of success. If success is impossible in the objective
situation "martyrdom" is the only acceptable course. On the
other hand, he is not in the least concerned with the effect of his
action on the prospects of realizing other values (for himself or
others), for other values simply do not count, or if they do they
are to be regarded as dangerous competitors of the supreme
value.[3] The matter of the results of his action is left to God,[4] it
is no responsibility of the actor's.

---

[1] See *Wirtsch. u. Ges.*, p. 13.

[2] *Cf. Religionssoziologie*, Vol. I, pp. 554 *ff.* on the *Spannungen* of a rationalized religious view in relation to other values. *Cf.* also Weber's *Politische
Schriften.*

[3] The basis of ascetic practices in a mystical religious position.

[4] The author is much indebted to personal conversations with Dr. von
Schelting for clarification of this distinction and its relation to Weber's two
types of rational action. Dr. von Schelting is not, however, responsible for
the views expressed here. The resemblance of this distinction to that of

Hence in the terms employed in this study the distinction between the two types of rational action is to be regarded as resting on that between two polar types of ultimate-end systems. There are, of course, all manner of possible transition types between them, especially mitigations of the rigor of the extreme absoluteness of a single value. Every hierarchy of values involves an element of *Gesinnungsethik*, while the opposite extreme is, for instance, the position taken by Bentham in the famous formula, "Pushpin is as good as poetry." Not only each individual but each value counts as "one and only one."

In respect to the means-end relationship the difference is not in its logical character, but in its "extensity." Certain considerations of the relations of means and ends which are essential to action of the *zweckrational* type become entirely irrelevant at the *wertrational* pole. But there is nothing in Weber's types in any way in conflict with the above scheme of the structural elements of rational action. His distinction cuts across this analysis of structure having to do especially with differences in types of concrete ultimate-end system. The present concern is not to criticize the distinction, which, on the contrary, is most useful, but merely to point out its differences from the scheme developed in this study.[1]

Even though he splits it into two types Weber's rational action involves positively defined normative elements. It differs from Pareto's "logical action" in that Weber's concepts refer to hypothetically concrete complete types and hence include the ultimate-end element, as well as ultimate means and conditions. It is not confined to the mode of means-end relationship as such, as is Pareto's concept (in the above interpretation). Hence residual elements of action if they exist for Weber—and they do— are to be approached in a somewhat different way from that in which Pareto would approach them. But the matter is further complicated by the fact that Weber positively defined another

Pareto between skepticism and faith is striking. There are however, also significant differences. See above, Chap. VII, pp. 284 *ff.*

[1] Weber's actual usage does not seem to be by any means consistent. *Zweckrationalität* often comes to be thought of in abstraction from any ultimate ends. But the above is the only clear meaning which can be extracted from his definitions. Departures from it can be interpreted as due to the pressures inherent in the logical situation toward bringing out the structure of a generalized system as well as types. See below, p. 660.

type of norm besides his two rational types—the traditional. It is necessary to discuss this before approaching the question of residual elements.

It has already been shown that the concept of traditionalism plays a very important part in Weber's empirical sociological work. In the passage quoted above he gives it only an extremely cursory definition—action is determined traditionally "through the habituation of long practice (*durch eingelebte Gewohnheit*)." This might even suggest that traditionalism for Weber was simply the expression of the psychological mechanism of habit. But, however important habit may be in explaining the *mechanisms* of a traditional order it seems to be quite clear that this interpretation is not by itself acceptable. In the first place, the example that was used extensively in the last chapter shows that traditionalistic fixation need not apply to the total complex of action—the term does not designate sheer "automatism" but relates only to certain *normative* aspects, in this case the fixed standard of living. On the other hand, by definition the adaptation of means to ends is, within these limits, rational. Traditional action is apparently a type of total action, its traditionalism consisting in the fixity of certain essentials, their immunity from rational or other criticism.

Weber nowhere gives a fuller definition of *traditional action* as such. He does, however, give further specification of the more general concept of traditionalism, which can throw light on the question. In his discussion of the concept of legitimate order[1] he holds that the legitimacy of an order may be attributed to it by the actors on account of tradition.[2] Tradition, then, serves as a sanction of what is definitely and explicitly a normative aspect of a social system. There is absolutely nothing normative about habit as such. It is either a mechanism or a concrete pattern of actual behavior, not a way men should act.

Moreover, in his fundamentally important discussion of types of authority (*Typen der Herrschaft*), one of the three main types of *legitimate* authority is the traditional. His definition may be quoted in full: "Authority will be called traditional, in so far as its legitimacy rests upon the sanctity (*Heiligkeit*) of an order,

---

[1] *Wirtsch. u. Ges.*, pp. 16 *ff*. This concept will be discussed at length below as it is of basic importance for present purposes.

[2] *Ibid.*, p. 19.

and this sanctity of the order and that of positions of authority within it, are believed in because they have come down from the past [have always existed]."[1] The interesting point for present purposes is the use of the term sanctity which combined with legitimacy again brings out the normative aspect. No habit as such is sacred. This strongly suggests the attitude of moral obligation found to be so central to Durkheim's thought. Finally, it may be recalled that Weber established a close connection between traditionalism and symbolism and ritual in his discussion of primitive religion.[2]

From all this it is legitimate to conclude, first, that traditionalism has little theoretically to do with the psychological concept of habit; second, that it has a great deal to do with the normative aspect of action. Its intimate relation to legitimacy and to sanctity establishes that beyond question. It is not, however, profitable to pursue the question farther until these concepts and the closely related one of charisma have been considered. It seems evident, however, that traditionalism is not one of the ultimate structural (or other) elements of action systems. It is rather formulated on a more descriptive level. Moreover, traditional action is defined as a *type*, though in this case even more than in the case of the two rational types, the difficulties of this procedure become apparent. In Weber's actual usage the more general concept seems to appear in two main contexts: (1) as the concrete content of norms taken over without rational criticism from the past (tradition) and (2) as a quality or property of certain concrete actions or relationships (the traditionalism of the piece-rate mowers or of authority). There seems to be an inherent difficulty in adequately describing a *total* concrete system of action by the one term traditional in the sense involving norms, which probably accounts for the suggestion of "habit" in Weber's definition.

Finally a few words must be said about the category of affectual action. The difficulties of considering this an adequate definition of a concrete ideal type seem to be even greater than those involved in the definition of "traditional." Apparently Weber had in mind such examples as an outburst of anger which was "irrational" seen in terms of the interests of the actor in his given

[1] *Ibid.*, p. 130.
[2] *Supra*, Chap. XV, pp. 565–566.

situation. There is, of course, no doubt that such instances occur and that it is possible to construct ideal types of specifically irrational action including them. But such ideal types, to be on the same level as the two rational types, would have to be positively defined. It is an important fact that Weber's definition here as in the definition of "traditional" is very sketchy and indefinite, in marked contrast to his treatment of the two rational types. Moreover, still more important, there is nowhere a positive *use* of the concept in Weber's empirical work at all comparable with the use even of traditionalism.

The obvious conclusion seems to be that affectual action is to be regarded as a residual category. This is the more likely since Weber nowhere states that the classification of the four types of action was not meant to be exhaustive. The path by which he probably arrived at this concept may be described as follows: His real starting point, as was Pareto's, was the concept of rationality of action. At the same time his methodological position pushed him in the direction of formulating type concepts. Then the two possible types of formal ethical attitude led him to the distinction of the two types of rational action—each thought of as a complete, though normatively ideal, type.

Apparently the traditional stereotyping of certain aspects of action and relationships was essentially an impressive empirical fact that he was continually encountering in his concrete researches. Being precluded by his methodological approach from relating it to a generalized system of action he simply took it as an ultimate irreducible fact. Largely in conflict with his empirical usage he tried to fit it, not altogether successfully, into a logically symmetrical scheme of types of action. This left over certain nonrational aspects of action which were at the same time not traditional. The positive approach to them was to be found in Weber's view that understandability is not confined to the rational.[1] Affect was accessible to an observer—for example, as an outburst of anger. Hence this nonrational, nontraditional residuum is formulated as the distinguishing criterion of a fourth type of action. No attempt will be made here to develop further what elements may be found to be included in it. It may be merely noted as a caution that especially in view of the residual character of the concept it is just as illegitimate to jump to the conclusion

[1] *Supra*, p. 641.

that it stands for psychological irrationality in the case of the outburst of anger, an expression of an instinct of pugnacity, for instance, as it was to identify traditionalism with habit. Psychological elements may well be involved, but *certainly* do not exhaust the matter. Above all, it is interesting to note that the basically important concept charisma makes no appearance at all in the four types of action. It may well prove to have something to do with the interpretation of affectual action.

From the four types of action Weber proceeds to the concept of social relationship.[1] This is defined as "a state of attitudes (*Sichverhalten*)[2] of a plurality of persons which according to their subjective meaning are mutually concerned with each other and oriented by virtue of this fact. The social relationship thus *consists* entirely and exclusively in the probability that there will in certain circumstances be social action of a meaningfully predictable sort, without reference to the grounds of this probability." It is not necessary to go into an analysis of this definition here, but only to note a few things about it. It comprises another way of looking at the same facts involved in the schema of action; it is, in fact, simply a way of looking at certain complexes of action. It is important because it is the unit in terms of which Weber later builds up most of his more complex categories. This course involves departure from the strict schema of action as such, though it involves it by implication.[3]

But in his treatment of social relationships there is implied the existence of elements of regularity in action itself in order that there may be a significant probability of such kinds of action occurring as to constitute a definable relationship.

MODES OF ORIENTATION OF ACTION

Among the elements of regularity those which interest Weber are the ones that are understandable in terms of subjective categories. He then takes a still further step in narrowing the range of consideration by confining his attention to what he calls "modes of orientation" of action. This form of expression

---

[1] *Wirtsch. u. Ges.*, p. 13.

[2] *Verhalten* and *Sichverhalten* are exceedingly difficult terms to translate. "Attitude" is a rough rendering.

[3] This is one important reason why the scheme of structure of systems of action remained implicit in Weber.

strongly suggests a focus of interest on the normative aspect of action systems, an impression which is strengthened by the general character of Weber's approach to the problems of action.

This is obviously the case with two of the three categories which Weber puts forward in this connection. Action may, he says, be oriented in terms of (a) usage (*Brauch*), (b) interest (*Interessenlage*) or (c) legitimate order.[1] "Interest" is the category in which uniformities are understandable in terms of the rational (*zweckrational*) orientation of the actors to similar expectations. The concept of legitimate order, on the other hand, involves the orientation of action to the idea (*Vorstellung*) on the part of the actors of the existence of such an order as a norm. A few further remarks relative to these two categories are in order here. The stability of regularities of action based on interest lies, he says, in the fact that any actor who does not consider the interest of the others in his action thereby calls forth their resistance, which becomes an obstacle to the attainment of his own ends.[2] Also, orientation to a legitimate order is not limited to the extent to which its rules are lived up to, but also includes their evasion and defiance. The point is, of course, that the existence of the order *makes a difference* to the action and that this difference may be imputed to understandable motives.

The normative character of these two elements of regularity is thus clear: With respect to one it is attributed to a norm of rationality in the pursuit of given ends; with respect to the other it is attributable to rules involving an element of legitimacy, or obligation. The status of the third category, usage, is more doubtful in this respect. Indeed Weber's own formulation, which is very brief, suggests that this is a catchall for non-normative elements. He says that usage involves uniformity of action "in so far as it is given as a matter of actual practice" (*durch tatsächliche Uebung*). This suggests the psychological mechanism of habit as the primary point that he has in mind. His actual treatment, however, shows beyond doubt that here also normative elements are involved. But they are involved in a manner that has not yet been analyzed in this study. Hence explicit discussion of the interpretation of this category will be postponed

[1] *Wirtsch. u. Ges.*, p. 15.
[2] *Ibid.*, p. 16.

until the two more closely related to the foregoing discussion have been dealt with.

The exact logical status of these three concepts is not very clear in Weber's own treatment. Two of them are qualified in his own definitions by the phrase "in so far as." The third is merely stated "Action . . . may be oriented to the idea of a legitimate order." It is possible to consider them as three ideal *types* of action. But why should there be a second classification of these in addition to the first without a word as to the relation of the two or as to why a second should be necessary? The most plausible interpretation seems to be that what Weber was really doing was putting forward, as a general framework for his classification of ideal types, an outline of the generalized structure of systems of action. If this interpretation is correct none of them would be, for the most part, meant as descriptions of even hypothetically concrete types of action.[1]

Usage in this connection seems at first sight to be defined only negatively. It is merely the way "things are done." All Weber says is that there is a distinction between things "being done" because they have "always been done that way" (*Sitte*) and because "it is the newest way to do it" (fashion). But in the descriptive characterization no specific motive—no means-end relationship[2]—appears to be involved. This is not in the least the same as saying that these uniformities will not turn out to be understandable as the results of complexes of motivation.[3]

The other two involve specific norms; the efficient adaptation of means to ends, on the one hand—norms of efficiency; the norm of legitimacy, or moral obligation, on the other. There is no reason whatever why these two, and usage as well, should not all be involved in the same concrete situation; indeed they so frequently are involved that when there is complete absence of any one of them from any concrete complex of action it is to be regarded as a limiting case. To avoid confusion one distinction

[1] The principal motive for introducing these concepts is probably, as was intimated in the last chapter, that he needed a framework for his systematic classification of ideal types. Methodologically he did not seem to be clear as to the significance of what he was doing in the context of interest here.

[2] There appears to be only some such element as what Pareto calls *la besoin d'uniformité*, a diffuse entity, not a motive.

[3] See above, Chap. X, on Durkheim.

should be pointed out,[1] that between the fact of *orientation* to a legitimate order and the motives for acting in relation to it. The two elements of interest and legitimacy are interwoven in a complex way. The fact that an order is legitimate in the eyes of a large proportion of the community makes it *ipso facto* an element of the *Interessenlage* of any one individual, whether *he* himself holds it to be legitimate or not. Supposing he does not, his action, to be rational, must be none the less oriented to this order. This ground has been thoroughly gone over in the discussion of Durkheim.

It seems, then, that the best interpretation that can be placed on these concepts is that they are parts of a structural framework of action. Weber's approach to them, however, is somewhat different from that worked out in the analysis of Pareto. It is more like Durkheim's approach. That is, the element of legitimacy, which undoubtedly directly corresponds to Durkheim's moral obligation, does not first appear in the form of an ultimate end of a particular means-end chain, but as a property of an *order*, that is, a system of norms, to which particular actions are oriented, but which stands in the relation of "condition" rather than means or end to the unit act. The attitude of the actor to these norms may vary; that is, they may, on the one hand, be morally neutral conditions to which he orients his action, as he would to the availability of any technical means, or, on the other hand, his attitude may be a "moral" one of acceptance and hence an obligation to live up to them, or rejection and a corresponding obligation to combat them.

This is in all essentials the same as Durkheim's approach to the same phenomena. It may, following the previous terminology,[2] be called the institutional approach as distinct from the direct action-element approach of Pareto. There emerge, then, by this approach three elements: the apparently non-normative merely factual element of order, usage, the efficiency-norm element and the legitimacy-norm element. A total concrete order normally involves all three.[3] The main task now is to analyze each of these to see if it is, in turn, further reducible to elements and in what relation these stand to the scheme of the

---

[1] Weber himself makes it quite clearly. *Cf. Wirtsch. u. Ges.*, p. 16.

[2] *Supra*, Chap. X, pp. 399 *ff.*

[3] *Cf.* especially *Wirtsch. u. Ges.*, p. 17.

structure of action already developed. But before embarking on this analysis it is well to remark on the nature of Weber's own course from here on.

He proceeds to develop step by step a system of ideal types of social relationship.[1] Starting with three elementary relations— conflict (*Kampf*), *Vergemeinschaftung* and *Vergesellschaftung*[2]— he builds them up into more and more complex structures culminating in such concepts as church and state. It is almost needless to say that this is not generalized theory in the present sense at all, but is the development of the other possibility of generalizing conceptualization—that of a system of ideal-type concepts. The unit of this systematization is the social relationship. The result is a scheme of "objectively possible" types of social structure. As such it is a monumental work, unique of its kind in its scope and refinement, and a mine for almost any kind of empirical research. It has, in the empirical uses to which Weber himself put it, the important result of bringing out into clear relief the structural differentiation of institutions. Where Durkheim saw clearly only the functional side of institutions, their relation to the determination of individual action, Weber saw their structural aspect on a tremendous "architectonic" panorama. It was the finest product of the historical relativism of the idealistic tradition. There is no space here to follow through this extraordinary type system. Certain aspects of it will be discussed later in illustrating the importance of the consequences of the alternative analysis. But the latter is the main concern now.

It is not necessary to dwell at any considerable length upon the analysis of what has been called the efficiency-norm element. But it is worth while to make certain points, above all that Weber made, even if in slightly different form, all the main distinctions of structural elements which have appeared in the foregoing analysis. In the first place, his definition of *Interessenlage* associates it directly with *Zweckrationalität*. This means that action is determined by interest only in so far as it involves adaptation of means to given ends, according to objective standards. It

[1] See *Wirtsch. u. Ges.*, pp. 20–30 for the bold outline, but throughout Part I carried out in more special respects.

[2] Explicit consideration of these two concepts will be postponed until the note appended to this chapter in connection with Toennies.

may be said that this is what orientation to efficiency-norms is. It is true that Weber's concept of *Zweckrationalität* does not directly abstract from the ultimate-end element. But in *this* connection his use of it involves no reference to any specific type of ultimate-end system, nor to its specific role. The reference is wholly to the character of the means-end relationship in a given situation, whatever the ultimate ends may be. These are not considered as variables for the present purposes. Hence it may be concluded that this structural *element* differs from the *zweckrational type* precisely in omitting consideration of the character of ultimate ends. It then becomes equivalent[1] to the intermediate intrinsic means-end sector.

But this is not all. The internal differentiation of this sector worked out above is also to be found, in essentials, in Weber. As would be expected this is clearest in connection with his discussion of the status of the economic element. Action is, he says, "economically oriented, in so far as it is concerned, according to its subjective meaning, with provision for the desire for 'utilities' (*Nutzleistungen*)."[2] "Economic action (*Wirtschaften*) is a *peaceful* exercise of power (*Verfügungsgewalt*) which is primarily economically oriented."[3] The second definition especially has a strong concrete-type leaning. But, in the first place, it explicitly excludes force as a means to economic action—possibly other modes of coercion. Secondly, the orientation to acquisition of utilities exactly corresponds to the above analysis. It is interesting to note that Weber still more explicitly excludes the specific nature of the ultimate ends of this utility-seeking element by stating that it must not be taken to be confined to consumption wants, since that would rule out "naked acquisition." The essential thing is that utilities are actually sought after, not why.[4] The importance of this distinction for the treatment of capitalism is obvious. Capitalistic acquisitiveness, its specific limitless character, is not to be explained on economic grounds alone.

Moreover, Weber draws essentially the same distinction between the economic and the technological elements which has

---

[1] Since it also abstracts from the character of any *specific* situation.

[2] *Wirtsch. u. Ges.*, p. 31.

[3] *Ibid.*

[4] *Ibid.* Unfortunately he does not work out the concept of utility further.

been made above.[1] He says: "Not every action which is rational
with respect to means should be called economic. Above all
'economy' is not identical with 'technology.'"[2] Rational technique is any employment of means which is consciously oriented
to experience and its analysis. There is thus a technique of
every kind of action,[3] *i.e.*, it is an element, not a type of action.
An economic element enters in only in so far as the comparative
scarcity of alternative means to a given end becomes relevant
to the choice between them. This is always a consideration in
addition to the technological, not in place of it. It means that
the costs of use of a given means for a given end are considered.
This, in turn, means that their comparative urgency for this and
alternative ends becomes involved.[4] Thus the fundamental
economic facts are scarcity, adaptation of means to alternative
ends and cost. The economic element involves the weighing of
the relative urgency of different uses of a given scarce means,
which the technological does not.

This gives all the main lines of distinction. The only qualification is that the status of the distinction as a matter of structural
elements, though strongly suggested, is not clarified. This is
related to the fact noted in the last chapter that Weber took
the concepts of economic theory as his leading case for the general
ideal type, hence involving all the methodological difficulties
found to be inherent in that concept. But considering this, and
the fact that Weber originally approached economics with the
antitheoretical biases of the historical school, he achieved a
remarkable degree of methodological clarification of the logical
status of economic theory—distinctly superior it may be said,
to the majority of present-day orthodox economists.

The status of coercive power in Weber in relation to the economic factor is a more complicated question than that of the
technological element. A fairly clearly definable line can, however,
be discerned. In the first place, by limiting "economic action"
to peaceful means Weber, as has been seen, explicitly excluded
the use of force.[5] For the rest in his systematic treatment he

[1] Chap. VI.

[2] *Ibid.*, p. 32.

[3] Including, for instance, prayer and mystical contemplation.

[4] *Wirtsch. u. Ges.*, p. 33. This is surely an unexpected place to find an
apparently independent version of the opportunity-cost doctrine.

[5] See also *Wirtsch. u. Ges.*, p. 32.

clearly separated in different chapters, The Sociological Fundamentals of Economic Life[1] and Types of Authority.[2] It is worth
while, then, to investigate his concept of authority (*Herrschaft*),
which he clearly did not think of as an economic category. He
defines it as "the probability of securing obedience to specific
commands on the part of a given group of persons."[3] It is a
narrower concept than that of power (*Macht*) which is "the
probability within a social relationship of being able to secure
one's own ends, even against opposition."[4] In this widest sense
power is by no means excluded from the economic element of
relationships, but authority is. In so far as a social relationship
involves economic considerations it is a matter of agreement,
not of command, on the one side; obedience, on the other.

Of course agreement in this sense by no means excludes in-
equality of bargaining power, hence coercion.[5] At the same time
it is perfectly possible to enter into a relationship that involves
submission to authority by voluntary agreement. Thus Weber
strongly emphasizes that the subjection to discipline in the
capitalistic enterprise is, in the strictest sense, subordination to
authority—although over a limited range. The worker must
obey orders.[6] But all this does not affect the central fact that
authority is a specific form of the exercise of power, involving
the possibility of coercion.

The concept of the "political" Weber makes still narrower,
tying it to authority exercised within a given geographical area,
on the one hand, and involving the application or threat of
physical coercion in case of need, on the other.[7] The important
distinction between political and economic elements cannot for
present purposes be found this far away from the central concern
of economics.

If then, the concept of authority be taken as the clear line
that Weber draws at the point where economic power stops[8] it

---

[1] *Ibid.*, pp. 31 *ff.*
[2] *Ibid.*, pp. 122 *ff.*
[3] *Ibid.*, pp. 28, 122. Irrespective of whether the obeyer likes the particular
content of the command or not.
[4] *Ibid.*, p. 28.
[5] *Ibid.*, p. 123.
[6] *Ibid.*
[7] *Ibid.*, p. 29.
[8] The exercise of authority for Weber may be either *Wirtschaftsorient-*

leaves the following situation: Once activities in pursuit of the acquisition and distribution of utilities take place in a situation involving social relationships, the question arises of the determination of the power relationships of the participants in the concrete activities. From the situation involving complete equality of bargaining power which seems to have been the starting point of the earlier classical economists,[1] there is a whole series of degrees involving more and more possibility of coercion of one party to such a relationship by the other parties.

Of these power relationships two types may be roughly distinguished. On the one hand, the departure from the completely economic norm may be due to the employment of what may be called noneconomic means. These may be defined as force, fraud and the exercise of authority (in Weber's sense). The upshot of Weber's treatment would seem to be to draw, in these terms, the line between economic and noneconomic power, taking authority as the "mildest" of these means.[2] On the other hand, this still leaves open the possibility of inequalities of power, not as a direct result of greater productivity, but entering in as a result of taking advantage of a better situation, *e.g.*, monopoly, etc., or of greater shrewdness and foresight in the use of economic means, that is, the securing of voluntary agreements to exchange goods and services.[3]

It is over this question that differences about the role of the power element play their principal part in the history of economic thought. At one pole stands the main classical position resting on the postulate of the "natural identity of interests," a position which altogether eliminates the coercive element. At the other is the Marxian type of economic theory, one of several theories that make it the *central* element. Weber leans rather to the latter

---

iert, concerned with securing utilities, or *Wirtschaftsrelevant*, affecting the distribution of utilities in the community, but it is not *Wirtschaften* as such. The distinction of these three things is very useful for concrete research.

[1] As Professor F. H. Knight says, the great discovery that lay at the basis of this development was that of mutual advantage in exchange. See his "Freedom as Fact and Criterion," *International Journal of Ethics*, Vol. 39, pp. 129 *ff.*

[2] Weber seems to have little concern with fraud in his conceptual framework. It is impossible to go into the question here.

[3] What Weber aptly calls "dominance through a constellation of interests." *Wirtsch. u. Ges.*, pp. 604–606.

than to the former school.[1] For the present purpose (which is
the distinction of the principal structural elements of action)
the issue is one of expediency rather than of fundamental principle. The exclusion of the noneconomic means from the positions
of variables in the system of *economic* theory seems clearly indicated.[2] On the other hand, it is clearly possible to formulate such
a system on the postulate of the natural identity of interests.
Whether the elements of economic coercion should be used to
define the same system, broadening its scope, or whether they
require separate systematic formulation can be decided only in
terms of the results of actual attempts to do the former. There is
no space here for critical analysis of what attempts have been
made.

In the meantime it must be sharply emphasized that considerations of the logical simplicity of a system of economic theory
that excludes coercion should not be allowed to obscure the enormous empirical importance of coercion in actual economic life.
In the work of the great majority of liberal economists this has
been conspicuously the case.[3] Weber is not subject to this criticism. He had a deep, almost tragic, consciousness of the importance of coercion in human affairs. Any study of his political
writings is sufficient to convince one of this.[4]

Legitimate Order, Charisma and Religion

It is time to return to the concept of legitimate order, or as
it has been put above, legitimacy norms, in relation to action.
The way in which Weber deals with this is of central interest.
In the first place he makes two classifications, the distinction
between which is not at first sight evident. The first[5] is of modes
in which "the legitimacy of an order may be guaranteed." The

---

[1] Of course he had no concern at all with the specific technicalities of
Marxian economic theory, such as labor theory of value, surplus value, etc.

[2] As Weber says, "Das Pragma der Gewaltsamkeit ist dem Geist der
Wirtschaft sehr stark Entgegengesetzt." *Wirtsch. u. Ges.*, p. 32.

[3] *Cf.* especially the remarks about Robbins and Souter in this respect in
Talcott Parsons, "Some Reflections on the Nature and Significance of
Economics," *Quarterly Journal of Economics*, May, 1934. Marshall is
another conspicuous example.

[4] See Weber's *Gesammelte Politische Schriften*.

[5] *Wirtsch. u. Ges.*, p. 17.

second[1] is of reasons why binding legitimacy is attributed to the order by the actors.

The basis of the distinction emerges from consideration of the actual content of the classifications. The guarantee spoken of in connection with the first may be purely subjective (*innerlich*), in which case it is (a) affectual, (b) *wertrational* or (c) religious. Or it may be external, which means in terms of "interest," certain expectations of external consequences. The terminology here used seems somewhat objectionable, but the essential meaning is clear. It is a classification of types of motive, hence of forces, by which actual adherence to the norms of the order in question is to be explained. In the terminology of this study it is preferable to say that these motives may be classified as disinterested and interested. In the one case the order is looked upon as an expression of values, hence to be lived up to because it is valued for itself or for the values it expresses.[2] In the other, its existence is part of the situation in which one must act—it takes the role of morally neutral means or conditions for the actor's own ends. Thus a communist who personally does not believe in free speech may invoke the right to free speech in court to keep himself out of jail and thus further his own cause. Such a right[3] is part of the legitimate order of present society, which he uses as means to his own ends. Weber may be interpreted as pointing out that even though interests may morally be quite neutral to the order they none the less may play a part in guaranteeing it, that is, in maintaining its function.

The other classification is on a different plane—it is that of the motives for which *legitimacy* is ascribed to the order, not why the order is upheld in action. Negatively the conspicuous fact is that interest drops out entirely. While interest may be a very important reason for conforming to an order, it has nothing to do with ascribing legitimacy—or illegitimacy—to it. Here only the disinterested motive elements have a place. But Weber's subclassification of these is somewhat different from the above. It is (a) traditional, (b) affectual, (c) *wertrational* and (d) held to be legal by positive institution (*Satzung*). It does not seem important enough to inquire here why Weber eliminated religious

[1] *Ibid.*, p. 19.
[2] Or combated for disinterested motives.
[3] Under certain restrictions.

motives and added traditional. On this last it may be noted only
that he says, "The legitimacy of an order by virtue of the *santifi-
cation* of tradition is everywhere the most universal and original
case."[1] This linking of traditionalism with *sanctity* is a conspicuous feature of his treatment of the former throughout.

It is interesting to note here a shift from the original meaning
of *wertrational*, directly corresponding to that previously noted
in *zweckrational*. Though the term absolute occurs,[2] in the context
the important thing seems to be not the absoluteness but the
"ultimacy" (in the sense of this study) of the value. This is
evident from the fact that *zweckrational* has become identified
with interest—concern with a thing or person only in so far as it
or he may be usable as a means or should be taken account of
as an intrinsically relevant condition. *Wertrational*, on the other
hand, becomes here identified with the disinterested attitude of
valuation of a thing for its own sake or as a direct expression or
embodiment of an ultimate value, which hence cannot, in so far,
simply be "used" as a means. In other words the distinction of
zweckrational and *wertrational*, originally one of hypothetically
concrete *types* of rational action, has stepped over into one of
structural elements of action systems, recognizable as properties
of attitudes. Occuring in the context where it appears this cannot
but be significant.

The fourth category, positive institution of norms held to be
legal, may from the present point of view be regarded as a category of derived legitimacy. The belief in legality implies that the
instituting agency has a right to institute such norms. It falls
for Weber into two subtypes—agreement and imposition (*Oktroy-
ierung*). In the former case, it should be noted, the mere fact that
persons with interests come to an agreement is not enough. In
order that there may be legitimacy there must be an obligation
assumed to carry out the terms of the agreement. This will be
found to involve one or more of the other three elements, above
all *Wertrationalität* (in the new sense). The connection of this
with Durkheim's analysis of relations of contract is obvious. The
element of legitimacy in agreements is a part of Durkheim's
"non-contractual element of contract."[3] Thus purely voluntary

---

[1] *Wirtsch. u. Ges.*, p. 19.

[2] Both here and in the classification in *Wirtsch. u. Ges.*, p. 17.

[3] *Supra*, Chap. VIII.

agreement is the limiting case where the element of legitimacy is reduced to a minimum. But this by no means implies that it is eliminated.

At the present moment it is not proposed to go further into the mutual relations of tradition, affect and *Wertrationalität* (in the *second* sense, which will be employed from now on). But already the analysis has gone far enough to justify certain conclusions. Legitimacy is for Weber a quality of an order, that is, of a system of norms governing conduct, or at least to which action may (or must) be oriented. This quality is imputed to the order by those acting in relation to it. Doing so involves taking a given type of attitude toward the norms involved which may be characterized as one of disinterested acceptance. To put the matter somewhat differently, for one who holds an order to be legitimate, living up to its rules becomes, to this extent, a matter of moral obligation.

Thus Weber has arrived at the same point Durkheim reached when he interpreted constraint as moral authority. Moreover, Weber has approached the question from the same point of view, that of an individual thought of as acting in relation to a system of rules that constitute conditions of his action. There has emerged from the work of both men the same distinction of attitude elements toward the rules of such an order, the interested and the disinterested. In both cases a legitimate order is contrasted with a situation of the uncontrolled play of interests.[1] Both have concentrated their special attention on the latter element. Such a parallel is not likely to be purely fortuitous.[2]

But the parallel extends much farther. The question arises whether it is necessary to leave the analysis of the motive elements involved in legitimacy at the pluralism of the three mentioned in Weber's classification[3] or whether it is possible to find in Weber any indication of a more general unifying conception in terms of which all three may be related to each other. Such a unifying principle is undoubtedly present in the concept of charisma.

---

[1] *Cf. Wirtsch. u. Ges.*, p. 648.

[2] The fact that both had juristic training probably has something to do with the similarity of their approaches in so far as they differ from that of Pareto.

[3] Tradition, affect, *Wertrationalität*.

Weber himself deals with this concept in a number of different contexts[1] which involve rather sharp differences of emphasis. There is, however, a definite thread of continuity running through them all which consists precisely in the relation of charisma to the concept of legitimacy. Tracing this will involve some interpretation beyond simple exposition, but it is of the sort that is unavoidable in such a situation.

The conception has already been dealt with briefly in connection with Weber's religious typology.[2] There it was noted that Weber takes as his point of departure the contrast with routine (*Alltag*). Charisma is, then, a quality of things and persons by virtue of which they are specifically set apart from the ordinary, the everyday, the routine.[3] It is interesting to note that Weber on several occasions specifically contrasts charisma with the economic element. It is, as such, "*spezifisch wirtschaftsfremd.*"[4]

This apartness is what characterizes charismatic things or persons. It is hence not immediately related as such to action—it is a quality of concrete things, persons, acts, etc. But a hint of the relation to action is given in the kind of attitude men take toward charismatic things or persons. Weber applies a number of terms, but two may be singled out. Applied to a person the charismatic quality is exemplary (*vorbildlich*)[5]—something to be imitated. At the same time recognition of it as an exceptional quality lending prestige and authority is a duty.[6] The charismatic leader never treats those who resist him or ignore him, within the scope of his claims, as anything but delinquent in duty. On the basis of this characterization it seems legitimate to conclude that charisma implies a specific attitude of respect, and that this respect is like that owed to a recognized duty. It is clearly the ritual attitude of Durkheim: charismatic authority is a phase of moral authority.

---

[1] The principal points are: *Wirtsch. u. Ges.*, pp. 140–148; 227 *ff;* 250–261; 642–649; 753–778; *Religionssoziologie*, Vol. I, pp. 268–269.

[2] *Supra*, Chap. XV, pp. 564 *ff*.

[3] Routine here clearly does not mean that habitually performed but rather "profane." Morning prayers, though carried out daily, are not *Alltag*.

[4] *Wirtsch. u. Ges.*, p. 142. Compare Durkheim's statement, "Labor is the profane activity par excellence," quoted above, Chap. XI.

[5] *Wirtsch. u. Ges.*, p. 140.

[6] *Ibid.*

In other words, charisma is directly linked with legitimacy, is indeed the name in Weber's system for the source of legitimacy in general. The principal difficulty of the concept arises from the fact that he did not, apparently, originally conceive it in these general terms in relation to a scheme of the structure of action. It was, rather, conceived of in terms of a much more specific theory of social *change* and developed from there. There has already been occasion to develop the theory in terms of its most important empirical example for Weber, the role of the prophet.[1]

The main context is that of a break in a traditional order. Hence two of the most prominent aspects of the concept charisma —its association with antitraditionalism as its revolutionary character[2] and its particularly close association with a specific person, a leader. The prophet is thus the leader who sets himself explicitly and consciously against the traditional order—or aspects of it—and who claims *moral* authority for his position, whatever the terms in which he expresses it, such as divine will. It is men's duty to listen to him and follow his commands or his example. In this connection it is also important to note that the prophet is one who feels himself to be reborn. He is qualitatively different from other men in that he is in touch with or the instrument of a source of authority higher than any which is established or any to which obedience can be motivated by calculation of advantage.

If the concept of charisma is oriented to this particular context, then the essential problem is that of the relation of prophetic charisma to the legitimacy of the orders which govern everyday life. In *this* revolutionary sense, Weber holds, charisma is in the nature of the case a temporary phenomenon. For the message of the prophet to become embodied in a permanent everyday structure, to become institutionalized, it must undergo a fundamental change. In this process the authority that the prophet exercises by virtue of his personal *charisma* may develop in one of two directions—a traditionalized or a rationalized structure.[3]

The crucial point in the concrete development comes with the question of succession at the passing of the original charismatic

---

[1] *Supra,* Chap. XV, pp. 567 *ff.*
[2] *Wirtsch. u. Ges.,* p. 759.
[3] See in general *ibid.,* Part III, Chap. X, *Die Umbildung des Charisma.*

leader. It is not necessary to go into the various concrete ways in which the situation may, more or less successfully, be met. Only the two main outcomes will be noted. In the one case the charismatic quality is transferred according to one of a number of possible rules, from one concrete person (or group of persons) to another. The most usual, though by no means the only possible, instance is hereditary charisma (*Erbcharisma*).[1] Then the element of sacredness, the qualification for certain functions, inheres in the particular concrete person by virtue of his birth, an act within the given sphere becomes legitimate by virtue of the fact that *he* performs it.

The correlate of this is some definition of the norm embodying the prophet's mission. In this case it takes the form of a traditionalized system of norms (a sacred law) which carry the same quality of sanctity, of charisma, as the person of the ruler. In this way there arise what are for Weber the two main characteristics of traditional authority[2]—a traditional body of norms held sacred and unalterable and, *within* the margin of freedom left open by these and the possibility of their interpretation, an area of arbitrary personal authority of the ruler, legitimized by his generally charismatic personal quality. By this process, from being the specifically revolutionary force charisma becomes, on the contrary, the specific sanction of immobile traditionalism.[3]

The alternative to this mode of routinization is a line of development which involves thinking of the charismatic quality as objectified and hence capable of divorce from the particular concrete person. It then becomes either[4] (*a*) transferable or (*b*) obtainable by a person by his own efforts or, finally, (*c*) not a quality of a person as such at all but of an office, or of an institutional structure without reference to personal qualities. The first two still tie it to particular persons, even though they are not independent prophets or blood descendants of them. In the third case, however, charisma becomes inherent only in the office or the objective system of rules. It is hardly necessary to note that this is the road which leads to bureaucratic organization and

---

[1] *Gentilcharisma* is a subtype of this.
[2] *Cf. Wirtsch. u. Ges.*, pp. 130 *ff.*
[3] *Ibid.*, p. 774.
[4] *Ibid.*, p. 771.

"legality" as the standard of legitimacy. The essential point is that the quest of the source of legality always leads back to a charismatic element, whether by apostolic succession, revealed law (Calvin's *Geneva*), divine right or a general will.

Thus it is evident that what changes in the shift from revolutionary prophecy to traditional or rational everyday authority is not the quality charisma as such but its concrete modes of embodiment[1] and its relations to other elements of the particular concrete complex. Indeed Weber's fullest treatment of legitimacy[2] leaves no doubt that there is no *legitimate* order without a charismatic element. In traditionalism this is always given in the sanctity of tradition.[3] This involves more than the mere fact that things simply *have been* done in a certain way and people consider it "a good thing" to continue in the same way. There is a definite *duty* to do them in the traditional way. Similarly in a rational bureaucratic structure there must always be a source of the legality of its order which is, in the last analysis, charismatic. Finally, the same is true of preprophetic traditionalism.[4]

Thus defined charisma covers a field considerably broader than what is generally called religion. But it has already been noted that the probable genesis of the conception in Weber's own mind started from the role of the prophet in the more specifically religious sense. What then, is its relation to religion? To answer this question it is necessary to go back to the place of charisma in primitive religion. As was noted[5] in that connection the special apartness of the quality of charisma is correlated with the conception of a world of supernatural entities in the specific sense of the above discussion.[6] Indeed, this sense of the supernatural is nothing but the ideological correlate of the attitude of respect. Corresponding to the dualism of attitude, which has been found running through the thought of both Durkheim and Weber, between that of morally neutral utilitarian use and moral or

---

[1] Regarded as a variable, the element itself remains unchanged through a range of different values.

[2] *Ibid.*, pp. 642 *ff.* This section is probably unfinished, as are many in this work.

[3] In speaking of traditionalism Weber almost always uses the term sacred (*heilig*).

[4] *Supra*, Chap. XV, pp. 565–566.

[5] *Supra*, Chap. XV, p. 565.

[6] And, note, *only* in this specific sense.

ritual respect, is one of "worlds" or systems of entities—in this most general sense, one of nature and the supernatural.[1]

Weber has defined religious action as action in relation to supernatural entities thus conceived. Then in the broadest possible sense religious ideas might be defined as any conceptions men have of these supernatural entities and their relations to man and to nature. Then on the symbolic level the question of meaning begins to be involved. Events do not merely "happen" and "happen to" men, but they may be interpreted as having a meaning in the sense of symbolizing or expressing the actions, will or other aspects of supernatural entities.

One further logical link is necessary to complete the chain. The discussion of Durkheim's treatment of religion brought out the central role of the active attitude of men toward the non-empirical aspects of the universe. In terms of Weber's ideas this relation may be analyzed somewhat further. Weber's religious "interests"[2] may be held to be another name for these active attitudes. The religious elements of action are concerned with men's relations to supernatural entities. Religious interests define the directions of these activities, the ends men may hope to accomplish by means of these acts.

On the "primitive" level religious actions remain a more or less unintegrated series of acts in pursuit of particular interests. The world of supernatural entities is not itself integrated into a fully rationalized system.[3] According to the exigencies of life as they arise and to the supernatural facilities provided in the traditional culture, these interests are defined and pursued. Here the question of the influence of religious ideas[4] is a difficult one. It is probably safest to speak of ideas, interests, value attitudes and acts as a single complex in which relations of priority

[1] When Durkheim rejected the definition of religion as concerned with supernatural things, the concept of supernatural was a different one from that used here. The latter is, as should be evident, entirely consistent with Durkheim's theoretical position.

[2] The use of this term in both this context and the above context where it is contrasted with disinterested is confusing. It is retained here because it is Weber's own usage. Interest in the religious context, however, is equivalent to a combination of the transcendental ends and ultimate-value attitudes of the above discussion.

[3] This is naturally a matter of degree. A completely unintegrated system would scarcely constitute a religion. *Cf.* Durkheim's definition.

[4] Which are primarily of the order of "myth." *Cf. supra*, Chap. XI, p. 425.

are exceedingly difficult to establish. Weber does not make a very great contribution to this question.

On the prophetic level, however, he has contributed very greatly to clarifying the relationships.[1] He has shown that, once the attempt to rationalize the meaning of the world into a rationally consistent system has been started in a given direction, there is an immanent dialectic of this process of rationalization. It may go at a more or less rapid pace; in one or several respects it may in a given development be carried to more or less radical conclusions or stopped at different points. But the main outline is clear. There is a limited number of mutually exclusive possibilities.

In the discussion of Durkheim religious ideas were treated in the main negatively, as ideas concerned with the nonempirical aspects of the world. Weber's results make it possible to define them more closely. They are ideas concerning not merely *how* the world works, but *why* in a teleological sense; they concern the "meaning" of the world. From this point of view religious ideas are inseparably bound up with human interests and vice versa. Weber has shown how the problem of evil, especially suffering, forms a central starting point for the formulation of the question of meaning. Conversely, what human religious interests *can* be, comes to be defined in terms of the conception of the meaning of the world.

This mutual relation is not altogether a completely relativistic circle. It is possible to say, in general, what kind of meaning and of interest is involved. The meaning is just that involved in the above teleological sense. If a friend is killed in an automobile accident the "how" is usually fairly clear in a scientifically satisfying sense. It is true that our knowledge of the physiology of death is by no means complete—and the friend of the deceased is not likely to be in possession of more than a small fraction of that knowledge. But this is not what is problematical to him. It is rather the "why" in a sense relative to a system of values. The question is, what purpose or value could his death serve? In this sense such an occurrence is apt to be felt as particularly meaningless.

The "meaning" in question, then, is that which is relevant to a teleological value context, not to a scientific explanatory context. The interests are those in the ultimate-value achieve-

[1] *Cf.* note appended to Chap. XIV, *supra*.

ments with which we identify ourselves. In this connection it must be noted that the religious ideas Weber is primarily concerned with are not as such exclusively value ideas, or ends of action. They are rather rationalized interpretations of the meaning of the world, including a complete metaphysical system. Out of these fundamental metaphysical postulates, then, is to be derived what meaning the world *can* have for man and, from this, in turn, what his ultimate values can "meaningfully" be.

It is rather that such ideas canalize religious interests—hence define ultimate ends and through them influence action. Their functional role may be thought of as analogous to that of institutions.[1]

They do not themselves constitute ends of action but rather a framework of ideal conditions under which ends may be pursued. What concrete ends will make sense depends on what is the structure of this framework. But for it to exert an influence on action it presupposes certain typical interests of men. The principal one relevant in the present context is the interest in giving their life a meaning. Correlative with this is the fact that all men respect or hold sacred certain things. The variations are not in this basic fact itself but in the concrete content of the sacred.

While the quest for a meaning of the world leads to one of the possible metaphysical positions, this is most emphatically not to be interpreted to mean that either the attitude of respect or the human interests correlative with such a theory are metaphysical entities. They are strictly observable empirical facts. Man is an entity that in relation to his nature and the kind of situation in which he is placed is known to develop metaphysical interpretations of his world. But whether he is this kind of entity or is placed in this kind of situation is not a metaphysical question but a question of fact. The position taken here, derived above all from Durkheim and Weber, is to be criticized and defended on empirical grounds.

It is now possible to make a reinterpretation of charisma. It is the quality which attaches to men and things by virtue of their relations with the "supernatural," that is, with the nonempirical aspects of reality in so far as they lend teleological "meaning" to men's acts and the events of the world. Charisma is not a

[1] In Weber's terms definable as "forms of legitimate order."

metaphysical entity but a strictly empirical observable quality of men and things in relation to human acts and attitudes.

Though its scope is broader than the religious in the usual sense there is inherent in the concept a religious reference. That is, men's ultimate-value interests are in the nature of the case inseparably linked to their conceptions of the supernatural, in this specific sense. It is hence through this religious reference that charisma may serve as the source of legitimacy. That is to say, there is an inherent solidarity between the things we respect (whether they be persons, or abstractions) and the moral rules governing intrinsic relations and actions. This solidarity is connected with the common reference of all these things to the supernatural and our conceptions of our own ultimate values and interests that are bound up with these conceptions of the supernatural. The distinction between legitimacy and charisma can be stated, in general terms as follows: Legitimacy is the narrower concept in that it is a quality imputed only to the norms of an order, not to persons, things or "imaginary" entities, and its reference is to the regulation of action, predominantly in its intrinsic aspects. Legitimacy is thus the *institutional* application or embodiment of charisma.

In concluding this discussion it is interesting to point out explicitly the extraordinarily close correspondence of Durkheim with Weber both in approach to this range of problems and in treatment of them. In spite of their differences—Weber's absorbtion in the problems of social dynamics and Durkheim's almost complete indifference to them, Weber's concern with action and, Durkheim's with knowledge of reality—in the basic conceptual framework at which they arrive their results are almost identical. The identity applies at at least two strategic points—the distinction of the moral and non-moral motives of action in relation to norms, and the distinction between the quality of norms as such (Weber—legitimacy; Durkheim—moral authority) and the broader element of which this is a "manifestation" (Weber—charisma; Durkheim—sacredness). The correspondence is the more striking in that the two started from opposite poles of thought—Weber from historical idealism, Durkheim from highly self-conscious positivism. Moreover, there is no trace whatever of mutual influence. There is not a single reference in the works of either to those of the other. It may be suggested that such an agreement is most readily explained as a matter of correct interpretation of the same class of facts.

Finally the correspondence extends to the sociologistic theorem, not only the theorem itself but the particular mode of its statement. It will be remembered that Durkheim's views on this subject were charged with being "made in Germany."[1] It has already been noted how extremely unlikely that is. But in the present context the relevant fact is that Weber was in conscious and explicit revolt against most of the prevailing organicism of German social theory which he largely identified with the intuitionist methodology that he criticized so severely. As against the realism of this trend, he was almost a militant social nominalist. A great deal of the German polemic against him has been based on this fact.[2]

Weber ruthlessly discarded from his work all nonempirical entities. The only *Geist* with which he will have anything to do is a matter of empirically observable attitudes and ideas which can be directly related to the understandable motivation of action. But in spite of this fact he definitely takes a sociologistic position. For one of his most fundamental results is that of the dominant social role of religious ideas and value attitudes— specific embodiments or values of charisma—which are *common* to the members of a great social movement or a whole society. Indeed only in so far as the attitudes derived from the doctrines of karma and transmigration are common to all Hindus is caste legitimized, and only in so far as the Protestant ethic was common to large numbers was there adequate motivation to rational ascetic mastery over everyday life. A society can only be subject to a legitimate order, and therefore can be on a non-biological level something other than a balance of power of interests, only in so far as there are *common* value attitudes in the society.

This, again, is exactly where Durkheim emerged in his interpretation of the possible meaning of the social reality. It is what is *left* after Weber's criticism of the historical organicism of German idealistic thought. Weber's individualistic treatment of charisma in connection with the role of the prophet in no way touches this

---

[1] *Supra*, Chap. VIII, p. 307.

[2] The most extreme case is Spann's review of *Wirtschaft und Gesellschaft*. See his *Tote und lebendige Wissenschaft*.

fundamental point. It merely serves to correct the principal defect which has been found in Durkheim's own statement due to his lingering sociologistic positivism. This was the implication that the empirical role of the value element was confined to sanctioning the institutional *status quo*. Weber, on the contrary, through his theory of prophecy and of the processes of routinization of charisma shows still another side of the picture. His position is not in the least in conflict with Durkheim's, but merely provides a further extension of its application which Durkheim failed to develop. This advance was due, above all, to Weber's comparative perspective and his correlative preoccupation with problems of social change.

Two other points should be mentioned before leaving the concept of charisma. It has already been noted[1] that Weber did not hold that the fully rationalized systems of ideas with which his comparative analysis of religion were concerned were, in the sharply formulated ideal-typical form in which he presents them, actually present in the minds of the great masses of the people he claims have been influenced by them. These rationalizations constitute polar-type cases—"exaggerations" almost—of the meaningful tendencies implicit in mass attitudes. This circumstance gives a clue to the general direction of interpretation of his views on the role of ideas and value elements. It will be remembered that among the motives of attribution of legitimacy to an order[2] he distinguished affectual and *wertrational*. The latter may be interpreted as referring to the formulation of the rational-type case. In harmony with the residual character of the category of affect, the affectual motive may be interpreted at least to include value elements in so far as they fall short of complete and consistent rational formulation.

This is particularly indicated by the close relation between the terms in which "affectuality" and charisma are characterized,[3] which makes it legitimate to conclude that Weber's "affect" is, in this respect, the counterpart of Pareto's "sentiment" and the ultimate-value attitude employed in this study. The distinction between this concept and *Wertrationalität* is the

[1] See Chap. XVI, p. 605.

[2] *Supra*, p. 659.

[3] "Affectual faith" is in the "validity of the newly revealed or the exemplary." *Wirtschaft. u Ges.*, p. 10.

counterpart of that in Pareto between the polar type of "residue," which is a principle clearly formulated and unambiguous, and a "sentiment," or in the terminology used here, an ultimate end and an ultimate-value attitude. The principal importance of this distinction is to note that it means that for Weber also the role of the value elements is *not* limited to the exceptional case of the clear, logical formulation of metaphysical ideas and ultimate ends. Departures from the rational norms are not to be interpreted *ipso facto* as evidence of the role of psychological factors. Indeed the concept charisma is so formulated as specifically not to involve this limitation.

Unfortunately, Weber does not give any extended analysis of the relations involved. To a certain extent doubtless ideas must be regarded as manifestations of the same basic elements as are attitudes and acts. But they are not wholly a function of sentiments. The cognitive element is certainly an indispensable independent element, however imperfectly rationalized. It is a function of true, not purely imaginary aspects of reality. But even less so than in the case of scientific ideas is it *wholly* this. As Weber shows, in the direction of interest and of the ways of putting the problems of the meaning of the world, a subjective element is involved. In working this out a concept of *Wertbeziehung* would become involved. Indeed this is the starting point for a *Wissenssoziologie* of metaphysical and religious ideas, as the concept of *Wertbeziehung* in his scientific methodology was for one of scientific ideas. The most general statement is that nonempirical reality (with particular reference to the teleological problem of meaning), our cognitive conceptions of it, nonrationalized value attitudes and the structure of the situations in which we act and about which we think, are elements in a relation of mutual interdependence upon each other. But this is more a statement of the problem than a solution. Such a solution would be beyond the scope of this study. It is one of the most fundamental fields for future analytical and empirical study.[1] Weber's importance lies in opening it up and formulating the elements of the problem in a way that promises to lead to tangible results. It lay on the frontiers of his thought.[2]

[1] No further analysis is attempted here. A broad statement of the problem of the role of ideas is made in the note appended to Chap. XIV, *supra*.

[2] As the residual character of the concept of affect shows.

Ritual

The one great exception to the remarkable correspondence of Weber and Durkheim in the basic categories of their sociological treatment of religion, is that of ritual. This element, so central for Durkheim has, curiously enough, no explicit place in Weber's system of concepts. It would, indeed, be a serious blow to the thesis of the essential similarity of the conceptual schemes of these two men if it turned out either that Weber had ignored the empirical facts of ritual entirely, or that he had put an interpretation on them radically inconsistent with that of Durkheim.

This is not, however, the case. On the contrary, though these elements are not explicitly brought together by Weber to constitute a theory of ritual, there are present in his thinking all the principal elements of a theory very close to that of Durkheim. All of them have been encountered in previous parts of the discussion. It remains here to discuss them in their relevance to this particular phenomenon.

In the first place, a glance back over the above treatment of Weber's comparative sociology of religion will immediately show that he by no means ignored the empirical facts of ritual, above all magic, but was vitally concerned with them. One of his two main directions of rationalization lay in the elimination of magical elements.[1] In his discussion of the failure of both the Chinese and the Indian religious ethics to develop a thoroughgoing rationalization of practical conduct, he laid great stress on the fact that both failed to attack the great mass of popular magic even though the elite themselves abstained from participation. The Puritan ethic, on the other hand, was characterized by a deep-rooted hostility, especially to magic, but also to ritual in general. To attribute sacredness to the means invoked was idolatry, and magic challenged the finality of the divine order which was an expression of God's will. Only where interference with it was revealed, as in the actions of predestined saints, was it to be assumed. The only rituals allowed to remain were those thought to be directly sanctioned by revelation, namely, baptism and communion.[2]

---

[1] *Entzauberung der Welt.* See especially *Religionssoziologie*, Vol. I, pp. 512–513.

[2] The Asiatic religious ethics may well have *transcended* magic. They never turned against it to root it out.

Secondly this failure to root out ritual, especially magic, is unquestionably very closely connected in Weber's mind with the failure to break through traditionalism.[1] This is so evidently the case that it may well be suspected that traditional action is the principal category in Weber's thinking where ritual is to be found hiding. But is this merely a suspicion, or is there further evidence for it?

There unquestionably is evidence of this. In the first place, it has several times been noted that Weber frequently applies the adjective sacred[2] to tradition. Indeed it is scarcely possible to speak of traditionalism as an element of his thought without this reference, for only with it does it become a form of *legitimate* order. Also it is only in this connection that it plays an important role in Weber's analytical scheme. For Durkheim ritual practices were "practices in relation to sacred things." Since sacredness, or the ritual attitude, is an essential characteristic of ritual, one source of the sacredness of tradition may well be that part of it, at least, is ritual tradition.

But the analysis may be pushed still farther. The concept of charisma, which is almost another name for sacredness, or for its source, is directly associated with both preprophetic and post-prophetic traditionalism. The traditionalization of a prophetic doctrine or message *is* precisely a process of transference of the charismatic quality from the person of the prophet to traditionalized norms and bearers of authority. The association of charisma and traditionalism is most intimate. There is no reason why this should not be applied to ritual.

But there is one final link in the chain. After the first, the mana stage of the embodiment of charisma, the question of meaning arises and with it symbolism enters into the picture. The things and events which have a meaning, then, are to be interpreted for this purpose as symbolic representations of supernatural entities. That is the source of the sanctity of these sacred things. They acquire, by virtue of this fact, a *charismatic* quality. Certainly among these "things" and events which are meaningful symbols of "supernatural" entities are included *actions*. In so far, then, is this not precisely Durkheim's definition of ritual as "actions in relation to sacred things"? Indeed this is just Weber's definition

---

[1] In the different branches of Christianity this relation is most striking.
[2] *Heilig.*

of a religious act except for the fact that Weber substitutes "supernatural entity" for "sacred thing"—that is, the thing symbolized for the symbol.[1] Moreover, fundamental to Weber's view is the most important thing in Durkheim's, the role of the symbolic relation. One could hardly ask for closer correspondence.

Finally, Weber holds that the first and universal effect of the entrance of symbolism into the situation is the stereotyping of tradition. Hence with this link with traditionalism the circle is closed. But why this intimate association between ritual, symbolism and traditionalism? Ritual involves both symbolism and sacredness. The element of sacredness forbids drawing an act into the ordinary utilitarian calculations of advantage—by virtue of that alone it would cease to be sacred.[2] Hence once a practice is "proved" efficacious, it becomes immediately stereotyped. Moreover, the symbolic element, especially in so far as it enters into the means-end relationship, makes it highly undesirable that it be subjected in intrinsic terms to rational criticism. For in so far as the relationship *is* symbolic it will by definition fail to meet such criticism.

In a context of action, which inherently implies the attempt to achieve ends, it may safely be assumed that the idea that it does not matter what ends are employed is deeply repugnant to the actor.[3] In the field of rational techniques an element of stability is provided by the objective intrinsic elements of the means-end relationship and the character of means and ends. At the same time there is no *inherent* obstacle to the alteration of such techniques in response to increasing knowledge of these intrinsic relationships. When ritual elements enter in there is a different situation. The sacredness, or meaning of sacred things is not an intrinsic, empirically observable property of them but something superimposed, a symbolic meaning. Similarly in so far as the means-end relationship is symbolic, there is then *no* intrinsic stabilizing element. These symbols can only function when the convention is accepted, that is, when they are traditionally

---

[1] In one possible symbolic relation. *Supra*, Chap. V, p. 211; XI, p. 419.

[2] *Cf.* "The sacred is that which is specifically unalterable," cited above from *Wirtschaft u. Ges.*, p. 231.

[3] That would be a "frivolity" incompatible with the "vie sérieuse" of which Durkheim speaks. *Formes élémentaires*, p. 546.

stereotyped. Traditionalism is the stabilizing element of symbolic relationships.[1]

This and not any incompatibility of philosophical doctrine is, it may be suggested, the main basis of the conflict between science and religion. The spirit of science is inherently that of critical skepticism in intrinsic empirical terms while, on the other hand, religion cannot do without symbolism.[2]

But, however this may be, there is undoubtedly a place in Weber's system for an element of the structure of action which involves charisma, and at the same time falls outside the ordinary intrinsic means-end analysis, above all through the fact that it involves symbolic elements in particular ways. These are the essential features of Durkheim's treatment of ritual for purposes of analysis of the structure of action. The correspondence between the two is complete.[3]

It is true that Weber did not develop a theory of the function of ritual at all comparable to Durkheim's. This and the fact that its analytical place was implicit rather than explicit is due primarily to Weber's focus of empirical interest. That is, he was concerned primarily with the dynamic aspect of religion embodied in the two aspects of charisma (in its prophetic embodiment) and rationalization. In this context the significance of traditionalism was mainly negative. It was that which stood in the way of these dynamic forces. He was not particularly concerned with "why"; to establish the fact that traditionalism had this effect was adequate for his purposes. Hence he did not pursue the analysis of traditionalism very far. It is significant that the lines of thought that have furnished the material for the above interpretation have been taken mainly from the section on the sociology of religion in *Wirtschaft und Gesellschaft*, where Weber attempted a systematic discussion of religion. Had he pursued this farther on the basis of a generalized system of theory, this conception of ritual would undoubtedly have become explicit. But he did not. And for the purposes of his empirical research on the relations of

[1] In the case of language as in every other.

[2] The application of this to Pareto's cycles is obvious. See above, Chap. VII.

[3] It should be obvious that the relation Durkheim established between ritual and the social, *i.e.*, the common value element, also applies to Weber. The above discussion of charisma is sufficient evidence.

religious ethics and capitalism, he did not need to. The results of this analysis only serve to confirm his conclusions in that context, not to alter them.

It almost goes without saying that for Weber as for the other writers here dealt with the factors formulable in nonsubjective terms, heredity and environment, play their part in the determination of concrete action. This is true both in the role of ultimate means and conditions of action and in the role of the sources of ignorance and error—the nonrational psychological factors in failure to attain and deviations from the rational norm. Nowhere does Weber take an extreme position denying the possibility of an important actual role for these elements. His own attention, however, is not focused on the analysis of this role, but on that of the other elements which have been discussed. It is merely mentioned here for the sake of completeness and to protect Weber against the unfounded charge of denying their role. He combated at many points exaggerated claims to complete determinism in terms of these factors. But he was open-minded as to the possibility of their providing significant elements of explanation on any particular problem.[1]

MATTERS OF TASTE

Finally, before this part of the discussion is brought to a close attention may be called to one further question which lies on the frontier of both the present analysis and that of all the writers treated in this study. Here it will only be introduced; it will receive some further consideration in the note appended to this chapter, in connection with Toennies. It will be remembered that Weber's scheme, with which this main analysis of his systematic theory started, contained not only two elements, efficiency norms of rationality and legitimacy norms, but also a third, usage (*Brauch*). Is this merely a chance formulation or will it repay investigation? Apparently being peripheral to Weber's own interest it is not central to any of his major concepts or conclusions. But none the less one line of thought associated with it is worth a brief development.

It will be remembered that the term usage was used to refer to uniformities of action in so far as they could not be held to involve either of the above two types of norm. The probability of a

[1] See especially *Wirtschaft. u. Ges.*, pp. 6 *ff.*

uniformity is given "purely through actual practice."[1] This is, like the definitions of affectual and traditional action, a somewhat indefinite formulation.

It might be inferred that it applied primarily to the uniformities of "automatism," the results of instinct, habit, etc. This interpretation, however, seems to be excluded by the fact that Weber quite explicitly limits his conceptual scheme to action in so far as it can be referred to subjectively understandable motives, that is, to action, in his technical sense. Usage, he quite explicitly says, is a "uniformity in the orientation of *social action*."[2] He is perfectly frank to admit that this regularity passes imperceptibly over into those oriented to a legitimate order—in this case, "convention."[3]

But this still leaves the problem unsolved. The principal example Weber uses is that of "tastes" in the time, modes and conditions of taking food. In Germany the "continental breakfast" is usage. It is what is "generally done." But there is nothing to prevent one having bacon and eggs or shredded wheat if he wishes—no sanctions will be visited on one who departs from the usage.[4] This gives the clue. Within the limits that are acceptable to the legitimate order of the society and are compatible with the needs of "efficiency," *e.g.*, physiologically adequate food at not excessive cost, there are elements of regularity which may be referred to as "matters of taste."

It is to be particularly noted that this element also involves *orientation to norms*. There are not merely factual regularities of action (as Weber's formulation would seem to imply) but standards of "good taste" in a society. The factual regularities, so far as they obtain, are to be interpreted as arising from common (or like) orientation to common norms. Reflection will show that this element has an extremely wide application in social life. It applies not only to matters of food, dress, daily personal habits, etc., but is a very prominent element in "art," "recreation," etc.

How is this to be interpreted in terms of the present scheme? In the first place this normative aspect alone radically shuts out a

---

[1] *Ibid.*, p. 15.

[2] *Ibid.*

[3] Which Weber distinguishes as a form of order enforced through diffuse sanctions of "disapproval" as opposed to "law," enforced through sanctions of coercion by a specially authorized *agency* of enforcement. See *ibid.*, p. 17.

[4] Within limits, of course.

"naturalistic" interpretation. There is every reason to believe that value elements are involved. On the other hand, it is a normative aspect of a distinctly different character from those thus far considered. The most conspicuous difference is the absence of a certain "binding" quality of the norms—at least in the same sense.

Efficiency norms and legitimacy norms are norms of action in a specific sense. They denote standards of the "right" relations of means and ends in a given context or the "right" modes of doing things with reference to binding values. Ritual, also, in its subjective aspect is to be regarded strictly as a means of accomplishing specific ends. The ritual manipulations are binding in the sense that they constitute the "right"—and the only "right" —way of achieving the end. But in practically all concrete acts, whether their principal context is predominantly utilitarian or ritual, there is to be found an element of embellishment in respects referable to standards of taste.

It may serve to clarify the question if an example is taken from each of these two fields. For the ancient Maori of New Zealand[1] bird snaring was one of the principal modes of gaining a livelihood. It is a universal fact that their bird snares are decorated with elaborate carving which demonstrably has absolutely no relevance to the efficiency of the snare in catching birds. There is a ritual aspect to this, since the carvings have magical significance, but, as the next example will show, this does not exhaust the question. Secondly, the Catholic mass is a typical ritual. But it may be performed in the most primitive circumstances with the simplest vestments of the priest, a wooden box for an altar, the rudest pottery for vessels. Or it may be performed with all the pomp and luxury of a great cathedral, the priest in rich, luxurious vestments, a highly decorated altar, vessels of gold studded with jewels, etc. The point is that the ritual element as such is conceived in both cases as exactly the same. The differences of appointments are precisely matters of taste. The pomp of the cathedral is not a bit more efficacious than the simplicity of a frontier or mission chapel.

Finally, there is a whole class of concrete acts that are spoken of normally as artistic creation and appreciation, on the one hand, and recreation, on the other, where the "taste" element

[1] *Cf.* R. FIRTH, *Primitive Economics of the New Zealand Maori.*

becomes predominant. It is true that all these activities involve "techniques"; once given a certain norm of taste, there are right and wrong ways of going about achieving it. These techniques may, then, be subjected to the ordinary means-end analysis. But the norm of taste is not itself a binding norm of the same character as the other two classes of norms discussed above.

It has already been noted that this normative character implies a value element. How is its relation to the other structural elements of action to be conceived? It seems that here the activities and their products are best regarded as modes of expression of value attitudes. The normative element is involved because of the fact that for these activities and their products to constitute an adequate expression they must in some sense be in conformity with the character of the values they express. But this conformity does not take the form either of subjection in the role of means or conditions to specific ends—considering the expressive activity as a total complex, in abstraction from the techniques involved, and from norms governing the means-end relationships—or of rules of legitimate order.[1]

It takes the form rather of meaningful correspondence between value attitude and concrete forms of activity and product. That is, these elements are to be interpreted as belonging together in a *Sinnzusammenhang* so that, on the one hand, the concrete activities and their products—works of art, etc.—constitute in this sense a coherent *Gestalt* and, on the other, motivational interpretation of them involves demonstrating their adequacy as expressions of the attitudes concerned. It is in this sense and only this that the style of Gothic architecture may be interpreted as an expression of the medieval Catholic *Geist* as formulated, for instance, in the *Summa* of Thomas Aquinas.[2]

In principle any and all attitudes can be expressed in terms of norms of taste in this sense and action oriented to them. But it should be evident that value attitudes[3] and above all common

---

[1] Involving moral sanctions.

[2] This is, I take it, what Professor Sorokin is fond of calling the "jigsaw method."

[3] Understood as the value element of concrete attitudes of course. Such elements belong together in a logical-meaningful unity. See P. A. Sorokin, "Forms and Problems of Culture Integration," *Rural Sociology*, June and September, 1936. Reprinted as Vol. I, Chap. I, of his *Social and Cultural Dynamics*.

ultimate-value attitudes will in general find expression in this mode as well as in the other relations to action which have been outlined. Conversely, any and all concrete action may be found to involve an element of this character—it is by no means confined to "art" in the popular sense.

This conclusion involves a most important methodological point. At the end of Chap. XVI was mentioned Dr. von Schelting's distinction between the understanding (*Verstehen*) of concrete motivational processes, on the one hand; of atemporal *Sinnzusammenhänge*, on the other. Dr. von Schelting shows that Weber's explicit methodological attention was confined to the former, but that at the same time he actually employed the latter in his empirical researches.

Its employment in the working out of systems of ideas as such is not relevant to the present context. But its further extension to concrete complexes of action is. This may, indeed, be interpreted precisely as the methodological counterpart of the empirical role of norms of taste and the action complexes oriented to them.[1] It is true that Weber's central interest, both analytical and methodological, was not in these phenomena but in the role of the other two types of norm. But on the periphery of his thinking it emerged on both levels—through the logical necessities of interpreting the empirical subject matter.

The place of this aspect of action systems—for it fully deserves to be called such—is, along with that of common ultimate values in the other context, the grain of truth in the intuitionist-emanationist social theories. It is no accident that such theories have always laid particular stress on this aspect of social life and have attempted to fit all the other aspects into the same schema. Weber's obliviousness to it is primarily to be explained in terms of his polemical attack on these theories, and his consequent concentration on the aspects of action they had patently misinterpreted. Its re-emergence from his own work is all the more significant on this account.

It may be emphasized that this sketch makes no pretense to being an exhaustive or adequate account of the role of norms of taste or still less to providing an adequate key to the understanding of such concrete phenomena as art, to which its applica-

[1] Though not alone of these. See note appended to this chapter, the discussion of *Gemeinschaft*, for another application.

tion is particularly obvious. Its purpose has been to characterize a part of the structure of action which impinges directly on those with which the previous analysis has been concerned. And, true to the general methodological character of the study, it has been dealt with precisely *in its relations* with the previous categories. This fact lends it an unavoidable residual character of which the reader by this time will have learned to be suspicious as it is probable that it covers up essential distinctions. It does not, however, seem expedient to attempt to press the analysis further at the present juncture. In the note appended to this chapter, however, something will be said in connection with the concept of *Gemeinschaft* about a class of concrete phenomena in which another element of the same type is prominently involved. The above sketch will serve as an introduction to this treatment.

The catalogue of the structural elements of action discernible in or directly inferable from Weber's systematic scheme of ideal types has now been completed. It has proved possible to identify and assign to a clear and definite role in the general scheme every single element of the previous analysis, especially as gained from the study of the work of Pareto and Durkheim. Moreover, every one of these elements, if it emerges in their work in clear-cut form at all, can be given a formulation that will fit both the theoretical schemes and the empirical interpretations of all three writers and do justice to what, according to the best interpretation a careful analysis has been able to put upon them, these writers themselves meant by their theories.[1] This definitely and finally establishes the convergence that it has been the principal object of this study to demonstrate. Finally, in Weber there has emerged still another structural element, the orientation of forms of expression to norms of taste, which fills a gap left in the other schemes.

It is not proposed here to enter upon the implications of the establishment of this generalized scheme of the structure of action for the problem of the construction of systems of general theory. A tentative essay in that direction will be attempted in the final chapter. Nor is it proposed to pursue the comparison of the three farther, or to recapitulate the essentials of the scheme.

---

[1] Put somewhat differently, making allowance for differing focuses of interest, the three conceptual schemes can be directly translated into terms of each other without essential change of meaning.

That will be attempted in the first of the two concluding chapters.

In closing this treatment of Weber it is essential merely to re-emphasize and make explicit beyond any possibility of doubt one thing. That is, Weber's whole position is definitely and fundamentally a voluntaristic theory of action, and neither a positivistic nor an idealistic theory. This has been found to be true at every essential point.

In the first place, his treatment of capitalism, of Protestantism and capitalism and more generally of the social role of religious ideas is understandable only on this basis. The role both of ideas and of the ultimate values associated with them is fundamental to Weber's thought. But equally so is the fact that these elements do not stand alone but in complex interrelations with other independent factors. Without the independence of heredity and environment, without the complex interrelations of ultimate values, ideas, attitudes, norms of different sorts with each other and with heredity and environment, concrete social life and action as we empirically know it, and as Weber treats it, is simply not conceivable or thinkable at all.

Secondly, the discussion of Weber's methodology has completely confirmed this interpretation of his empirical work. His methodological interest has been found to be focused mainly on those aspects of the logic of science which are significant for the understanding of action and neither of "nature" nor of atemporal complexes of meaning.[1] And, deeper still, Weber has demonstrated that the conception of objective scientific knowledge in any sense, of any empirical subject matter, is indissolubly bound up with the reality both of the normative aspect of action and of obstacles to the realization of norms. Science itself cannot be methodologically grounded without reference to the value element in the relation of *Wertbeziehung*. Without it there can be no determinate selection of *relevant* data, hence of objective knowledge in distinction from the "stream of consciousness." The very conception of science itself implies action.[2] Furthermore it is this basic solidarity of science and action which is the ultimate justification of the starting point of this whole study, the role in action of the norm of rationality in the sense of a scientifically verifiable intrinsic means-end relationship. If,

[1] See Chap. XIX, p. 727.
[2] This is, as has been noted, one grain of truth in pragmatism.

then, there is to be science at all there must be action. And if there is to be a science of action it *must* involve the norm of intrinsic rationality in this sense; it must, in fact, revolve about this as the pivotal point. Denial of this fundamental relationship from either side inevitably leads sooner or later to subjectivism and skepticism which undermine both science and responsible action.[1]

There is another aspect of Weber's methodology which has been briefly touched upon which fits directly into the present context; that is, one principal aspect of the ideal type is its normative character. It is not, of course, a norm for the observer, but the observer understands action partly in terms of the norms he has evidence for imputing to the actor as binding for the latter's action. Weber uses for explanatory purposes mainly rational-type cases but in any case pure type cases, which imply hypothetical full realization of the norm. It is further instructive to recall that in his polemical opposition to intuitionist theories Weber took special pains to emphasize the *unreality* of ideal types in this sense.

The above disagreement with Weber over the ideal type did not affect this normative character at all, but only the fact that Weber failed to distinguish concrete norms (the hypothetically concrete type-element) from normative elements of a generalized theory of action, and confined his explicit methodological attention to the former category. But from his point of view his insistence on their unreality was perfectly sound, and the strongest possible indication that he was dealing in terms of a voluntaristic theory of action. For while the normative elements are absolutely indispensable to action it is equally true and important that they cannot stand alone but can only acquire their meaning in their relations to non-normative elements; the reification of these ideal types, that is, the normative elements, *ipso facto* disposes of action itself—the theory becomes idealistic.[2]

Third, the discussion of the present chapter has shown that there is, at least as far as the present analysis has gone, a complete

---

[1] A recognition of this fundamental truth, though not always clearly, is one of the principal merits of Professor W. Y. Elliott's interesting *Pragmatic Revolt in Politics*. This paragraph may be regarded as a philosophical excursion rather than part of the strictly scientific argument.

[2] *Cf.* supra Chap. XI, in connection with Durkheim.

account of the structure of action systems identifiable in Weber's own conceptual scheme. And this is true in spite of the fact that his methodology had not clarified the logical nature of a generalized theoretical system. This total system of structural elements cannot acquire meaning at all except in the context of a voluntaristic theory of action; on the other hand, it is also to be maintained that such an approach inevitably leads to these elements in some form.

Finally, another emergent aspect of Weber's theory may be remarked upon which was passed over earlier because it was not in the center of his attention. It is, however, highly significant in the present context, indeed finally clinches the proof both that his position was a voluntaristic theory of action and that once such a theory is built up certain empirical conclusions flow from it. The above treatment of the problem of social change has followed Weber's central interest in the mutual relations of prophecy, rationalization and traditionalization.

There is, however, another aspect of social change, an account of a radically different kind of process to be discerned in his work —which may be called "secularization." The most prominent point at which it is evidenced is in his conception of adventurers' capitalism. The emergence of this phenomenon is due to a process of emancipation from ethical control, the setting free of interests and impulses from normative limitations, traditional or rationally ethical. It appears in the mitigation of ascetic rigor in the later stages of the development of the Protestant ethic—in general in the process of accomodation on both Protestant and Catholic bases. It appears in what Weber refers to as the "secularizing influence of wealth," which he emphasizes so strongly in the *Protestant Ethic*.[1] It appears finally in other spheres than the economic, for instance in the development of erotic enjoyments into a fine art.[2]

This is the centrifugal "bombardment of interests and appetites," their tendency to escape control, which has already been referred to at length. It is essentially the process involved in Pareto's process of transition from dominance of the residues of persistence to those of combination,[3] equally in Durkheim's

---

[1] *The Protestant Ethic and the Spirit of Capitalism*, p. 174, especially.

[2] *Cf. Religionssoziologie*, Vol. I, pp. 556 *ff.* especially.

[3] *Supra*, Chap. VII, pp. 284–285.

transition from solidarity or integration to *anomie*.[1] It is a process the possibility of which is inherent in the voluntaristic conception of action as such. Its complete absence from Weber's thought would have given grave reason to doubt the accuracy of the above analysis. But it is there. Only, like the explicit role of ritual, it is pushed out of the foreground of attention by the peculiarities of Weber's own empirical interest.

Unlike Pareto, Weber did not set out to build up a generalized theoretical system in the social field. Indeed there is little evidence that he had any clear conception either of the possibility of doing so or of its usefulness if it could be done. He was, rather, deeply absorbed in specific empirical problems and conceived theory directly as an aid to empirical research, never to be pursued for its own sake, but only as a means of forging tools for the empirical tasks directly in view. But his empirical research was not carried on with any dry-as-dust pedantry, investigating obscure and esoteric problems. He attacked the most significant questions he could find, with a range of perspective and an imaginative scope that few have equaled. It is indeed significant that in doing this he was in fact led, though without full self-consciousness, to develop the outline of a generalized theoretical system in at least one of its main aspects. The structural outline of a generalized system of action in his work is the most complete of any encountered thus far. It has previously been repeatedly emphasized that general theory, properly understood, is not sterile dialectical argument, but of the utmost consequence for the interpretation of empirical problems. The study of Max Weber shows most strikingly, conversely, that empirical research, if it has the scope and imagination to be genuinely important to the deeper problems of the time, leads directly into generalized theory with or without explicit methodological intention. The solidarity of general theory and empirical knowledge, one of the principal theses of this study, could scarcely be more impressively shown.

Note on *Gemeinschaft* and *Gesellschaft*[2]

After setting forth the classification that formed the main starting point for the analysis of the last chapter, of modes of orientation of action as to

[1] *Supra*, Chaps. VIII and X.

[2] These terms have become practically internationalized in their German form so it seems futile to attempt to translate them.

interest, legitimate order and usage, Weber proceded to set up a further threefold classification, *Kampf* (conflict), *Vergemeinschaftung* and *Vergesellschaftung*, which is the primary basis of the subsequent system of relationship types. The above analysis was not pushed to this point, as it is here that Weber turns from direct consideration of action to that of social relationships. Moreover, what is theoretically significant for present purposes could be brought out without considering this. There is, however, one point which should be briefly elucidated—that the aspect of social systems which has been called above modes of expression of attitudes, is not confined to matters of taste but extends over into the institutional sphere. For the purpose of showing this, the phenomena designated by the concept of *Gemeinschaft* as it has been developed in German sociological literature are convenient. But it is more convenient to discuss these phenomena in terms of the formulations of Toennies[1] who introduced the concept, on which Weber modeled his own, than it is to follow Weber farther. Toennies employed this dichotomy as the basis of a classification of social relationships.

Both *Gemeinschaft* and *Gesellschaft* are what are sometimes referred to as positive types of social relationship, that is, modes in which individuals are bound together. Thus both types specifically exclude conflict elements— indeed, as has been noted, Weber made conflict a third basic relationship element. With this issue it will be unnecessary to be concerned.

Gesellschaft for Toennies is the type of social relationship which has been formulated in the utilitarian school of social thought. It is significant that in the personal history that led to his theory Toennies was much preoccupied with the thought of Hobbes and deserves much credit for helping to revive interest in Hobbes. Indeed Hobbes and Marx may be considered the writers who influenced most his formulation of the concept of *Gesellschaft*. Next to these influences is that of Sir Henry Maine's concept of contract.

The keynote of *Gesellschaft* is the "rational pursuit of individual self-interest." The relationship is to be regarded subjectively as a means by which the individual attains his own ends. The motive for entering into such a relationship is that it is the most efficient means to his end that is available in the situation. All this presupposes the essential *separateness* of the parties to the relationship with respect to their own systems of ends or values. At least in so far as the relationship is of the *Gesellschaft* type whatever the parties may have in common beyond the specific elements directly spoken of is irrelevant to this conceptual analysis. And a total system of relationships approaches the *Gesellschaft* type precisely in so far as in understanding it such common elements may in fact be disregarded.

Toennies divides relations roughly into those among equals (*genossenschaftlich*), on the one hand, and those involving authority (*herrschaftlich*), on the other. Of the former class the typical *Gesellschaft* relations are exchange and the voluntary limited-purpose association.[2] In the case of exchange the parties act in the relation of means to each other's ends. *A* can supply something that *B* wants and vice versa. In the association relation they

---

[1] See F. TOENNIES, *Gemeinschaft und Gesellschaft*, 5th ed.

[2] *Verein* in the German terminology.

share a common immediate end, but only in matters related directly to this specific limited end can they be said to have common interests. Finally, authority on a *Gesellschaft* basis takes the form of a hierarchical relationship of superiority and subordination within a specific limited sphere. Bureaucratic authority in Weber's sense is a type case.

In each of these three cases the specific characteristic of *Gesellschaft* is a fusion of interests over a specific, *positively defined* area. Within that area it involves a "compromise" of interests of the parties, but it only mitigates their deeper-lying separateness, which in essentials remains untouched. Toennies goes even farther, following Hobbes, to say that there remains a latent conflict which is only patched up by compromise within this specific limited area.[1]

Toennies does not state the concept of *Gesellschaft* in such a way as to exclude institutional elements. On the contrary, the Marxian influence on his thought is particularly prominent in this respect. The compromises of *Gesellschaft* are arrived at within a framework of rules and are not purely *ad hoc* agreements in the sense of the Spencerian contractual relations. But in a very important sense the institutional rules are external to the relations in question, regulating them from the outside. They constitute conditions according to which men must enter into agreements to exchange or associate themselves for a common end or submit themselves to authority.

Toennies, in view of the role of the institutional element in *Gesellschaft* and of the role of *Gemeinschaft* generally, is of course not to be considered as belonging to the utilitarian school of social thought. But, with the qualifications necessary to take account of the institutional element, it is in the category of *Gesellschaft* that the elements of action of which the utilitarian position takes account find their main formulation in his theory.[2] Of course Toennies does not postulate that ultimate ends are *in fact* random, merely that in so far as relationships are of the *Gesellschaft* type what other ends the individual parties may entertain besides those involved immediately in the relationships become irrelevant. In particular it is irrelevant whether the ultimate-value systems of the parties are integrated. When a man walks into a store in a strange city to make a purchase his only relevant relation to the clerk behind the counter concerns matters of kind of goods, price, etc. All other facts about both persons may be disregarded. Above all it is not necessary even to know whether the two have any further interests in common beyond the immediate transaction.

Over against this Toennies sets *Gemeinschaft*. He uses a number of terms to characterize it of which only a few need be employed here. Above all, it is a broader relationship of solidarity over a rather undefined general area of life and interests. It is a community of fate (*Schicksal*). One may say that

---

[1] The similarity of Toennies' characterizations to those of Durkheim in this connection is striking. Toennies' book (1887) antedated the *Division of Labor* (1893).

[2] *Gemeinschaft* and *Gesellschaft* are for him *concrete* types of relationship. Hence the intermediate sector of the intrinsic means-end chain is involved in *Gemeinschaft*, too, but in a different way.

within the area of the relationship the parties act and are treated as a unit of solidarity. They share benefits and misfortunes in common, not necessarily equally, because *Gemeinschaft* relations perfectly well admit both of functional and of hierarchical differentiation. But it is the specific field of application of the communistic principle, to each according to his needs, from each according to his abilities.

Toennies tended to lay stress in this connection on the involuntary character of adherence to such a relationship, taking that of parent and child, for instance, as a type case, by contrast with voluntary entrance into a contractual relationship. This does not seem to be the important line of distinction, but rather to confuse the issue, since both friendship and marriage are in our society entered into mainly voluntarily, yet are most definitely in "ideal" relationships of the *Gemeinschaft* type.

The main criterion seems to lie rather on another plane, that of the way in which it is possible to speak of the parties having a "purpose" in entering into or adhering to the relationship. In the *Gesellschaft* case it was a specific limited purpose, a specific exchange of goods or services, or a specific immediate end held in common. In the *Gemeinschaft* case it is never this.[1] If it is possible to speak of an "end" for which a party enters into the relation, or for which it exists, this is of a different character. In the first place, it is of a general, indefinite character comprising a multitude of subsidiary specific ends, many of them as yet entirely undefined. If one is asked "Why did you marry?" he will generally find it an exceedingly difficult question to answer in the usual teleological terms. If on the other hand, he were asked why he went into a certain store he would reply without hesitation, "To buy some cigarettes." But the case of marriage—one is in love, perhaps; one wants a home, would like to have children, companionship, the "psychic security" which goes with these things, the combination of receiving benefits and being responsible for one's own share in maintaining the common enterprise

In so far as such a relationship is entered into by voluntary agreement it is an agreement to pool interests over a certain more or less well-defined general area of life. There are usually certain rather definitely understood minimum points—thus in marriage, that there should be sexual relations and a common household maintained. But even these do not define the relationship in the same sense that the specific ends of the parties do in the contractual case.

Of course there is an institutional aspect to *Gemeinschaft* relations as well as *Gesellschaft*. But there is a specific and typical difference in at least two important respects. In the *Gesellschaft* relation the parties to the relationship are held to obligations, morally in the first instance, but enforced by sanctions if necessary. But in this case the obligations are typically limited by the terms of the contract, that is, in entering into the relationship a party has assumed certain specific, positively defined obligations.[2] And, above all, in any new situation that may arise the presumption is against the inclusion

---

[1] These are, of course, polar types so there is a transition between them.

[2] *Gesellschaft* relations do not by any means involve *only* the "interested" motives of the earlier discussion.

of a new obligation unless it can be shown to be "in the contract" or implied in its terms.[1] The burden of proof is on him who would require the perform- ance of an obligation not obviously and explicitly assumed.

Gemeinschaft obligations, on the other hand, are typically unspecified and unlimited. If specified at all it is in the most general terms. Thus in the mar- riage oath each assumes the obligation to "love and cherish, for richer for poorer, in sickness and in health." It is a blanket obligation to help in what- ever contingency may arise in the course of a common life. The burden of proof is on him who would evade an obligation arising in any such contin- gency. One of the most striking examples is care for sickness. On the basis of contractual relations one does not, in general, feel obligated to assume the burden of care for an employe, or a business associate or customer who falls sick and whose own resources will not suffice. If one does it is from other motives, such as friendship or charitable feeling, not those inherent in the business relationship as such. But for a member of one's own family such care is a first obligation even though the object of it has done nothing to deserve it and he is personally disliked.

Though the obligations attached to a *Gemeinschaft* are unspecified and in the above sense unlimited, in another they are limited. But it is an entirely different kind of limitation from that given in the *Gesellschaft* relation. This is a corollary of the fact that the same person stands in a plurality of *Gemein- schaft* relations and others involving ethical obligations. Hence the claims of any one are limited by the potentially conflicting claims of others. There is implied a hierarchy of values, and a *valid* reason for refusing an obligation claimed by the other party to a *Gemeinschaft* relation is its incompatibility with a higher obligation. Thus a husband may reject claims of his wife on his time and attention because, being a doctor, they would force him to neglect the interests of his patients. But the point is that the higher obliga- tion here must be explicitly invoked; in the *Gesellschaft* case such consider- ations are irrelevant. If a storekeeper attempts to collect more than is owed him on his bill, it does not even matter if the debtor squanders the extra money on useless or even pernicious things, while the storekeeper "needs" it. The important thing is that the debtor's refusal to pay more would be upheld by the moral sanction of the community even without inquiry as to whether the storekeeper would put the money to better use than he, accord- ing to the standards of that community.

The second important difference in the institutional aspect lies in the point at which institutional norms apply. In the *Gesellschaft* relation the institu- tional norms constitute a body of contingent rules: *If* you enter into an agreement you are obligated to carry out its terms faithfully. You are equally obligated to remain within certain limits in securing assent of the other party, in refraining from fraud, duress, etc., even if you have the power to perpe- trate them. All these rules touch the specific means, ends and conditions of the actions or complexes of them.

[1] Qualified by the considerations discussed by Durkheim. *Supra*, Chap. VIII.

The *Gemeinschaft* relation is essentially different. There is none the less a system of institutional control in this sphere. But it does not in general take the form of norms directly regulating the specific ends, means and conditions of actions within the relationship. Where this occurs it is generally at the periphery. Certain things will be regarded as indispensable minima for the relationship to exist at all. Thus in the case of marriage general condemnation will strike the wife who will not allow her husband sexual access to her, and the husband who deserts or is guilty of nonsupport. But in general, and these cases are not really exceptions, institutional sanction is concerned rather with attitudes than with specific acts. The latter are judged primarily as expressions of these attitudes. This is especially clear from a consideration of gossip as a mode of social control in such matters. What we enjoin primarily are attitudes such as "love," "respect," "filial piety" and the like. The acts formally forbidden are those held to be particularly incompatible with the "proper" attitudes, those formally enjoined a minimum expression of such an attitude.[1] In the *Gesellschaft* relation on the other hand, attitudes are specifically irrelevant. It is the sphere of "formal legality."

This brings out what is in the present context the central point. In the *Gesellschaft* case the specific relationships are, within a framework of institutional norms, *ad hoc* for the specific acts or complexes of action. In that sense they are to be regarded as resultants of the immediate action elements. In a certain sense, as Toennies often remarks, the relation is mechanistic. The *Gemeinschaft* relation is, on the other hand, in the corresponding sense, specifically organic. For in order to understand the specific acts they must be seen in the context of the wider total relationship between the parties which by definition transcends these particular elements.

The relationship, then, is not to be regarded as a resultant of these immediate elements alone but as involving a wider framework within which they are placed. What carries the relationship is not these *ad hoc* elements taken alone but the relatively permanent and deep-seated attitudes of which these may be held to be expressions. It is owing to this fact that we always inquire into the attitude behind an act within a *Gemeinschaft* relationship as we do not in the other case.

In one sense the category of *Gemeinschaft* is strictly "formal." There may be a wide variety of different content involved. For instance, within the family even today there is a considerable amount of economic exchange of services incident to the maintenance of a common household. But this cannot be isolated from the wider framework of relationships and attitudes into which it fits, as it can be in the case of an ordinary market. This is not to be taken to mean that economic categories of analysis are inapplicable to such a situation, only that they cannot be taken alone. This has, indeed, been rather widely recognized by economists.

At the same time, whatever the reasons for it, there are certain types of concrete action which normally appear in a *Gemeinschaft* framework which strong moral feelings inhibit from being radically carried over into the

---

[1] Another aspect of these will be spoken of presently.

Gesellschaft context. This seems to be particularly true, at least in our society. of the sexual relationship. The connotations that the term prostitution has acquired are particularly striking in this respect. In its original reference prostitution refers to sexual intercourse precisely in abstraction from such a wider context of relationship—as an *ad hoc* transaction. It does not matter how "honest" the parties are, how considerate, how free from a desire to exploit one another. There may be a strong element of "workmanship," a disinterested performance of service, but it is still prostitution.

This same example brings out another thing. In our society not all extramarital sexual relations count as prostitution. We specifically distinguish from it those which occur in a context of friendship. No matter how severely the latter may be condemned in our mores they are never treated in the same way as prostitution. This is because friendship is also a *Gemeinschaft* type of relationship.

It follows that in so far as acts fall within such a system of *Gemeinschaft* relations they constitute particular modes of expression of deeper-lying, more permanent attitudes. This means *ipso facto* that they take on a symbolic significance in addition to the intrinsic significance. There can be no doubt of the enormous importance of this fact in social life. Sentiments cluster about such acts, they acquire a meaning for those who perform them. Without being able to discuss them with any fullness one or two of the specific applications may be mentioned.

In the first place it seems probable that this explains a large part of the relatively easy acceptance of tasks of drudgery. A woman doing housework will find tasks relatively bearable which are not intrinsically interesting when they are part of the necessary maintenance of her own family. The same tasks would probably appear much more as sheer drudgery if she were performing them as a hired maid in someone else's house.[1]

The sexual relation brings out a somewhat different aspect. Here its symbolic aspect in terms of a wider relation, in marriage, for instance, gives it a "meaning" which is, of course, not usually necessary as an incentive for people to enter into it. But this framework serves in most important ways as a mode of controlling what are in themselves strong impulses difficult to manage. These impulses are, both in marriage and in friendship, canalized in specific directions which, in so far as the control is effective, prevent their development into dangerously all-absorbing modes of hedonistic gratification.[2]

The role of symbolism in this as in other contexts involves that of traditionalism. Toennies often remarks on the close connection between *Gemeinschaft* and traditionalism. From the analysis of the previous chapter the reasons for the connection should be evident. In turn, there is a particularly

[1] For a related case, see the very interesting monograph by Roethlisberger and Dickson, *Technical vs. Social Organization in an Industrial Plant*, Harvard School of Business Administration, Studies in Industrial Research, 1934. See also T. N. Whitehead, *Leadership in a Free Society*.

[2] Romanticism, in this context, may be regarded as an exaggeration of this symbolic aspect of sexual relations.

close relationship between *Gemeinschaft* and religion owing primarily to the fact that common to both is a certain type of attitude, of disinterested devotion involved in a fusion of interests over an area, and the prominent role of symbolism. This comes out with especial clearness with reference to the relations of religion and the family, a major though by no means the only concrete field of *Gemeinschaft* relations. It may be stated[1] as an empirical generalization that religious and family interests may be very closely integrated with each other, or may be acutely opposed; they are never mutually indifferent.

The most important point is that here in the phenomena of *Gemeinschaft* is to be found another case where acts may best be interpreted as modes of expression of attitudes rather than as means to specific ends.[2] Thus *Gemeinschaft* norms are norms closely analogous to the norms of taste discussed in connection with Weber's concept of *Brauch*. They are, however, analogous and not identical. For the way in which Weber distinguished legitimate order and *Brauch* threw the moral element entirely over into the category of legitimate order. This, however, as was natural enough, he analyzed predominantly in terms of the institutional aspect of the intrinsic means-end schema.

It is quite clear, though, that *Gemeinschaft* involves the moral element, as the nature of community attitudes toward a breach of marriage customs, for instance, definitely proves. By this criterion, then, it is definitely institutional but in other respects it is closer to the norm of taste. The attitudes expressed within the framework of *Gemeinschaft* relationships though concrete attitudes, involve a value element, of which a major component, in turn, is that of value attitudes common to members of the same community. Adherence to the norms regulating *Gemeinschaft* relationships is by no means purely a matter of taste.

Then the category of "modes of expression" has been broadened out to include, in a different relation, the same elements that have been central to the intrinsic and the symbolic means-end relationships. This has the methodological implication that, like action oriented to norms of taste, action in a *Gemeinschaft* context must be understood by the jigsaw method. The concrete motivation elements must be placed in the wider context of the relation, or complex of them, as a whole.

This is the essential reason for the importance in this context of the relationship schema. Statement of the facts in its terms throws emphasis immediately and directly on the organic aspects of the phenomena in a way in which the action schema does not. Thus it provides an important corrective to any biases of perspective which may arise from exclusive concern with the action schema.

But it should be emphasized again that this importance of the relationship schema is primarily descriptive, not analytical. For Toennies, *Gemein-*

[1] This statement has already been made in another place. See Talcott Parsons, "The Place of Ultimate Values in Sociological Theory," *International Journal of Ethics*, April, 1935, p. 312.

[2] Always making allowance, as in the cases discussed in the last chapter, for techniques within such activities.

schaft and *Gesellschaft* are ideal types of *concrete* relationship. His scheme is in this sense a classification. Its importance here lies in its stating and classifying the facts in such a way as to bring out with especial clarity what are for the present analytical purposes highly significant points. Above all it shows the limitations of the understanding of complexes of action in terms of the immediate ends and situation of each particular act taken alone.

But for the explanation of *Gemeinschaft* as well as *Brauch* the generalized theory derived by developing the action schema is the most important. The conception of modes of expression is not a repudiation of the schema of the structure of action but an *extension* of it into what were for its less extended forms residual categories. Above all, what is "expressed" is the same attitudes that have been encountered before, with ultimate-value attitudes as the component of greatest theoretical interest. The fact that this leads, methodologically, into channels that have been used most by theories on another basis than the voluntaristic theory of action, that is, idealistic theories, is not to be wondered at nor objected to. As has been seen, in this as in other respects, both the general positions with which this study has been concerned (but with which it differs) have left permanently valid precipitates, both empirical and methodological, which it has been possible to incorporate into another scheme. The fact that this element is here made use of does not constitute putting forward either an idealistic or a positivistic theory.

Weber, it has been noted, used a concept closely related to Toennies' *Gemeinschaft*. He used it, however, mainly on a descriptive level, and its implications that are important for present purposes do not come out so clearly in his case as they do in the case of Toennies. Hence it has seemed preferable to use Toennies' work as a basis for this discussion. But its main conclusions may be applied directly to Weber[1] and tied in with the previous analysis of this work.

But this discussion of *Gemeinschaft* and *Gesellschaft* should not be taken to mean that these concepts are unreservedly acceptable as the basis for a general classification of social relationships or, indeed, that it is possible to start from *any* dichotomy of only two types. The basic types cannot be reduced to two, or even to the three that Weber used. To attempt to develop such a scheme of classification would be definitely outside the scope of the present study. Such an attempt would, however, have to make a critical examination of the schemes of Toennies, Weber and some others one of its main tasks.

However, the aspects of Toennies' classification with which this discussion has been concerned do involve distinctions of basic importance for any such scheme and would hence have to be built into the wider scheme, which would probably involve considerable alteration in their form of statement. For the present purpose, however, that of demonstrating another application of the concept of mode of expression of attitudes, their formulation in Toennies' terms has sufficed.

---

[1] Weber, of course, in his discussion of these problems owed much to Toennies.

PART IV
CONCLUSION

CHAPTER XVIII

EMPIRICALLY VERIFIED CONCLUSIONS

In the first chapter it was stated that this study should be considered as an attempted empirical verification, in a particular case, of a theory of the process by which scientific thought develops, the theory that was there outlined. The point may here be reiterated with all possible emphasis. This study has attempted throughout to be an *empirical* monograph. It has been concerned with facts and the understanding of facts. The propositions set forth have been based upon facts, and direct references to the sources for these facts have been given throughout in footnotes.

That the phenomena with which the study has been concerned happen to be the theories that certain writers have held about other phenomena does not alter matters. Whether or not they have held, as here interpreted, the theories that have been discussed is just as much a question of fact as any other, to be verified by the same method, that of observation. The facts in this case have reference to the published works of these writers. They belong to a class of facts, linguistic expressions, about which there has been necessarily a good deal of discussion. Observation of this class of phenomena involves interpretation of the meanings of the linguistic symbols employed in these works. It must be granted that this is empirical observation, otherwise not only this study but all the works of the writers here discussed, and all others which involve the subjective aspect of action, must be denied scientific status. After the discussion of the previous chapters there is no need to insist upon this point further. But short of radical and consistent behaviorism the status of the material as observable empirical fact can scarcely be doubted.

It is true that this study has not been concerned with theories only as empirical phenomena; it has also done some explicit theorizing on its own account. But according to the view of science here maintained, not only is this right and proper in an empirical monograph, it is altogether indispensable. The facts do not tell their own story; they must be cross-examined. They must be carefully analyzed, systematized, compared and interpreted. As is the case with all empirical studies this one has had as much to do with working out the implications of certain facts as with the establishment of the original facts. Observation and theoretical analysis have stood in close relations of interdependence. Without a theory of interpretation many of the facts about these writers' theories on which the greatest stress has been laid would not have been important and, if they had been observed at all, would have led to no theoretical conclusions. But equally the theory would have remained sterile if it had not been continually verified by observation. Of course, in the process of development of the study the theory itself has undergone continual modification and restatement. As is usual in such studies only the final version has actually been stated.

In these terms, then, the concluding remarks will be divided into two parts. The present chapter will be devoted to a statement of the evidence for certain conclusions which it will be maintained have been definitely established on empirical grounds by the foregoing study. The following, the final, chapter will be concerned with developing a few of their methodological implications. These are, as far as can now be seen, legitimate implications of the empirical conclusions arrived at. But it is not claimed that they are established by empirical evidence in the same sense. Hence the two groups of conclusions should be kept clearly distinct.

Summary Outline of the Structure of Action

But before stating the first group of conclusions, empirical demonstration of which is claimed, it will be well for the last time to summarize briefly the main line of analytical argument of the study as a whole. Thus the reader will have all the main points of the evidence freshly in mind and be in a better position to judge whether the theses stated are adequately proved.

Rationality and Utilitarianism

The starting point, both historical and logical, is the conception of intrinsic rationality of action. This involves the fundamental elements of "ends," "means" and "conditions" of rational action and the norm of the intrinsic means-end relationship. The rationality of action in terms of the latter is measured by the conformity of choice of means, within the conditions of the situation, with the expectations derived from a scientific theory[1] applied to the data in question and stated, as Pareto puts it, in the "virtual" form. Action in these terms is rational in so far as there is a scientifically demonstrable probability[2] that the means employed will, within the conditions of the actual situation, bring about or maintain the future state of affairs that the actor anticipates as his end.

Historically, this concept of rationality of action, not always clearly and unambiguously stated, has played the central role in what has been called the utilitarian branch of the positivistic tradition. In spite of differences due to varying assumptions about the environment in which rational action operates, it has been, in its essential structure, a constant structural element of the systems of thought considered here. The two radically positivistic polar positions do, however, alter its status in essential respects. The rationalistic position does so by erasing the distinctions between ends, means and conditions of rational action, making action a process only of adaptation to given conditions and predictions of their future state. The anti-intellectualistic position in its really radical form alters the status of rationality still more fundamentally; at the pole, indeed, eliminating it altogether. Both radical positivistic positions, however, involve insuperable difficulties—methodological and empirical.

The utilitarian type of theory concentrated on the means-end relationship and left the character of ends on the whole uninvestigated. This was sound. But in so far as it tended to become a closed system on a positivistic basis it was forced to the assumption that ends were random relative to the positivistically determinate elements of action. On this basis any attempt to bring order into this random variation led in the direction of radical positivistic determinism. In the cases of hedonism, the theory of natural selection, etc. several of these attempts have been reviewed and their consequences worked out. The utilitarian

---

[1] However elementary and empirical.

[2] This mode of statement makes allowance for error due to limitations of available objective knowledge.

assumption, explicit or implicit, of random ends is the only possible way to uphold on a positivistic basis the voluntaristic character of action, the independence of ends and the other normative elements of the structure of action from determinism in terms of heredity and environment.

Within the range of the utilitarian tradition and variations from it in the direction of the radical positivistic pole, there have appeared all the main relations of the norm of intrinsic rationality to the elements formulated in the radical positivistic theories, that is, to heredity and environment.[1] These may be seen in two main contexts. In so far as action is conceived as a process of rational adaptation of means to ends, they appear in the role of ultimate means and conditions of action. The qualification "ultimate" is made necessary by the fact that what are means and conditions to any given concrete actor may be in large part results of the other action elements of other individuals. To avoid reasoning in a circle it is necessary to think in terms of what are ultimate analytical conditions of action in general, abstracting from the concrete conditions of a particular concrete act. Failure clearly to make this distinction has been shown to be a prolific source of confusion. Another warning of the same order may be repeated. The same elements of heredity and environment play a part in determining the concrete ends of action. Such a concrete end is an anticipated concrete state of affairs, involving elements of the external environment and of heredity. Hedonism clearly illustrates this situation. Pleasure as an end of action was plausible because the psychological mechanisms that produce pleasurable feelings in certain circumstances are, in fact, expected to operate in the process leading to the desired state of affairs. But this has nothing to do with the analytical concept of end as part of a generalized system. It is a feature of the organism which we know by experience we can count on to operate in certain ways, and which hence belongs analytically to the conditions of action. To speak of ends as determined by the mechanism of pleasure is to that extent to eliminate ends from the generalized theoretical system.

---

[1] Used here, it will be remembered, in the technical sense defined in Chap. II, as a convenient summary for those elements bearing on action capable of formulation in terms of nonsubjective categories.

Secondly, the same elements of heredity and environment appear in relation to failure to attain the rational norm. From the objective point of view they appear mainly as reasons why action either falls short of or deviates from the norm, what have been called the resistant and the deviating factors, respectively. Subjectively the same factors in the same role appear as the sources of ignorance and error. Error in this sense is not random, but rather the existence of a bias of error in a particular direction is *ipso facto* evidence that a nonrational deviating factor is at work. Above all, within the positivistic framework, departures from the norm of rationality must be reducible, from the subjective point of view, to terms of ignorance or error or both.

Finally, it is not to be forgotten that there may well be hereditary elements which "drive" behavior in conformity with a rational norm but without the independent agency of the actor which is basic to the voluntaristic conception of action. In so far as this is true, whatever subjective aspect there is to action will turn out, on thorough investigation, to be reducible to terms of nonsubjective systems.[1] The test is always whether an adequate explanation of the concrete behavior in question can be attained without reference to the elements formulated in concepts with an inherent subjective reference.

Thus it is seen that both the norm of intrinsic rationality itself, and its main relations to heredity and environment in all three of the modes just outlined, could on the whole be adequately formulated within the general framework of the positivistic theoretical system, so long as it does not go over to the radical positivistic pole. It has, however, been shown that the utilitarian position is inherently unstable, and that in order to maintain it within a positivistic framework it is necessary to employ an extrapositivistic, metaphysical prop, which in the cases analyzed here has taken the form of the postulate of the natural identity of interests. Hence the more rigorously and systematically the implications of the positivistic position have been carried through, the more precarious has become the status of the normative elements of action which could find adequate formulation within a positivistic framework.

[1] It was noted above, Chap. XVII, p. 642, that Weber explicitly took account of this.

Indeed it may be held that the growing pressure of this increasingly rigorous systematization of the remoter implications of the positivistic approach to the study of human action has played an important part in the movement of thought which has occupied this study. The form of primary interest here is an increasingly sharp presentation of the "utilitarian dilemma": either a really radical positivistic position or the strictly utilitarian. The former course involved abandoning completely the means-end schema as analytically indispensable, the latter meant increasing dependence on extrascientific metaphysical assumptions. In the generally positivistic state of opinion all the weight of "hard-boiled" scientific prestige seemed to lie on the radically positivistic side. But at the same time the utilitarian tenets rested on sound empirical insight which could not readily be explained away. Hence the stage was set for a radical theoretical reconstruction that would transcend the dilemma altogether. Part II has been concerned with analyzing three different processes by which this reconstruction has occurred. They may be reviewed briefly.

Marshall

Marshall[1] took only one step, and that he took without clear self-consciousness of what he was doing. He inherited the conceptual scheme of the utilitarian tradition. And precisely the elements of it in which this study has been interested were central to his own further development of it in his utility theory. The conceptions of utility, of marginal utility and the principle of substitution are all completely dependent on the means-end schema, rational choice and the analytical independence of ends. This alone is sufficient to account for his failure to follow the trend, so important in his day, to radical positivism.

But at the same time he was quite clear about the inadequacy of a rigidly utilitarian position for explaining certain facts of economic life, those relating to the phenomena of free enterprise. The course he took was partly determined by his sound empirical insight, partly by his own ethical predilections. He broke through a rigidly utilitarian theory of economic life mainly at two points. First, he refused to accept the assumption of independence of wants even for the heuristic purposes of

[1] Analyzed in Chap. IV.

economic theory. This assumption he held applicable only to one class of wants, which he called, with a strongly derogatory connotation, "artificial" wants. For the class he was primarily interested in, "wants adjusted to activities," it would not hold. Secondly, he refused to accept the view that the concrete actions of economic life should be considered solely as means to want satisfaction, even for purposes of economics. They are at the same time fields for the "exercise of faculties" and the "development of character."

These two departures from the utilitarian schema are brought together under the concept of activities. This is not very clearly defined by Marshall; indeed, in relation to his inherited conceptual scheme, it is mainly a residual category. Certain things can, however, be said about it. It is quite clearly not primarily a new form of statement of the elements of heredity and environment. The explicit distinction between wants adjusted to activities and biological needs excludes this interpretation in one direction; it is excluded in a second direction by the clear impossibility of making out Marshall as a hedonist; and in still a third direction by his complete failure to question the rationality of action in the name of antirationalist psychology.

There can then be no doubt that activities constitute a residual category in the value direction. Both the wants adjusted to activities and the modes of activity themselves are to be regarded in the terms of this study primarily as manifestations of a single, relatively well-integrated system of value attitudes. The extraordinarily close resemblance of these attitudes to those involved in Weber's spirit of capitalism, particularly in its ascetic aspect, has been remarked upon.

"Activities" in this sense become for Marshall an important empirical element of the economic order. Along with increasing rationality and the accumulation of empirical knowledge, the development of this value system becomes to him the primary moving force of social evolution. But here Marshall stops. His consideration of integrated value systems as distinct from random ends is limited to this one system. He fails to develop the logical possibilities of there being others in other societies. He also fails to develop the theoretical possibilities of its relation to concrete action beyond the two points where it impinged directly on his utility theory. Thus the theoretical importance of his departure from tradition, and the empirical implications of a further development in this direction remained hidden, both to himself and to his followers. But in spite of this limitation he did take the crucial step, introducing an integrated value system, common to large numbers, which had no place in either the utilitarian or the radical positivistic framework.

Pareto

In the treatment of Pareto the same problems were considered from a different point of view. In the first place, his general methodological position cleared the way for the explicit development of a voluntaristic theory of action. For his skepticism had divested scientific methodology of the implication that a theory, to be methodologically acceptable, had to be positivistic. Indeed, of the four writers Pareto, in his general methodological requirements of scientific theory,[1] came much the closest to formulating a view that can be considered acceptable for the purposes of this study. Above all he thoroughly disposed of the fallacy of misplaced concreteness which has so persistently dogged the footsteps of positivistic social theory.

Pareto also was an eminent economist and as such developed essentially the same kind of utility theory as did Marshall. He furthermore shared with Marshall the conviction of its inadequacy for the scientific explanation of concrete human action even within the economic field. But his way of dealing with this situation was different from Marshall's. Rigidly limiting economic theory to the utility element he proceeded to supplement it with a broader synthetic sociological theory.

In his explicit conceptual scheme he did this by a double use of residual categories. The starting point is the positively defined concept of logical action. It is concrete action *in so far as* it consists of "operations logically united to their end" from the points of view both of the actor and of an outside observer. Nonlogical action, on the other hand, is definitely a residual category— action in so far as it fails, for whatever reason, to meet the logical criteria. Finally the concept of logical action is explicitly broader than the economic, but there is no positive systematic treatment of the noneconomic logical elements. They are enumerated, not defined. The principal task of further analysis

[1] As distinct from those peculiar to the theory of action.

of Pareto's work lies in following out what happens to both these residual categories in a structural context.

Pareto's explicit analysis of nonlogical action may first be summarized.[1] It is inductive and starts with a distinction of two classes of concrete data—overt acts and linguistic expressions. Pareto is directly concerned only with the latter and as a result of the analysis of nonscientific "theories" in this sense arrives at the categories of residue and derivation, the relatively constant and variable elements of these theories respectively. Thus the residue is a *proposition*.

Pareto developed the conception of the residues and derivations directly as variable elements in a theoretical system without explicit reference to the problem of structure. Having defined the concepts he proceeded to classify their values, without attempting, until a much later stage, to consider concrete systems of action. The concern of this study has, on the other hand, been to work out the implications of his treatment for the structure of the systems to which Pareto's analysis of elements is applicable.

In the first place, it was shown that the way in which he defined the concepts was such as to cut across what has been the major dichotomy of the present study, the distinction of the normative and the conditional aspects of systems of action. In particular, the residues must be held to manifest not one but both of these categories of elements. The result would be, in Pareto's own terms, to introduce into his classification of the residues, another basis, cutting across those he used. Many of Pareto's secondary interpreters have held that his "sentiments" were essentially the drives or instincts of antirationalist psychology. But the study of the way in which he approached his analysis has shown that there is no warrant in the logic of his position for this exclusive interpretation, and it has been shown to be specifically incompatible with certain important features of his work, particularly with his treatment of Social Darwinism and of the question, Do the residues correspond to the facts?[2]

This general bifurcation of structural elements is the basis for the further analysis.[3] The conception of logical action was the starting point for investigating the general question, What

---

[1] Treated in Chap. V.

[2] Treated in Chap. VI, pp. 219 *ff.*

[3] *Supra*, Chap. VI, pp. 228 *ff.*

are its implications for the structure of the total system of action in which it has a place? First, one element in the residues is that of the ultimate ends of action in the intrinsic means-end chain which, at the fully rationalized pole, is a clearly formulated, unambiguous principle[1] guiding action. The fact that ultimate ends belong in the nonlogical category makes it possible to interpret logical action as the intermediate sector of the intrinsic means-end chain. It has been possible to verify this interpretation of one element of the residues in terms of the role Pareto assigns to "faith" in the residues of persistence of aggregates. On no other hypothesis known to the present writer is this aspect of his cyclical theory understandable.

Secondly, it appears quite clearly that the value element is not exhausted by that of this particular type of residues, but that this is a rationalized polar-type case. Short of this there is a vaguer, less determinate value element discernible in the sentiments which is manifested in other residues, in derivations and in various ways in overt behavior. To designate this element and distinguish it from others involved in Pareto's sentiments the term ultimate-value attitudes has been introduced. Similarly to distinguish the residues that constitute governing principles of rational action from others they have been called ultimate ends. Here has appeared a distinction between two elements within the broader value category which was not contained in Marshall's concept of activities.

Third, it has turned out that logical action, or the intermediate intrinsic means-end sector is not, in systems of action structurally homogeneous but must be subdivided. On the basis of an analysis of the implications of Pareto's concept of logical action for such systems distinctions have been made between three such elements of the intermediate sector. On the principle of the progressive introduction of the broader relations of a given act to the rest of an action system there have been distinguished the technological, economic and political subsectors. It has also been possible to verify these lines of distinction in most striking fashion in terms of Pareto's theory of social utility. The hierarchical series of different levels on which he holds that the utility problem may be considered is the statement of the same distinctions

---

[1] "Le principe qui existe dans l'homme" as Pareto himself put it at one point.

in a somewhat different form. It is significant that these distinctions emerged in the synthetic part of Pareto's work where he is considering action systems as a whole, while they are not to be found in his explicit analytical scheme where only isolated unit acts are considered. Thus in place of a mere enumeration of the content of logical action has been introduced a scheme of systematically related structural elements.

Finally, to crown the hierarchy, in connection with the same theory of social utility there has been found to emerge a version of the sociologistic theorem. At the rationalized pole, with which Pareto is there concerned, it takes the form of the conception of the "end a society should pursue by means of logico-experimental reasoning." This may be restated to the effect that the actions of the members of a society are to a significant degree oriented to a single integrated system of ultimate ends common to these members. More generally the value element in the form both of ultimate ends and of value attitudes is in a significant degree common to the members of the society. This fact is one of the essential conditions of the equilibrium of social systems.

Thus as a result of Pareto's explicitly non-positivistic methodology and the much higher degree of historical relativism in his empirical views there is to be found implicit in his thought a differentiation of the structural elements of action systems far beyond the point to which Marshall carried it. The latter did not even clearly distinguish analytically the norm of intrinsic rationality from the value element—they were treated together in his conception of free enterprise. This distinction is explicit in Pareto—the one is logical, the other nonlogical. With this goes the clear differentiation of the ultimate-end element from the intermediate means-end sector. The latter, in turn, becomes differentiated into three subsectors, the lines of distinction of which did not come out at all clearly in Marshall. He tended to fuse them all with activities in his economic category, and thereby to suppress the element of coercive power entirely. Then the ultimate-value element itself differentiates into three distinguishable aspects, ultimate ends as such, value attitudes and both in so far as they are common to members of a community. Finally, there appears on the horizon a phenomenon as yet not explicitly analyzed but of great empirical importance to Pareto, which became analytically central for Durkheim, namely, ritual. Thus, though Pareto's starting point was not markedly different from that of Marshall, yet, by analyzing the stage that he reached, it is possible, from the present viewpoint, to make an enormous advance beyond Marshall.

Durkheim

Durkheim, in relation with Pareto, provides the first impressive example of convergence. It is true in a sense that they were both, even from the beginning, concerned with a very closely related set of problems. But the terms in which they approached these problems were so radically different that, prior to the present study, they have been thought to have little in common except that they were both sociologists.

Durkheim never dealt at all with matters of economic theory in the technical sense. But it has been shown that in his earlier empirical work he was greatly interested in the questions of economic individualism. Moreover, the theoretical terms in which Durkheim dealt with these problems have very much to do with the status of the utilitarian position. But here the immediate resemblance stops.

In one sense Durkheim's approach is through the action schema, but it was used in a peculiar way. The methodological counterpart of his empirical criticism of the utilitarian theories, in respect both to the *Division of Labor* and to the *Suicide*, is the assertion that they rest on an unsound teleology. In the terms of this study this means essentially that he thinks in terms of the utilitarian dilemma and having decisively rejected the utilitarian solution he is thrown back on the radical positivistic alternative. In subjective terms this means that the decisive factors must appear as facts of the external world to the actor, hence as conditions of his action. This is the genesis of "exteriority" and "constraint" as criteria of "social facts."

But with the extension in the *Suicide* of his empirical criticism from the utilitarian position to the whole group of theories involving the factors of heredity and environment a further set of problems developed. For the criteria of exteriority and constraint clearly included these elements as facts to the actor. Social facts became a residual category arrived at by elimination. This included the nonutilitarian aspects of action—that is, facts to the actor which were *not* a matter either of heredity or of the nonhuman environment. They constituted hence another kind of environmental factor, the *milieu social*.

The formulas to which Durkheim's name is still most widely attached—that "society is a reality *sui generis*," that it is a "psychic" entity and that it consists of "collective representations"—were framed, as has been seen, in the effort to define this residual category. All these efforts, but especially the synthesis argument, represent indirect attacks on the problem rather than developments out of the schema of action, which was his starting point.[1] In respect to this he remained in an impasse.

This impasse was finally broken through. The decisive step was the distinction of *social* constraint from naturalistic causation. The social milieu constitutes a set of conditions beyond the control of a given concrete individual, but not beyond the control of human agency in general. In fact from this point of view its most conspicuous aspect turns out to be a system of normative rules backed by sanctions.

Up to this point, having rejected utilitarian teleology, Durkheim still thinks of the actor passively on the analogy of a scientist studying the conditions of his situation. He entirely fails to consider the voluntaristic aspect of action and the role of ends. The next step, however, radically alters this situation. It is the recognition that fear of sanctions constitutes only the secondary motive for adherence to institutional norms; the primary is the sense of moral obligation. With this the primary meaning of constraint becomes moral obligation and a clear-cut distinction is drawn between social constraint and that of natural facts. The social reality has ceased to be merely a residual category.

But this brings Durkheim back to the voluntaristic aspect of the action schema which he had apparently deserted with his rejection of the utilitaran position. It is literally the synthesis that transcends both thesis and antithesis. For the sense of moral obligation toward a norm is clearly a value attitude in the above sense. Moreover, since the social milieu for Durkheim involves an integrated system of such norms, his position involves the existence of a common system of ultimate-value attitudes. The individualism of the utilitarian position has been transcended,

---

[1] It has been shown that the concept of collective representations did arise out of this schema, but in the particular rationalistic form Durkheim gave it rather than from a means-end analysis like that developed in Chap. VI.

but after this is done, the value element can return. Durkheim, having enunciated the sociologistic theorem at the beginning, has arrived by a process of its progressive reinterpretation, at essentially the same version as Pareto's; the social element involves the existence of a common value system.[1]

There is, however, one important difference. Pareto, approaching the problem through the direct development of the means-end schema and its generalization at the rational pole, formulated the social element as the "end a society should pursue." Durkheim's approach was different. Instead of generalizing the means-end schema for systems of action he thought of the individual acting in a social environment and went on to analyze the elements of this environment. Here he encountered a common system of normative rules as one of its principal features. Then he came to the sense of moral obligation first as a motive for individual obedience to a given rule, and at last he came to see that the maintenance of a common system of rules rested on a set of common values.

Thus Durkheim illuminated the institutional aspect of action systems, one which had been latent in Pareto's analytical thought, though there were strong suggestions of its role in his empirical work. But Durkheim brings it into clear relief as a distinct feature of the structure of action systems approached in terms of the intrinsic means-end schema. It turns out that action in the intrinsic means-end chain has at least a double normative orientation, as with Weber, both to efficiency norms and to legitimacy norms.

This new orientation has the further effect of bringing utilitarian elements back into the picture in the form of "interests" tending centrifugally to escape normative control. The most conspicuous formulation of this kind of conception in Durkheim's work so far considered is in the concept of *anomie*.[2] It bears a striking resemblance to Pareto's conception of the "interests" in relation to the residues of combinations. But on the whole relatively little of Durkheim's attention was centered on the intrinsic means-end schema as such, above all, on its intermediate sector. Hence the distinctions of elements in the latter which were found to be implicit in Pareto's work remained latent in

---

[1] Stated in Chap. X, pp. 381 *ff*.
[2] *Supra*, Chap. VIII, pp. 334 *ff*.

Durkheim's. His own further development of the action schema was of revolutionary importance but it lay in another direction, in aspects which had remained for Pareto, theoretically speaking, latent.

This important new development came in Durkheim's study of religion.[1] Considering his peculiar previous use of the subjective point of view it is not surprising that he started with the question of what "reality," that is, empirical reference of a class of facts to the actor, underlay religious ideas. But though his question is formulated in the same terms as before, his answer had revolutionary consequences. In the problem of institutions he gradually moved in his interpretation of the social milieu from considering it a set of facts of "nature," to a set of rules of moral obligation. But such rules are still empirical facts the importance of which lies in their intrinsic relation to action as agencies of control.

The specific objects of religious ideas, however, he found to be entities with one property in common—they were "sacred." Those with which theories of religion had been primarily concerned were mainly "imaginary" entities, gods, spirits, etc. But Durkheim showed that this property was shared with a large group of concrete objects and also actions, persons in certain circumstances, etc. Then the question arises, what is there in common between all sacred things which accounts for the common property of sacredness? The previous attempt had been to find an intrinsic source of this property. Durkheim takes a radically different course. The only property common to all sacred things is sacredness, and this does not lie in their intrinsic properties at all, but they have it only by virtue of the particular attitude men take toward them, the attitude of "respect."

If this be true, then, men respect sacred things not for themselves but because of their relations to something else they respect. What, then, is the character of this relation? It cannot be derived from the intrinsic properties of sacred things, but it is symbolic. Sacred things are sacred because they are symbols with a common symbolic reference to a source of sanctity. This symbolic relationship is something entirely new in the theory of action as considered up to this point.[2]

---

[1] Treated in Chap. XI.

[2] It was introduced in the discussion of Pareto, but he did not explicitly consider it in a systematic theoretical context.

Then arises the question, what is this common reference? It must be, says Durkheim, something we can respect in this specific sense, and in this sense we respect *only* moral authority. Hence the source of the sacredness of sacred things is the same as that of obligation to moral rules. It is "society." This synthesis of what had been before regarded as quite disparate aspects of human life was a stroke of genius on Durkheim's part—of revolutionary importance.

But this position is in need of further interpretation to clear up the difficulties left by Durkheim's lingering positivism. Society in this context is not a concrete entity; it is, above all, not the concrete totality of human beings in relation to each other. It is a "moral reality." The further analysis has shown that religious ideas have to do with men's cognitive relations with certain nonempirical aspects of the world, what has been called in a *special* sense, in the study of Weber, the "supernatural." Associated with these ideas are certain "active attitudes," as Professor Nock calls them, in part determined by these ideas but in part determining them, in turn. These active attitudes turn out to be the ultimate-value attitudes of the previous discussion, and, in so far as they constitute "society" in Durkheim's sense, are common value attitudes. The *source* of sacredness is the supernatural; our symbolic representations of it are sacred things; the attitude of respect to them is, along with respect for moral obligations, a manifestation of our ultimate-value attitudes which are social in so far as they are common.

But this is not all. The active attitudes associated with religious ideas are manifested not only in "ideas" but in certain actions or "behavior," and these actions share the quality of sacredness and involve relations to sacred entities. This whole class of "actions in relation to sacred things" Durkheim calls rituals. They are actions in the strictest sense, modes for the actor of attaining specific ends. As Durkheim puts it, they are part of the *vie sérieuse*.[1] But they differ in two fundamental respects from the actions the analysis has previously been concerned with. They are sacred and hence carried out only under special conditions, specifically removed from the ordinary utilitarian calculations of advantage—they are performed with the "ritual attitude." Further, they involve the manipulation

[1] See *Formes élémentaires*, p. 546.

of sacred symbols, what has been called a symbolic means-end relationship. In both these respects, measured by the standard of the intrinsic norm of rationality, they are not *ir*rational but *non*rational. The standard simply does not apply.

Finally, ritual to Durkheim was not merely a manifestation of value attitudes, but of great functional importance in relation to social "solidarity," a mode of revivifying and strengthening the common value elements, which are ordinarily more or less latent in the course of profane activities. In this connection the centrifugal tendencies of "interests" make a striking reappearance in Durkheim's thought. Ritual is one of the fundamental defense mechanisms of society against the tendency to *anomie*.

There was thus a steady process of development in Durkheim's thought about society. From a concrete reality it became a complex of elements of action existing only "in the minds of individuals." From a category of the "facts of nature," in the role of conditions of human action, it became a common value system involving a nonempirical reference. This latter tendency culminated in his sociological epistemology. This constituted the final break with the methodology of positivism, but brought new difficulties of its own. It represented a trend of Durkheim's thought in a definitely idealistic direction which in his final phase was warring with the voluntaristic theory of action. Reinterpreted in terms of the latter its essential truth is that which came out in more acceptable form in Weber's concept of *Wertbeziehung*, introducing as it did an element of relativity into knowledge and at the same time providing a point of departure for analysis of the social factors in its development.

It should be emphasized that in the respects relevant to the present context there is *nothing* important in the theories of Pareto which is incompatible with those of Durkheim, and vice versa. Their differences are complementary, lying in the different points at which they differentiated the elements of the structure of action. Pareto brought out,[1] as Durkheim did not, the internal differentiation of the intermediate intrinsic sector and the ultimate-value element so far as it is not integrated in a common system. Durkheim, on the other hand, brought into clear relief the role of the institutional element in relation to the intrinsic means-end chain and carried out a much further

[1] In the theory of social utility.

differentiation of the structure and modes of manifestation of the ultimate-value system, which for Pareto had remained residual.

This was done in the concepts of the sacred, of the role of symbolism and of their relations to ritual action and its function. In the concept of the sacred there is implied the nonempirical reference of ultimate values, and hence the relation of value attitudes to "ideas" is much more clearly evident than in Pareto. Furthermore, the symbolic relationship, which is central to representations of the supernatural turns out, along with the concept of sacredness, to provide the analytical key essential to the understanding of a whole class of actions, ritual, which had been highly important to Pareto empirically but for his systematic theory had remained residual. These concepts of Durkheim's are to be regarded as a further specification of the content of Pareto's categories of nonlogical action and sentiment.

That the conceptual elements which have been differentiated in the course of analyzing the work of Pareto and of Durkheim really do belong to the *same* theoretical system, and that the work of the two really did converge, is conclusively demonstrated by the fact that it has been possible to show that *all* of them and one other are to be found in the work of Weber. This is true in spite of the fact that Weber's work was entirely independent of that of either of the other two, and that Weber's methodological position was such as seriously to obscure the status of a generalized theoretical system. It is, above all, remarkable that a German historical economist should have come to a conception of the place of the economic element almost identical with that of the neoclassicist Pareto and that Weber, an idealist (in background), should have come to a *point-for-point* correspondence in the distinctly complex system of structural categories relating to religious ideas, institutions, ritual and value attitudes, with the outspoken positivist Durkheim. It is legitimate to maintain that in these fundamental respects the convergence has not merely been suggested or made to seem likely but has been *demonstrated* as a matter of empirical fact. It can only be doubted on the ground that the work of the three men has here been radically misinterpreted, and that is a question of fact.

Weber

The work of Weber should be sufficiently fresh in the reader's mind for it to be unnecessary to give it more than a very brief recapitulation. Empirically his main attack was on Marxian historical materialism which, as has been shown, constituted, analytically considered, in essentials a version of the utilitarian position, placed in a historical context. Over against this he placed a theory of the role of value elements in the form of a combination of religious interests, *e.g.*, value attitudes, in their relation to systems of metaphysical ideas. This was, however, placed in the context of a voluntaristic theory of action, not of idealistic emanationism. Value elements for Weber exert their influence in complex processes of interaction with the other elements of a system of action, not by simply "becoming real." All this was worked out in great detail in his empirical studies of the relations of religious ethics to economic life.[1]

The methodological counterpart of his refusal to regard the social influence of religious ideas as a process of emanation was his attack on the methodological views growing out of idealistic philosophy.[2] Their common characteristic was a denial of the possibility or validity of general concepts in the field of human action. As against them Weber sharply vindicated the indispensability of general theoretical concepts for the demonstration of any objective empirical proposition in any field.

While sharply rejecting their views of the logic of social science he salvaged out of the wreckage certain elements of basic importance to his own substantive position. Idealistic theories of intuition were sound in suggesting the subjective reference of the theory of action, the indispensability of the subjective point of view. The freedom argument left the norm of intrinsic rationality as basic to action. The organic aspect of intuitionism left the concept of a value element in its double relation, in *Wertbeziehung*, as methodologically indispensable to theory and as central to action itself. Above all the methodological vindication of general concepts is essential to the concept of action since science and rationality of action are indissolubly bound up together.

At the same time, due to circumstances which have been reviewed, there were from the present point of view two serious limitations in Weber's methodological position. First, in trying to defend a line of distinction between the *logical* character of the natural and the social sciences, which has here been held to

[1] Treated in Chaps. XIV and XV.
[2] *Supra*, Chap. XVI, pp. 581 *ff*.

be indefensible, he was driven to a fictional view of the nature of general concepts in these fields which tended to obscure the role of the essentially nonfictional generalized system of theory. Secondly, this and the circumstance that general concepts were for him a residual category obscured what is for this study the vital distinction between his hypothetically concrete type concepts and their empirical generalization, on the one hand, and the categories of a generalized theoretical system, on the other. Only the former are fictional in the social field, a fact that is due to the important degree of organicism of the subject matter.

Thus his explicit systematic theorizing tended to run off in a direction different from that of the main present interest, that of a systematic classification of structural ideal types of social relationship.[1] But in spite of these methodological limitations it has been possible to elicit by analysis a definite scheme of the structure of a generalized system of action which appears at the most strategic points of Weber's work and, though he did not clearly recognize its logical nature, this scheme was absolutely essential to Weber's specific results both empirical and theoretical. Thus the complexities in the category of general concepts brought to light by the previous analysis have been verified by the demonstration that *in fact* his actual systematic theorizing involves the different types that would be expected if the analysis is correct. It is not necessary to recapitulate the structural outline of this generalized system and the ways by which Weber arrived at its elements so fully as has been done in regard to Marshall and Pareto. The logical starting point is again the standard of intrinsic rationality embodied in the norm of efficiency. This involves essentially the same relations to heredity and environment which have been found to exist in every case. The intermediate sector of the intrinsic means-end chain is differentiated in essentially the same way as was worked out in the study of Pareto.[2] The line between the technological elements and the economic is the same as that drawn before and is perfectly explicit. That between economic and political involves more complex questions but, in drawing it as Weber did

[1] This is formal sociology in Simmel's sense. See G. SIMMEL, *Soziologie*, Chap. I.

[2] *Supra*, Chap. XVII, pp. 653 *ff.*

with the use of the concept of authority, there is both a clear recognition of the importance of coercive power as exercised by a variety of means, and a recognition that there is a definite limit to the extent to which these may be made to fit into ordinary economic categories of analysis.

The ultimate-value element came into Weber's work in the first instance with the systems of value attitudes associated with religious ideas. Its status in the role of ultimate ends of the intrinsic means-end chain comes out theoretically in connection with the types of rational action, *zweckrational* and *wertrational*. Its institutional relation to the intrinsic means-end chain is expressed in the concept of legitimate order, the direct equivalent of Durkheim's rules possessing moral authority. Its nonempirical "religious" reference is formulated in the concept of charisma, corresponding to Durkheim's sacred. By analyzing this it was possible to clarify the reciprocal relation between value attitudes, generally called by Weber in this context religious interests, and religious ideas. Consideration of the question of "meaning" in relation to these ideas, and to things and events in the world, leads to the central role of symbolism, and for Weber undoubtedly there was a class of actions to an eminent degree involving both charisma and symbolism, that is, ritual. This was not explicitly analyzed as by Durkheim but all the elements of Durkheim's analysis are present.

In all these respects there is a remarkable point-for-point correspondence between Weber and Durkheim.[1] There are, in this range of questions three main differences, none of them disagreements but all differences of emphasis. The categories relating to ritual, which were explicit and central for Durkheim, were largely implicit for Weber. On the other hand, the mutual relations of value attitudes and ideas of the supernatural, which had to be worked out by inference from Durkheim's position, are quite explicit in Weber, in a way that directly verifies the inferences made from Durkheim's position. Third, the role of value elements in dynamic processes of change from the *status quo*, which was almost completely latent in Durkheim, comes into the center of the stage for Weber in his theory of prophecy, thus correcting a seriously one-sided impression given by Durkheim as he himself left his work.

[1] *Supra*, Chap. XVII, pp. 661 *ff.*

Finally, in Weber is to be found another emergent aspect of action systems, that which has been called "modes of expression" of value attitudes, which has nowhere else been found. It turns out to be emergent on both the methodological and the theoretical levels. In the study of Weber it has been analyzed in one context, that of orientation of action to norms of taste. But in the discussion of Toennies the same kind of analysis is found to be applicable to institutional phenomena in the case of *Gemeinschaft*, where the norms in question contain a moral element and are not merely matters of taste.

The elements of structure of a generalized system of action thus outlined are seen to fall into three relatively well-defined groups. The first is heredity and environment, seen subjectively as the ultimate means and conditions of action and as the sources of ignorance and "determinate" error. These are the elements the scientific understanding of which is possible in terms of categories not involving a subjective reference.[1] They constitute data for the sciences of action.[2] Knowledge of their nature and behavior is the "permanently valid precipitate" for the theory of human action, left behind by the radically positivistic social theories.

The second is the group included in the intermediate intrinsic means-end sector. This group constitutes the permanently valid precipitate of the utilitarian theories. The atomistic character of utilitarian thought prevented the internal differentiation of this sector from coming out clearly, but the lines can be discerned. The general concept of rationality of action, common to them all, formulates the technological element. Utilitarian theories on a social level under the postulate of the natural identity of interests have formulated the economic element. In conceptual refinement this has reached its culmination in the marginal-utility analysis of modern economic theory since Jevons and Marshall. Finally, the element of coercive power received its classic formulation on a utilitarian basis with Hobbes and has since appeared in various forms whenever the postulate of the natural identity of interests has been broken down.

The third is the whole group of elements clustering about the ultimate-value system in so far as it is integrated and not reduc-

---

[1] Qualified for the psychological elements to be discussed in the next chapter.

[2] See the next chapter.

ible to the random ends of utilitarianism.) It is, as has been shown, emergent from the positivistic tradition and the process of its emergence is that of the breakdown of the positivistic tradition in its transition to a voluntaristic theory of action. In some form it has always been indigenous to the idealistic tradition and for the development of the theory of action, this is the permanently valid idealistic precipitate. But until recently the positivistic-idealistic dualism of modern social thought has created, both methodologically and theoretically, a hiatus which has prevented its integration with the other elements into the description of a single comprehensive general system of action. Only the corresponding breakdown of the idealistic methodology which has been traced in the study of Weber has made possible the bridging of this hiatus and the convergence of the two developments.

Finally, there is an element which does not fall within any of these three structural groups as such but serves rather to bind them together. It is that which has been encountered at various points and called "effort." This is a name for the relating factor between the normative and the conditional elements of action. It is necessitated by the fact that norms do not realize themselves automatically but only through action, so far as they are realized at all. It is an element the analytical status of which in the theory of action is probably closely analogous to that of energy in physics.

Verified Conclusions

It may be submitted that the propositions included in the above outline and the discussions in the body of the study of which they form a brief summary, constitute, with one exception, adequate proof of the five theses about to be stated. The one exception is that within the scope of this study it has been impossible to include all the empirical evidence on which the theories under discussion have been based. In the above outline none could be included, but in the body of the study the attempt has been made to bring forward a fair sample of this evidence, and the reader who is sufficiently interested can turn to the works of the writers themselves for the rest. The five theses are:

1. That in the works of the four principal writers here treated there has appeared the outline of what *in all essentials*, is the

same system of generalized social theory, the structural aspect of what has been called the voluntaristic theory of action. Theoretically important differences between these writers can be reduced to three circumstances: (*a*) Differences of terminology, different names for the same thing (for instance Pareto calls "logical" what Weber calls "rational"). (*b*) Differences in the point to which the structural analysis has been carried in order to arrive at the explicit distinction of all the major elements. In this respect Marshall represents hardly more than a beginning of the advance beyond the utilitarian position. But it is a beginning at such a strategic point as to be of great interest here. (*c*) Differences in mode of statement due to the different empirical centers of attention and theoretical approaches of the different writers. Thus the moral element appeared for Pareto first as ultimate ends, one element of the residues; for Durkheim as institutional norms.

2. That this generalized system of theoretical categories common to the writers here treated is, taken as a total system, a *new* development of theory and is not simply taken over from the traditions on which they built. It is not, of course, a creation *ex nihilo* but was arrived at by a gradual process of critical re-examination of certain aspects and elements of the older systems, a process standing in closest relation to empirical observation and verification. Indeed, given the diversity of starting points, the fact alone that it is essentially the same system precludes its being simply taken over from the older systems. Above all, it does not contain only elements common to all the previous traditions. Though every one of its major groups of elements had some place in at least one of the other traditions as something more than part of a residual category, this is not true of the system as a whole looked at as a specific total structure of conceptual elements. The completed structure is at some vital point incompatible with each of these older systems.

3. That the development of this theoretical system has in each case stood in the closest relation to the principal empirical generalizations which the writer in question formulated. First, negatively, the closeness of Marshall's empirical views to those dominant in the utilitarian tradition is possible only by virtue of the relatively slight extent of his departure from their theoretical system. To take only one crucial instance, if from his

insight into the role of one common value system he had come to see the possibilities of different value systems, he could not have upheld linear evolutionism in the sense he did. In the cases of Pareto and Durkheim their departures from all the major positivistic empirical theories, such as linear evolutionism, *laissez faire*, Social Darwinism, religion and magic conceived as pre-science, are most intimately related to the voluntaristic theory of action. In part, their development of this theory is due to the criticism of positivistic theories which has followed from their new empirical discoveries and insights; in part, their new theoretical ideas have led them to new factual insights. The same is true of Weber, with the exception that he was fighting on two fronts—on the one side against idealistic, emanationist views and the empirical theories associated with them; on the other against the positivistic tendencies of Marxian historical materialism.

Above all, the important empirical interpretations of none of the three thinkers could be adequately developed or stated in terms of either a positivistic or an idealistic conceptual scheme. It is to be remembered that their "theories" in this sense are not merely such bald propositions as "Social change follows in certain respects a cyclical pattern" or "There are social factors in suicide" or "The Protestant ethic had an important effect on Western economic development." All these propositions could be fitted into other schemes. The "empirical interpretations" here spoken of are rather their specific accounts of the modes, processes and relations of elements of the phenomena concerned, which underly these most general propositions. The more deeply one goes into the detail of their explanations of these things the more central do the categories of the voluntaristic theory of action become.

4. That one major factor in the emergence of the voluntaristic theory of action lies in correct observation of the empirical facts of social life, especially corrections of and additions to the observations made by proponents of the theories against which these writers stood in polemical opposition. It has naturally been impossible, within the scope of this study, to present all the empirical evidence which each writer studied brought forward himself or which could be introduced. Hence the possibilities of empirical proof of this proposition have not been exhausted. The

evidence that has been presented is, however, adequate. In the first place a considerable amount of this evidence has been cited and on the whole found to be sound. Secondly, various criticisms brought against these empirical theories have been considered and found to be lacking in conclusiveness. Finally, there is the very impressive fact of convergence, that the work of these men who started from markedly different points of view converges upon a single theory.

It is, of course, conceivable that the convergence does not exist at all, but that its appearance in this study is the result of an accumulation of errors of interpretation by the present author. It is also conceivable, though very improbable, that it is the result of an accumulation of random errors on the part of the various theorists themselves. If either of these possibilities is to be considered, it might be instructive to calculate the probabilities that this might occur, considering the number of different elements and their combinations to be taken into account.

That it is due to a congruence of purely personal sentiments seems highly improbable in view of the great diversity of the four men in these respects which was noted in the first chapter. For instance, the anticlerical, radical humanitarianism that was at the basis of Durkheim's personal values was the commonest target for Pareto's biting irony. Finally, the diversities of individualistic positivism, sociologistic positivism and the idealistic social theories as conceptual schemes are so great as to eliminate as an adequate explanation the immanent development of previous theoretical systems without reference to the facts. Each of these theoretical systems could have developed in any one of several different ways— there was no general predetermination in favor of a voluntaristic theory of action. Above all, the utilitarian position could have developed, and did develop, into radical positivism, especially the theory of natural selection and psychological anti-intellectualism. Equally a critique of Marxian historical materialism in favor of the role of "ideas" could perfectly well have developed into a radically idealistic emanationist theory, and, with Sombart, did so develop.

In the matter of convergence, then, there remain two other possible explanations. One is the determination of the convergence by the adequacy of the theories to the facts. The other is that it is due to certain features of the total movement of European thought, independent of the facts observed by scientists, but common to all the intellectual traditions considered here out of which the voluntaristic theory of action has emerged. It is by no means argued that the latter element cannot be involved at all—it certainly is involved—but only that, taken by itself, it cannot serve as the exclusive or an adequate explanation.[1] In addition to the evidence already presented the following may be noted: Eliminating observation of the facts as an important element in the development of the theory of action really amounts to eliminating action itself, unless there be a purely fortuitous harmony between the outline of the theory and the facts to which it refers. For action itself in the relevant sense is not conceivable without some degree of correctness in observation of facts. This would place the whole problem of the nature of science itself, to say nothing of this particular set of scientific ideas, on so radically different a footing from the position taken here that the whole study would fall to the ground.[2]

This is, then, the basic thesis of the study. On it the whole structure must stand or fall. There is no possible explanation of

[1] It is presumably the common source of the similarity of *Wertbeziehung* which is essential to such a theoretical agreement.

[2] The thesis that there has been convergence between the theorists treated in this study on the structure of the same generalized system of social action is so crucial that, at the risk of boring the reader by repetition, he may here be referred to the principal points at which the main stages of its demonstration are to be found. In the first place, the distinction of the two principal elements of Marshall's work, utility theory and activities as genuinely independent rather than, as Marshall himself treated them, as tied together in the development of free enterprise, is verified directly by the results of structural analysis as applied to Pareto's system, in Chap. VI, pp. 264 *ff.* In Chap. IX (pp. 343 *ff.*) it is shown that the analysis of action from the subjective point of view in terms of the methodological schema of science is applicable to Durkheim as well as to Pareto. Indeed all the main thread of analysis of Durkheim's theoretical development has been couched in these terms. By following this it has been demonstrated (Chap. X, pp. 381 *ff.*) that the independence of the value elements from those of the intermediate sector of the intrinsic means-end chain is a necessary basis for interpreting Durkheim's later position. The analysis of the internal differentiation of the intrinsic means-end chain, developed independently of any of the writers, was verified by its correspondence with Pareto's analysis of social utility (Chap. VI, pp. 241 *ff.*). Durkheim's mode of treatment of religious ideas and ritual, and the version of the sociologistic theorem at which he arrived were shown to be consistent with the same elements considered in relation to

this convergence into a single theoretical system which does not include the proposition that correct observation and interpretation of the facts themselves constitutes a major element.

This conclusion is particularly important for the following reason: If this be true, and it is reasonable to think that it has been demonstrated, then the concepts of the voluntaristic theory of action must be sound theoretical concepts. It is not, of course,

---

Pareto. In the former connection, however, Pareto did not develop the main distinctions explicitly. (Compare Chap. VI, pp. 256 *ff.* and Chap. XI, pp. 414 *ff.* See also Chap. X, pp. 386 *ff.*)

Finally, in Chap. XVII it has been possible to show in detail that Weber's analysis of the intrinsic means-end system corresponds directly with that developed and verified in relation to Pareto (Chap. VI) while the general categories dealing with religion correspond point for point with those to be found in Durkheim (Chap. XI). Though some of the structural elements important to this study are explicit in some writers, others in others, it can be said that, with the exception of Marshall, who hardly began the transition from the utilitarian position, no element has been identified and found to be verifiable in the scheme of one writer which could not be fitted into that of the others. In so far as the interpretation of all three makes any sense it follows that, in the respects important to this study, the three writers all use the same generalized system. It has, however, been necessary to disregard certain aspects of the work of some of them in order clearly to bring out this consequence.

To avoid all possible misunderstanding a word may be said about the possible meaning of the term demonstration. In the most rigorous sense a conclusion may be said to be demonstrated (1) when every statement of fact on which it logically depends can be verified by a completely determinate, unambiguous operation and (2) when every step in logical inference can be derived with mathematical rigor. It cannot be claimed that this convergence has been demonstrated in quite so rigorous a sense. That the writers in question have actually written what it is claimed they have written can be verified by a perfectly definite operation—reading their texts. But the total number of relevant statements of fact is very large and unfortunately it is impossible to apply mathematical methods to the logical inferences from these facts. The problem is one of fitting these facts into a general pattern which makes sense. Short of mathematical demonstration there is no way of convincing a critic who simply refuses to see the facts in relation to the total pattern here presented and stubbornly asserts that this is the wrong interpretation of them. But it is claimed that no other interpretation of these facts, taken all together, which could be seriously considered has ever been put forward, though some of them may well fit into other schemes. Seen in terms of the scheme employed here the facts fall into a consistent pattern such that the evidence for convergence is adequate. No one who considers all the facts *together in relation to this scheme* can evade this conclusion.

asserted that they are in the present formulation final and will never develop further. But they have been through the test and proved to constitute a conceptual scheme usable in empirical research. Hence they furnish a feasible starting point for further theoretical work, since science always develops further from a given theoretical point of departure. To advocate the use of this scheme, then, is not to lay down a Utopian program of what the social sciences should do but never have done. It is, on the contrary, to take the position that what has proved useful in the past and has greatly contributed to the attainment of important empirical results is likely to continue to do so in the course of its future use and development.

5. That the four above conclusions, taken together, constitute the hoped-for empirical verification, for this particular case, of the theory of the development of scientific theory stated in the first chapter. It is, indeed, impossible to understand the processes of scientific change which have been demonstrated on any other basis. In particular it has been shown that this change cannot be understood adequately (a) as the resultant of a process of accumulation of new knowledge of empirical fact arrived at independently of the statement of problems and the direction of interest inherent in the structure of the initial theoretical systems; (b) as resulting from processes of the purely "immanent" development of the initial theoretical systems without reference to the facts; (c) as only the result of elements external to science altogether such as the personal sentiments of the authors, their class position,[1] nationality,[2] etc. That leaves the mutual interdependence of the structure of the theoretical systems with observation and verification of fact in a position of great, though by no means exclusive, importance.[3]

[1] A Marxian might say that since no proletarian is included this element has not been eliminated. Granted; but that could make no difference to the general conclusion. There is too much positive evidence for the importance of elements other than class position.

[2] It need hardly be recalled that all four writers were of different nationalities.

[3] It may be explicitly pointed out that this conclusion goes beyond the thesis that the scheme is empirically valid. It maintains that the fact of its empirical validity has been demonstrated to constitute *one* important factor in the explanation of why it has developed. Many other factors are involved of course, but it is here claimed that had it not been for the fact

It is worth while pointing out that if the last conclusion be accepted, especially in combination with the other four, this study has a legitimate claim to be considered, not only as a contribution to the understanding of certain social theories and their processes of development, but also as a contribution to social dynamics. For in view of its exceedingly close relations to rational action, which have constituted a main theme of the study as a whole, the development of empirical knowledge must be considered a factor of major importance in social change; the rationalistic positivists erred only in making it of exclusively dominating importance. This is as true of knowledge of human action as it is of that of nature. Hence an understanding of the kind of processes by which such knowledge, particularly in the form of science, develops is an indispensable preliminary to any accurate comprehension of its social role. Of course this study has not solved these problems, but it may lay claim to have contributed to their solution.

that its authors observed correctly, and reasoned cogently about their observations, the theory, as it has here been presented, would not have developed. Only by virtue of this thesis can the study claim to make a contribution to social dynamics.

Chapter XIX

TENTATIVE METHODOLOGICAL IMPLICATIONS

It would, indeed, be rash to maintain that the outline of the structure of action presented in the last chapter was complete, even in the mere enumeration of distinguishable elements, to say nothing of the modes of relation between them. This can only be decided as a result of the continual testing of the theory in actual scientific use over a long period. It is in far too early a stage of development for any claim to be made that a definitive statement of it in either of these two respects has here been attained. It is not proposed to attempt in this study to carry these questions any farther. The limited task set for it has already been accomplished.

The development of the system has, however, been traced far enough to establish definitely its identity as a system, and as one distinct from other systems prominent in the thinking of contemporary social scientists, particularly those by modification of which its development has taken place. Whether in its present state it is a logically closed system, only time and much critical analysis can tell.[1] Above all, the main concern here has been with the definition of structural elements. This has naturally involved a great deal of reference to their mutual interrelations. But there has definitely been no attempt to investigate this latter question systematically, even to the extent to which the works of these writers could throw light on it. And this would be necessary before the question of logical closure could be settled even on the structural level.

All this must be left for the future; it transcends the scope of this study. Before closing it will, however, be advisable to

[1] Could it be stated as a system of simultaneous equations, this would be easy to tell. But even though the variables can be satisfactorily defined, it is quite another thing to attempt to state a sufficient number of demonstrated modes of relationship between them to furnish such a test. This study has been confined to certain preliminaries without even attempting such a statement.

attempt to do two things. In the first place certain methodological questions have run through the study as a whole. The reader will be left with a clearer impression if these are brought together in the form of a more systematic statement of the issues than has been provided in the body of the study, since there discussion of each of these issues has been limited by its relevance to the immediate questions of interpretation under consideration at the time. Second, the study considered in its earlier chapters the problem of the status of the conceptual scheme of one of the principal social sciences—economic theory. The problem of its status was, it was seen, of crucial methodological importance. At other points various other questions relating to the status of other social sciences have been mentioned. Hence it will be instructive to inquire, now that all the evidence has been presented, whether a basis is available for further systematic clarification of these issues.

EMPIRICISM AND ANALYTICAL THEORY

Though this has been explicitly claimed to be a scientific, not a philosophical study, it has not been possible, for the reasons discussed in the first chapter, to avoid the consideration of certain philosophical problems. One group of these problems which has been touched upon at several points is a phase of the epistemological problem, that of the status of scientific concepts in relation to reality. In particular, it has been necessary to criticize, in terms of their unfortunate empirical implications, a group of views which have been brought together under the term empiricism.

It will be remembered that under this heading three different positions have been included. The first has been called positivistic empiricism and consists in the reification of general theoretical systems of the logical type of the classical mechanics. This means either that the concrete phenomena to which the theory is applicable are held to be exclusively understandable in terms of the categories of the system, or, in the less radical version, that all changes in such phenomena must be predictable from knowledge of the values of the variables of the system. The latter position makes room for certain constants, that is, assumptions necessary for the concrete application of the theory. But in so far as the empiricist position is adopted these constants are held to be constant not merely for the immediate scientific purposes in hand, but as part of the "nature" of the phenomena in question. In other words, the theory applies only when the "experimental conditions" are given in which predictions from its "laws" alone work out with concrete exactitude. The law of falling bodies is held to apply only in a vacuum. The most conspicuous example of such reification in the social field is the interpretation of the classical economics as a theory applicable only to a regime of perfect competition. The heuristic assumptions necessary for the doctrine of maximum satisfaction then become the constants, which are asserted, in the extreme case, to be necessary truths about concrete reality.

The other two modes of empiricism involve the repudiation of the validity of general theoretical concepts in this sense for any purpose in relation to the concrete phenomena in question. One form is what has been called particularistic empiricism, the doctrine that the only objective knowledge is that of the details of concrete things and events. It is impossible to establish causal relationships between them which are analyzable in terms of general concepts. They can only be observed and described, and placed in temporal sequence. It is clear that this is the methodological counterpart of Hume's skepticism in epistemology. It is quite clear that such a view is unacceptable here, since it would destroy the whole purpose of this study, which is to work out the outline of just such a system of general theoretical categories, having demonstrable empirical validity.

The third form of empiricism is what has been called (following Dr. von Schelting) intuitionist empiricism. It permits a conceptual element in social science, but maintains that this can be only of an individualizing character; it must formulate the unique individuality of a concrete phenomenon, such as a person or a culture complex. Any attempt to break down this phenomenon into elements that can be subsumed under general categories of any sort destroys this individuality and leads not to valid knowledge but to a caricature of reality. It is equally clear that this view is unacceptable for purposes of the present study since it denies to its central task any legitimacy as a scientific aim.

The first form, reification, is unacceptable for a different reason. It is correct in insisting on the scientific legitimacy of general theoretical concepts, but wrong in its interpretation of their status in relation to concrete reality. This study has presented abundant evidence for the view that the understanding of human action involves a plurality of such theoretical systems. There can be no doubt of the applicability of the systems of the physical sciences to human action, but attempts to exhaust its explanation in such terms have broken down. More narrowly, conclusive evidence has been presented to show that the assumptions necessary for a theory of economic *laissez faire* cannot, for the general purposes of social science, be assumed to be constant features of all social systems, but such systems are found to vary in ways subject to analysis in terms of other, noneconomic elements of the theory of action. In so far as this is the case, the single system of economic theory is inadequate to the broader theoretical task.

A fourth attitude toward scientific concepts and their relation to reality which has been encountered in the study is that they are not reflections of reality, but "useful fictions." The principal example was Weber's own formulation of the status of his ideal-type concepts, a formulation that was arrived at in conscious reaction against all three of the forms of empiricism just outlined. There is, as has been shown, an element of truth in this view as applied to certain types of concepts but, when applied, as Weber was inclined to apply it, to all general concepts of social or any other science, it also is untenable.

In opposition to all four of these untenable views may be set the epistemological position that seems to be implied throughout this study—analytical realism. As opposed to the fiction view it is maintained that at least some of the general concepts of science are not fictional but adequately "grasp" aspects of the objective external world. This is true of the concepts here called analytical elements. Hence the position here taken is, in an epistemological sense, realistic. At the same time it avoids the objectionable implications of an empiricist realism. These concepts correspond, not to concrete phenomena, but to elements in them which are analytically separable from other elements. There is no implication that the value of any one such element, or even of all those included in one logically coherent system, is completely descriptive of any particular concrete thing or event. Hence it is necessary to qualify the term realism with "analytical." It is the possibility of making this qualification which renders the resort to fictionalism unnecessary.

The mere statement of the general position which seems to be implied in the findings of this study and its relation to the other possibilities rejected, is not, however, enough. It is necessary to consider further what analytical realism means when it is applied to a detailed consideration of the conceptual structure of the theoretical system here developed, the voluntaristic theory of action, and the various kinds of concepts which must be discriminated in understanding how it is to be applied to problems of empirical research. This will involve taking up again the thread of the discussion of types of concepts which was begun in the first chapter.

THE ACTION FRAME OF REFERENCE

It has been seen throughout the study that it is necessary to distinguish two different levels on which the schema of action with all its main features may be employed; these have been called the descriptive level and the analytical level. Any concrete phenomenon to which the theory is applicable may be described as a system of action, in the concrete sense. Such a system is always capable of being broken down into parts, or smaller subsystems. If breakdown, or analysis, is followed far enough on this plane, it will eventually arrive at what has been called the unit act. This is the "smallest" unit of an action system which still makes sense as a part of a concrete system of action.

Though this unit act is the ultimate unit which can be thought of as a subsystem of action it is still not, from the point of view of the theory of action, an unanalyzable entity but is complex. It is to be thought of as composed of the "concrete" elements of action. It takes a certain number of these concrete elements to make up a complete unit act, a concrete end, concrete conditions, concrete means, and one or more norms governing the choice of means to the end. All these concepts have been discussed before and there is no necessity to repeat. It need only be noted that while each of these is, in a sense, a concrete entity, it is not one that is relevant to the theory of action unless it can be considered a part of a unit act or a system of them. A chair is, for instance, in a physical context a complex of molecules and atoms; in an action context it is a means, "something to sit on."

It is essential to distinguish from the concrete use of the theory of action, in this sense, the analytical. An end, in the latter sense, is not the concrete anticipated future state of affairs but only the difference from what it would be, if the actor should refrain from acting. The ultimate conditions are not all those concrete features of the situation of a given concrete actor which are outside his control but are those abstracted elements of the situation which cannot be imputed to action in general. Means are not concrete tools or instruments but the aspects or properties of things which actors by virtue of their knowledge of them and their control are able to alter as desired.

The fundamental distinction of these two different applications of the theory of action raises the problem of their relations to each other. This may be put most generally by saying that they involve a common frame of reference. This frame of reference consists essentially in the irreducible framework of relations between these elements and is implied in the conception of them, which is common to both levels, and without which talk about action fails to make sense. It is well to outline what the main features of this frame of reference are.

First, there is the minimum differentiation of structural elements, end, means, conditions and norms. It is impossible to have a meaningful description of an act without specifying all four, just as there are certain minimum properties of a particle, omission of any one of which leaves the description indeterminate. Second, there is implied in the relations of these elements a normative orientation of action, a teleological character. Action must always be thought of as involving a state of tension between two different orders of elements, the normative and the conditional. As process, action is, in fact, the process of alteration of the conditional elements in the direction of conformity with norms. Elimination of the normative aspect altogether eliminates the concept of action itself and leads to the radical positivistic position. Elimination of conditions, of the tension from that side, equally eliminates action and results in idealistic emanationism. Thus conditions may be conceived at one pole, ends and normative rules at the other, means and effort as the connecting links between them.

Third, there is inherently a temporal reference. Action is a process in time. The correlate of the teleological character is a time coordinate in the relation of normative and non-normative elements. The concept end always implies a future reference, to an anticipated state of affairs, but which will not necessarily exist without intervention by the actor. The end must in the mind of the actor be contemporaneous with the situation and precede the "employment of means." And the latter must, in turn, precede the outcome. It is only in temporal terms that the relations of these elements to each other can be stated. Finally, the schema is inherently subjective, in the sense of the above discussion. This is most clearly indicated by the fact that the normative elements can be conceived of as "existing" only in the mind of the actor. They can become accessible to an observer in any other form only through realization, which precludes any analysis of their causal relation to action. From the objective point of view alone all action is, it will be remembered, "logical."

These underlying features of the action schema which are here called the "frame of reference" do not constitute "data" of any empirical problem; they are not "components" of any concrete system of action. They are in this respect analogous to the space-time framework of physics. Every physical phenomenon must involve processes in time, which happen to particles which can be located in space. It is impossible to talk about physical processes in any other terms, at least so long as the conceptual scheme of the classical physics is employed. Similarly, it is impossible even to talk about action in terms that do not involve a means-end relationship with all the implications just discussed. This is the common conceptual framework in which all change and process in the action field is grasped.

Thus the action frame of reference may be said to have what many, following Husserl,[1] have called a "phenomenological" status. It involves no concrete data that can be "thought away," that are subject to change. It is not a phenomenon in the empirical sense. It is the indispensable logical framework in which we describe and think about the phenomena of action.[2]

This is not true of the components of concrete action systems, or of the values of analytical elements, the specific content of ends and the like. They are of the empirical order of existence and are subject to analysis in terms of causality and concrete empirical process. The distinction between the action frame of reference and the concrete data is vital.

[1] E. HUSSERL, *Logische Untersuchungen.*
[2] So long as the conceptional scheme employed here is used at all.

The fact that wherever the general action schema is used at all phenomena are described in terms of this common frame of reference means that whatever level of analysis is employed there is a common structure of all systems of action. It is this common structure which it has been the main task of this study to analyze. The ultimate unit is always the unit act with the fundamental structure of the elements that make it up. Then there are inherent in the frame of reference a certain number of "elementary" relations between the various unit acts in any system. These are mainly derived from the fact that the existence of other units in the same system is necessarily a feature of the situation in terms of which any one unit is to be analyzed. Finally there are the emergent relations of units in systems. These are not logically inherent in the concept of a system as such, but they are empirically shown to exist in systems beyond certain degrees of complexity. Indeed, by contrast with the utilitarian system, it is primarily recognition of the empirical importance of these emergent aspects of total systems which characterizes the voluntaristic theory of action. The primary interest of the preceding analysis has been in them.

This elucidation of the status of the frame of reference of action in its relation to the structure of systems makes it possible to state a needed qualification of the term concrete, as applied to such systems and their components. This leads to certain questions of the nature of the data of science and their relation to a theoretical system. The descriptions of even the concrete components of action systems, unit acts, their parts and aggregations, do not comprise all the possible facts that can be known about the phenomenon in question, but only those which are relevant within the action frame of reference. But even these facts, the data of the theory of action, fall into two classes. The distinction and the relations between the classes can best be elucidated in terms of an example showing the mutual interrelations of two alternative frames of reference for statement of the facts about the same phenomenon, the spatiotemporal and that of action.

In dealing with a case of suicide by jumping off a bridge, the *social* scientist will describe it as an "act"; the physical scientist as an "event." For the social scientist it has a "concrete" end, death by drowning—the actor anticipates "himself, dead in the water." The means is "jumping." The "conditions" include the height of the bridge, the depth of water, the distance of the point of striking from shore, the physiological effects of impact, of the filling of the lungs with water, etc. The actor "orients" himself to phenomena understandable in terms of the physical-spatial schema. He knows that *if* he jumps he will fall, and *if* he does not swim he will drown. When the facts are stated in terms of the action schema these physical facts are assumed as "data." But *given* these data the problems set for the social scientist lie in the "ifs" italicized above. The reasons why, *if* he jumps, the man will fall, do not interest the social scientist. He is interested only in the facts *that* the man will fall, *that* the would-be suicide knows it and knows the probable consequences to himself.[1]

To the *physical* scientist studying this particular phenomenon interest is focused on the "event" of the fall. He will apply to it the law of falling bodies, etc. *That* the man jumped is to him a *given* fact, he does not inquire why. Or if he does, in terms of "motive," he is no longer talking in terms of a "physical" frame of reference. That is, he is no longer describing his data in terms relevant to the particular theoretical system, of physics.

Then in the descriptions of concrete action are included facts relevant to theoretical systems other than that of action. In fact, they must be if the action frame of reference is to be considered capable of serving as a descriptive schema. But they are stated differently from their mode of statement in another schema for other theoretical purposes. This difference may be stated broadly as follows: The scientific function of a descriptive frame of reference is to make it possible to describe phenomena in such a way as to distinguish those facts about them which are relevant to and capable of explanation in terms of a given theoretical system from those which are not. The latter enter into the descriptions as one class of "data." To the social scientist it is a relevant but unproblematical fact that if a suicide jumps he falls. What is problematical is *why* he jumps. To the physicist, on the other hand, it is a relevant but unproblematical fact that the suicide *does* jump. What is problematical to him is why, having jumped, he fell as he did, with the rate of acceleration, the velocity and momentum on striking the water, etc. For the statement of "data" in this sense there is only the requirement that they should be "adequate" to the context. Both the social

---

[1] *Cf.* Durkheim's definition of suicide which is precisely as an "act," in this sense.

scientist and the suicide must know enough about the "physical aspect" to be able to predict that the jump will probably result in death. Otherwise the term suicide is meaningless as applied to the act. This may be called "motivationally relevant adequacy" of physical data. Similarly, the physicist must know enough about the jump to know that the jumper was actually detached from the bridge and *would* fall. This would constitute physically relevant adequacy of knowledge of the action data of the physical problem. To yield empirically valid conclusions every theoretical system must be able to describe these data as facts "adequately," in this sense. But, beyond establishing this adequacy, it need not pursue inquiry into why the data are as they are.[1]

This does not, however, exhaust the category of data of a science, if by that is meant all the observed facts about a concrete phenomenon describable within a given frame of reference, as is the general usage. It includes, rather, only what is usually referred to in the physical sciences as the constants of a problem. In addition there are the values of the variables. In the case of the suicide the physically relevant values are distance from the place of the jumping to the water line, etc. The socially relevant values are certain particular features of the situation of the actor, his ends and the like.[2] These data, like the constants, are always given in any particular concrete situation. They can never be deduced from theoretical concepts, but must be determined by observation. All deduction from theory can do is to help us mutually to verify different sets of data by drawing their respective implications for each other. And if, for example, we have the values in a given case for three variables out of four in the system we can, given the requisite logical or mathematical technique, deduce that of the fourth.

Thus the data of any concrete problem fall into the two classes, "constant" data and the values of variables. One of the most important functions of the frame of reference is to enable the distinction to be drawn.[3] Constants can *only* be described in terms of this frame of reference; their further analysis requires

---

[1] For *its* theoretical purposes.

[2] They are analyzed in Durkheim's monograph. See also *supra*, Chap. VIII.

[3] It is not, however, enough, as Marshall's experience shows.

a different set of terms. The description of values of variables, on the other hand, is the starting point for analysis.[1] This brings the discussion to the next step.

SYSTEMS OF ACTION AND THEIR UNITS

This concerns the construction *within* the frame of reference of concrete historical individuals and their various possible modes of subdivision into parts or units, on the one hand, and, on the other, the various objectively possible combinations of these units into more and more complex structures. In this connection a large number of exceedingly complex methodological problems are raised which it is impossible even to begin to discuss adequately here. Such discussion would require an extensive methodological treatise of its own. Only a few points essential to the immediate context can here be touched upon.

In the first place, if the above view of the essential role of the frame of reference is correct, it follows that the criterion of relevance to such a schema sets a definite limit to the extent of useful subdivision of the phenomena into units or parts. It is to be remembered that such a unit must be a "part" of the phenomenon in the sense that it can be conceived of as concretely existing in isolation from the other parts; whether or not it is practically possible to carry out the isolation experimentally *in concreto* is not methodologically important. In the classical physics, at least, it is safe to say that a unit of matter had to be conceived as itself a physical body, a particle. In the unit sense all physical bodies must be thought of as made of such particles and all physical processes must be conceived of as changes that "happen to" these units or combinations of them.[2]

In the case of phenomena describable in terms of the action schema, the "smallest" unit which can be *conceived* of as concretely existing by itself is the "unit act." This further involves the minimum "concrete elements" that have been spoken of—a concrete end, concrete means, concrete conditions (including

---

[1] Hence to make the distinction the variables must also be defined, that is, the analytical elements.

[2] The present author does not feel competent to say what difference the quantum theory may have made in this respect. The impression is that there has been a *correlative* change in conceptions both of the unit of matter and of the frame of reference in terms of which physical "bodies" and processes are described. If this be true it confirms the general view presented here.

institutional rules) and a concrete norm governing the means-end relationship. These are, in a sense, concrete units but they cannot be thought of in a form relevant to the action schema except as elements or parts of an act,[1] which further implies an "actor," that is, a "personality," the identity of which transcends any one of its particular acts.

Description of the same phenomena in terms that isolate these elements or, in turn, further subdivided parts of them, from their relation to an act in this sense, destroys the relevance to the action schema so that if the facts are relevant to any scientific theory it must be a theoretical system other than that of action. Thus in the suicide example the bridge, which in several respects constitutes a condition of the act, may from a physical point of view be "broken down" into parts all the way from towers, suspension cables, etc., on a macroscopic level to the molecules and atoms of the chemical substances of which the steel and concrete are composed. These units are relevant to the schema of action only in the particular concrete combination that we call a "bridge." Indeed the word bridge in everyday speech gets its primary meaning precisely from its relation to the action schema. It is a structure over a body of water or some other barrier, over which people or vehicles may go. It is defined functionally by its relation to action not physically as an aggregation or as a determinate structure of atoms.

This is the limitation on abstraction in one direction which was mentioned above.[2] A definite limit to the scientifically useful subdivision of concrete phenomena into units or parts is set by their relevance to the frame of reference. In the theory of action it is their capability of being thought of as acts or concrete elements of acts. One principal criterion of this capability is that the subjective point of view can be employed. Failure to see this was one of the main reasons why Weber was so afraid of abstraction and hence did not even attempt to develop a generalized theoretical system.

It will be asked whether breaking up concrete phenomena into parts or units in this sense is a process of abstraction at all.

---

[1] Abstracted from this they can all be placed in other descriptive frames of reference. Thus a tool which in the action schema is a "means" may also be described as a physical object.

[2] *Supra*, Chap. XVI, p. 633 *ff.*

The answer is that it is so precisely in so far as the phenomenon in question is organic. This is preeminently true of systems of action as they have been treated in this study. It is true that in the last analysis all such systems are "composed" of unit acts. But it is necessary to be careful in interpreting what this means. It does not mean that the relation of the unit act to the total system is closely analogous to that of a grain of sand to the heap of which it is a part. For it has been shown that action systems have properties that are emergent only on a certain level of complexity in the relations of unit acts to each other. These properties cannot be identified in any single unit act considered apart from its relations to others in the same system. They cannot be derived by a process of direct generalization of the properties of the unit act.[1] In so far as this is true, the conceptual isolation of the unit act, or of other parts constituting combinations of them, is a process of abstraction. This is the type of concept which is really and necessarily fictional, in the sense that Weber attributed to his ideal types. The questions of the organicism of systems of action, of the place of emergent properties of such systems which is a corollary and of the sense in which unit or part concepts that omit consideration of these properties are abstract need further elucidation.

It is best to begin with the simplest example of an emergent property which has been encountered in this discussion. It is impossible, from the data describing a single rational act with a single clearly defined immediate end and a specific situation with given conditions and means, to say whether or in what degree it is economically rational. The question is meaningless, for the economic category involves by definition the relation of scarce means to a plurality of different ends. Economic rationality is thus an emergent property of action which can be observed only

---

[1] "Direct" generalization may be taken to mean, the implications of the mere fact of the presence of a plurality of units in the same concrete system, derivable from the fact that certain relations between units, if there are more than one, are inherent in the frame of reference. A system composed of unit acts with only these elements of generalization is an atomistic system.

It is true, as was noted in the first chapter (footnote 1, p. 32), that mechanical systems have properties as wholes which the parts do not have in isolation. But in such a case all such properties (such as entropy) can be derived from those of the units with the aid of the considerations just discussed.

when a plurality of unit acts is treated together as constituting an integrated system of action. To carry unit analysis to the point of the conceptual isolation of the unit act is to break up the system and destroy this emergent property. So long as analysis is confined to the unit act, in talking of the rationality of action it is impossible to mean anything but the technological aspect of the property of rationality.

Thus, on the one hand, unit analysis is limited by the relevance of the unit formulated to the frame of reference being employed. On the other hand, so far as this mode of analysis is used, it is not, when applied to organic phenomena limited in the same sense, but must be used with caution because it involves a certain kind of abstraction. This abstraction consists in the progressive elimination, as the breaking down into parts is carried farther, of the emergent properties of the more complex systems. Limiting observation of the concrete phenomenon, then, to the properties that have a place in the unit act or other subsystem leads to indeterminacy in the theory when empirically applied to complex systems. This indeterminacy, a form of empirical inadequacy, is the fundamental difficulty of atomistic theories when applied to organic phenomena. They cannot do justice to properties such as economic rationality which are not properties of "action as such," that is, of isolated unit acts or of atomistic systems, but only of organic systems of action beyond a certain degree of complexity.

The methodological problem is thus a matter of the relation of the unit or part concept to the analysis of systems. The abstraction involved in the former consists in the impossibility of taking account of certain features of the latter and the concrete effects of variation in them in terms of such units and of the unduly simple elementary relations between them alone. The problem may be further clarified by reversion to a figure employed earlier in the study. It will be remembered that when the conception of an integrated system of rational action was outlined the figure of a "web" of interwoven strands was used. This provides a mode of visualizing what is meant by the organic character of systems of action. Thinking of such a system as made up of unit acts in the atomistic sense would involve the possibility of unraveling the web into concretely separable threads. Dropping the metaphor, means-end relations would be identifiable only as connecting a given concrete act with one ultimate end through a single sequence of acts leading up to it. In fact, however, the same concrete immediate end may be thought of as a means to a variety of ultimate ends, so that from this point ahead the "threads" branch out in a number of different directions.[1]

A given concrete unit act is to be thought of, then, as a "knot" where a large number of these threads come momentarily together only to separate again, each one to enter, as it goes on, into a variety of other knots into which only a few of those with which it was formerly combined enter with it.[2]

Even here, however, the metaphor may be misleading in one respect. A concrete web of threads can, in fact, be untied, the threads unraveled from each other. In the present case, and, if Professor Jennings is right, the genetic case, this cannot be done even conceptually. The web must be thought of as composed only of analytically, not in any sense concretely, separable units.

[1] This may be illustrated graphically:

Time ↑ ⊁ Unit act

Means-end chains

[2] A close parallel to the logic of this situation in another science is that involved in the principle of segregation, in genetics. Here the hereditary constitution of a given individual organism is to be regarded as the meeting point of a large number of analytically identifiable "strands," that is, genes, which are relatively constant through a large number of generations. Looking back from a given individual the sources of these gene elements segregate out into more and more numerous elements, the number doubling with each generation to which the analysis is pushed back. Similarly looking forward in the progeny of the individual they will be *re-segregated* out with each successive generation. It is only by tracing a sufficient number of generations that the units can be identified. See H. S. Jennings, *The Biological Basis of Human Nature.*

Professor Jennings' account suggests a further extension of the parallel. What he calls the unit character theory of inheritance reified these gene elements by identifying them with concrete somatic characters of the mature organism. This led to the logical difficulties of the "mosaic" theory of development that he so clearly brings out. The atomism just warned against is a strict parallel to this. It involves the *identification* of the analytical elements of action with the concrete action elements of unit acts; it is logically the same kind of reification. The result is similarly a "mosaic" theory of action systems. We have seen (*supra*, Chap. XVI) Weber falling into a similar "mosaic" fallacy. The difference is that he uses another much more complex unit than the unit act.

The unraveling is a process of making *analytical* distinctions and following through the relations of the values of the elements thus arrived at in a series of concrete cases.

But if certain of these elements can only be given values by describing emergent properties of organic systems, what is the empirical basis of their inclusion at all in a scientific theory? Is it not true that only units really exist? The answer is to be found in the fact of independent variation. The basis for distinguishing the economic from the technological elements of rationality is the fact that they vary in value independently of one another. A maximization of either one does not imply a corresponding maximization of the other. But how is this independent variation to be demonstrated? It is possible only through comparison of different concrete cases. This is not true of the description of a unit which can be formulated independently of comparison.

The role of comparison in distinguishing elements is best brought out by a specific case. Given comparable technologically relevant conditions there is no essential difference between the technological efficiency of producing electric power by water power on the Colorado River (Boulder Dam) and, for instance, on the Ohio River near Pittsburgh. But the fact that Boulder Dam is a very long distance from coal supplies while Pittsburgh is in the center of a great coal field is reflected in the fact that near Pittsburgh it is cheaper to produce electric power by steam. Many further qualifications would have to be made to make the two cases strictly comparable, but the principle is clear. In each of these cases there are available two acceptable technological methods of attaining an end—electric power by water power or by steam. In any two different cases the choice between them might be made differently, not on technological but on economic grounds. The immediate economically relevant fact is the lower cost of coal at one place, its higher cost at the other. By spending less money at Boulder Dam for water-power electricity than for electricity produced from coal, there is involved less sacrifice of satisfaction of other wants than if the same amount of power were produced, delivered at the same point, by steam. This comparison demonstrates independent variation of the technological and the economic aspects of rationality of action.

Thus can be seen the essential methodological basis for not merely the validity, but the indispensability of the comparative method for all the analytical sciences. Experiment is, in fact, nothing but the comparative method where the cases to be compared are produced to order and under controlled conditions. Weber's insistence on comparative study, by contrast for instance with Sombart's genetic method, was thus deeply symptomatic. Without the comparative method there can be no empirical demonstration of the independent variation of the values of analytical elements.

Before leaving the question of the status of the descriptive unit or type-part concept in the sciences of action, a brief sketch may be made of some of the different kinds of such concepts the social scientist may be expected to encounter and of their relations to each other. Two preliminary remarks are in order. First, that causal explanation, as has been seen in connection with Weber, *always* involves breaking down a historical individual into structural units or parts, on the one hand, perhaps also into values of analytical elements, on the other. Precisely in so far as a phenomenon is indivisible, in either or both of these two senses, it must be considered inaccessible to science. Second, it has been shown that systems in the social field are to a highly important degree organic and hence certain of their properties are only identifiable when there are present sufficiently complex combinations of the more elementary units. It is as different ways of looking at these relatively complex combinations that the different possible descriptive schemata applicable to human society may be distinguished.

It has already been stated that the smallest elementary unit of human action which is still relevant to the action schema is what has been called the unit act. These unit acts may be conceived of as combined to constitute more and more complex concrete systems of action. These systems are organic in the sense that they have structurally and analytically important emergent properties which disappear when the breakdown of the systems into units or parts is carried far enough. Neither economic rationality nor value integration is a property of unit acts apart from their organic relations to other acts in the same action system. But allowing for this organic character the action schema may, descriptively, be carried out to the highest conceivable degree of complexity of concrete action systems.

When a certain degree of complexity is reached, however, to describe the system in full in terms of the action schema would involve a degree of elaboration of detail which would be very laborious and pedantic to work out. This is true even if description is limited to "typical" unit acts and all the complex detailed variations of the completely concrete acts are passed over. Fortunately, as certain degrees of complexity are reached, there emerge other ways of describing the facts, the employment of which constitutes a convenient "shorthand" that is adequate for a large number of scientific purposes.

This takes the form of confining attention to what may be called "descriptive aspects" of the concrete action system. These can be held to be functionally dependent on the concrete action system so that substituting them for the full concreteness is not, within certain limits, a source of error. This isolation of descriptive aspects can take place in two main directions which, in this particular case,[1] may be called the "relational" and the "aggregational." They are complementary, not exclusive.

The first has already been dealt with in connection with Weber. There it has been seen that the acts and action systems of different individuals, in so far as they are mutually oriented to one another, constitute social relationships. In so far as this *inter*action of the action systems of individuals is continuous and regular these relationships acquire certain identifiable, relatively constant properties or descriptive aspects. One of them is the structural.[2] Another is involved in the relative priority of *Gemeinschaft* and *Gesellschaft*. No attempt will be made here to give it a specific name as a property.[3]

The important thing is that so far as the relationship schema is employed for the observation and description of the facts of human life in society it sets a standard of what are adequate observations. It is not necessary to observe *all* the acts of the parties to a relationship, or all their attitudes, etc., but only enough to establish what is for the purposes in hand the relevant "character" of the relationship. For such observation to be facilitated as much as possible, there should be available in each relevant descriptive aspect a classification of types with adequate

---

[1] Perhaps more generally. No attempt will be made to go into this.

[2] Simmel's "form."

[3] In the earlier stages of defining quantitatively variable analytical elements the tendency is to give different names to the *poles* of variation. Thus, bodies are "light" or "heavy." Science tends to substitute for this a single entity, as "mass," thought of as capable of variation in value within a range.

criteria so that the observer may fit his observations into a conceptual scheme. Precisely in so far as such classifications have become established and verified is it possible to limit observation to a small number of "identifying" facts. How much observation is necessary for identification can, however, never be laid down a priori but depends on the particular facts and the current state of knowledge of the field in question. But the tendency of scientific progress is to *reduce* them continually. This takes place by a double process. First, some facts can be eliminated as irrelevant. Thus for purposes of the theory of gravitation the density of a body is irrelevant and need not be measured. Second, it is possible to establish connections between the relevant facts so that when some are observed it may be inferred that others exist without the trouble of observing them. Thus to identify an object as in a biological sense a "man" it is not necessary to open his skull to see whether he actually has a human brain.

Thus the primary function of such a secondary descriptive schema as that of social relationship is one of scientific economy, of reducing the amount of labor of observation and verification required before adequate judgments may be arrived at. A second function has already been noted, to state the facts in a way that will prevent carrying unit analysis to a point where it would destroy relevant emergent properties. That the relationship schema is secondary to that of action is proved by the following consideration: It is quite possible to isolate (conceptually) unit acts from a social relationship. But it is quite impossible to isolate even conceptually a social relationship from the actions of the parties. It is a descriptive aspect of action systems involving a plurality of individuals and their acts.

Attention has already been called to the fact that the schema of action implies an actor. This is as fundamental to the concept of action as is the assumption of a knowing subject to that of knowledge. It is impossible even to conceive of "knowledge" except as something *known by* a subject. Similarly action is a series of acts *of* one or more actors. It is not necessary for present purposes to become involved in the exceedingly difficult philosophical problems relative to the concept of the ego or self. A very few considerations will suffice in the present context.

First it may be noted that this implication of the concept of action points again to the organic property of action systems.

From the present point of view the implication of an actor constitutes a mode of relation of different unit acts to each other. In so far as it holds, the knowledge of the intrinsic properties of a conceptually isolated unit act is not enough for understanding it. It is necessary, in addition to know whose act it is and what relation it bears to other acts of the same actor. Thus in describing any given concrete action system one possible principle of descriptive organization of the units is their grouping according to the actor whose acts they are.

Thus arises the concept of an individual or a personality. The logic of the situation here is essentially the same as in the case just discussed. For present purposes, then, the concept of "personality" is to be regarded as a descriptive frame of reference for stating the facts of human action. In this sense a personality is nothing but the totality of observable unit acts described in their context of relation to a single actor. But this is to a greater or less degree an organic system of action and as such has in its totality emergent properties not deducible from those of the unit acts taken atomistically.

In so far as this is true, it is possible to employ a similar kind of descriptive "shorthand" to that employed in connection with the relationship schema. It is not necessary to observe all the unit acts of the person in question but only enough to identify him as a given theoretically relevant kind of person. Objectively these identifying properties may be referred to as character traits, subjectively as attitudes. They will be identifiable in terms of a classification as in the relationship schema. Thus for present[1] purposes the personality schema is another secondary descriptive schema of action. It is an organized system of unit acts brought together by their common reference to the same actor.

This process of "aggregation" can, however, be pushed forward another step. When action systems involving a plurality of actors are present they may be described as groups; that is, a larger aggregate may be thought of as made up of persons as their unit. The person, in this context, becomes a member of a group. There is no reason to doubt that groups, in this sense, also have emergent properties not derivable from those of persons

---

[1] This is, above all, not necessarily the same as the psychological concept of personality.

taken in conceptual isolation from their group membership. In any event, group properties can certainly be described without detailing all the character traits and attitudes of their members, hence further descriptive economy is achieved.

It is true that the individual person is the unit of composition of group structure. But it does not follow that the same person cannot at the same time be a member of a plurality of groups. On the contrary he generally is a member of many at the same time. Thus his whole personality is not involved in any one group. At the same time there are, of course, limitations to the compatibility of different group memberships. One cannot be a member of both the Catholic and the Baptist churches at the same time. This is a question of the particular concrete groups or of types of groups, and the relations of their characters to each other.

At the same time in the present context the group schema is also to be regarded as secondary to the action schema. There are no group properties that are not reducible to properties of *systems* of action and there is no analytical theory of groups which is not translatable into terms of the theory of action. The case of Durkheim is most striking. His analysis of the nature of social groups led directly to the schema of action and the generalized theory of action.

After what has already been said, it is unnecessary to insist that the generalization of these unit or part concepts[1] on all these levels can, with proper precautions and for properly limited purposes, yield empirical generalizations adequate to explain many things. The principal cautions are two. These concepts can hold only for ranges of variation of circumstances not too large to invalidate the assumption that for practical purposes the particular constant relations between the values of analytical elements which these type concepts in the concrete case represent, will not be so unreal as to exceed an acceptable margin of error. Second, it has been stated repeatedly that precisely in so far as the whole is organic its parts or units are not real entities but abstractions. Hence their use requires a particularly high degree of caution to avoid the kind of reification which creeps in when

[1] That is, not only unit acts, but social relationships, persons and groups may serve as units of social systems.

this is forgotten and these units are treated as constant real parts through complicated processes of change. The result is to reduce the organic wholes to a "mosaic" of unit parts.

Enough has been said to show the very close relation of the unit concept at all these different levels of complexity to the frame of reference of action. Such concepts have no meaning for the theory of action unless they are capable of description in terms of the latter—as concrete elements of action, as unit acts in some combination. This has been found to be true even though the facts are not stated directly in terms of the action schema but in that of the relationship, personality or group schemata. For all three of these are here held to be secondary to the action schema in the sense stated. The requirements of the frame of reference set a definite limit to the meaningful subdivision of historical individuals into unit parts, for they cease to be meaningful for the theory of action as soon as they lose their relevance to its frame of reference. In this sense it sets a limit to abstraction.

The Role of Analytical Elements

At a number of points in the foregoing discussion phases of the role of analytical elements have been encountered. On this subject only a very few words are called for. In the first place, it should be repeated with emphasis that element analysis and unit analysis are not stages of scientific abstraction but two different *kinds* of abstraction on two different planes. To use Simmel's figure of speech, they draw "lines through the facts" not in the sense that the first is the sector of the same line farthest from the concrete, the second, nearest, nor that the lines are parallel, but that they cut across each other. To use another figure, unit analysis unravels the warp of empirical reality, element analysis the woof.

From the point of view of element analysis every unit or part, concretely or conceptually isolated, constitutes a specific *combination* of the particular values of one or more analytical elements. Every "type" is a constant set of relations of these values. The element, on the other hand, may be the universal (1) of which the particular unit as a whole is a particular, (2) of which one or more facts describing it are particulars, (3) which corresponds to one or more emergent properties of complex combinations of such units. Any atomistic system that deals only with properties identifiable in the unit act or any other unit will of necessity fail to treat these latter elements adequately and be indeterminate as applied to complex systems.

A word should also be said about the sense in which the term emergent is here used since it has acquired various connotations elsewhere. Here it has a strictly empirical meaning, designating general properties of complex systems of phenomena which are, in their particular values, empirically identifiable and which can be shown by comparative analysis to vary, in these particular values, independently of others. So far they are no different from any other general properties. What distinguishes the emergent from the elementary properties is *only* the fact that upon unit analysis of the system in question beyond a certain point they evaporate and are no longer observable. This has been amply illustrated for the case of economic rationality. The existence and empirical importance of emergent properties in this sense is, as has been seen, a measure of the organicism of the system. They are basically important to action systems.

Above all, it is not to be inferred that in some sense the ultimate relevant unit, in the present case the unit act, with its elementary properties, alone is "real" and the emergent properties are in some sense "derived" or "fictitious." That would be a definite departure from the empirical basis of science.[1] In distinguishing analytical elements the facts must be taken as they are found. The criterion is always empirically verifiable independent variation in values. Where this is demonstrable there is a "real" element whether it be elementary or emergent. Indeed in science there is no other criterion of reality. It is just as possible to argue that the unit act is a fiction. Like Aristotle's concept of hand, the unit act is a "real part" of an action system "only in an equivocal sense." There is no mysticism whatever about this concept of emergence. It is simply a designation for certain features of the observable facts.

It can now be understood how analytical elements tie in with the other two kinds of conceptualization which have been discussed. Every actually or hypothetically concrete entity, described in terms of a frame of reference, must have properties. This is one of the ultimate necessities of thinking about empirical reality, a phenomenological fact. Within a given frame of refer-

[1] A *metaphysical* atomism.

ence there will be found to be a limited number of these properties which, taken together, are adequate[1] to the description of the phenomenon in question. The number of those necessary for adequacy may in organic phenomena increase with the complexity of the phenomena.

The element of order in concrete phenomena, seen from the analytical point of view, consists in the fact that though these are, in their particular values, variable properties, their values stand in certain constant modes of relation to each other. The order consists in these modes of relation plus the constancy of definition of the elements of the theoretical framework within their range of variation.

Now the values of analytical elements are concrete data, facts of observation or combinations of facts. The processes of their variation are processes of concrete change in time. Hence the action schema in its form of a framework of analytical elements takes on a different meaning from that which it has as a descriptive schema. Its elements have causal significance in the sense that variation in the value of any one has consequences for the values of the others. Above all, the means-end schema becomes the central framework for the causal explanation of action. Furthermore it is the specific peculiarity of this schema that it has a subjective reference. It involves a real process in the mind of the actor, as well as external to it.

On this level then the action schema, including its central means-end component becomes more than phenomenological, it takes on not merely descriptive but also causal significance, and in so doing involves references to "real subjective processes" of motivation. It becomes, in Husserl's sense, "psychological."[2] But its phenomenological aspect, as a frame of reference, does not

[1] The standard of "adequacy" is set by the questions which, within the framework of the theoretical system, must be answered in order to attain a determinate solution of the problem in hand.

[2] *Cf.* HUSSERL, *op. cit.* This meaning is certainly not the one that can be involved in the definition of any analytically distinguishable science of psychology. It implies only (1) that the existence of the phenomena is empirical not "ideal" as is, for instance, that of a mathematical proposition; (2) that they are accessible to analysis in terms of subjective categories, in the sense employed throughout this study. To make psychology the science of psychological phenomena, in Husserl's sense, would be to make it the synthesis of all the sciences of action.

disappear; it remains implicit in any use of the action schema. Indeed it is this element which binds the descriptive action schema and the analytical action schema together. For purposes of explanation the analytical theory of action is applicable only to systems the facts about which can be stated in terms of the descriptive action schema or of one of its secondary derivative schemata, and so to phenomena ultimately divisible by unit analysis into unit acts and systems of them. Thus all three kinds of conceptualization are most intimately bound together.

It has repeatedly been stated that this study has not attempted a systematic treatment of what is, in this sense, the analytical aspect of the theory of action. It has been limited, rather, to working out the structural outline of the generalized systems of action to which such an analytical theory would be applicable. The two modes of conceptualization often overlap, however, so there has had to be much talk of variables, of analytical elements. But no attempt has been made to consider the problem of setting up a *system* of variables. The other has proved to be a quite sufficiently formidable task without the additional complications which the inclusion of the latter would have entailed. Moreover, it provides certain indispensable preliminaries to the systematic prosecution of the other task. Among other things, by showing that the conception of a generalized system is useful in its structural aspect, it has demonstrated that the task of setting up a corresponding system of elements and their relations is not logically impossible.[1]

In order not to leave the reader feeling that the formulation of analytical laws on the basis of the system here worked out is in the structural context impossible, it may be useful to suggest tentatively that there already exists the basis for the formulation of such a law of wide scope and high significance. The law may be tentatively formulated as follows: "In any concrete system of action a process of change so far as it is at all explicable in terms of those elements of action formulated in terms of the intrinsic means-end relationship can proceed only in the direction of approach toward the realization of the rational norms conceived as binding on the actors in the system." That is, more briefly, such a process of action can proceed only in the direction of increase in the value of the property rationality.

[1] Weber would, it has been shown, have held a contrary opinion.

Stated in this way this brings immediately to mind a striking analogy to the second law of thermodynamics. That also is a statement of the directionality of change in a system, this time a physical system; it must be in the direction of increasing entropy. Potential energy is converted into kinetic energy, into action, in the physical sense. Rationality occupies a logical position in respect to action systems analogous to that of entropy in physical systems (at least on the basis of classical physical theory). Effort energy is, in the processes of action, converted into realization of ends, or conformity with norms. Rationality is one, at least, of the properties in terms of which the extent of this change is to be measured for any *given* system at any given point in the process of change.

This conception of a law of increasing rationality as a fundamental generalization about systems of action is, of course, not original. It is the most fundamental generalization that emerges from Weber's work, his conception of the process of rationalization. Action systems do not, in his view, differ with regard to this basic character. The principal differences which he takes account of are two: the concrete content of the ends and norms toward the realization of which action is rationalized, and the formidability of the obstacles to the progress of the process. It is to be noted, though, that the latter differences, formulated by Weber mainly in the concept of traditionalism, are differences touching only the *rate* of the process of rationalization, not its direction.[1]

There is a further interesting parallel between Weber's process of rationalization and the second law of thermodynamics. In the framework of the classical physics this law has been made the basis of fatalistic conclusions about the "running down" of the physical universe. It is a striking fact that Weber's process of rationalization was both by himself and by his interpreters thought to lead to closely analogous fatalistic conclusions. These have taken a parallel form; in Weber's terms a stock of charismatic energy, as it were, was in process of being consumed in the course of a rationalization process and would leave behind it at the end a "dead mechanism."

---

[1] Weber's generalization is in need of qualification, for the fact that the intrinsic means = end relationship is not the only norm governing action systems in this general way.

It may be suggested very tentatively that the fatalistic conclusions in both cases go back to the same order of causes, to reification of theoretical systems. Professor Whitehead has shown the effects of this, the fallacy of misplaced concreteness, for the classical physics. It has been seen above how Weber similarly tended to reify his ideal type concepts. There can be little doubt of the connection of this tendency with the fatalistic interpretation of the process of rationalization. There is unfortunately no space here for further discussion of this interesting parallel.

THE GENERAL STATUS OF THE THEORY OF ACTION

Having indicated the general epistemological position implied in the results of this study, that called analytical realism, and discussed its application to the various forms of theoretical conceptualization, this part of the methodological discussion may be concluded by a brief word about the most general philosophical status, usually called ontological, of the type of scientific theory considered here.[1] The position is realistic, in the technical epistemological sense. It is a philosophical implication of the position taken here that there is an external world of so-called empirical reality which is not the creation of the individual human mind and is not reducible to terms of an ideal order, in the philosophical sense.

The systems of scientific theory under consideration are obviously not this external reality itself, nor are they a direct and literal representation of it, such that one and only one such representation is in any sense valid. They stand, rather, in a functional relation to it, such that for certain scientific purposes they are adequate representations of it. It is possible to indicate a few of the features of this relation.

In the first place, the applicability to it of scientific theory implies that empirical reality in this sense is a factual order. Furthermore its order must be of a character which is, in some sense, congruent with the order of human logic. Events in it

---

[1] This discussion is, in strictness, outside the scope of the study, but it is inserted so that the reader who is interested in the possible philosophical implications of the position taken here may be able better to relate it to a philosophical universe of discourse. None of the empirical conclusions of the study depend on the following considerations.

cannot occur simply at random, in the sense which is the negation
of logical order. For a common feature of all scientific theory is
the logicality of the relations between its propositions.

But, in the second place, scientific theory is not itself an
empirical entity; it is an ideal representation of empirical phenomena or aspects of them. It is thus subject to the limitations
inherent in this fact. It is not a justified assumption that reality
is exhausted by its congruence with the kind of ideal systems
accessible to the human mind in its scientific phase, such as
what we call logic. The same kind of argument may be applied
to limitations inherent in the humanly available mechanisms of
observation. If the term be interpreted broadly enough it is
correct to say that factual elements can find a place in science
only when there is a humanly possible operation by which they
can be determined. The limitations to which human observation
is subject may well be purely fortuitous seen in relation to the
totality of external reality.

For both these reasons it may be inferred that humanly
possible knowledge is not identical with that conceivably possible
to a mind freed from these human limitations. But at the same
time the fact of verification, that scientific theory "works,"
is proof that, though limited, the propositions of human science
are not completely arbitrary but are adequately relevant to
significant aspects of reality. There is and must be as a limiting
concept a totality of humanly possible scientific knowledge which
is not that of "external reality itself" but adequate to a significant part of it. In so far as science progresses actual knowledge
approaches this limit asymptotically.

But in addition to the limitations on complete realism necessitated by common human limitations, there are others which
determine the fact that knowledge at any given time in any given
field is less than this totality of humanly possible knowledge.
These may be said to be of two orders: those inherent in the
nature of the cognitive aspect of the human mind and those owing
to the fact that this cognitive aspect is never completely isolated
from the other aspects; man is never exclusively Homo sapiens.

In the first connection the concrete entities dealt with by the
scientist are never "fully" concrete even in the humanly possible
sense but are what Weber called historical individuals. They are
constructed entities, the construction being determined by the

structure of the frame of reference employed. Hence the realism of the description of concrete entities must be modified to take account of this element of descriptive selection. Secondly, in so far as description in this sense is applied not to a total concrete system, but to parts or units of it isolated from their context, a further element of abstraction enters in to the extent that the system is organic and has emergent properties. There is no a priori reason to limit the number of important emergent properties as such systems increase in complexity. Finally there is the abstraction involved in the concept of an analytical element. The empirical reference of such a concept is not necessarily a concrete phenomenon even in the above relative sense, but may be one aspect of it; the particulars corresponding to the general concept may constitute only a small part of the many facts ascertainable about the phenomenon in question.

Hence a given system of generalized theory must be interpreted in the light of this threefold abstraction from the totality of humanly possible knowledge. It is capable of explaining only part of the facts important within the given frame of reference. The others, the values of constants, can be explained, if at all, only in terms of other analytical systems. But the facts that are important in terms of a given frame of reference are by no means all those which can be known about the concrete phenomenon. Only when it has been adequately described in terms of all known frames of reference, and all the data subsumed under analytical concepts of some system, and all these different ways of analyzing it systematically related to one another, can it be said to have been as fully explained as is possible in the state of scientific knowledge of the time. But these various levels of abstraction do not imply unreality, in the fictional sense. This is proved by the fact that the results of analysis on the different levels, in terms of the various frames of reference, etc., are capable of being integrated into a coherent body of knowledge which, as a whole, has the realistic implications that have been outlined. In so far as this happens the various parts of this body of knowledge serve to reinforce each other and to strengthen the evidence in favor of any one proposition in it.

At the same time, evidence has been presented in this study that though scientific knowledge is an independent variable in human action it is interdependent with the other variables. In so far as the others determine the human limitations on the knowability of reality which have been mentioned, they have already been taken account of. But there are, at the same time, other limitations. Those connected with the direction and limitations of scientific interest in relation to value systems are, perhaps, the most significant. In so far as the range of empirical interest has, in fact, been limited by these factors it may be inferred that the humanly possible approaches to empirical phenomena have not been exhausted. But as the possible variation of human values is actually approached, the scientific range is also broadened. It has been noted that if this element of relativism in science is not to lead to skeptical consequences, it is necessary to postulate that in this sense the possible points of view are of a limited number. With the accumulation of value experience the totality of knowledge approaches the asymptote.

The particular ontological status of the system of the theory of action is to be understood as a special application of these general considerations.

In the first place the action frame of reference is certainly one of those in which certain of the facts of human action can be for certain scientific purposes adequately described. It is not the only one of which this is true, but the critical results of this study show that, for certain purposes, which cannot but be considered scientifically legitimate, it is more adequate than any of the alternative frames of reference which have been considered here, such as the natural science schema of space-time and the idealistic schema. Within that frame of reference it has been possible to work out systematically points of articulation with both these other frames of reference through considering the status of the constant data of the problems of action. Furthermore it has been demonstrated that within the range of what must be considered variables from the point of view of the action system, there are several subgroups that constitute relatively independent subsystems. The necessity of taking account of all of these for concrete purposes has been shown.

It cannot be maintained either that in the formulation attained in the present study this theoretical system is complete, or that it will not, with the further development of the social sciences, be superseded by one as radically different from it as it is from the systems from which it has emerged. But its empirical usefulness as recounted in this study is such that it is quite safe to say that if and when it is superseded it will be found to have left a substantial permanently valid precipitate of knowledge which, with the appropriate restatement, it will be possible to incorporate into the future broader system. This, and this only, is the sense in which it is claimed that it has given us valid knowledge of empirical reality.

The Classification of the Sciences of Action

The general position regarding the relation of theoretical concepts to concrete phenomena which is implied in the findings of this study has been called analytical realism. In one respect this view is contrasted with the empiricist reification of theoretical systems. The latter view implied that only *one* system of analytical categories could be applicable to the understanding of any given concrete class of phenomena. By contrast with this implication the position taken here involves the theorem that the adequate understanding of many concrete phenomena may require the employment of analytical categories drawn from more than one such system, perhaps from several.

Secondly, this study has considered at length one particular case of a theoretical system with reference to which the problem of reification, in this sense, has been acute in much scientific discussion, that of orthodox economic theory. The conclusion reached is that, as Pareto rightly saw, it must be interpreted as the formulation of the relations of a limited group of analytical elements in the broader concrete system of action. Concrete phenomena, even those capable of description in terms of supply and demand, involve other variables not included in the system of economic theory. Empirical evidence has been presented sufficiently ample to prove this point beyond question. Furthermore it has been possible to go farther than merely to state that this group of elements is abstract, one among several in concrete social phenomena. In the sense used by Pareto and in one part of Marshall's theory, it has been placed in systematic logical relations to the other elements in the structure of the wider system here called action.

This wider system, the voluntaristic theory of action, has, in turn, been found to involve at another remove a similar kind of abstraction. In particular, its concrete application has been found to involve constant data that are capable of description, but not analytical explanation in terms of the action frame of reference. One set of these data fit into another of the broader frames of reference of contemporary science, called in the broadest sense the "physical," which describes phenomena as spatio-temporal things or events. Indeed one of the main polar positions with which the analysis here has had to be concerned is that at which the action schema loses explanatory relevance altogether and becomes merely descriptive. When this happens it turns all data into constants in the above sense. And at one pole, the radical positivistic, analytical treatment of these data involves the physical frame of reference, the positive criterion of which is spatiality, the negative criterion, analytical irrelevance of subjective categories. Complementary to this tendency for the theory of action under certain circumstances to slip over to a radically positivistic theory, is the tendency for it to slip over to the opposite, the idealistic pole. Ideas may be said to be constant data for the theory of action in the same methodological sense as are physical data. They are not, as such, variables of the action system.

Finally, in discussing Weber's methodology there has been encountered the bifurcation of scientific interest, in the one direction toward the understanding of concrete individual phenomena as such, in the other to the building of theoretical systems of general validity.

Consideration of all these questions has been necessary to the elaboration of the conceptual structure of this study. Each of them is important to the structure at some point. Moreover in connection with several there has had to be raised the question of the status, in relation to the whole, of a more restricted conceptual scheme, which is widely referred to as constituting the theoretical aspect of a specific science. Thus the economic theory in question is the theoretical preoccupation of economic science as a unified discipline. Also the question of the physical data of action systems has involved, in some sense or other, that of the relation of the natural and the social sciences.

A great deal of the confusion into which this study has attempted to introduce some order has been due to the failure of scholars clearly to discriminate between these various conceptual schemes and adequately to investigate their mutual logical relations. Wherever, in any empirical problem, more than one of them becomes involved, it is essential in the interest of clarity that the student of the problem should know what he is doing; to know when he is employing one scheme, when another and what the shift from one to another implies. If a basic theorem of the present discussion be accepted, that in a large proportion of empirical problems in the action field more than one of these theoretical systems is involved, it follows that the questions of their relations cannot be evaded; they are scientifically important questions in the strict sense.

It is clear what this means: the study of these relations is the attempt to develop a systematic classification of the empirical sciences and an outline of this, so far as it bears upon the problems of the present study, is the final task to be undertaken.

There is a great deal of current protest against attempts to set up boundaries between the sciences, to divide them into neat compartments. We are told that all knowledge is one, that the way of progress is to break down divisions, not to set them up. It is possible to sympathize generally with the spirit of this protest. For concrete empirical research it is clearly impossible to adhere to any neatly separated fields. The empirical scholar will follow his problems wherever they may lead and refuse to be deterred by any signs which read, "Foreign Territory." Indeed this study, by demonstrating the extent to which different conceptual schemes must be called upon to unravel the complexities of the same empirical field, has given a direct justification to the advocacy of such scientific *Wanderlust*. But, at the same time, such an attitude, pushed to the extreme of refusing even to discuss the problems of systematic relationship of theoretical systems involved in the classification of the sciences, becomes a case of the kind of empiricist evasion of theoretical problems which has been shown again and again to be scientifically disastrous. It is an excellent thing to travel in many countries, but the traveler who refuses to take any cognizance of the local peculiarities and customs of the countries he visits is likely to get into trouble. Many a traveler has lost his life through sheer ignorance of these things. Such an attempt, then, is not mere pedantry; it is a deduction from the general scientific precept, "It is a good thing to know what you are doing." The attempt is further justified here by the fact that these problems have been touched upon in fragmentary fashion at various points in this study, and in these connections have been shown to be important to it. Their systematic treatment will provide an opportunity to bring out with greater clarity than before the main outline of the conceptual structure which has emerged as the principal outcome of the study as a whole. It will place its results in a clearer perspective than has been attainable in the summary contained in the previous chapter.

All the distinctions that will be made use of have already been encountered; it is necessary only to point out their relation to the present context. The first to be recalled is the line between the historical and the analytical sciences. The object of the first group is to attain the fullest possible understanding of a class of concrete historical individuals or of one of the class. This distinction holds regardless of whether the historical individual concerned is a natural object or event, a human individual, an act or system of acts, a system of social relations or a type of social group. In each case the explanation in question will involve, by implication if not explicitly,[1] reference to the theoretical categories of one or more analytical sciences. How many and what ones will depend on the particular scientific purpose in hand, the aspects of the phenomenon, changes in which require explanation. One such system may prove adequate but in no case is there an a priori presumption of such adequacy. Full explanation may be found to involve all the theoretical categories of all the analytical sciences.

On the other hand, there are the analytical sciences, the aim of which is to develop logically coherent systems of general analytical theory. The unit of reference for such sciences is not a particular historical individual nor a class of them, which may for purposes of the science in question be considered essentially the same, but a closed system of theory. Wherever such a closed system exists which is not translatable into terms of another it is possible to speak of an independent science.

The role of what has been called the frame of reference introduces a complication into this classification. For its use necessitates a distinction, implicit or explicit, between two classes

---

[1] Depending on whether, for empirical adequacy, it is necessary to go beyond structural or unit analysis. Only if it is necessary to do so does the distinction of analytical systems involved have to become explicit.

of data—those which are problematical and those which are unproblematical to the corresponding analytical system, the values of variables and of constants, respectively. On this basis it is best to distinguish between a "fully" and a "relatively" historical discipline. To illustrate: most history is written in terms of the action schema and its secondary derivatives. The data, for instance, of the geographical environment are taken simply as unproblematical data, are noted and their consequences worked out for the particular historic process in mind. This is a relatively historical procedure. It would become a fully historical one in so far as the historian attempted to explain changes in these data in terms of geology, climatology, etc., as well as the data of heredity, race, for instance, in terms of natural selection. Most actual historical disciplines are, in this sense, relatively rather than fully historical. Thus history generally confines its problems to data relevant to the action schema, meteorology to those relevant to the schemata of physics and chemistry. If, for instance, a meteorologist finds that smoke in or near a large city significantly alters the climate there, he takes the smoke production for the area as a fact without attempting to enter into an economic or a sociological explanation of it. He merely works out its meteorological consequences.

Unit or part concepts as such can hardly constitute the basis of independent sciences. In their descriptive and nonanalytical explanatory use they are adjuncts to the historical sciences. Further analysis of them, on the other hand, leads over to the analytical sciences. They constitute the principal conceptual link between the two.

It is not difficult to see that an empiricist methodology favors (1) the general classification of the sciences on a "historical" basis, according to the classes of concrete systems dealt with; (2) the limitation of the development of theory to the type-part concept and its empirical generalization. Any attempt at analytical theory on an empiricist basis leads to the reification of the theoretical system. Where, as in physics, the main concrete historical individuals studied are scientifically interesting to men almost entirely in the respects relevant to such a theory, for example the stars, and the processes going on in laboratories for atomic research, the consequences may not become serious until an advanced stage in the analysis. Where, as in the field of human behavior, almost any concrete historical individual is a meeting ground for the application of a number of such systems, the consequences become serious at an early stage. The fate of orthodox economic theory faced with institutionalist criticism is a vivid case in point. On an empiricist basis there is a complete deadlock.

On an analytical basis it is possible to see emerging out of this study as a whole a division into three great classes of theoretical systems. They may be spoken of as the systems of nature, action and culture.[1] It should be further noted that the distinction is one of theoretical systems, not one of classes of concrete historical individuals. Only the first two are systems of *empirical* scientific theory in the usual sense; the third occupies a special status.

This is because an empirical science is concerned with *processes in time*. The problematical data of the theories of both the nature systems and the action systems concern such processes; those of the culture systems do not. The line of distinction which may

---

[1] The closest approach to this classification is that of Freyer (*Soziologie als Wirklichkeitswissenschaft*) into *Naturwissenschaft, Wirklichkeitswissenschaft* and *Logoswissenschaft*. The present formulation owes a good deal to his scheme, though it differs in certain respects.

It will be noted that in this final classification the qualifying adjective, "voluntaristic" as applied to the theory of action has been dropped and reference is made simply to the sciences of action as distinguished from those of nature and of culture. It is true that in this study the conception of a positivistic theory of action has been employed and has been useful in analyzing and classifying theories. It has been applied to theories stated in terms of the action schema, but having positivistic implications. Here, however, the object is not to analyze others' theories but to set up the most nearly correct classification which is at present attainable.

It is a legitimate conclusion from the analysis of this study that in the sense of having independent causal importance there can in the last analysis be no such thing as a radically positivistic theory of action. It is always possible to state the facts in terms of the action frame of reference, but when the advance from description and unit analysis to element analysis is made, it turns out that the action categories are not analytically significant. The causally relevant variables can always be adequately stated in terms of a natural science system. In this sense a positivistic position always reduces the explanation of action to natural science terms.

It follows that if a theory of action is to have the status of an independent analytical system at all, it must, in the nature of the case, be a voluntaristic theory. Hence the qualifying adjective, originally introduced to distinguish the system this study was concerned with from a positivistic theory, becomes superfluous and can be dropped from the final classification.

be drawn between the first two is that the nature systems involve time in relation to space in the frame of reference, the action systems in relation to the means-end schema. Physical time is a mode of relationship of events in space, action time a mode of relation of means and ends and other action elements. *All* known empirical scientific theory apparently involves one or the other of these two basic frames of reference, physical space-time or the means-end schema of action. Action is *non*-spatial[1] but temporal.

The culture systems are distinguished from both the others in that they are *both* non-spatial and atemporal. They consist, as Professor Whitehead says, of *eternal* objects, in the strict sense of the term eternal, of objects not of indefinite duration but to which the category of time is not applicable. They are not involved in "process."

Concrete spatial objects and temporal events may have a cultural aspect, in this sense, but in so far as they are physically understandable it can only be as symbols. Eternal objects constitute the meanings of symbols. As objects they exist only "in the minds" of individuals.[2] They in themselves are not to be found by external observation, only their symbolic manifestations.

It cannot, however, be denied that the cultural systems have the status of science if by that is meant a body of objectively verifiable propositions. For if it is granted, as it must be, that the meanings of symbols are observable, it is necessary also to grant that there is verifiable knowledge of eternal objects. But this cannot take the form of causal understanding of events. Beyond the grasp of the immediate meaning of a particular isolated symbol it can only mean a grasp of the interrelations of eternal objects in meaningful systems.

Of these systems there are presented to our experience many kinds which it is not possible here to attempt to analyze and classify. The reader may, however, be reminded that the systems of scientific theory with which this study has been so intensively concerned are among such systems. As such they are neither physical objects nor events. There are also other kinds of culture systems as of "ideas," "art forms" and many more.

---

[1] Of course every *concrete* event occurs in space, *too*. But this fact is an unproblematical datum to the analytical *sciences* of action.

[2] Or "embodied" in systems of symbols the "understanding" of which implies a mind.

The relations of culture systems to action are highly complex. Here it is necessary to state only that they may, on the one hand, be considered as *products* of processes of action; on the other, as conditioning elements of further action, as for instance is true of scientific and other "ideas." The sciences of action can no more avoid concern with them than they can with "physical" facts. But the logical relation is essentially the same. They constitute unproblematical data, knowledge of which is essential to the solution of concrete problems.[1]

On both sides there is one exception. Though these three kinds of systems must be clearly distinguished from each other, they all constitute parts of a consistent whole of objective knowledge. Hence the presumption is that there exist important interrelations. It goes without saying that a vast number of physical objects may be considered in part products of processes of action.[2] Action, that is, changes the physical world as well as being conditioned by it. Similarly, culture systems are in part[3] products of action as well as in turn conditioning action. Both these borderline cases would naturally give rise to borderline disciplines. On the borderline between action and culture there is already a quite well-developed and recognized discipline, generally known in Germany as *Wissenssoziologie*. Its concern is with culture systems as products of action, the influence of action elements upon them and their concrete processes of development.

Leaving aside the "sciences" of culture[4] the empirical analytical sciences may then be divided into the two great groups of the natural sciences and the sciences of action. The latter are distinguished negatively by the irrelevance of the spatial frame of reference, positively by the means-end schema and by the indispensability of the subject aspect, hence of the method

---

[1] It should be noted that physical phenomena are also often the products of action.

[2] Usually called *artefacts*.

[3] From the causal point of view we must grant to them the relation to action a certain *Eigengesetzlichkeit*. A thought process which *is* a process of action is canalized by logical considerations. The system of logic, a culture system, is a causal element in the concrete result.

[4] Such as logic, mathematics, systematic jurisprudence, etc. One great branch constitutes what are sometimes called normative sciences. This term should be taken cautiously, however.

of *Verstehen*,[1] which is specifically irrelevant to the natural sciences.

Each of these groups constitutes in a sense *one* great system since there is a common basic frame of reference and in all probability a definite systematic relation of all the analytical and structural elements relevant to this frame of reference. But within each of these groups there have developed well-marked subsystems that enjoy a degree of independence of each other. It can be said with some definiteness what is the main principle of subdivision in the action group; with much less definiteness, in the natural science group. The main principle is that, with increasing complexity of concrete systems, there appear successively new emergent properties which give rise to new theoretical problems not relevant to the more elementary systems. No attempt will here be made to enter into the question as it concerns the natural sciences except to note that a somewhat similar doctrine of "emergence" is rather widely held among biologists. According to this doctrine what is peculiar to biological theory is the problems raised by the properties of organisms which are not to be found in their constituent physicochemical elements or parts. And surely the line between the physicochemical and the biological group is the clearest line of subdivision within the natural sciences.

But in the action group it is possible to be much more specific. It has been seen that certain fundamentals are to be posited of the elementary unit act. The first emergent property that arises with increasing complexity of action systems is, in one direction, that of economic rationality. Now the whole methodological discussion of this study in this connection has started with the fact that the ramifications of this element in its various relations to the concrete facts of action have given rise to a well-integrated theoretical system, that of economic theory. If one such emergent element can be made the basis of a coherent theoretical system there seems to be no clear prima-facie reason why others should not also, if others there be.

For it must be evident that, if the analysis is pushed no farther, the results of the discussion of the status of economic theory are

---

[1] Culture systems are obviously *only* understandable by this method. In the sciences of action we combine *both* *Verstehen* and observation of "behavior," that is, of the external spatial course of events.

anomalous. This is well illustrated by the position in which Pareto left the question. He is quite clear that what he called pure economics is to be regarded as an abstráct theoretical system. Its status is precisely that which has been accorded here to an analytical system. But he leaves it as the *only* positively defined analytical science applicable to action. The only other social science he mentions is sociology, which, though he explicitly refused to define it rigorously, appears to include two aspects. One is an analytical aspect, the analysis of the nonlogical elements of action, the other a synthetic, the total account of concrete action generally, including the economic element. It is clear that sociology for Pareto must be considered, in the analytical sense, a residual science since it is concerned with a residual category of action elements.[1] On this basis it surely could not hope to be a closed system in the sense that mechanics has long been. From this it seems legitimate to conclude, either that the course Pareto took in defining the status of economic theory was wrong and an entirely different basis must be found or that it is necessary to proceed from his position, which involves only one positively defined analytical science of action, to the construction of a coherent system of the analytical sciences of action. Since the economic element of Pareto's treatment has a definite place in the wider scheme of elements of action here developed, it is reasonable to think that the latter will provide a practicable basis for the more comprehensive scheme of classification. This study is naturally definitely committed to Pareto's view of the status of economics.

Thus the principle employed is to classify analytical sciences according to which structural element or group of elements of a generalized system of action constitutes the focus of attention of the science in question. It must be remembered that this structural analysis may or may not coincide with the most convenient selection of analytical elements or variables. Thus, in the economic case, the relevant subsystem of the theory of action will include all the variables that are most significant in accounting for changes in actions attributable to the fact that these systems are economically rational to a high degree. One of these

---

[1] This may be, and probably was regarded by Pareto as, a first approximation. As such it was a great advance on the position for instance, of Marshall. Now, fortunately, it is possible to proceed to a second approximation.

may be the valid knowledge of their situation possessed by the actors. But in so far as the same systems are rational in respects other than the economic, namely the technological and the political, the same variable will probably be included in other subsystems. Though the analytical systems are, as a whole, distinct from each other, it does not follow that in the choice of particular variables they are mutually exclusive. On the contrary, they are almost certain to overlap. Any group of variables may constitute an analytical system which it is convenient to treat together in relation to empirical problems. Since the main structural features of the differentiation of action systems with which this study has been occupied form some of the most conspicuous features of the concrete phenomena of action, it is probable on general grounds that the variables which are the most closely related to each in the manner outlined will have a set of such close mutual interrelations that it is for many purposes convenient to treat them together as a system. This general presumption is greatly strengthened by the fact that the most closely articulated analytical system in the action field, that of economic theory, does, in fact, fit very closely one of these main distinguishable structural aspects of action systems.

The economic concept makes sense only for systems of action, but it is applicable to the system of action of a particular individual—"Crusoe economics."[1] The next conceptually important step in increasing complexity of systems of action comes with the inclusion of a plurality of individuals in the same system. This has a double consequence. On the one hand, it introduces the possibility of coercive power entering into the relations of the individuals within the system. This is a property not included in the economic concept. The action system of an individual may have not only economic rationality but also coercive rationality.

But this coercive rationality has a peculiar characteristic. It cannot be a property of the *total* action system[2] involving a plurality of individuals; it can only apply to some individuals or groups within such a system *relative* to others. Coercion is an

---

[1] All its fundamental conceptual elements are to be found on this level.

[2] In this respect it is analogous to the economic conception of value. The idea of a "general level of values" is nonsensical because value is a *relative* concept. Power is also a relative concept.

exercise of power over others. At the same time this possibility of coercion opens up a new set of problems, the problems of social order stated in classic form by Hobbes as a result of his exploration of the consequences of an unlimited struggle for power. In order that there may be a stable system of action involving a plurality of individuals there must be normative regulation of the power aspect of the relations of individuals within the system; in this sense, there must be a distributive order. This double aspect of *social* action systems, the problem of power relations and order in so far as it may be regarded as a solution of the struggle for power, gives another relatively well-marked set of emergent properties of action systems. These may be called the political action elements.

The Place of Sociology

Third, it has been seen that the solution of the power question, as well as of a plurality of other complex features of social action systems, involves a common reference to the fact of integration of individuals with reference to a common value system, manifested in the legitimacy of institutional norms, in the common ultimate ends of action, in ritual and in various modes of expression. All these phenomena may be referred back to a single general emergent property of social action systems which may be called "common-value integration." This is a clearly marked emergent property readily distinguishable from both the economic and the political. If this property is designated the sociological, sociology may then be defined as "the science which attempts to develop an analytical theory of social[1] action systems in so far as these systems can be understood in terms of the property of common-value integration."

Thus, in terms of the emergent properties of action systems beyond those attributable to the elementary unit act, it is possible to distinguish three well-defined emergent levels. With each of these is associated a group of emergent properties that, on the one hand, disappear when the system is broken down by unit analysis beyond this level of complexity and, on the other hand, can no longer be thought of as standing alone when the construction of such systems is carried beyond the given stage of com-

[1] Involving a plurality of actors mutually oriented to each other's action.

plexity. Thus the three analytical social sciences of organized action systems, economics, politics[1] and sociology may reasonably be distinguished by their respective relations to these three emergent properties of such systems.

This leaves the unit act. In itself its basic properties do not constitute the subject matter of an independent analytical science. They constitute, rather, the common methodological basis of all the sciences of action, for it is really these basic elementary properties of the unit act in their mutual interrelations which constitute the common frame of reference of all the sciences of action. It is no more true that the unit act defines an independent science of action than that there is an independent natural science of space-time.

At the same time there are two points at which systematic theorizing in connection with action is not exhausted by the three systematic sciences just mentioned. In the first place, nothing has been said about the problems arising from the fact that action elements and processes involve a reference to an actor. This is another organic aspect of action systems not included in the three sets of emergent properties so far discussed. It has already been mentioned in connection with the aggregational organization of action systems, involving the concept of personality.

Reflection shows that concrete personality can be in part explained in terms of the analytical systems of these three social sciences. That aspect may be called the social component of personality. Application of this social analysis will, however, leave a residuum unexplained within the limits of relevance of the action frame of reference. In so far as this residuum can be abstracted from the specific content of the concrete ends and norms of unit acts, which is environmental, it will be found to be referable to heredity. There are, then, certain emergent properties of action systems, in part at least, understandable with reference to the hereditary basis of personality. There is an important place for a systematic analytical science concerned with these properties. In no other way can psychology be defined in terms of the general scheme employed here—as an

---

[1] In arriving at this conception of the place of politics the present author has been greatly influenced by discussions with Professor C. J. Friedrich of Harvard University. He is not, however, responsible for the above specific formulation.

analytical, not a historical[1] science. It would then be the analytical science concerned with the variable properties of action
systems derivable from their reference to the hereditary basis of
personality.

This makes psychology definitely a science of action and, in
spite of the common reference to heredity, draws a clear line
between it and biology.[2] Its categories refer to properties of action
systems with special reference to the subschema of personality.
They are thus *non*-spatial. They are modes of function of the
organism as a whole. But they abstract from social relationships,
and hence from the properties of action systems that emerge
only on the social level.

Secondly, the general properties of the unit act, in abstraction
from economic, political and sociological considerations, may be
studied with special reference to the concrete content of immediate ends, norms and knowledge. Since the general properties of
the unit act do not constitute the basis of an independent
analytical science but, rather, the common basis of all the
sciences of action, there will arise out of this study not so much
one discipline as a plurality of disciplines according to classes
of concrete ends.[3] These disciplines may be called the technologies.
They will be highly important concretely, but they add relatively
little to the systematic analytical theory of action.

Common to all these five analytical disciplines is the basic
action schema on both the descriptive and the analytical level.
The facts relevant to them all can be translated into terms of
the action schema as a frame of reference. But, at the same time,
it is in general convenient to operate, for most of their purposes,
with more specialized subschemata. In regard to economics
it is primarily the supply-and-demand schema. In the political
discipline it is primarily the social-relationship schema in the
special form of power relationships, secondarily the group[4]
schema. In sociology the relationship and group schemata are
particularly suitable. In psychology the personality schema is

---

[1] Two of the current definitions quite definitely make it a historical science
in our sense as, the science of "behavior" and the science of "mind," or of
"subjective processes."

[2] *Supra*, note appended to Chap. II, pp. 85–86.

[3] Such as industrial, military, scientific, erotic, ritual, ascetic, contemplative, artistic, etc.

[4] As for instance in the theories of political pluralism.

obviously central.[1] Finally, the technologies can in the nature of the case operate only in terms of the elementary means-end action schema.

History may be regarded primarily as the general historical science concerned with human action.[2] As has already been pointed out it tends to be a relatively rather than a fully historical discipline. Besides its subdivisions according to periods and concrete social units, peoples, nations, etc., it also tends to subdivide into the study of classes of concrete fact *particularly* relevant to one or another of the analytical sciences of action. Thus there are economic history, political history, social (perhaps, sociological) history, biography and histories of the various concrete technologies. History of religions would for obvious reasons, be included primarily in the sociologically relevant group. The main criterion of distinction between these various branches of history would be consideration of the facts in terms of one or another of the descriptive subschemata of action. Thus a biography is the history of a personality. It should be noted that history is here treated *only* so far as it claims empirical scientific status; in other words in so far as it attempts to arrive at empirically verifiable judgments of fact and of causal relationships. Any other aspect of concrete historical works, as works of art, for instance, is beyond the scope of the present discussion.

While in the interest of clear thinking it is essential to maintain the logical distinctions between the various analytical sciences of action, it is none the less true and important that since they all constitute subsystems of the same great and inclusive system of theory their interrelations are exceedingly close and the working scientist cannot afford to neglect them.[3] Above all, there seems to be no possibility that scientific work on a high level can be done by a man in any one of them who does not have a working knowledge of the others. This becomes particularly true at the

---

[1] Thus a basic psychological concept is that of attitudes. But it is quite clear that concrete attitudes are not the exclusive concern of psychology, but are relevant to all the sciences of action.

[2] As distinguished from what, reviving an old term, may be called natural history, on the one hand, history of ideas and other cultural systems, on the other.

[3] These interrelations will naturally give rise to borderline fields analogous to physical chemistry and biochemistry, *e.g.*, social psychology, social economics, etc.

higher levels of emergence. A sociologist can no more hope to do satisfactory work, empirical or theoretical, without a knowledge of psychology, economics and politics than can a biologist without a knowledge of physics and chemistry. The reasons are much the same. The "mechanisms" of the processes that a sociologist is interested in will always prove to involve crucially important elements on these "lower" levels. This fact has been largely obscured by empiricist methodology and the closely related elementary level of analytical thinking in the sciences of action. Over against this has to be set the fact that in these fields common sense is by no means of negligible value. Good common sense often yields better results than bad theoretical analysis.[1]

It will be noted that the place given to sociology in this classification makes it a special analytical science on the same level as economic theory. This procedure runs counter to the bulk of methodological tradition in the matter. The dominant view in the past has been the encyclopedic, which would make sociology a fully historical science in the above sense. Weber, defining it as the science of social action would make it either a relatively historical science, or a synthetic analytical science of action, including economics and politics.

The starting point from which this conclusion has been reached is the view of economic theory as a special analytical science, at which Pareto arrived. Once this is accepted it is, as has been stated, anomalous to stop there for purposes of more than first approximation and speak of only one such science in the action field. This is particularly true since other structural elements of action have been defined which are part of the same broader system as the economic and occupy methodologically the same logical status as emergent properties of action systems. The logical course, then, seems to be to carry the analysis through to the point of outlining a complete system of the special analytical sciences of action. The only alternative would be to go back to the empiricist basis of classification which has become, as a result of the preceding analysis, untenable.

The procedure here is not, however, altogether without precedent. Simmel's[2] was, perhaps, the first serious attempt

---

[1] Which does not prove its results are better than would be those of *good* theoretical analysis.

[2] SIMMEL, *Soziologie*, Chap. I.

to gain a basis for sociology as, in this sense, a special science. His formula is unacceptable for reasons that cannot be gone into here. But it was founded on sound insight and the view just stated may be regarded as a restatement of its sound elements in more acceptable terms. The main difficulty for Simmel was that the view he took of the other social sciences precluded relating his concept of sociology to other analytical social sciences on the same methodological level. To him sociology was the only abstract analytical science in the social field.[1]

Moreover, Durkheim's thought was progressing to a point where, had his conception of action continued to develop in the voluntaristic direction he might well have reached a similar outcome. Long before the close of his career his concept of society as a *"reality sui generis"* could no longer be considered a concrete entity but only an abstract element or group of elements of concrete reality. His conception of society also tallied well with the above view of emergence. Finally, its specific content in his thought makes it quite legitimate to identify it with the emergent property of common-value integration. The view taken here is the logical outcome of placing Durkheim's substantive results in a systematic scheme of the structure of action.[2]

It can easily be seen why such a view has had to wait upon a relatively full development of the generalized theory of action. This concept of sociology could not develop on a positivistic basis. For at the radical positivistic pole all empirical sciences become natural sciences in the above sense. Short of that, on a utilitarian basis action systems could only be considered on levels at which the property of common-value integration was not yet emergent, or, in concrete application, was present at best as a residual category, taking the form generally of implicit assumptions such as that of the natural identity of interests. If anything beyond psychology, economic theory and political theory of the Hobbesian type was to be given a place at all it had to be as a "synthetic" science.[3]

[1] It is interesting to compare this opinion with the corresponding status given to economics in Pareto's scheme.

[2] Another view similar in a number of respects, is that set forth by Professor Znaniecki in his *Method of Sociology.*

[3] Spencer's system is so definitely utilitarian that this may serve as an explanation of why he regarded sociology as an encyclopedic science.

On an idealistic basis, on the other hand, the *facts* of value integration were clearly seen, but the inherent tendency was to assimilate them to culture systems in the above sense, and thus to end up in some kind of emanationist theory. Freyer, in his book cited above, has analyzed this tendency with great acumen. Thus, as long as social thought has remained divided between the positivistic and the idealistic systems there has been no place for an analytical sociological theory in the sense in which it has just been defined. The possibility of giving it a place is, perhaps, the deepest symptom of the great change in social thinking the process of convergence here traced has brought about.

One final word. There has been of late a strong current of pessimism in the thought of students of the social sciences, especially those who call themselves sociologists. We are told that there are as many systems of sociological theory as there are sociologists, that there is no common basis, that all is arbitrary and subjective. To the present writer this current of sentiment has two equally unfortunate implications. On the one hand, it encourages the view that the only sound work in the social field is detailed factual study, without benefit of theory. On the other hand, for those who refuse to be satisfied with this, it encourages a dangerous irrationalism which lets go of scientific standards altogether. We are told sociology is an art, that what is valuable in it is to be measured by the standards of intuition and inspiration, that it is not subject to the canons of rigorous logic and empirical verification.

It is to be hoped that this study may contribute to the combating of both these dangerous tendencies. It may claim to do so in two principal respects. First, it has shown that, within the field it has covered, the differences are not so great as they appear at first sight. There is a substantial common basis of theory if we will but take the trouble to dig deep enough to find it. The opinion may, indeed, be ventured that it will be found to be the more substantial the more eminent the men whose work is studied. It would be quite possible to cite the four men here studied as examples of this lack of agreement. Yet it is a legitimate conclusion from the evidence here presented that this would be a superficial judgment. Their agreement far outweighs the differences that occur on the more superficial levels. What has happened in the minds of these men is not the appearance of an unorganized mass of arbitrary subjective judgments. It is part of a great deep stream of the movement of scientific thought. It is a movement of major proportions extending far beyond the works of the few men here considered.

Secondly, if the interpretation of the nature of scientific development here formulated be accepted even only in its application to this particular case, another conclusion follows. What has been traced is not merely a movement of thought of major proportions; it is scientific progress; indeed, notable scientific progress. One of its main aspects is a clearer, sounder understanding of a broad range of the facts of human action. The whole theoretical work here reviewed is oriented to and justified by this achievement. It could not have been done without the systematic theoretical thinking which forms the basis and is the subject of this study.

It is not, therefore, possible to concur in the prevailing pessimistic judgment of the social sciences, particularly sociology. If attention is centered not on the average achievement but, as is fully justified in such a case, on the best, we certainly need not be ashamed of our science. Notable progress on both empirical and theoretical levels has been made within the short space of a generation. We have sound theoretical foundations on which to build.

BIBLIOGRAPHY[1]

CHAPTER XIII. THE IDEALISTIC TRADITION

COHEN, MORRIS R.: *Reason and Nature*, Harcourt, Brace & Company, New York, 1931.

DILTHEY, WILHELM: *Einleitung in die Geisteswissenschaften*, Duncker und Humblot, Leipzig, 1883.

FREYER, HANS: *Soziolozie als Wirklichkeitswissenschaft: Logische Grundlegung des Systems der Soziologie*, B. G. Teubner, Leipzig, 1930.

VON GIERKE, OTTO: *Das deutsche Genossenschaftsrecht*, 4 vols., Weidmann, Berlin, 1868–1913.

GRÜNWALD, ERNST: *Das Problem der Soziologie der Wissens*, W. Braumüller, Vienna and Leipzig, 1934.

VON JHERING, RUDOLF: *Der Geist des Römischen Rechts*, 2 vols., 2d edition, Breitkopf & Härtel, Leipzig, 1866–1869.

MEINECKE, FRIEDRICH: *Die Entstehung des Historismus*, 2 vols., R. Oldenbourg, Munich, 1936.

PARSONS, TALCOTT: "'Capitalism' in Recent German Literature: I, Werner Sombart," *Journal of Political Economy*, Vol. 36, pp. 641–661, 1928.

ROTHACKER, ERICH: *Einleitung in die Geisteswissenschaften*, J. C. B. Mohr (P. Siebeck), Tübingen, 1920.

SOMBART, WERNER: *Der Bourgeois; Zur Geistesgeschichte des modernen Wirtschaftsmenschen*, Duncker und Humblot, Munich, 1913.

——— "Capitalism," *Encyclopedia of the Social Sciences*, Vol. III, The Macmillan Co., New York, 1930.

——— *Die drei Nationalökonomien*, Duncker und Humblot, Munich and Leipzig, 1930.

——— *Die Juden und das Wirtschaftsleben*, Duncker und Humblot, Leipzig, 1911.

——— *Der moderne Kapitalismus*, 3 vols., 2d ed., Duncker und Humblot, Leipzig, 1916.

——— *Der proletarische Sozialismus*, 2 vols., G. Fischer, Jena, 1924.

[1] This bibliography is not meant to be exhaustive. It includes three classes of works: (1) The principal works of the authors treated. No attempt is made to include all their minor articles and book reviews. (2) A selected list of secondary references dealing with each author's work. (3) Other works which the present writer has either actually cited in the text or found particularly useful in connection with the subject matter. Though not exhaustive it is quite sufficient to lead any interested reader into any phase of the field he wishes to investigate further.

—————— *The Quintessence of Capitalism*, trans. and ed. by M. Epstein, E. P. Dutton & Company, Inc., New York, 1915.

TROELTSCH, ERNST: *Der Historismus und seine Probleme*, Vol. III of *Gesammelte Schriften*, J. C. B. Mohr, Tübingen, 1922.

WHITEHEAD, ALFRED N.: *Science and the Modern World*, The Macmillan Company, New York, 1925.

WINDELBAND, WILHELM: *Präludien*, J. C. B. Mohr (P. Siebeck), Tübingen, 1884.

CHAPTERS XIV TO XVII.   MAX WEBER

A. Works

A complete bibliography of Weber's works is contained in Marianne Weber's *Max Weber, Ein Lebensbild* (see reference below).

WEBER, MAX: *General Economic History*, trans. by F. H. Knight, George Allen & Unwin, Ltd., London, 1927.

—————— *Gesammelte Aufsätze zur Religionssoziologie*, 3 vols, J. C. B. Mohr (P. Siebeck), Tübingen, 1920–1921.

—————— *Gesammelte Aufsätze zur Sozial- und Wirtschaftsgeschichte*, J. C. B. Mohr (P. Siebeck), Tübingen, 1924.

—————— *Gesammelte Aufsätze zur Soziologie und Sozialpolitik*, J. C. B. Mohr (P. Siebeck), Tübingen, 1924.

—————— *Gesammelte Aufsätze zur Wissenschaftslehre*, J. C. B. Mohr (P. Siebeck), Tübingen, 1922.

—————— *Gesammelte Politische Schriften*, Drei Masken Verlag, Munich, 1921.

—————— *Grundriss der Sozialökonomik*. III. Abteilung: *Wirtschaft und Gesellschaft*, 2 vols., J. C. B. Mohr (P. Siebeck), Tübingen, 1925.

—————— *The Protestant Ethic and the Spirit of Capitalism*, trans. by Talcott Parsons, George Allen & Unwin, Ltd., London, 1930.

—————— *Wirtschaftsgeschichte*, ed. by S. Hellman and M. Palyi, Duncker und Humblot, Munich, 1923,

WEBER, MARIANNE: *Max Weber, Ein Lebensbild*, J. C. B. Mohr (P. Siebeck), Tübingen, 1926.

B. Secondary Sources

1. *Religion and Capitalism*

BARKER, ERNEST: *Church, State and Study*, Methuen & Company, Ltd., London, 1930.

BRENTANO, LUJO: *Die Anfänge des moderne Kapitalismus*, K. Bayrische Akademie der Wissenschaften, Munich, 1916.

—————— *Der wirthschaftende Mensch in der Geschichte*, F. Meiner, Leipzig, 1923.

BRODRICK, JAMES: *The Economic Morals of the Jesuits: An Answer to Dr. H. M. Robertson*, Oxford University Press, London, 1934.

FANFANI, AMINTORE: *Cattolicisimo e Protestantesimo nella formazione storica del capitalismo*, Società editrice "Vita e pensiero," Milan, 1934.

—————— *Protestantism, Catholicism and Capitalism.* Sheed & Ward, London and New York, 1935.

FRIEDRICH, CARL J. and TAYLOR COLE: *Responsible Bureaucracy*, Harvard University Press, Cambridge, 1932.

FULLERTON, KEMPER: "Calvinism and Capitalism," *Harvard Theological Review*, Vol. 21, pp. 163–195, 1928.

HALBWACHS, M.: "Les origines puritaines du capitalisme moderne," *Revue d'histoire et philosophie réligieuses*, Vol. 5, pp. 132–134, 1925.

HALL, THOMAS C.: *The Religious Background of American Culture*, Little, Brown & Company, Boston, 1930.

HAUSER, HENRI: *Les débuts du capitalisme*, F. Alcan, Paris, 1927.

HONIGSHEIM, PAUL: "Zur Religionssoziologie des englischen Protestantismus," *Kölner Vierteljahrshefte für Soziologie*, Vol. 11, pp. 401–411, 1932, 1933.

KNIGHT, FRANK H.: "Historical and Theoretical Issues in the Problem of Modern Capitalism," *Journal of Economic and Business History*, Vol. 1, pp. 119–136, 1928.

KRAUS, JOHANN B.: *Scholastik, Puritanismus und Kapitalismus*, Duncker and Humblot, Munich and Leipzig, 1930.

MAURER, H. M.: "Studies in the Sociology of Religion. I. The Sociology of Protestantism," pp. 257–286, II. "Religion and American Sectionalism. The Pennsylvania German," pp. 408–438, *American Journal of Sociology*, Vol. 30, 1924.

MERTON, R. K.: *Science, Technology and Society in Seventeenth Century England*, to be published in *Osiris, History of Science Monographs*, Vol. IV, ed. by George Sarton, Cambridge.

OFFENBACHER, MARTIN: *Konfession und soziale Schichtung*, J. C. B. Mohr, Tübingen, 1901.

PARSONS, TALCOTT: " 'Capitalism' in Recent German Literature. II. Max Weber," *Journal of Political Economy*, Vol. 37, pp. 31–51, 1929.

———— "H. M. Robertson on Max Weber and His School," *Journal of Political Economy*, Vol. 43, pp. 688–696, 1935.

PIRENNE, HENRI: *Les périodes de l'histoire sociale du capitalisme*, Hayez, Brussels, 1914.

RACHFAHL, FELIX: "Kalvinismus und Kapitalismus," *Internationale Wochenschrift*, Bd. III, pp. 1217–1238, 1249–1267, 1287–1299, 1319–1334, 1347–1366, 1909.

ROBERTSON, HECTOR M.: *Aspects of the Rise of Economic Individualism: a Criticism of Max Weber and His School*, University Press (John Wilson & Son, Inc.), Cambridge, England, 1933.

VON SCHULZE-GAEVERNITZ, G.: "Die geistesgeschichtlichen Grundlagen der anglo-amerikanischen Weltsuprematie, III. Die Wirtschaftsethik des Kapitalismus," *Archiv für Sozialwissenschaft und Sozialpolitik*, p. 61.

SEÉ, H.: "Dans quelle mesure Puritains et Juifs ont-ils contribué au progrès du capitalisme modérne?", *Revue historique*, Vol. 154, pp. 57–68, 1927.

———— *Les origines du capitalisme moderne*, A. Colin, Paris, 1926.

SOMBART, W.: *The Jews and Modern Capitalism*, trans. by M. Epstein, T. F. Unwin, London, 1913.

TAWNEY, RICHARD H.: *Religion and the Rise of Capitalism*, Harcourt, Brace & Company, New York, 1926, 2d ed., 1929.

TROELTSCH, ERNST: *Die Bedeutung des Protestantismus für die Enstehung der moderne Welt*, R. Oldenburg, München, 1911.

——— *The Social Teaching of the Christian Churches*, trans. by Olive Wyon, 2 vols., The Macmillan Company, New York, 1931.

WOOD, H. G.: "The Influence of the Reformation on Ideas Concerning Wealth and Property," *Property; Its Duties and Rights, Historically, Philosophically and Religiously Regarded*, with an introduction by the Bishop of Oxford (Charles Gore), Macmillan & Company, Ltd., London, 1913.

2. *Methodological and General*

ABEL, THEODORE F.: "Systematic Sociology in Germany," *Studies in History, Economics and Public Law*, edited by the Faculty of Political Science of Columbia University, No. 310, Columbia University Press, New York, 1929.

BENNION, L. L.: *Max Weber's Methodology*, Dissertation, University of Strasbourg, Imprimatur, Les presses modernes, Paris, 1933.

BIENFAIT, W.: *Max Webers Lehre vom geschichtlichen Erkennen*, Ebering, Berlin, 1930.

ENGEL-REIMERS, CHARLOTTE: "Der Methodenstreit in der Soziologie," *Schmollers Jahrbuch*, Vol. 56, pp. 87–103, February, 1932.

FECHNER, ERICH: "Der Begriff des kapitalistischen Geistes bei Werner Sombart und Max Weber und die soziologischen Grundkategorien Gemeinschaft und Gesellschaft," *Weltwirtschaftliches Archiv*, Vol. 30, pp. 194–211, 1929.

——— "Der Begriff des kapitalistischen Geistes und das Schelersche Gesetz vom Zusammenhang der historischen Wirkfaktoren (Vergleich und Ausgleich zwischen Sombart und Max Weber)," *Archiv für Sozialwissenschaft und Socialpolitik*, Vol. 63, pp. 93–120, 1930.

FREYER, HANS: *Soziologie als Wirklichkeitswissenschaft*, B. G. Teubner, Leipzig, 1930.

GINSBERG, MORRIS: "Recent Tendencies in Sociology," *Economica*, February, 1933.

GRAB, HERMANN J.: *Der Begriff des Rationalen in der Soziologie Max Webers*, Sozialwissenschaftliche Abhandlungen, Vol. III, Karlsruhe, 1927.

HALBWACHS, MAURICE: "Max Weber, un homme, une oeuvre," *Annales d'histoire économique et sociale*, Vol. 1, pp. 81–88, January, 1929.

HINTZE, OTTO: "Max Webers Soziologie," *Schmollers Jahrbuch*, Vol. 50, pp. 83–95, 1926.

HONIGSHEIM, PAUL: "Max Weber als Soziologie," *Kölner Vierteljahrshefte für Soziologie*, Vols. 1–2, pp. 32–41, 1921.

——— "Der Max Weber-Kreis in Heidelberg," *Kölner Vierteljahrshefte für Soziologie*, Vols. 5–6, pp. 270 ff., 1925–1926.

JASPERS, KARL: *Max Weber*. Rede bei der von der Heidelberger Studentenschaft veranstalteten Trauerfeier, J. C. B. Mohr (P. Siebeck), Tübingen, 1921.

——— *Max Weber*. *Deutsches Wesen im politischen Denken, im Forschen und Philosophieren*, G. Stalling, Oldenburg, 1932.

KELSEN, HANS: *Der soziologische und der juristische Staatsbegriff, kritische Untersuchung des Verhältnisses von Staat und Recht*, J. C. B. Mohr (P. Siebeck), Tübingen, 1928.

KLÜVER, H.: "Max Weber's Ideal Type in Psychology," *Journal of Philosophy*, Vol. 23, pp. 29–35, 1926.

LANDSHUT, S.: *Kritik der Soziologie*, Duncker und Humblot, Munich, 1929.

—— "Max Webers geistesgeschichtliche Bedeutung," *Neue Jahrbücher für Wissenschaft und Jugendbildung.*, Vol. VII, pp. 507–516, 1931.

LENNERT, RUDOLF: *Die Religionstheorie Max Webers*, Kohlhammer, Stuttgart, 1935.

LIEBERT, ARTHUR: "Max Weber," *Preussische Jahrbücher*, Vol. 210, pp. 304–320, 1927.

LÖWITH, KARL: "Max Weber und Karl Marx," *Archiv für Sozialwissenschaft und Sozialpolitik*, Vol. 67, pp. 53–99, 175–214, 1932.

MEINECKE, FRIEDRICH: *Staat und Persönlichkeit*, E. S. Mittler und Sohn, Berlin, 1933.

MEITZEL, E. P. C.: "Max Weber," *Handwörterbuch der Staatswissenschaften*, 4th ed., vol. VIII, p. 926, Lieferungen 102–112.

VON MISES, L.: "Soziologie und Geschichte," *Archiv für Sozialwissenschaft und Sozialpolitik*, Vol. 61, pp. 465–512, 1929 (on Weber, pp. 470–497).

OPPENHEIMER, HANS: *Die Logik der soziologischen Begriffsbildung mit besonderer Berücksichtigung von Max Weber*, J. C. B. Mohr, Tübingen, 1925.

PALYI, MELCHIOR (ed.): *Erinnerungsgabe für Max Weber*, 2 vols., Munich: Duncker und Humblot, 1923.

PARSONS, TALCOTT: Review of von Schelting's "Max Webers Wissenschaftslehre," *American Sociological Review*, Vol. 1, pp. 675–681, 1936.

RICKERT, HEINRICH: "Max Weber und seine Stellung zur Wissenschaft," *Logos*, Vol. 15, pp. 222–237, 1926.

SALOMON, ALBERT: "Max Weber's Methodology," *Social Research*, Vol. 1, pp. 147–168, 1934.

—— "Max Weber's Political Ideas," *Social Research*, Vol. 2, pp. 368–384, 1935.

—— "Max Weber's Sociology," *Social Research*, Vol. 2, pp. 60–73, 1935.

SCHELER, MAX: *Schriften zur Sociologie und Weltanschauungslehre*, P. Reinhold, Leipzig, 1923.

VON SCHELTING, ALEXANDER: "Die logische Theorie der historischen Kulturwissenschaften von Max Weber und im besonderen sein Begriff des Idealtypus," *Archiv für Sozialwissenschaft und Sozialpolitik*, Vol. 49, pp. 623 *ff.*, 1922.

—— *Max Webers Wissenschaftslehre*, J. C. B. Mohr (P. Siebeck), Tübingen, 1934.

SCHUHMACHER, H.: "Max Weber, Nationalökonom," *Jahrbuch der deutschen biographie*, Deutschen Verlags-Aust., pp. 593–615, Stuttgart.

SCHÜTZ, ALFRED: *Der sinnhafte Aufbau der sozialen Welt*, Julius Springer, Vienna, 1932.

SOROKIN, PITIRIM A.: *Contemporary Sociological Theories*, Harper & Brothers, New York, 1928.

SPANN, OTTMAR: *Tote und lebendige Wissenschaft*, 2d ed., Gustav Fischer, Jena, 1925.

STOLTENBERG, H. L.: " 'Tote und lebendige Wissenschaft' (on Ottmar Spann and Max Weber)," *Zeitschrift für die Gesamte Staatswissenschaft*, Vol. 85, pp. 133–141, 1928.

TROELTSCH, ERNST: *Der Historismus und seine Probleme*, Vol. III of *Gesammelte Schriften*, J. C. B. Mohr (P. Siebeck), Tübingen, 1922.

——— "Max Weber," *Deutscher Geist und Westeuropa*, J. C. B. Mohr (P. Siebeck), Tübingen, 1925.

WACH, JOACHIM: "Max Weber als Religionssoziologe" (appendix to his *Einführung in die Religionssoziologie*), J. C. B. Mohr (P. Siebeck), Tübingen, 1931.

WALTHER, ANDREAS: "Max Weber als Soziologe," *Jahrbuch für Soziologie*, Vol. II, pp. 1–65, 1926.

WILBRANDT, R.: "Max Weber als Erkenntniskritiker der Sozialwissenschaften," *Zeitschr. für die Gesamte Staatswissenschaft*, Vol. 79, pp. 583–674, 1925.

WOLF, ERICH: "Max Webers ethischer Kritizismus und das Problem der Metaphysik," *Logos*, Vol. 19, pp. 359–375, 1930.

C. Other Relevant Works

BLUNT, E. A. H.: *The Caste System of Northern India*, Oxford University Press, London, 1931.

DEVEREUX, E. C., JR.: "Gemeinschaft and Gesellschaft in Tokugawa Japan," unpublished thesis, Harvard University, 1934.

ELLIOTT, WILLIAM Y.: *The Pragmatic Revolt in Politics; Syndicalism, Fascism, and the Constitutional State*, The Macmillan Company, New York, 1928.

GRANET, M.: *La pensée chinoise*, La Renaissance du Livre, Paris, 1934.

GRÜNWALD, ERNST: *Das Problem der Soziologie des Wissens*, Wilhelm Braumüller, Vienna and Leipzig, 1934.

KNIGHT, FRANK H.: "Freedom as Fact and Criterion," *International Journal of Ethics*, Vol. 39, pp. 129–147, 1928–1929.

KOFFKA, KURT: *Principles of Gestalt Psychology*, Harcourt, Brace & Company, New York, 1935.

MANNHEIM, KARL: *Ideologie und Utopie*, F. Cohen, Bonn, 1929; trans. by Louis Wirth and Edward Shils, Harcourt, Brace & Company, New York, 1936.

PARSONS, TALCOTT: "Some Reflections on 'The Nature and Significance of Economics,'" *Quarterly Journal of Economics*, Vol. 48, pp. 511–545, 1933–1934.

RICKERT, HEINRICH: *Uber die Grenzen der naturwissenschaftlichen Begriffsbildung*, 5th ed., J. C. B. Mohr, Tübingen, 1929.

ROBBINS, LIONEL: *The Great Depression*, Macmillan & Company, Ltd., London, 1934.

ROETHLISBERGER F J and W. J. DICKSON: *Management and the Worker; Technical vs. Social Organization in an Industrial Plant*, Harvard

School of Business Administration, Studies in Industrial Research, Boston, 1934.

SOROKIN, PITIRIM A.: "Forms and Problems of Culture Integration," *Rural Sociology,* Vol. 1, pp. 121–141, 344–374, 1936; Reprinted as Chap. I of his *Social and Cultural Dynamics,* 3 vols., American Book Company, New York, 1937.

TÖNNIES, FERDINAND: *Gemeinschaft und Gesellschaft,* Fues's Verlag (R. Reisland), Leipzig, 1887.

VEBLEN, THORSTEIN: *The Instinct of Workmanship,* The Macmillan Company, New York, 1914.

WHITEHEAD, T. N.: *Leadership in a Free Society,* Harvard University Press, Cambridge, 1936.

CHAPTERS XVIII AND XIX, CONCLUSION

FREYER, HANS: *Soziologie als Wirklichkeitswissenschaft,* B. G. Teubner, Leipzig, 1930.

FRIEDRICH, C. J.: *Constitutional Government and Politics,* Harper & Brothers, New York, 1936.

HUSSERL, EDMUND: *Logische Untersuchungen,* 2 vols, M. Niemeyer, Halle, 1900–1901.

JENNINGS, HERBERT SPENCER: *The Biological Basis of Human Nature,* W. W. Norton & Company, New York, 1930.

SIMMEL, GEORG: *Soziologie,* Duncker und Humblot, Leipzig, 1908.

WHITEHEAD, A. N.: *Science and the Modern World,* The Macmillan Company, New York, 1925.

ZNANIECKI, FLORIAN. *The Method of Sociology,* Farrar & Rinehart, Inc., New York, 1934.

INDEX